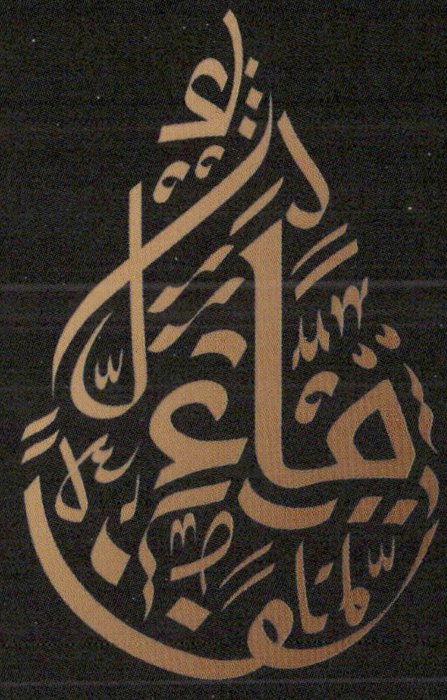

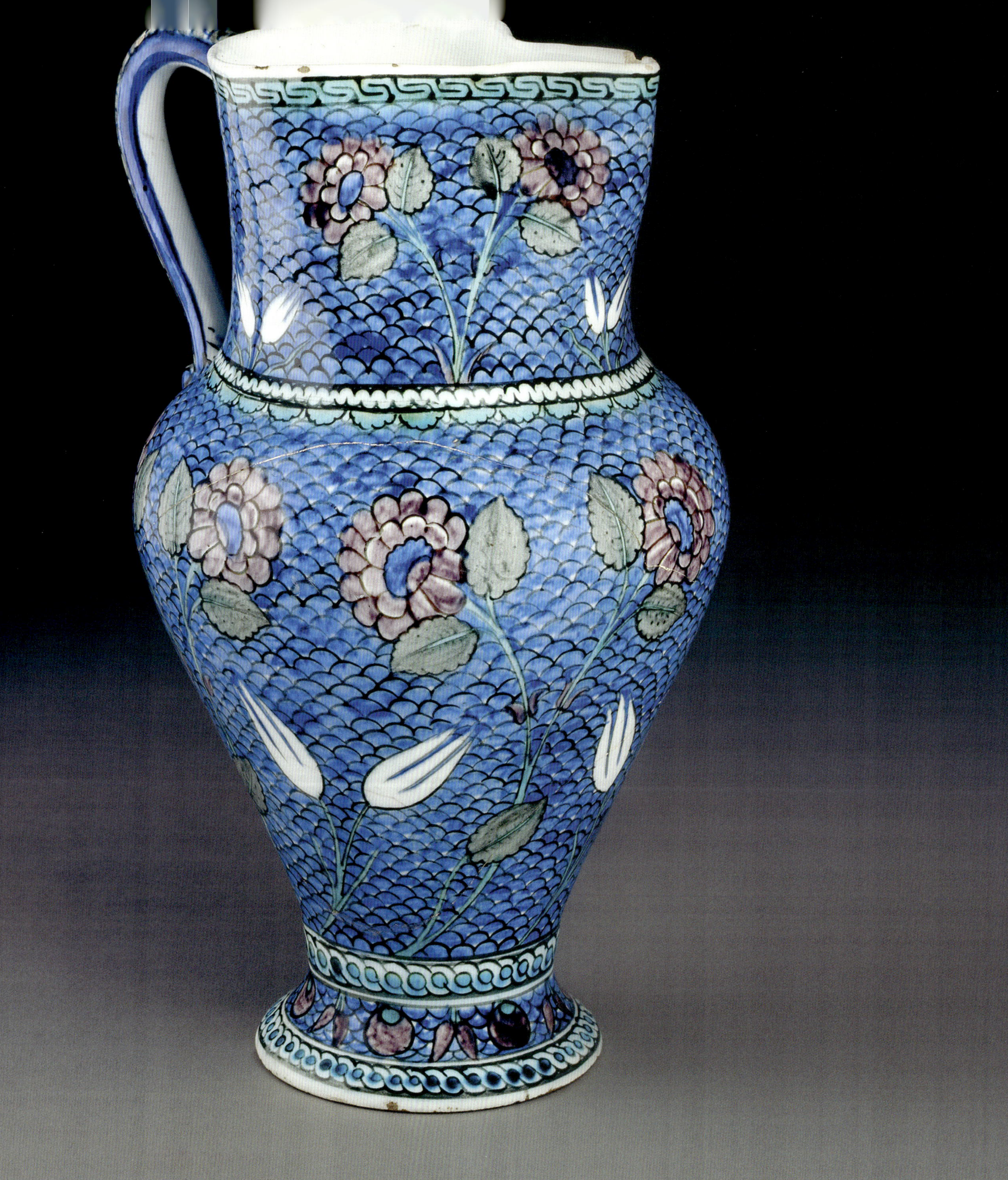

WATER, ISLAM AND ART

*Drop by Drop,
Life Falls from the Sky*

SilvanaEditoriale

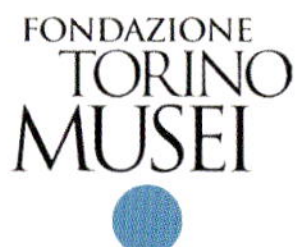
FONDAZIONE
TORINO
MUSEI

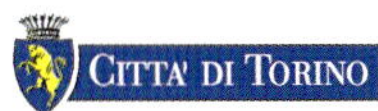

Mayor
Chiara Appendino

Local Chief of the Department of Culture
Francesca Leon

Director of the Cultural and Administrative Services Division
Emilio Agagliati

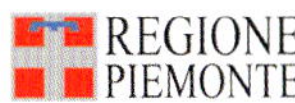

President
Sergio Chiamparino

Local Chief of the Department of Culture and Tourism
Antonella Parigi

Director of the Cultural, Touristic and Sportive Promotion
Paola Casagrande

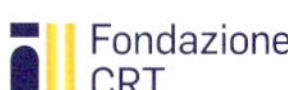

President
Giovanni Quaglia

Vice Presidents
Anna Beatrice Ferrino
Anna Chiara Invernizzi

Secretary General
Massimo Lapucci

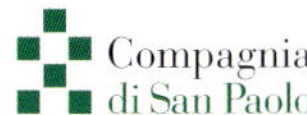

President
Francesco Profumo

Vice President
Licia Mattioli

Secretary General
Alberto Anfossi

List of Lenders
The Aron Collection;
The Ashmolean Museum, University of Oxford, Oxford, United Kingdom;
Benaki Museum, Athens, Greece;
Biblioteca Apostolica Vaticana, Città del Vaticano;
Biblioteca dell'Archiginnasio, Bologna;
Fondazione Musei Civici di Venezia, Museo Correr;
Galleria Moshe Tabibnia, Milan;
Instituto de Valencia De Don Juan, Madrid, España;
L.A. Mayer Museum for Islamic Art, Jerusalem, Israel;
MIC, Museo Internazionale delle Ceramiche in Faenza, Faenza;
Musei del Bargello, Florence;
Museo delle Cappelle Medicee, Insigne basilica di San Lorenzo, Florence;
Museo Civico Medievale, Bologna;
Museo del tessuto e della tappezzeria "Vittorio Zironi", Bologna,
Museo d'Arte Orientale - MUCIV, Rome;
Museo de la Alhambra, Patronato de la Alhambra y Generalife, España;
Museo e Real Bosco di Capodimonte, Naples;
Museo Poldi Pezzoli, Milan;
Polo museale della Sardegna - Pinacoteca nazionale di Cagliari;
Private collection;
Private collection, Brussels, Belgium;
Private collection, Genoa;
Private collection, Sanremo;
Private collection, Turin;
Zaleski collection;

The MAO wishes to express its gratitude to the following lenders, with whose contribution the realisation of this exhibition and catalogue were possible:

The Ashmolean Museum, University of Oxford: Aisha Burtenshaw, Mallica Kumbera Landrus, Ilenia Scerra, Alexander Sturgis;
The Aron Collection: Martina Massullo, Armando Tagliacozzo;
Benaki Museum, Athens: Irini Geroulanou, George Manginis, Mina Moraitu, Haris Siampanis, Greta Vasileiou;
Biblioteca Apostolica Vaticana: Amalia D'Alascio, Riccardo Luongo, Valerio Mancuso, Claudia Montuschi, Adalgisa Ottaviani, Reverendissimo Cardinale Pietro Parolin, Monsignor Cesare Pasini, Sua Eccellenza Monsignor Monsignor José Tolentino de Mendonça, Ambrogio M. Piazzoni;
Biblioteca dell'Archiginnasio, Bologna: Elisabetta Arioti, Alessandra Curti, Clara Maldini, Anna Manfron, Sonia Venturi;
Fondazione Musei Civici di Venezia, Museo Correr: Gabriella Belli, Valeria Cafà, Dennis Cecchin, Mariacristina Gribaudi, Sofia Rinaldi;
Galleria Moshe Tabibnia: Margherita Barziza, Virginia Giuliano, Lucia Pirovano, Moshe Tabibnia;
Instituto de Valencia de Don Juan, Madrid: Rafael García Ormaechea, Cristina Partearroyo Lacaba, Maria Angeles Santos;
L.A. Mayer Museum for Islamic Art, Jerusalem, Israel: Eli Khan, Deena Lawi, Anat Michaeli, Idit Sharoni, Nadim Sheiban;
MIC, Museo Internazionale delle Ceramiche in Faenza: Giorgio Assirelli, Claudia Casali, Elena Dal Prato, Elena Giacometti, Valentina Mazzotti;
Musei del Bargello, Museo delle Cappelle Medicee, Insigne Basilica di San Lorenzo: Monica Bietti, Reverendo Priore Monsignor Marco Domenico Viola;
Museo Civico Medievale, Bologna: Irene Faranda, Antonella Mampieri, Massimo Medica;
Museo d'Arte Orientale - MUCIV: Francesca Manuela Anzelmo, Gabriella Di Flumeri, Filippo Maria Gambari, Micheal Jung, Gabriella Manna;
Museo de la Alhambra, Patronato de la Alhambra y Generalife: Reynaldo Fernández Manzano, Purificación Marinetto Sánchez;
Museo del tessuto e della tappezzeria "Vittorio Zironi", Bologna: Giancarlo Benevolo, Antonella Mampieri, Massimo Medica;
Museo e Real Bosco di Capodimonte, Naples: Sylvain Bellenger, Concetta Capasso, Lucio Fiorile, Marina Morra, Patrizia Piscitello; Maria Rosaria Sansone;
Museo Poldi Pezzoli, Milan: Maurizio Delsale, Andrea Di Lorenzo, Martina Franzini, Annalisa Zanni;
Polo museale della Sardegna - Pinacoteca nazionale di Cagliari: Roberto Concas, Silvia Caracciolo, Giovanna Damiani, Gerlinde Tautschnig; Zaleski collection.

Our gratitude also goes to the lenders who expressed the wish to remain anonymous, to institutions and the many people who contributed in several different ways to the realisation of this exhibition:
Marco Biscione; Beatrice Campi; Marco Galateri di Genola; Eric Grunberg; Paolo Leone Kadjar; Giovanna Murgolo; Fabiano Panzironi; Elisabetta Raffo; Claudia Ramasso; Paola Ruffino; Generoso Urciuoli; Roberta Vergagni.

WATER, ISLAM AND ART

Drop by Drop, Life Falls from the Sky

MAO Museo d'Arte Orientale, Turin
13th April - 1st September 2019

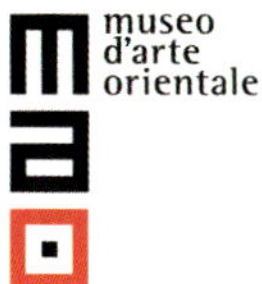

Director
Marco Guglielminotti Trivel

Curator
Claudia Ramasso

Exhibitions and Events Department
Delia Malfitano

Press and Communication Office
Raffaella Bassi

Educational Department
Mia Landi
Eva Morando

Technical and Security Department
Patrizia Bosio

Information and Booking
Tiziana Nosek

Human Resources
Veronica Mantovani
Simona Trombetta

www.maotorino.it

Exhibition curated by
Alessandro Vanoli

Assistant Curator
Ilaria Bellucci

Scientific Committee
Giovanni Curatola, *President*
Ilaria Bellucci
Marco Galateri di Genola
Claudia Maria Tresso
Alessandro Vanoli

Project Managers and Coordinators
Arianna Bona
Delia Malfitano
with the collaboration of
Giulia Vitellaro

Installation Project and Design
Simonetti Architettura

Graphics
Sara Fortin Design

Translations
Emily Ligniti

Set-up
Fargofilm Srl

Fundraising
Carla Centonze

Shipping and Set-up
Apice, Milan

Insurance
AGE Assicurazioni Gestione Enti srl
Assicurazioni Generali S.p.A.
BiG Broker Insurance Group, Ciaccio Arte, Milan
Blackwall Green, London

High readability font biancoenero®
of Bianconero editions, designed by Umberto Mischi. The font is free for the non-commercial use.

Technical Sponsor
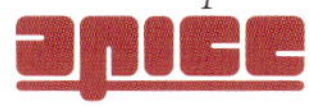

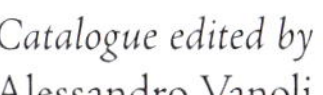
Catalogue edited by
Alessandro Vanoli

Coordinators
Delia Malfitano
with Giulia Vitellaro

Essays
Giovanni Curatola
Marco Galateri di Genola
Alessandro Vanoli

Cataloguing entries
Francesca Manuela Anzelmo *F.M.A.*
Ilaria Bellucci *I.B.*
Gabriella Di Flumeri *G.D.F.*
Gabriella Manna *G.M.*
Michael Jung *M.J.*
Laura Parodi *L.P.*
Loredana Pessa *Lo.P.*
Alessandro Vanoli *A.V.*

The Fondazione Torino Musei is delighted to present today the exhibition Drop by Drop, Life Falls from the Sky. Water, Islam and Art *at the MAO Museo d'Arte Orientale (Museum of Oriental Art) in Turin.*

Possibly the largest ever organised on this theme with its multitude of meanings, the exhibition offers a specific interpretation – the Muslim one – on a universal element like water, which indistinctly unites all cultures, traditions and civilisations. This mesmerising project wouldn't have seen the light without the precious participation of several national and international museums and the collaboration with important local institutions.

The exhibition showcases how in Islam water had not only an ordinary purpose, but also more profound meanings, which inspired philosophers, thinkers and religions through the centuries. In this specific context, water witnesses its greatest expression of the dualism between sacred and ordinary, a dualism reflected in several different mirrors all tied together by atavistic notions, such as birth and destruction; sensuality and purity; silence and noise. Ruled with the qanat*; ritualised with the* hammam*, worshipped as a celestial gift and feared as a divine punishment, Muslim civilisation evolved without neglecting any of these multifaceted aspects. It is not a coincidence that the conceptual and practical sustenance of this civilisation led it to get involved with a broader universe of more complex symbols, traditions and rites, allowing future cultures and civilisations to blossom.*

But the blossoming should not only be conceived as symbolical and metaphorical, but also literal. The destiny of plants and of men is inevitably tied to water in a very tight knot; their stories cannot but be constantly intertwined. In parallel to the development of society, one can witness the creation of lush gardens, pivotal sites in Islam as directly inspired by the representation of Paradise. This exhibition aims at offering not only a thorough excursus on the concept of water in Islam, but also an occasion to reflect on broader social topics connected to contemporaneity.

We whole-heartedly thank the museums, the collectors, the public institutions and the curators who made this project possible by sharing their precious resources and their cultural expertise.

Maurizio Cibrario
President Fondazione Torino Musei

Turin is an open-minded city that looks towards the future; a future that must not ignore our relationships with the people and countries of other continents with a view to bringing our different cultures closer. Our relationship with predominantly Muslim countries is very important for this Administration in terms of international cooperation, given that it is considered strategic for our city's economic and cultural growth. To cite just two examples: Turin has participated several times in the Dubai Global Islamic Economy Summit; and the guest of honour at the 2019 International Book Fair will be the Emirate of Sharjah. Last year, the MAO Museo d'Arte Orientale also took its exhibition of Asian puppets and marionettes, Le figure dei sogni - Figures of dream, *to the same Emirate, where it was hosted by the Museum of Arab Heritage. Initiatives of this type show how pivotal the city's museums are in initiating collaborations with key areas in today's world.*
So let us welcome this important exhibition of Islamic art promoted by the MAO: another important piece in the increasingly lively cultural panorama that surrounds us, with an eye not only to increasing tourist attractions, but also to the integration aspired to by this Administration in a multi-ethnic reality such as Turin's. The transformations that have affected the very fabric of this city over the past twenty years lead us to interact and deal positively with a vaster world than we have ever known before.
The Drop by Drop, Life Falls from the Sky. Water, Islam and Art *exhibition, with its new approach to a millennium-old culture, goes beyond the* clichés *through which we – as Westerners – tend to see the Islamic world. A world that is full of contradictions, it is true; that at times is controversial, and too often manipulated. But that at heart is a kaleidoscope in which we can all, as human beings, recognise ourselves.*
Because it is worth pointing out that we are all, without exception, made mostly of water.

Chiara Appendino
Mayor of the City of Turin

With the exhibition Drop by Drop, Life Falls from the Sky. Water, Islam and Art, *the MAO Museo d'Arte Orientale is also ushering in the second decade of its own existence in a spirit of innovation and originality.*

Although we can count on a magnificent collection of works from the Islamic countries of Asia, most of which are on permanent display on the Museum's fourth floor, for the first time since we opened the MAO is putting on an exhibition on Islamic art. And it is not just any exhibition, but an important project on an international scale with a highly original slant, that aims – through the medium of art – to explore the significance of water in the Islamic world. From many points of view, this is the most demanding our institution has mounted to date: not only because of the resources involved, and the number and variety of lenders, but also because of the range of perspectives. Furthermore, an increased focus on Islamic culture obviously holds particular significance in the historic moment we are living in, and this exhibition once again highlights the importance of the social role that the MAO is called to perform because of its natural calling as a "bridge between cultures".

Another of the show's innovative elements is the fact that it was conceived as a new MAO product that may appeal to other museums, both in Italy and elsewhere. In this way, we can consolidate our position as a museum that is strong, capable of making itself better known at the international level, while at the same time taking deeper root in our home ground. The exhibition will in fact represent an important opportunity to look at both present and future using an interdisciplinary approach: thanks to the collaboration and networking with other bodies and institutions, it has been possible to explore issues related to challenges that the modern world must tackle in managing water resources, thereby also touching on geopolitical, technological and economical aspects.

This project is also the first part of a cohesive three-pronged plan that will continue with the most important exhibitions of 2020 and 2021, with a view to planning an agenda that looks far and deep. The aim is to explore the complexity of Eurasian globalisation from a historical perspective, analysing the methods and objects of exchanges – whether these be artistic and cultural, commercial, political or social – by means of three points of reflection. Starting from the Western end of the maritime Silk Route, we will continue with its Eastern end, and will ideally bring these two extremities together with the third of the shows we have planned. Water, in many respects, will be the unifying factor in this process. Not just the water of the seas as a conveyer of transoceanic communication that then branches into the capillary networks of river navigation, but also as a metaphor for the flow of knowledge that results from exchanges between different cultures. Drop by drop, the shape of water also becomes that of the container that holds it: in the same way, individual societies selectively define a heritage that belongs, without discrimination, to the entire human race.

Marco Guglielminotti Trivel
Director, MAO Museo d'Arte Orientale, Turin

Contents

17 The Drop of God
Giovanni Curatola

23 Water and Islam
Spaces and Interpretations
Alessandro Vanoli

34 Religion
56 Hammam
90 Drinking Water
152 Gardens

177 Damascus:
the Lost Garden of Eden
Marco Galateri di Genola

182 Bibliography

The Drop of God

Giovanni Curatola
University of Udine

... and We created every living thing from water.
Qur'an, Surah Al-Anbya, 21:30

Water. Islam. Art. Every culture, civilisation, religion, philosophy, location, history, life and world is connected to water. This element is and means everything to us, it's the very condition of our existence. On Mars, there is water. Whether this is true or not, whether factual or speculative this may be, water is in its scentless, colourless and tasteless form the pure essence of our being, not only in the human realm but also in the vegetal, animal and mineral ones.

Through the centuries, water yielded itself to a pivotal function in the history of human and religious evolutions. Its fundamental role may be translated in different facets and nuances, but it is always undeniably linked to the sphere of sacred. Islam, the third great monotheistic religion, which similarly to Judaism and Christianity developed from and within the desert, couldn't possibly be an exception in this scenario. Water is infinite, as sand grains and rocks are; but all the infinite drops of water flow into each other and constitute our oceans, seas, lakes and rivers, appearing thus as the true embodiment of God's oneness. In its raw and pristine form, water was sacred in several ancient religions, first and foremost in the Zoroastrian faith, the ancestor to the above-mentioned monotheisms. And it is surely not a coincidence that the great civilisations of the past flourished and thrived thanks to their nearby big rivers, such as the Fertile Crescent in Mesopotamia with the Tigris and Euphrates; the Nile in Egypt; the Indus and Ganges in India; the Yangtze and Yellow Rivers in China; the Amu Darya and Oxus River, flexible or at least superable borders of the Iranian world. And last but not least, us, with the Tiber and Rome. The importance and sacredness of water are universal values, which Islam embraced from its very first steps. In the Qur'an, the sacred text of Islam containing the revelation from God (Allah) to Prophet Muhammad through the archangel Gabriel (Jibril), several suras (chapters) clearly mention the water element and its relevance. However, the story of water and Islam is way more complex and nuanced than this. In telling this story, one should refrain from trying to codify Islam under a specific category. This would be a futile exercise, a form of cultural cross-sightedness. There is never only one way of looking at things, although our society, in its constant hunger for homologation and simplification, seems to be thinking that it's better to feed one distorted vision rather than multiple partially complete truths. But in the same way that a rainbow never repeats itself in the exact same proportion of colours in another rainbow, water too takes on different shapes and forms. With almost a millennium and a half worth of history and a vast geographic spread, reaching from Spain to the Far East, Islam is like a kaleidoscope. Scholars honour its multi-faceted forms, which are all interwoven into a common thread, or to put it another way, a trunk which at times rises to strong branches bearing ripe fruits, and others to weak and infected ones bearing rotten fruits. The reference here to episodes of iconoclastic fury, violence and terrorism is deliberate and intentional.

With strains and often incoherent and convoluted paths, history taught us that some routes are more clearly laid out for us and constitute the essence of a civilisation, its core values. That said, generalisations remain and they are the toughest obstacles to overcome. Firstly, each of us comes with his / her own perspectives and personal predispositions; life experience, education, family environment, personal inclinations - all of these elements influence the way we think and observe the world. Secondly, enlarging one's horizons to distant shores can often end up in a nebulous, hazy exercise, which leads to confusion and lack of substance, mortifying one's intelligence and thirst for knowledge. We ought to overcome these obstacles for a bigger and better good.

One of the common features presented in several writings on Islam is the duplicity of signs, the existence of a latent dualism (surely not of Mazdean origin) which can be easily found in a series of both synchronic and diachronic dichotomies, such as spoken word / scripture; nomadic / sedentary; villages / cities; collective / individual; stones / clay bricks; and so on. These dichotomies may sound confusing at first, but as Niels Bohr stated thirty odd years ago:

> *[...] it is indeed possible to understand an event through two different interpretative angles, which are concurrently complimentary and mutually exclusive. It is through their juxtaposition that the phenomenal content can be truly grasped.*

If the method of Bohr (noble father of quantum physics) is accepted as a suitable scientific methodology for "exact sciences", why should it not be applied to humanities as well?

The Drop of God is a captivating title which refers to and honours the great philosopher Raimon Panikkar's masterly reflection: "A book is a drop in the public opinion's ocean. A truthful pray is a glass of water, but a book ripened through profound contemplation can become a bounteous rain" (18th February 1996)[1]. This reminds me of an early Islamic parable. On a rainy day, a drop of water fell in the Ocean. By seeing such a vast expanse of water below itself, the single drop immediately felt tiny and immeasurably infinite at the same time. "I'm nothing", said the drop, "nothing compared to the One who created all of this!". God heard the drop's comment and to reward her wise awareness, He transformed her in a magnificent pearl lying on the bottom of the sea. Since then, it would be rather immodest and ambiguous to proclaim oneself a drop in the ocean of human knowledge!

One could carry on talking about water in Islam till the end of days. Water is a link and a constant and has often a legal notion too. Not only in the Qur'an, but also in popular religious practices, which often incorporate traditions rooted in pre-Islamic times, water is considered a common good as well as an instrument for implementing the will of God (the Legislator). An example of that can be found in the traditional hydric distribution system in the important city of Fez, Morocco. The very first water that springs in the city goes straight to the congregational mosque (masjid jāmi'), where every Friday (al-jume'a) the community (ummah) gathers to pray together at midday. Nearby, visitors are welcomed into several hammams, the public baths, direct heirs of the great Roman tradition. A brief digression on Roman civilisation seems now due. Every location where the Romans asserted their power and established themselves, they built great public works, i.e. roads and aqueducts. They were particularly keen on ensuring a capillary and effective distribution of water throughout the city and they were among the first to build large public bath complexes, fundamental structures for the society's hygiene, health and overall well-being. In this sense, Islam resumes and is inspired by Rome; an example of this can be found in the beautiful mosaics of the Western riwaq (portico) in the Great Umayyad Mosque in Damascus.

Coming back to Fez, subsequently to the mosque, water would be served firstly to the Muslim community and secondly to the Christian and Jewish ones. Lastly, when it started filling up with impurities, the remaining water would be channelled into several areas of productivity, such as dyeing and tanning. These activities, so important to the upkeep of Medieval economy, undoubtedly needed the support of the precious liquid but given how

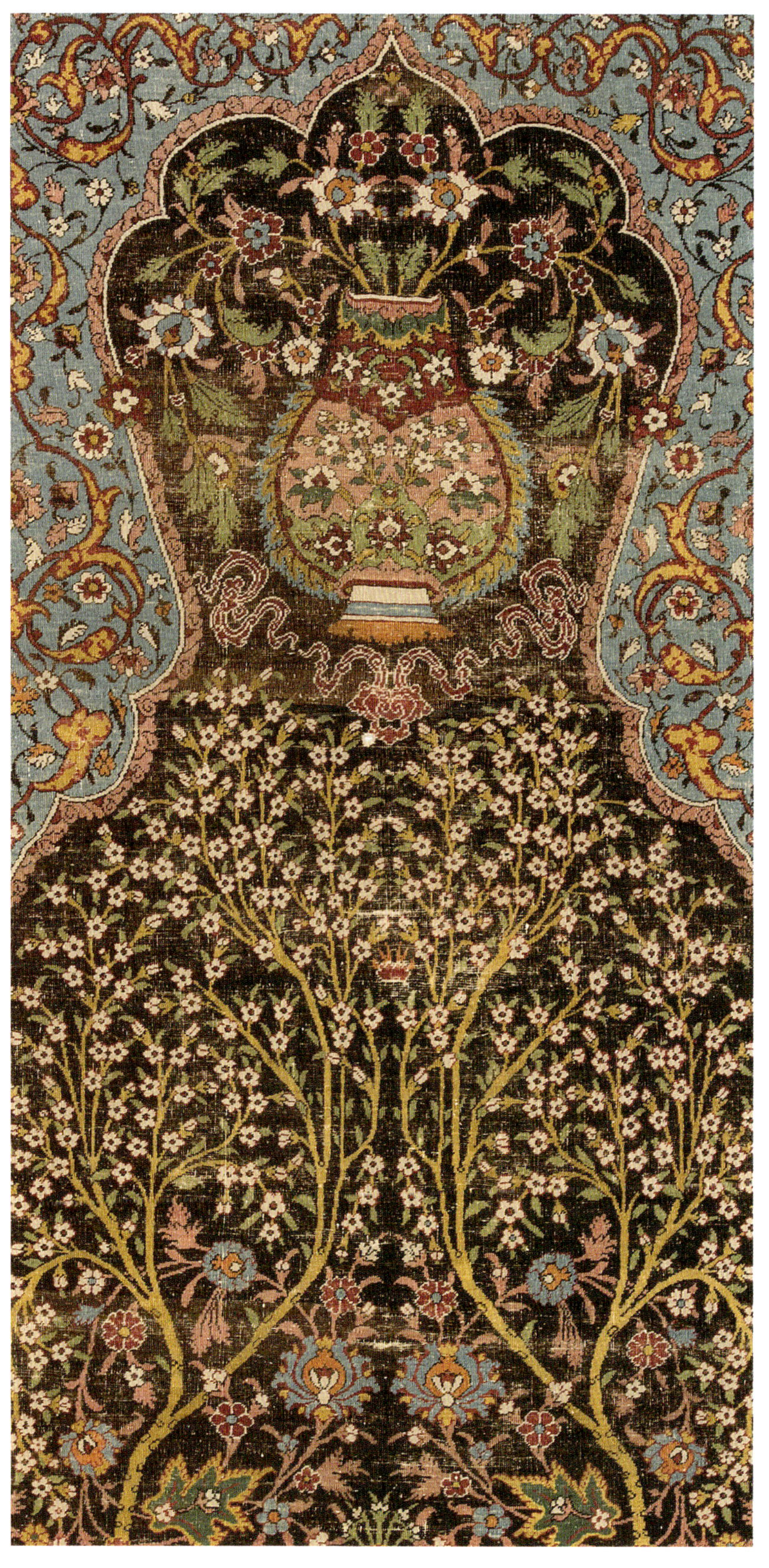

polluting they were and that often they were carried out by groups living on the margins of society (the Jews). This looks to me like an interesting model, very rational and not discriminatory at all, documenting the urbanist and social building and shaping up of a complex civilisation.

The relationship with water varies from one necessity to the other, from one territory to the other. It's like a litmus test with a vast array of gradations that eventually all confirm the superiority of water through its neutrality. That said, there are some inescapable constants provided by the law and by the Qur'an. The first and foremost constant is obviously the use of water for daily ablutions five times a day before the prayer, which is symbolised by myriads of jugs and ewers so commonly encountered in a vast array of contexts in the Islamic world. Water is surely a purifying element. However, it is worth noting that in its absence Muslim believers can replace it with sand, demonstrating thus that the purification is not only an act of the body but most importantly a symbolical gesture connected to the heart and mind of the pious. The second constant is the presence of a continuous supply of fresh water through either public fountains or water deposits with large unglazed clay jars, preserving the freshness of this precious liquid in absence of free-flowing running water in the surroundings. The institution, safe-keeping and maintenance of these fountains are privileges and obligations with which the caliph, or his viziers, must comply at all times in order to honour the subtle balance between them and the community, of which they have been proclaimed the head. And often, waqfs (pious foundations) are the perfect instrument to achieve this, acting as reminders that we have to give back some of what we own, as in the end everything belongs to God and we are only temporary administrators in his unfathomable plan.

In the paradigm of a desert monotheism, where at times too much emphasis is drawn onto the oasis, by far not the only Islamic landscape worth of mention, the offer of water is a must. The fountains in the cities strictly echo the shape of wells, one of which deserves a special mention here, the sacred Well of Zamzam near Mecca. This well, described in the Genesis (21; 8-21) and renowned in the Islamic tradition too, is believed to be a miraculously generated source of water which God created thousands of years ago in the middle of the desert to quench the thirst of Ibrahim's infant son Isma'il, the ancestor of Muslim people, who had been left there with his mother, Hajar. Another well that is part of the Muslim collective memory and specially significant to Shiah believers, is the one near Karbala, not far from Kufa in Iraq. Here, in 680 AD Hussain, son of 'Ali and grandson of the Prophet, and his family were firstly tortured by the Umayyad troops by blocking their water supplies and subsequently slaughtered. Water is pivotal in a culture such as the Islamic one that digs its roots in the nomadic context of the desert. An example of this may perhaps be found in the so-called Umayyad "desert castles" (7th-8th century AD). Although historical, archaeological and landscape studies have long confirmed that these structures were often neither castles nor in the middle of the desert, their construction and shape act as witnesses of the Bedouin nostalgia for a raw natural habitat. The intimate relationship of water in Islam with its polyhedral realities is deeply interconnected with the relation between different worlds, one created by God's will and the latter by human's revelation; between politics and nature; between environment and society; and lastly, between power and its very balance. For those who wish to delve further into these themes, the Hadith (a collection of sayings and deeds of the Prophet Muhammad after the Revelation, which are considered one of the primary sources of the Shari'a law) present itself as an interesting literary inspiration, introducing Muhammad as a true role model and ecological precursor.

Coming back to our exhibition, it is worth pointing out that the original idea behind it was to tell the story of a kaleidoscopic Islam through water. It goes without saying that our curators had to pick and choose, and at times limit, the specific angles explored in this exhibition, given the rather broad - potentially infinite - nature of the main subject. Their main aim has been throughout to introduce the wider, non-specialised public to an exhibition which made a peculiar and justified choice: to discover the intrinsic relation of water in Islam through the universal language of art. Indeed, Islamic art is often an expression of multiple realities and dimensions, exactly like water is.

The exhibition itinerary develops around four main sections, each of which is interconnected with the preceding one. Firstly, the visitors will explore water in the religious context and delve into its close affiliation with the mosque. Subsequently, they will proceed into the world of hammams and the practice of ablution. The third

third section will expose them to the daily use of water and its more mundane, domestic context. Here a specific mention will be made to the lavish and opulent courts of the caliphs, emblems of the power and luxury of the time. The fourth and final section will sing the praises of the Islamic gardens, which on its own could have easily been the subject of an entire exhibition. The team of experts that worked on this exhibition has deliberately chosen to break free from those overly romanticised atmospheres of One Thousand and One Nights and instead to privilege the clear and crisp transparency of facts. Certain Islamic spaces, such as hammams and gardens, have often been distorted in the West under an Orientalist light, charging them with sensuality and erroneously interpreted erotism. This exhibition distances itself from previously showcased discourses on figurative Orientalism, from those fairs and exhibitions that at times not only misrepresented Islamic art and culture but even butchered it and distorted it to the point of creating new concepts and fake truths. This exhibition is simply about three elements: Islam, Water and Art. Three powerful ingredients, which wisely measured in this exhibition and mixed in an unexpected and innovative solution, provide a different vision of what Islam is, a culture that although so intertwined with our society, we know so little of and that we tend to judge on the basis of prejudices and media distortion. In our modern society, it is fundamental, if not essential, to stubbornly emphasise the importance of learning more about the multi-faceted realities of Islam, especially on its artistic merits. "*Gutta cavat lapidem, non vi sed saepe cadendo*" [Dripping water wears out a stone not with its strength, but with its constancy].

[1] R. Panikkar, *L'acqua della goccia. Frammenti dai Diari,* edited by M. Carrara Pavan, Milano, Jaca Book, 2008.

Water and Islam
Spaces and Interpretations

Alessandro Vanoli

Introduction

Water belongs to our deepest dreams. This precious element epitomises life, birth, maternity, cleansing, purity, sensuality, and even death in a multitude of cultures and societies around the world. However, specifically in the Islamic world, water always held an important role both on the practical level and on the religious, spiritual and artistic ones. The context of its climate unfolds only one side of these complex relations. Besides the secular bond with arid and desert lands, water in Islam digs deeper and finds its roots into the cultural and religious inheritance of past civilisations and the varied sociological reasons articulating specific historical developments in each individual territory.

When telling the story of water and Islam, one is bound to take all of this into consideration, starting with the very word for water, *ma'*.

The word for water in Arabic, *ma'*, stems from an ancient root fairly common in Semitic languages (Akkadian *ma'a* and Hebrew *may*), bearing a similar meaning: water in all its forms and facets, in its generic and practical sense, and in its ritual and purifying dimension too.

The goal of this exhibition is to narrate the relation between water and Islam, from its most ancient roots to its varied complex developments, coming all the way to the present day, with its modern challenges and locations where this precious primary element is increasingly becoming a rare resource. The story we are telling aims to highlight the similarities, but also the cultural and regional differences existing in this relationship. To do so, we built an exhibition itinerary articulated around specific broad themes. The starting point is water in its religious and ritual context, as it is described in the Qur'an and in religious literature. The following necessary stop is in the world of *hammams*, the bath as an intimate place with its religious, hygienic and social connotations, for both purifying oneself and gathering with others. We then move on to observe water in its everyday context, in the houses and palaces, that perfect balance between sustenance and conviviality. Here we also tackle the theme of water supply and hydric technologies, such as aqueducts and fountains. Our journey ends in the open air, in the contexts of agronomy and gardens, speaking of countryside, oasis, and the neighbouring domestic and public spaces. Our story is being told through images, objects, archaeological finds, manuscripts and miniatures intertwining technology, ordinary life and art thanks to the medium of water. The exhibition also aims to raise awareness on the present condition of the Islamic lands where nowadays water is increasingly becoming a frail though essential resource, whose supply causes internal tensions and frictions.

Religion

Have not the unbelievers then beheld that the heavens and the earth were a mass all sewn up, and then We unstitched them and of water fashioned every living thing?
(Qur'an, Surah Al-Anbya, 21:30)

In Islam, water is the ultimate life-giving element. In the Qur'an, the noun *ma'* (water) is used more than sixty times, appearing in its varied shapes (rain, dew, spring, well, sea, river, etc.). First and foremost, water is considered one among thousands of extraordinary elements God yielded the universe: water is therefore a sign and only those with intellect can grasp its pure sense. God used water to create all living things and the gardens of Paradise are filled with fresh running water (*ma' maskub*, 56:31) presenting itself in the shape of abundant rivers, fountains, springs – some scented with camphor. Water is a fundamental part of the Muslim believers' afterlife. Indeed, "*the pious will be in gardens with fresh springs*" (15:45); instead, hell is characterised by one single large spring of hot water and the infidels will shout and plead the guests of paradise to throw upon them some fresh water (7:50).
On Earth, water is the fundamental tool God uses to imbue life: he brought the rain to penetrate the soil, fertilise it, and yield plants and vegetables; he also raised springs (*'uyun*; 26:134) to the ground and created rivers (*nahar*; 18:33).
On these premises, juridical and religious scripts started appearing. Rain, springs, wells, hail, snow, river and sea are all resources that the believers are allowed to use, and these manuscripts proceed debating who specifically could use them and how to administer their fruition, adding a series of normative elements detailing the relation between water and society, which will be discussed in depth in another chapter.
In terms of its purifying properties, water became one of the traditional elements offered to the dead. Being a vehicle for sacredness and purity, water also became a pivotal element to several divinatory and geomantic practices. A particularly good example of this is given by the so-called "medical" or magic bowls, where water would be poured onto Quranic calligraphic verses and would thus be imbued with special thaumaturgical properties. But water could also be dangerous at times. Hot springs were often believed to be haunted by *jinn*[1] (demons) and due to the very nature of springs, they were often considered portals to the underworld. Ponds with stagnant water were the favoured abode for demons.
Besides popular beliefs, water became tightly intertwined to fundamental Islamic ritual and religious practices, as testified by the attendance to the Zamzam well during Hajj and daily ablutions. Ablutions and ritual purity practices are common themes in almost all religions, but definitely acquire a special value in the three monotheistic religions. The crucial role played by water in Islam is acknowledged in the Qur'an more than once (see also 4:43):

> *O believers, when you stand up to pray wash your faces, and your hands up to the elbows, and wipe your heads, and your feet up to the ankles. If you are defiled, purify yourselves; but if you are sick or on a journey, or if any of you comes from the privy, or you have touched women, and you can find no water,*
> *then have recourse to wholesome dust and wipe your faces and your hands with it. God does not desire to make any impediment for you; but He desires to purify you, and that He may complete His blessing upon you; haply you will be thankful.* (5:6)

Impurity is a fact of nature rather than a moral concept. According to Quranic proscriptions and local traditions, the Muslim jurists explain that the degree of impurity can be greater (*hadath akbar* or *junub/janaba*) when one has intercourse, and for women when they have menstruation or are in the postpartum period; but it can also be minor (*hadatha sghar*) when caused by sleep, physiological needs, loss of blood, ingestion or contact with impure substances. Those who are in a state of impurity cannot attend the daily prayer, they cannot and should not in any circumstance touch or recite the Qur'an, nor practice the *tawaf*, the ritual circumambulation around Ka'ba during Hajj. Before every ablution, the believers need to mentally express their intention (*niyya*) of cleansing themselves, to which the recital of the *bismillah al-rahman al-rahim* ("in the name of God, the most Gracious, the most Merciful") follows. To remove greater impurity one has to carry out a total body ablution (*ghusl*), whilst for minor impurity one has to perform the following actions three times: wash the hands; wash the mouth; clean the nostrils inside; throw water on the face with the palm of the hand; wash the forearms up to the elbows; pass a wet hand over the head and on the neck and over the beard, if applicable; cleanse the ears with a finger;

and lastly, wash the feet up to the ankles (*wudu'*). In absence of water or in specific cases where the use of water is discouraged for sanitary reasons, it is accepted to perform an abridged version of the ablution ritual with sand or dust (*tayammum*), which involves beating the hands on the ground, shake them and pass them on the face and arms. This concession epitomises the symbolical nature of this rite and legitimises the use of water in other institutions connected to the religious practice such as the *hammams*.

Hammam

Everything begins with heat, a very particular type of heat released from the ground through deep waters. The Greeks used to call it *balaneion* (hot water bath) but archaeological evidence in Crete leads to believe that this concept already existed in the Minoan and Mycenaean times. We know very little about those ancient times, but it is generally acknowledged that since 6th century BCE, the practice of immersing oneself in hot water baths became rather widespread. The root of this practice digs into a simple basic idea leading to the development of the four temperaments theory. The human body is made of four main "*humours*" – blood, phlegm, yellow and black bile. When the four humours are well-balanced and mixed, the body is healthy; as soon as there is an imbalance, the body gets sick and weak. Originally, it was believed that this lack of balance could be caused by the external environment in the form of the four elementary atmospheric conditions (hot, cold, dry, humid) or the change of the seasons. Among the multitude of remedies, thermal hot waters offered a vast array of options, from sweating to fumigates, and full body immersions in hot or cold waters. This led to the rise of new medical traditions and practices. Heating techniques and architectures became more and more sophisticated with time and by the end of 2nd century-beginning of 1st century BCE, the *balaneia* had developed into true artworks, as the Olympia hot bath testifies. Around that time, the Romans started becoming aware of these practices and inspired by another Greek word, *thermós*, they established a new name for it: *thermae*, thermal baths. A proper revolution of morals and habits took place: since the late Republican Era, going to the baths, these grand public complexes, became an everyday activity, a widespread and shared practice done at ease. Usually, the garments would be left in the *apodyterium*, the changing room, often richly ornate and equipped with masonry benches. From there, the visitors had direct access to the gym, where they used to play ball games and work out. Once the physical activity was over, the sweaty and strained visitors would leave the gym and proceed into the *laconicum*, the sauna. Here the routine would be as follows: the visitors would firstly enter an often circular *calidarium* equipped with a masonry tub filled with hot waters; they would then proceed to a *tepidarium* with an intermediate temperature, where they could pause, rest, and spread natural ointments onto their bodies; and lastly, they would end the routine with an immersion in the *frigidarium* with tanks of reinvigorating ice-cold water. Every room was filled with statues, marbles, rich mosaics, recreational spaces, places where the visitors could converse, read, listen to music and admire works of art.

It is hard to imagine something more Roman than thermal baths. Those structures reached every corner of the Empire, from Naples to Bath (the name itself bears the memory of the past), all the way to several provinces in Asia. Particularly in the East, like in Byzantium, classical thermal baths kept on being in use for the whole period of the Middle Ages, even though their shape, design and dimensions had downsized by then. It is likely to believe that the Arabs and Turks first saw them there[2].

The Arab *hammams* came to light when several different elements finally merged and converged into one: ancient traditions; same locations; same deep, hot waters; and a new religion putting great emphasis on the necessity of maintaining a constant ritual purity through water. Indeed, when the Arabs spoke about baths, they used an old Semitic root, *hm*, whose meaning was "warm". The same root appears in Akkadian *ememu*, Aramaic *hamam*, and in biblical Hebrew *hom*, all with a similar meaning. As the Arabic version was *hamm*, it is likely to hypothesise the name for these baths became very spontaneously *hammam*, a noun describing the place where heat is released.

Not much is known on the early *hammams* until approximately 9th century CE. Arab sources tend to keep their existence quiet and archaeological remains have not yield further hints so far. Thus, one could speculate whether *hammams* originated as private spaces, prerogative of the caliphs only, like at the Umayyad complex of Qusayr 'Amra in Jordan (8th century). That said, from the 9th century onward, *hammams* became one of the most characteristic and traditional architectural structures in Islamic cities. Already

in 10th century, Arab accounts tell us (exaggerating!) that Baghdad had at least 10,000 baths and that in large cities such as Cordoba and Isfahan there were hundreds of them. Notwithstanding regional stylistic variations, the core structure of Arab *hammams* is still very much indebted to its Greek and Latin counterparts – a succession of halls, more or less spacious, serving the purpose of spreading and taming the heat to ensure its homogenous progression from the coldest hall, *bayt al-barid* (literally the "house of cold", similar to the *frigidarium*) to the hottest one (*bayt al-sukkun*, similar to the *calidarium*). In between these two halls, according to the type of *hammam* and its importance, there would be one or more lateral rooms connecting the two ends called *wastiyāt*, the equivalents of the Latin *tepidarium*. Similarly to the Greeks and Latins, Muslims also believed that water had purifying and healing properties. Water should be conceived as a material manifestation of God's blessing and mercy, as the Qur'an reminds us: "God created all living things from water" (24:45) and "[…] poured down blessed rain from the sky and made grow thereby gardens and grain from the harvest and lofty palm trees, having fruit arranged in layers as provision for the servants" (50:9-11). There is a religious meaning underlining all of this, which yields the very origin of the *hammam* and its spread in the Islamic world. Indeed, the *hammam* symbolises ritual purity and thanks to its cleansing water, the pious Muslim can attend his/her daily rites. At the *hammam*, the believers can perform *ghusl*, greater ablution, or *wudu'*, minor ablution, achieving thus the indispensable degree of ritual purity necessary for the *salat*, the daily prayer.
Besides this strong religious connotation, water is also deeply linked with the more ancient ideas of purification and care in medical terms. All these connotations mingled together through the centuries, and by not replacing each other, but rather complementing, they entailed the survival of ancient traditions[3]. In the same way to Roman *thermae*, the *hammam*'s hot waters have healing properties. Often called *al-tabib al-bakkush*, the silent doctor, baths were considered in popular traditions places where any illness could be healed, from respiratory problems to rheumatisms, thanks to the heat, the vapours, and the abundant sweating. For centuries, Islamic doctors, Ibn Sina in particular, reminded in their scripts of the healing properties of full body immersions in hot or cold waters together with applications of aromatic substances and reinvigorating drinks. Washing, purifying, healing: *hammams* were the active centres where these functions could be performed and their meanings amplified. It shouldn't surprise thus that *hammams* were so central in the urban lives of the Islamic lands. Inside them, one could wash, relax and take care of his/her self: men would dye their beards and hairs with privet; women would paint intricate arabesques on their hands and feet, put make up on their eyes made with *khol* or *daghba*. But above all, inside the *hammams* people had the occasion to meet, strike deals, make business, arrange weddings, respecting at all times a rigorous separation between men and women.
The word *hammam* meant for centuries all of the above and it adapted through time to the specific local requirements, cultures and traditions of the Islamic lands. A great example of that is given by the Turkish-speaking Ottomans, heirs at once of both the Byzantine and the Islamic traditions. They embraced the public baths' tradition and name with enthusiasm (*hamam* with one single 'm' though). According to Evliya Çelebi's travel diaries, by the mid of 17th century Constantinople was already boasting sixty-one *hammams* in the city centre and other fifty-one in the suburbs (not to mention all the private ones!). Substantially, public baths were prime places for social gatherings. There were specific opening hours for men and for women, and some *hammams* even had special times for the infidels. On their doorsteps, one could often see street vendors selling depilatory creams or even barbers, offering their hair and beard cutting skills. Baths were so heavily attended that soon after their establishment, they ended under the direct surveillance of the *muhtasib*, the censor and supervisor of public and commercial morality[4].
It was indeed through the Ottoman empire that Westerners made their encounter with the *hammam*; explaining why it is called to this very day "Turkish bath". That said, little they saw, a lot they imagined. The sensuality of baths and their erotic connotation were already well-known and understood in the Islamic world[5]. However, Western travellers brought these elements one step forward and associated *hammams* with the promiscuity and lust they attributed to Oriental cultures. In the 19th century though, the progressive encounter with Western ideas and the adoption of their technologies changed radically the morphology of Islamic society. The appearance of running water and the changes on urban settings dedicated to public health caused the decline of the *hammams*, by then considered retrograde and

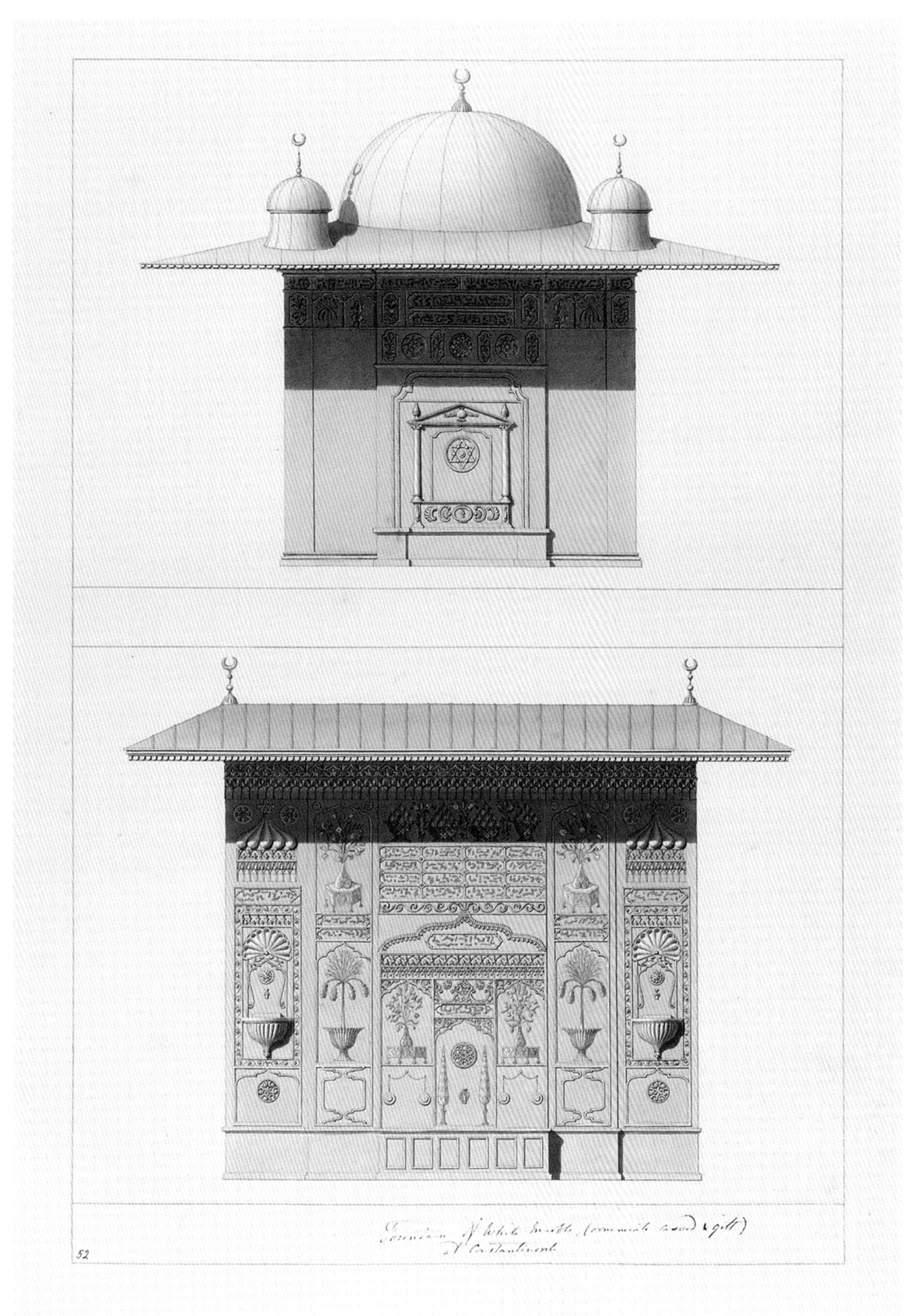
52

obsolete places with appalling hygienic measures and more and more associated with male and female prostitution.
Until a few decades ago, it was difficult to imagine a renewed global interest for Turkish and public baths. But today things seem to be developing differently, a new chapter of foreign investments, re-openings, restorations, discoveries of historical affairs and artistic spaces has started. Water, mud, thermal baths and massages are regaining their pivotal place in contemporary culture. Once again, *hammams* have changed their names and morphology, becoming part of larger complexes focused on wellbeing and good shape, commercial spaces detached from a specific cultural or regional identity. In Cairo like in Istanbul, the difference can be felt; the *hammam* as social necessity has now left its turn to the *hammam* as a sightseeing stop for tourists or, if private, as a personal weekend treat. This of course doesn't mean that its past social and religious function has completely vanished. No meaning ever disappears from the word *hammam*; simply new, modern connotations mingle with old concepts and practices. And that's exactly what water is – an atavistic, precious element in constant transformation, flow and evaporation. But it very rarely loses its connections with its own and our origins.

Drinking Water: Public Use and Social Gatherings

Public Use

At the origin of any discussion on water, it lies the realistic problem of how to make use of it given certain climates and territorial circumstances. Such problem is way older than Islam itself: canals and aqueducts were already in use in Mesopotamia since the 3rd millennium BCE[6]. The ancient Persians invented a successful system of hydric infrastructures, called *qanat*, which ensured the distribution of fresh water to great distances from the spring, crossing even dry and hot areas. Indeed, *qanats* are made of a series of vertical tunnels, similar to wells, all interconnected to a slightly sloping underground tunnel. These tunnels would draw water from a distant aquifer and move it where it was needed by exploiting the force of gravity.
The Romans are also renowned for their grand infrastructural projects. Firstly, they built underground tunnels, which moved large portions of water by exploiting the natural slope of the surroundings. Then, massive aqueducts on arches would draw the water from these tunnels and make it flow for dozens of kilometres. By the Imperial period, these aqueducts turned into real masterpieces with complex grids of lead and terracotta pipes, inside which the water was pumped and moved through by a system of gradients, water towers and tanks. This infrastructural technology became widespread in every part of the Roman Empire, from its northern borders in rainy Britain all the way to the most arid areas in Northern Africa and the Middle East. With the fall of the Empire and the rise of Islam, most of these infrastructures and techniques have been adopted, re-utilised and innovated by the Muslims.

To grasp the pivotal role water had in the life of early Islamic cities, one should read the travellers' and geographers' accounts of the time like the one on the towns of the Tunisian coast written by the traveller Al-Muqaddasī in the 10th century[7]:

'Asfaqs (Sfax) and Susa (Sousse) are two maritime cities, both surrounded by fortified, clay and stone walls. Their inhabitants access drinking water through wells and cisterns.
Al-Mahdiyya lies next to the sea and is surrounded by fortified walls; its inhabitants drink from wells and tanks where rainwater gathers.
Tabarqa is a seaside town dominated by a mountain; its ruinous fort no longer holds its people, who moved nearby. They drink from local wells; the town is crossed by a salt water river.
Marsā l-Kharaza is a town on a peninsula; there is only one way to get there. This is also the only place where you can fish beautiful examples of coral, to be found in the nearby sea.
Buna (Bône) is a seaside town surrounded by fortified walls; there people extract iron and drink from wells.
Baja (Béja) is located between Al-Qayrawan and the sea; it is rich in cereals; in the city centre there is a spring of fresh water which supplies the whole city.

From this extract, it is evident how water and its supply were considered the primary concern for urban settlements. All towns' descriptions written by Arab geographers enumerate in detail how many tanks, cisterns, springs, pipelines, hydric systems each city implemented and their individual supply methods, deeply connected with the logic of sustenance and survival[8].
Some cities resolved the problem by settling near great rivers

such as Baghdad, Mosul and Cairo. Here water was drawn through a system of canals and large *norias* (water wheels with buckets attached, used to raise water from a fresh water stream). Moreover, the vicinity to the river spurred the development of a new job, "the water carriers" or *saqqā'īn*, who in Baghdad used to draw water from the Tigris; and in Mosul used to travel to the nearby river and bring back large quantities of water on a donkey's back[9]. In Cordoba, the water supply guaranteed by the Guadalquivir river with the Albolafia noria soon became insufficient to satisfy the needs of the rapidly expanding city. Therefore, around the mid of 19th century, 'Abd al-Rahman II had to restore the ancient Roman aqueduct, drawing water from the nearby mountains.
Similar cases can be noticed in other cities of Arab Spain such as Jaen and Helva, or even in Tunis, where the Hafsid governors had to restore the vast majority of the local Roman hydraulic system. That said, the vast majority of Islamic cities drew their supply from small streams and springs and to do so, they often had to go back to and perfect the *qanats'* technique. In 10th-century Persia, for instance, between Isfahan and Qom one could admire a proper network of *qanats'* canalisations, built and looked after by the local governors[10].
However, once water reached the cities, other problems had to be tackled such as where to store it and how to organise its distribution. Since their early days, Muslim governors distinguished themselves for their grand cisterns like the one in Kairouan and Marrakesh. Every city improved, enlarged and strengthened its underground network of canals. As an example, the Muslim traveller Ibn Hawqal wrote that in Palermo there were several fountains, orchards and water mills; drinking water was drawn from wells dug in each house. That said, he also commented that at times those wells would yield heavy and unhealthy water[11]. Similarly, in Marrakesh the water supply was guaranteed by nearby creeks and by a system of underground galleries, called *khettara*[12].
It goes without saying that the concern about water distribution rose important legal issues. The most obvious was to establish to whom did the water belong. According to a famous *hadith* mentioned by Ibn Hanbal, water should be considered common property of the society – "Muslims share the possession of three assets: water, fire and pastures"[13]. Such pronouncement proved way too simplistic and insufficient to settle the infinite questions connected to water and its ownership. So Muslim jurists had to entertain long discussions to come up with a detailed classification of all waters, their infrastructures and subsequently, who could use them, who had to administer them, who had to take care of them and so forth.
Running and underground waters were voted common property and did not belong to anyone in particular (*ghayr mamluk*). In theory, they should be used freely by any member of society[14]. What could be owned though were the means used to draw water. Thus, the jurists recognised the property right to certain categories that either owned, built or looked after hydraulic structures (canals, wells, norias) or to those who owned the lands where the spring or river were [15].
In Damascus, Aleppo, Fez and other big Islamic cities, public canalisations were funded by *waqf*, an endowment made by a Muslim to a religious, educational, or charitable cause. According to the Muslim doctrine, the temporal power had the duty to ensure and maintain public order and to protect the believers. Ensuring the society's common good, what we would call today *welfare*, was not among its main duties. To oversee the lack of such administrative care, charitable foundations such as *waqfs* started appearing. In large Islamic urban centres, *waqfs* were the primary – if not the only – facilitators through which rulers, governors and officials managed to provide basic public services to the locals, including the restoration and maintenance of the water network.
That said, the management of the city's water system was often one of the major concerns for Islamic rulers. Managing water trickled down to a question of power: it was both a ruler's obligation, but also a tool for rulers and governors to show their benevolence to the people. In this sense, special attention was directed to large mosque complexes. Indeed, the pious and praiseworthy nature of every action dedicated to the mosque and the great consumption of water that took place in this structure were both circumstances that called for the temporal power's attention and participation. Some jurists of the time once wrote: "[…] the water of these tanks is reserved to the use of the mosque and nobody should make a personal use of it in their abodes. Whoever uses the water of the mosque by infiltrating into the canal system replenishing the tank, must contribute to its maintenance and repairing it in the same proportion of the profit earned".
Among the structures showcasing the ruler's benevolent action, public fountains (*sabil*) were at the top of the list. At times simple, other times lavish and opulent, fountains are undoubtedly a recurrent element in the urban landscape

of Islam. In the Ottoman provinces, the sultans undertook grand hydraulic works, constructing large public fountains like in Jerusalem; repairing aqueducts in Cyprus and Algieri; digging canals in Iraq and Egypt; and even changing the direction of rivers like in Bursa. For local authorities, water works were a duty towards the society, but also a source of income and religious merit. The easier way to manifest one's power or perhaps, to be forgiven for a mistake were to multiply the public fountains in a city and claim merit through an inscription over their marble.

Gardens

An Ancient Inheritance

Islamic hydraulic technologies and irrigation systems derived from a complex and varied experience[16]. In this sense, Roman and Persian traditions played a crucial role, but Islamic civilisations also tried to experiment and introduce significant innovations. Agriculture (*filaha* in Arabic, from whose root the well-known term *fallah*, farmer – peasant, comes) underwent substantial changes with the introduction of new technologies, irrigation systems and intensive plans of crop rotation[17].

For instance, there are several Arabic manuscript referring Sicily as an incredibly fertile island, rich in woods, forests and especially water. One of the most precious accounts comes from the already-mentioned Ibn Hawqal, an Arab 10th-century traveller. In his scripts, he confirmed the advanced level of local agriculture achieved through a capillary water supply system reaching Palermo's countryside, rich in fenced farms (*mahall*) and springs with a multitude of water mills wisely located near the main streams. Among the common crops and cultures locally available, he enumerates watermelons, papyrus, Persian canes, cotton, hemp, several vegetables and vines, and the production of very high quality linen. Although he did not write about citrus fruits, already a century later other accounts clearly testify their importance in Sicilian agriculture. In this regard, an account by Ibn Makkī is particularly relevant, given that he wrote a treaty on the linguistic mistakes the Sicilians used to make when speaking Arabic. Ibn Makkī invites them to rectify the popular pronunciation *laranj* and *aranj* to *naraj* (orange) and *lumia* and *limuna* to *laymūna* (lemon).

That said, the most relevant testimonies about the agronomic tradition in the Mediterranean come from Arab Spain, from al-Andalus. An example is the *Kitab al-qasd wa l-bayan* by the Andalusian writer Ibn Bassal (second half 11th century), where he explains with anecdotes and in-depth details the local customs regarding cereals sowing, harvest and cultivating different vegetables and cotton (*zira'a al-qutn*). Other significant scripts in this field are the ones by the Sevillian author Abu l-Khayr al-Ishbili or Ibn al-'Awwam.

Speaking of innovations, a special mention to Islamic gardens seems now due[18]. In Islamic cosmogony, the garden was conceived first and foremost as an imitation of Paradise. Such association is explicitly rendered in the Qur'an, where the terms used for garden, *janna* and *firdaws*, are the ones usually referred to Paradise, the garden reserved to Muslim believers after their death.

Janna, the most recurrent word, harks back to the root of "what is covered", in green in this case. When plural, *jannat*, it clearly refers to the gardens on Earth – "And We placed therein gardens of palm trees and grapevines and caused to burst forth therefrom some springs so that they could eat His fruits" (36:34-35). The term *firdaws* has an analogous meaning. It comes into Arabic from ancient Persian and it phonetically recalls the biblical Hebrew and Aramaic *fardés*, which appears in the Old Testament with the meaning of garden, orchard surrounded by fortified walls or tall hedges (Ct. 4:12, Two Kings 25:4). The common derivation for all these languages is the Avestan *pairidaeza*, a term which originally referred to royal hunting grounds and reserves. It then entered Greek with *parádeisos*, and from there it became part of several Indo-European languages.

On a functional level, Arab gardens tend to conform to precise requirements and most specifically, to the image of the oasis with its dichotomies of plants–desert, cultivated land–nobody's land, nomadic and sedentary. Thus, the garden was also perceived as a peaceful fenced oasis. The shade of palms, the scent of a rose garden, the hushing of a fountain all express the same necessity –take a break from the heat and share a moment of togetherness in a refined, tranquil context. Beyond symbolical and literary connotations, the Islamic garden was not only a place where to rest and where plants and streams were aesthetic icons; gardens had to be manned and looked after.

Islamic historians started exploiting juridical literature to cast light on the historical development of the early urban settlements. Collection of *fatwas* (juridical opinions) became relevant landmarks in the social and urban landscape of the time. In these scripts, gardens are often mentioned and although they may lose part of their literary charm, they acquire new shades from everyday life, otherwise hard to come by.

It is through these texts that we discover that in the caliphal Cordoba of 10th century, a consistent problem faced in the gardens was water evacuation. For example, if there were two funds placed at different heights, the owner of the lowest one was obliged to receive rain water and was not allowed to build structures preventing its free flowing. The walls surrounding a garden (*jinani*), for instance, or the hydric canalisation system (*qanat*) managing the outflow of water were constantly subject to inspections and in case they were to become an obstacle and prevent the water from getting through, they could get demolished[19]. Indeed, the concerns rising from the management of the water canalisations between gardens and public places shall remain one of the most debated and thorny subjects in Islamic jurists' discussions[20].

Possibly, the most well-known Islamic gardens are the monumental kind, normally to be found in royal complexes and illustrious residences. The chronicles and poetry of the time reserve them a special place, not to mention the archaeological evidences and architectural remains. In those gardens, courtiers would rest, drink together, flirt, listen to music and be merry. Often they were the primary background to special banquets and *mujalasa*, gatherings where literary works were recited and read aloud. For a long time, these gardens became the main source of the transmission of knowledge in the Arab-Islamic world.

Let's not forget that monumental gardens not only guaranteed society an acknowledged place of merriment; they also played and accomplished an important political role. This is perhaps one of the reasons why they are all so varied. It would be difficult to attribute this variety solely to religious inclinations. Indeed, at times the gardens' internal divisions seem to be mirroring the territorial divisions of the surrounding agricultural landscape, rather than an idealised image of Paradise crossed by four rivers. In a similar way, the choice of plants arranged in these gardens often hides the foregoing agronomic experimentations and the intentions of a world run by commerce and exchanges, finding their reasons to be in spices, scents and ointments.

These monumental gardens were therefore grand representations of power as well. Their elegantly balanced shapes often conceal to our inexpert eyes what would have once been immediately clear to the contemporaries: besides the pleasures and delights these gardens granted, one should also remember that men and women experiencing these gardens were often moved by concrete necessities and very human needs. After all, water in its simplicity has always been the perfect answer to thirst.

[1] Ph.J. Baldensperger, *Peasant Folklore of Palestine*, Palestine Exploration Fund Quarterly Statement, London 1893, p. 210.

[2] R. D'Amora, S. Pagani, *Hammam, le terme nell'islam*, Olschki, Firenze 2011.

[3] M.H. Benkheira, *La maison de Satan. Le hammam en débat dans l'islam médiéval*, in "Revue de l'Histoire des religions", 220 (4), 2003, pp. 391-443.

[4] D'Amora, Pagani, *Hammam* cit.

[5] M.H. Benkheira, *Hammam, nudité et ordre moral dans l'islam médiéval*, in "Revue de l'Histoire des religions", 225 (1), 2008, pp. 75-128.

[6] M. Liverani, *Paradiso e dintorni. Il paesaggio rurale dell'antico Oriente*, Laterza, Roma-Bari 2018, pp. 33-52.

[7] A. Vanoli, *I cammini dell'Occidente*, Cleup, Padova 2001, pp. 21-22.

[8] T. Madani, *L'eau dans les villes islamiques médiévales*, in M.I. Del Val Valdivieso, O. Villanueva Zubizarreta (edited by), *Musulmanes y Cristianos frente al agua en las ciudades medievales*, Universidad de Castilla-La Mancha, Santander 2008, pp. 49-76.

[9] A. Raymond, *Grandes villes arabes à l'epoque ottomane*, Sindbad, Paris 1985, pp. 127, 156.

[10] H. Goblot, *Les qanats, une tecnique d'acquisition de l'eau*, Mouton, Paris 1979, p. 78.

[11] A. Ibn Hawqal, *Kitab surat al-ard*, edited by J.H. Kramers, in *Bibliotheca Geographorum Arabicorum*, vol. II, Brill, Leiden 1938, pp. 22-23; A. Vanoli, *La Sicilia musulmana*, il Mulino, Bologna 2012, pp. 136-138.

[12] P. Pascon, *Le Haouz de Marrakech*, vol. I, Éditions marocaines et internationales, Rabat 1977, p. 64.

[13] D. Santillana, *Istituzioni di diritto musulmano malichita con riguardo anche al sistema sciafiita*, vol. I, Istituto per l'Oriente, Anonima Romana Editoriale, Roma 1926, p. 304.

[14] M. Norvelle, *Water Use and Ownership according to the Texts of Hanbali Fiqh*, tesi, McGill University, Montréal 1980, pp. 23-29.

[15] D.S. Powers, *Law, Society, and Culture in the Maghrib, 1300-1500*, Cambridge University Press, Cambridge 2002, pp. 103-105.

[16] A. Touwaide, P. Dendle (edited by), *Health and Healing from the Medieval Garden*, Boydell Press, Woodbridge 2008.

[17] A.M. Watson, *Agricultural Innovation in the Early Islamic World*, Cambridge University Press, London - New York 1983; E. Burke, *Islam at the Center: Technological Complexes and the Roots of Modernity*, in "Journal of World History", 20 (2), 2009, pp. 165-186.

[18] J.B. Lehrman, *Earthly Paradise: Garden and Courtyard in Islam*, University of California Press, Berkeley - Los Angelese 1980; D.F. Ruggles, *Islamic Gardens and Landscapes*, University of Pennsylvania Press, Philadelphia 2008.

[19] Ch. Mazzoli-Guintard, *Vivre à Cordue au Moyen Âge*, Presses Universitaires de Rennes, Rennes 2003, p. 171.

[20] F. Vidal-Castro, *Agua y urbanismo: evacuación de aguas en fatwa-s de al-Andalus y el norte de Africa*, in P. Cressier, M.I. Fierro, J.-P. Van Staëvel (edited by), *L'urbanisme dans l'Occident musulman au Moyen Âge, aspects juridiques*, Casa de Velázquez, Consejo Superior de Investigaciones Científicas, Madrid 2001.

Religion

In the Qur'an, the miracle of water is mentioned several times:

Let Man consider his nourishment.
We poured out the rains abundantly,
then We split the earth in fissures
and therein made the grains to grow
and vines, and reeds,
and olives, and palms
and dense-tree´d gardens,
and fruits, and pastures,
an enjoyment for you and your flocks.
(Qur'an, Surah 'Abasa, 80:24-32)

Similarly, in the arts of the Islamic world water took on different shapes and forms like the lush rivers of Paradise, presented in carpets and miniatures; and the several vessels and decorative patterns used during the daily ablution rites. Water and its iconographic expression are particularly relevant in the context of *Hajj*, the annual Islamic pilgrimage to Mecca, one of the five pillars of Islam, constituting a mandatory religious duty for Muslims to be accomplished at least once in their lifetime. The believers attending *Hajj* need to undergo a series of practices involving ablutions, haircuts, cutting their nails shorter, cladding themselves with only two white cloths; and several other ceremonies such as walking around Ka'ba in circles seven times, running between two small hills, and throwing stones to low pillars and steles embodying a demon. After this circumambulation, all pilgrims then walk to the Zamzam well, to commemorate a passage from the Qur'an in which Hājar and her son Isma'il were miraculously able to quench their thirst thanks to this well. -It is commonly believed that the water from this well is rich of beneficial properties; even the Prophet's *hadīths* define the Zamzam well's water "*the best one on earth*". It is thus not surprising that every year visiting pilgrims pour some of this water in small flasks and take it away with them.

In several maps of the *Masjid al-Haram* (the Great Mosque of Mecca), the Zamzam well is clearly pictured and it is often mentioned in *Hajj* literature too like prayer books, illustrated guides, and lithographed pilgrimage certificates and maps produced by local artists of the Hijazi area for the pilgrims.

The sacredness attributed to water by popular beliefs led this element to be a primary one in magical practices, such as divination. Though rejected by several Muslim theologists, the use of magic bowls to tell the future was rather common.

These bowls would be inscribed with Quranic verses to the interior. The water, by flowing against these verses, would be imbued with special powers. Often, Quranic tablets were placed in these bowls, water would be poured onto them to melt the ink away, and the ink mixed with the sacred water would be given to drink to heal illnesses. Distinguished families of the time secretly owned and used these vessels and also collected manuscripts about magic and supernatural powers, following at times the therapeutic practices there described. There are numerous 'magic' bowls used to heal different illnesses, each one inscribed with specific thaumaturgical formulae that, when in contact with water or other liquids, release their healing properties to them.

Especially with the rise of the Safavid dynasty (16th-17th century) to power, interest in divinatory practices and in the art of divination seem to have been very widespread, coinciding with a large production of these magic bowls.

1

Basin

Iran-Afghanistan (Khorasan),
Ghaznavid period, second half
12th century
Copper alloy, with engraved decoration
h. 11.7 cm, Ø 43.8 cm
Museo d'Arte Orientale - MUCIV
inv. n. 8390

Of stellar shape, resting on a plain base, with flared walls with fourteen indented lobes, the decoration incised and located only to the interior, consisting of three concentric registers, the centre with an eight-lobed flower sprouting an interlocking stellar geometric motif contained within a circular frame; the spaces created by the ribbons' knotwork filled with figural representations of harpies and pseudo-epigraphic bands in Kufic; the third band with a frieze of interlocking arches ornate with tri-lobed flowers and a cursive pseudo-epigraphic band against a vegetal and floral spiralling ground located along the upper portion of the wall, organised in fourteen rectangular cartouches, alternating with small arches emerging from the space created by the wavy profile of the cartouche's frame, the rim with engraved S-shaped motifs. Basins with flared walls and stellar profiles are confidently attributed to the Khorasan area and they could be considered the most quintessential expression of the Eastern Iranian metalware production dating from 12th to 14th century (Scerrato 1961; Laviola 2016, pp. 103-111, 466-474). The lobes are generally shallow and in the later productions, their number increases from 12-16 to 18-20. The MAO basin is a significant representative of this Eastern Iranian production, from both the formal and decorative points of view with the typical compositional scheme and characteristic motifs (Scerrato 1961; Allan 1976, p. 253).

F.M.A.

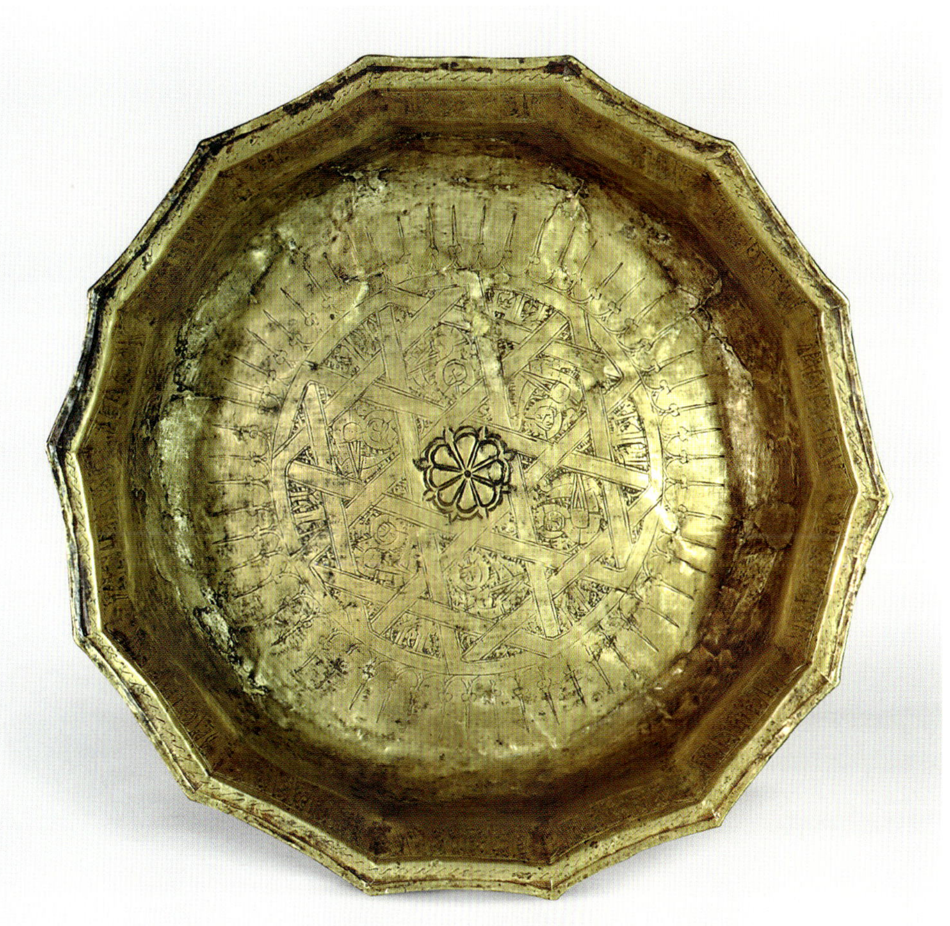

1

2

Chaharbagh garden carpet

Northwest Persia, 17th century
Cotton warp, wool weft, asymmetric wool knot
242 × 208 cm (a fragment)
Zaleski collection, Courtesy Galleria Moshe Tabibnia, inv. n. 156809

The following entry also refers to cat. n. 102 Chaharbagh garden carpet
Northwest Persia, early 18th century
Moshe Tabibnia collection,
inv. n. 154021
see page 155

Large carpet fragments (at times, the dimensions of a single carpet can reach 10 meters.). On the borders a continuous decorative band with fir-like trees interspersed with other trees with large leaves topped by pairs of birds. The central decoration divided in four parts by rivers flowing from an octagonal fountain with fish located in the centre, each rectangle depicting gardens with lush trees and flowers within eight-pointed star designs emerging from the intersection of two squares.
These carpets portray in their warps and wefts the features of a lush garden, an essential element in the noble abodes of Safavid Iran. Gardens were so central to Iranian culture that they were often depicted in Persian miniature paintings and they even provided the title to many poems.

Bibliography: 156809 appears in Burns 2002, pp. 144-145. For a better preserved example, refer to *Civiltà islamica*, 2015, cat. 141, pp. 168-169.

I.B.

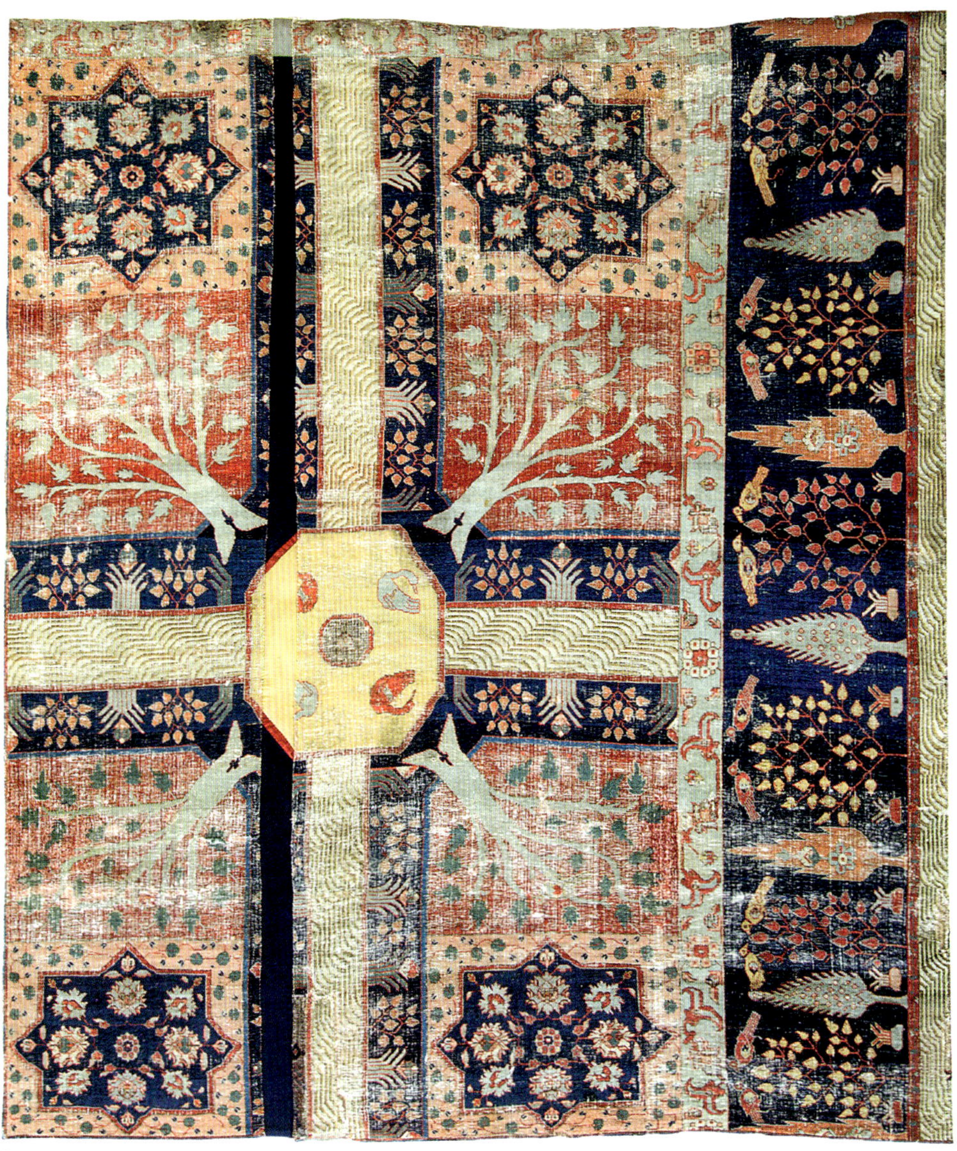

2

3

Basin of al-Malik an-Nāsir Muhammad b. Qalāwun

Egypt or Syria, first half 14th century
Brass with silver and gold damascene
h. cm 21.6, max. Ø 50.5 cm, base Ø 39 cm
Museo e Real Bosco di Capodimonte, Napoli, inv. n. 112109/1145
(previously Borgia collection)

Of large circular shape, on a flat base, with flat walls, flared rim and splayed mouth. Both the interior and exterior incised with a large epigraphic band filled with large *thuluth* inscriptions against fine floral and vegetal grounds, interspersed with three large polylobed medallions decorated with peonies and rosettes leading to a central roundel with the name of the Sultan.
The interior mirrors the same decorative arrangement of the exterior epigraphic band, the base with dense floral tendrils and vegetal ornaments.

Outer inscription:

Glory upon our Lord the Sultan al-Malik / al-Nasir
Rescuer of the world and of religion, Muhammad Ibn al-Malik al-Mansur ibn Qalawun al-Salihi

Inner inscription:

Glory upon our Lord the Sultan al-Malik / al-Nasir
Rescuer of the world and of religion, slayer of the unbelievers and of the polytheists Muhammad ibn Qalawun al-Salihi, may your victories be full of glory
(S. Carboni, in *Eredità dell'Islam* 1993, p. 316).

The stye of the decoration and the content of the calligraphic medallions place this artwork at the time of Muhammad ibn Qalawun (r. 1293-1341 with two minor interruptions).
In Mamluk art, inscriptions boasting and praising the Sultan's deeds and qualities are common. But typical of Qalawun's period is the inclusion of his name in the central polylobed medallions, replacing a figural image of the sultan himself.
The most well-known example of monumental Mamluk basin is the one preserved at the Louvre Museum in Paris, called the "Baptistère de Saint Louis". At the Louvre, there is also another basin very similar to the one in this exhibition, inv. n. MAO 101. Lastly, another basin commissioned by ibn Qalawun and bearing his name is preserved at the British Museum in London (inv. OA 1851.1-4.1).

Bibliography: Scerrato 1966, n.56; Scerrato 1967, n. 12, fig. 1; *Eredità dell'Islam*, 1993, cat. n. 182, pp. 316-317; Martino et al., 1996, p. 38; Martino L., *Le quattro parti* 2001, p. 150; Spallanzani 2010, pl. 5, p. 124; Drake Boehm, Holcomb 2016, cat. n. 129c., pp. 254-255; *Islam e Firenze*, 2018, cat. n. 48, p. 222.

I.B.

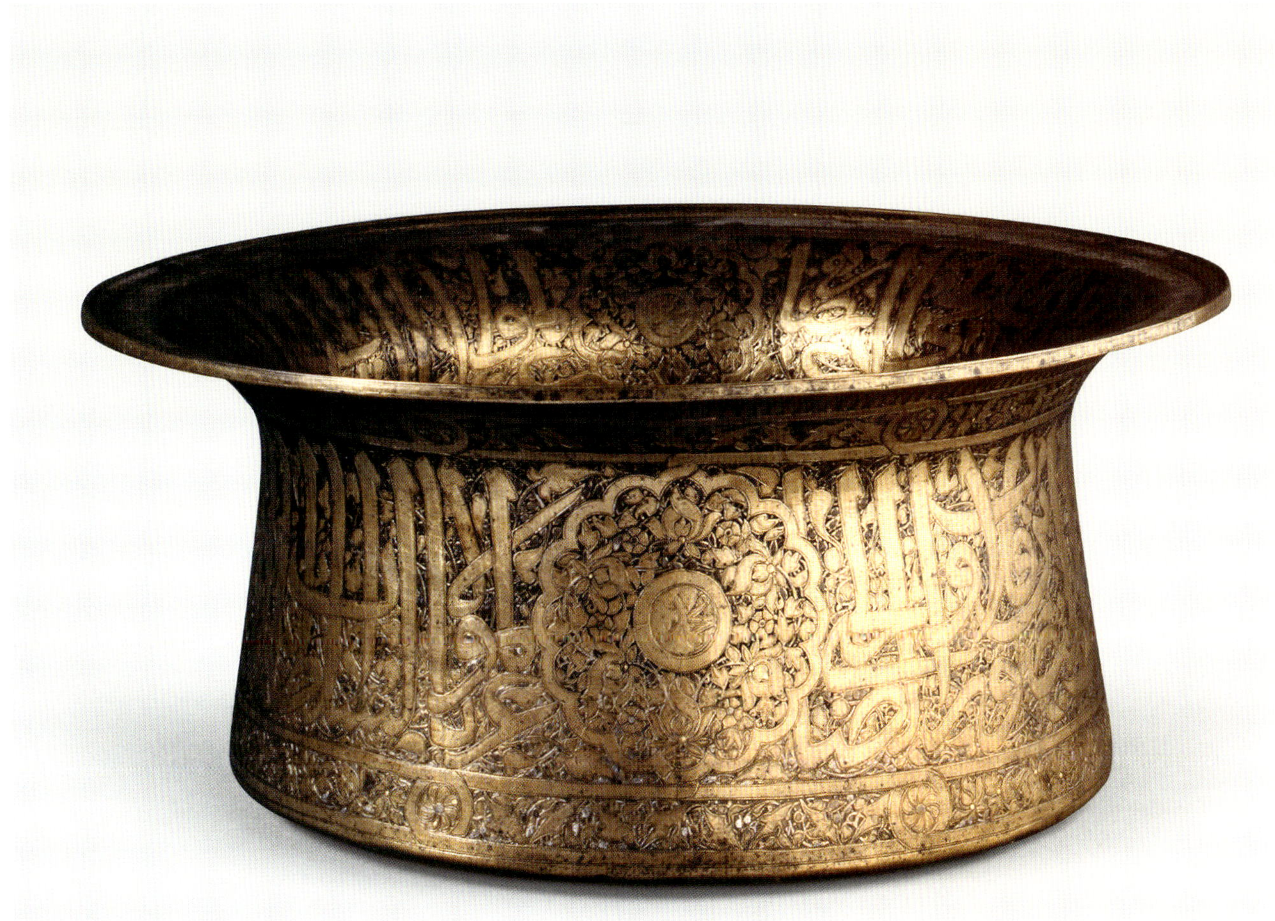

3

4

Prayer rug

Central Persia, second half 16th century
Cotton and wool warp, cotton and silk weft, Persian asymmetric wool knot, 174 × 118 cm
Courtesy Galleria Moshe Tabibnia, inv. n. 195011

Of rectangular format with concentric decorative bands, on the outer perimeter lobed cartouches filled with *thuluth* calligraphic Quranic inscriptions, similar lobed cartouches towards the base. The centre with a cusped niche is filled with a colourful floral triumph.

Inscriptions:

Bismillah, two verses from the second sura, *Surah Al-Baqarah*, *Ayatul Kursi* (2:255), the *shahada* in its Sh'iah format, *Surah Al-Ahzab* (33:56), and an auspicious prayer to the Fourteen Infallibles. The four star-shaped medallions are inscribed in squared Kufic with invocations to Allah, Muhammad and 'Ali.

For an in-depth discussion on the flower vase' symbolism, please refer to cat. n. 5. It is worth noting that on the base of the vase, there are no inscriptions. This would be the area where the believer would kneel and against which he would rest his knees, an area too unremarkable to contain celestial references.

Bibliography: Eiland et al. 1999, vol. V, cat. 51, p. 99; *Amos Gitai* 2014, pp. 48 and 52.

I.B.

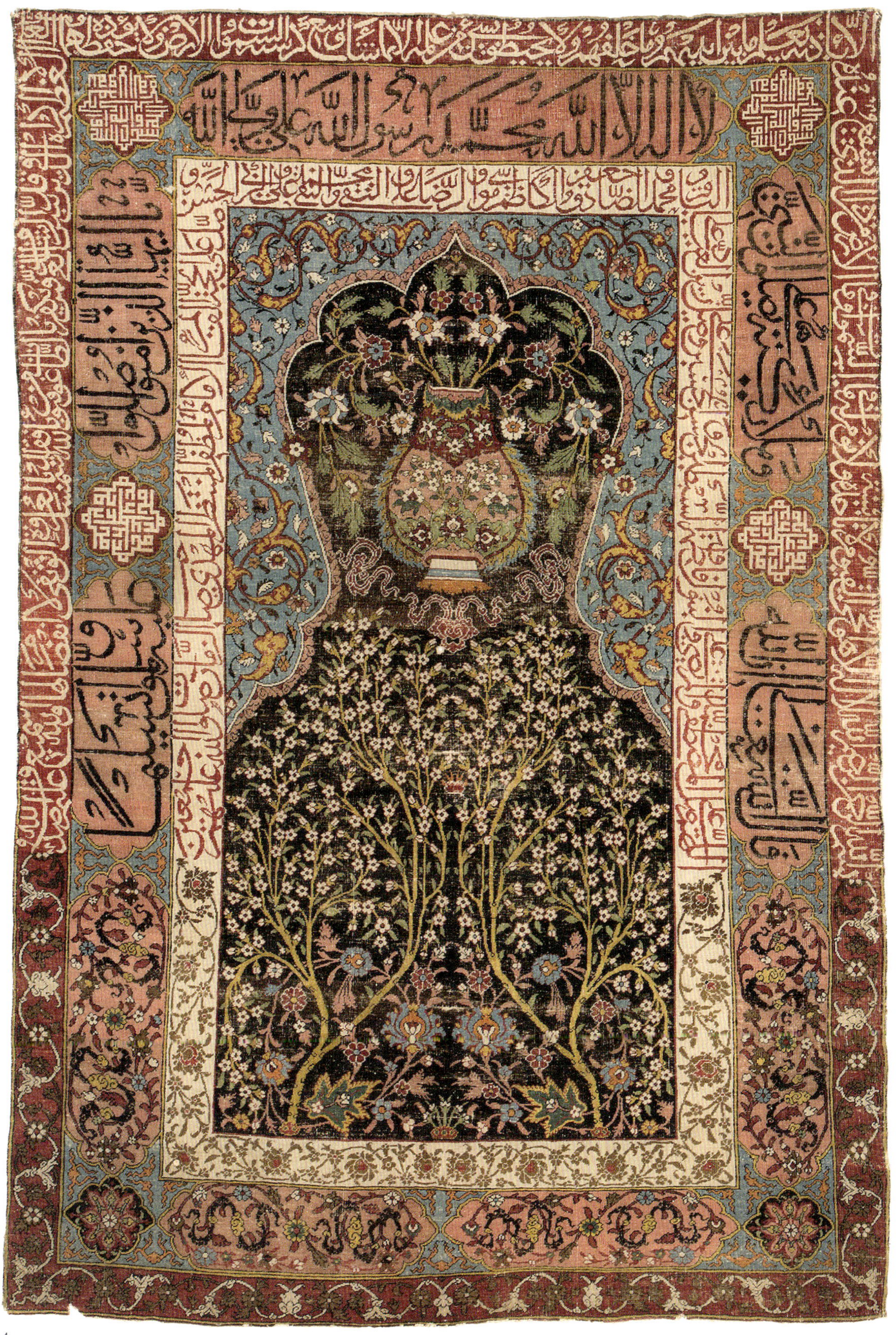

4

5

Iznik Plate decorated with an ewer

Turkey, last quarter 16th century
Fritware, with polychrome underglaze painting
25.5 × 4 cm
MIC, Museo internazionale delle Ceramiche in Faenza, inv. n. 6299

Comprising a dish of circular shape, resting on a circular foot, with shallow cavetto and slightly splayed rim, the decoration of the cavetto with a crown of *saz* leaves interspersed with prunus leaves in blue and yellow and of the rim with the typical Chinese rock and weaves motif, the centre with a red-painted large ewer and the surrounding composition enhanced by small touches of bole red in relief, the exterior with small blue roundels.
This example fits into the varied Iznik wares production, of which in this exhibition several other examples are showcased allowing to trace the interesting chronology of this kiln. This dish can be dated to the last quarter of the 16th century due to the presence of the bole red in the palette, a colour added only in 1545. It took a few years before the local craftsmen mastered the technique of stabilising this colour during the firing process, producing thus a brilliant and bold red in relief, evident here, and glazed with a glossy lead-alkaline glaze.
For an in-depth discussion on Iznik wares, please see the appendix to cat. n. 83.

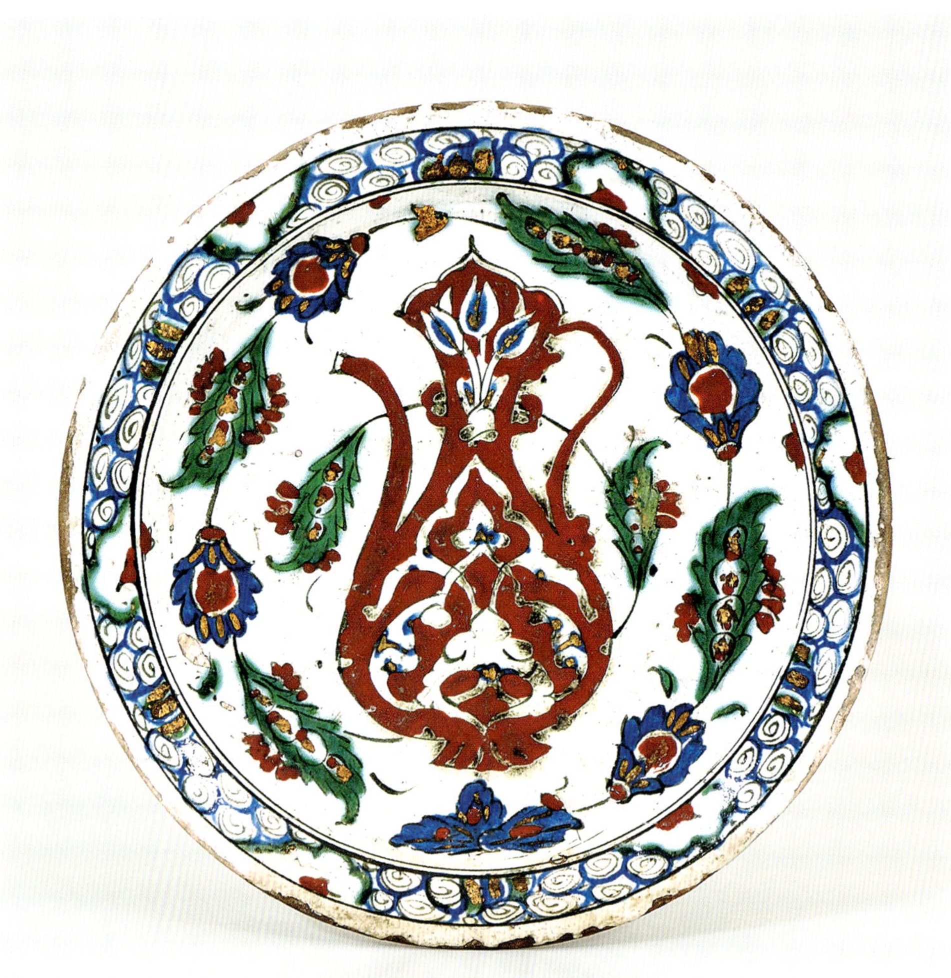

5

The symbolism of the vase and ewer

The iconography and symbolism of the ewer digs its roots in the both poetical and religious contexts. Due to the climate, water always had a place of honour in the Muslims' priorities list, even more so portable water, the personal supply which can be taken around and tamed.
Further to this, the Qur'an - always concerned with hygienic measures with the aim to carry out a social function - prescribes the ablution before the prayer and to wash one's hands before several daily activities. Even the Quranic description of Paradise as a garden links it to water, as it goes without saying the existence of a garden depends very much on the presence of water, without mentioning here all the other passages hinting at the enlivening properties of water.
In Persian poetry, rich of strong metaphors and personifications, the human body is symbolised as an ewer with five spouts (reference to the five senses), containing the water of the divine grace. For all these above-mentioned reasons, the depiction of ewers and flower vases act as synecdoches of the water element and are among the most recurrent decorative motifs in Islamic architecture and art.
In the architectural context, for instance, this motif can be found in the extraordinary pieta-dura marble inlays of Mughal India or in the *Chini Kana* (ceramics niches), where the niche is often in the shape of the vase there located. Even in Safavid Iran there are several *cuerda seca* tiles decorated with flower vases. In miniature painting, vases and ewers are always present on terraces, banquets and lovers' garden and picnics scenes. Lastly, in the ceramic production, as in this case, it can be found as a decorative element on its own.

Bibliography: Ravanelli Guidotti 1987, cat.n. 194, pp. 304-305. For similar examples, see Atasoy and Raby, 1989, cat. n. 741-779 and Watson, 2004, cat. T.21, p. 443.

I.B.

6

Tombak basin and ewer

Turkey, first half 19th century
Gilded copper (*tombak*), engraved
h. 40 cm (ewer), Ø 64 cm (basin)
Private collection, Brussels

Comprising a pyriform ewer (*ibrik*), resting on a circular foot, with a domed lid topped by a small pommel resting on a vegetal ground, both the spout and the handle S-shaped; and a large circular basin, with a wide splayed rim designed to gather the water poured by the ewer, both objects decorated with a similar lozenge-shaped, spearhead-like pattern. Similar objects are likely to have been produced as lavish commodities in an exclusive, possibly courtly, context to be used during ritual ablutions. At the Ottoman court, the association water-Paradise is very often mirrored in the objects' symbolical decorative vocabulary. For instance, the *ibrik* became a true icon of water and was then reproduced on prayer rugs, to remind the believers to purify themselves before practicing the prayer.

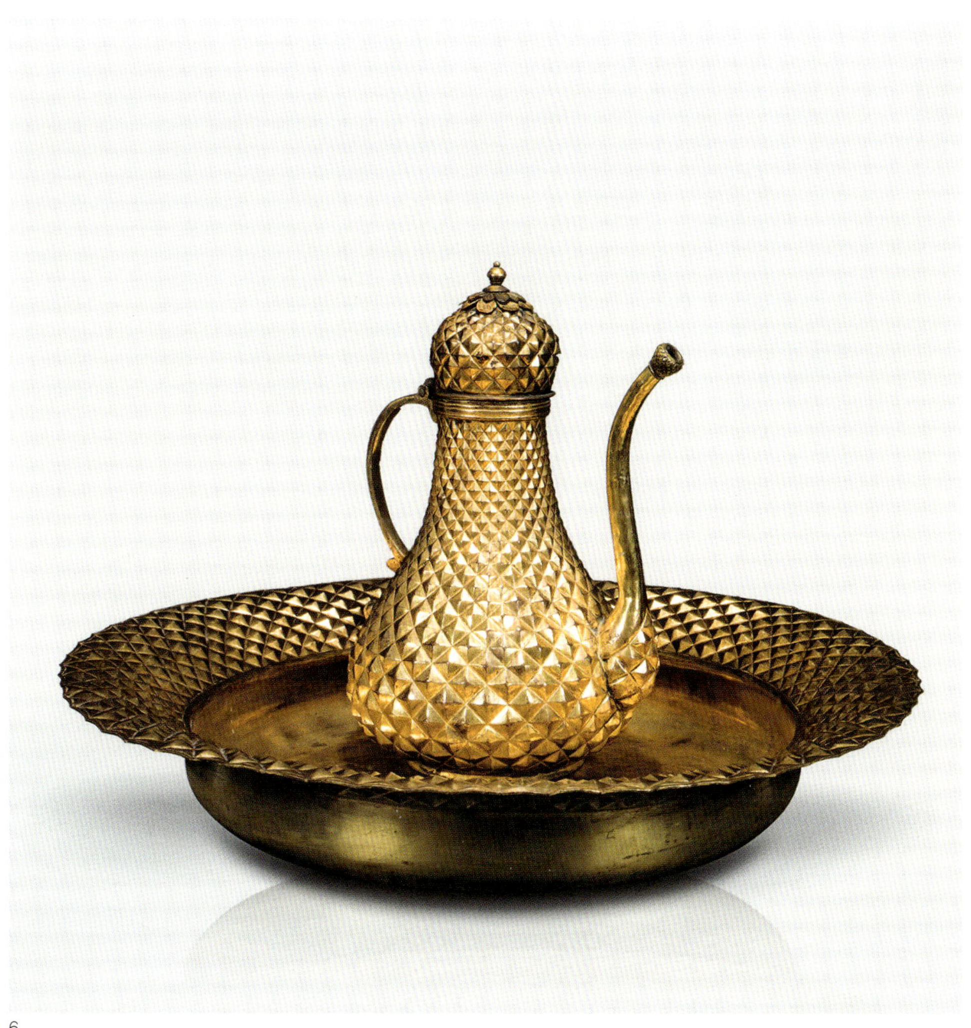

6

Provenance: antique art market.
Bibliography: a similar example is preserved at the Museum of Islamic Art, Istanbul, inv. n. 21 in *Topkapi à Versaille*, 1999, p. 151, n. 103; and Sahin, 2009, pp. 300-302.

I.B.

7
Al-Barun Al-Mukhtari
Qibla finder, Mecca marker

Turkey, dated 1738 AD
Ink and tempera on wood
Closed triptych holder
76.5 × 36 × 4 cm
86 × 44 × 6.5 cm
Fondazione Musei Civici di Venezia,
Museo Correr, inv. n. Cl. XXIX, n. 53

... this miserable servant, looking for a refuge in the one and only of his time, the most virtuous and clever next in line at court, the most beloved and courteous Mustafa Efendi ...
... for the pious practitioners who wander through the streets on this Earth, determining the Qibla was a primary necessity in their daily religious practice, even if the direction was never thoroughly accurate; thus, the need to design a universal pointer with new rules of practical use ...
... the paper represents the flat projection of the terrestrial hemisphere constituted by the Seven Climates, Asia, Africa and Europe ...
... for each country, the most well-known cities are marked and show their latitude and longitude coordinates ... similar to a proper mirror of the world.
Moreover, once one knows the Qibla of a specific place by following the correct rotation instructions on this pointer, they also know where the holy Ka'ba *is, which looks like a* mihrab *in the upper edge of the paper, overlooking the whole hemisphere.*
... The miserable servant el-Barun was the first who conceived and built with his own hand this universal Qibla finder, may God save him from any affliction. In the city of Istanbul, the year 1151 (1738).
(G. Bellingeri in *Eredità dell'Islam*, 1993, p. 1)

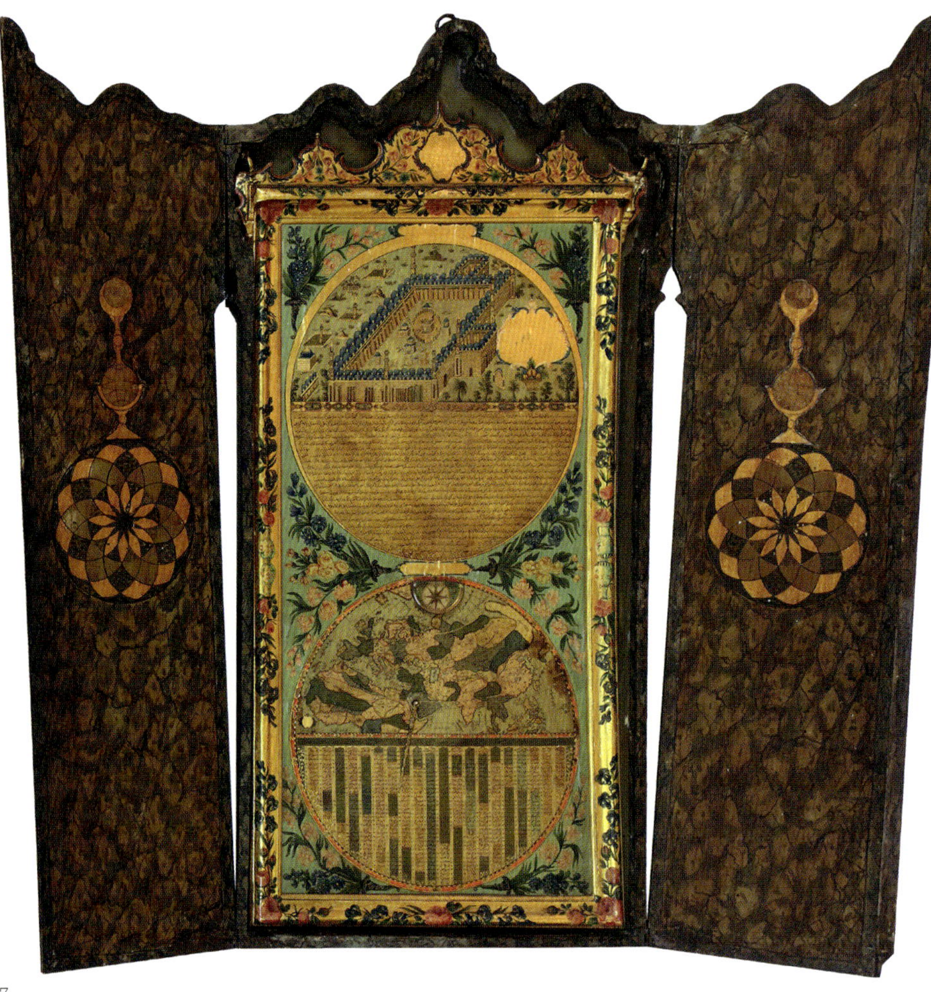

7

The long inscription on this Qibla finder, located in the upper roundel of the southern hemisphere, portraying in half the sacred enclosure of Mecca, serves as its own description. All the above-mentioned elements lead to believe that this was indeed a universal scientific tool in use to determine the direction of the prayer towards Ka'ba. A more integral version of the inscription delving further into the instructions on how to use it, the maker and the date of production can be found in Bellingeri in Concina, 2006, pp. 188-190 or Curatola in *Eredità dell'Islam*, 1993, cat. n. 260, pp. 406-407.

Curatola (ivi, p. 407) speculates that the name of the maker, El-Barun Al-Mukhtari, may suggest that the object was conceived by the genius of the Armenian crafts community in Istanbul. Bellingeri (in Concina, 2006, p. 190) tries to rebuild the story of this pointer and believes that it was thanks to the Abbot G. Toderini that it landed in Venice. In his major work, *Letteratura Turchesca* (Venezia 1787), Toderini provides a detailed description of this tool, by then owned by Baroni and later on purchased at auction by Toderini. In this description, the pointer is defined as "mirror of the world" and it is rather curious that the work was successively mounted as a 19th-century dressing table with two doors opening like a casket and whose decoration emulates marbled paper.
The internal wooden frame showcases rather baroque vegetal elements, clearly European in its inspiration. Some analogous examples of Qibla pointers can be found at the Chester Beatty Library, and at the Gallery of Oriental Art (inv. n. MS 443) in Dublin, also dated around 1738.

Bibliography: Toderini, 1787, pp. 121-129; *Eredità dell'Islam*, 1993, cat. n. 260, pp. 406-407; Q Adamjee, in *Venise et l'Orient*, 2006, pp. 108-109, 312 cat. 48; Concina, 2006, pp. 188-190; Q Adamjee, in *Venezia e l'Islam*, 2007, pp. 128, 327-328 cat. 28; G. Bellingeri in *Armenia* 2011, pp. 216-217 n. 63.

I.B.

8

Ms Ross 878, Sacred area of Mecca

18th century
Manuscript
Opaque polychrome tempera on paper
173 × 110 × 10 mm
Ross 878, f. 12r © Biblioteca Apostolica Vaticana

An illustration part of an Al-Jazuli's (d. 869) *Dala'il al-Khayrat* (The Demonstrations of Excellence) manuscript, the Maghribi author of the text the founder of the Jazuliyya sect, comprising a small collection of prayers addressed to the Prophet Muhammad, the description of his sepulchre and of his names, the calligrapher Isma'il, also known as Sayyadizade, belonging to the Istanbuli entourage and pupil of Husayn known as Khaffaf-zade of Yedikule, a renowned calligrapher (d. 1741); the illustration on f. 12, 118 × 68 mm, depicting the sacred area of Mecca, the *Masjid al Hara*, and Ka'ba, a landscape of clear Western influence especially in the rendering of the mountainous landscape and the clouds behind it.

Bibliography: *Catalogo dei codici* 2014.

A.V.

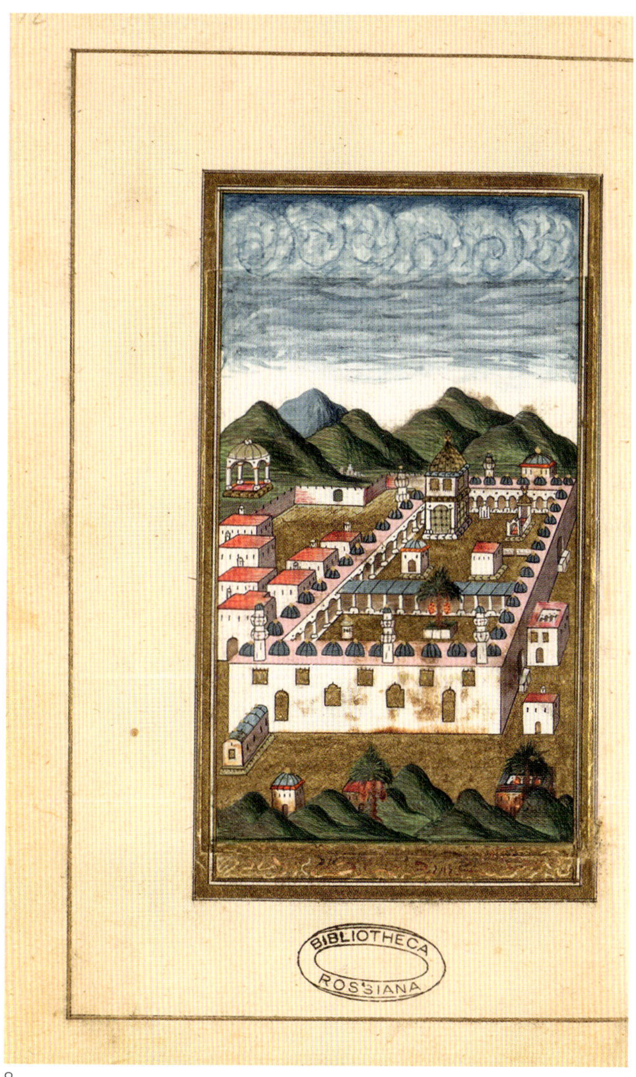

8

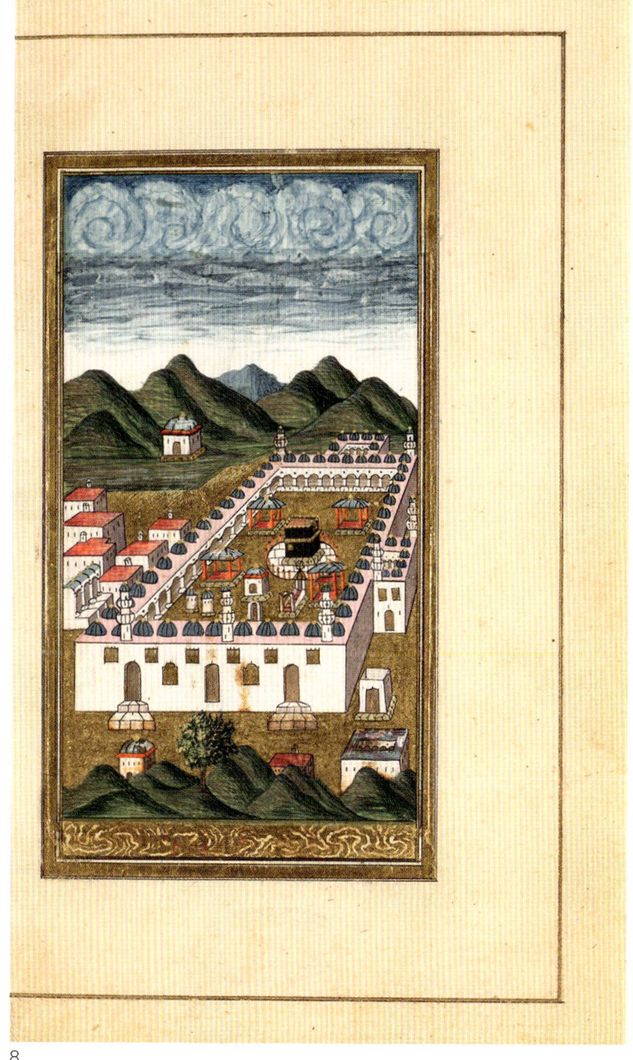

8

9

Rock crystal bottle, subsequently used as a reliquary

Bottle: Egypt, 10th century
Renaissance mounting: Bernardo Baldini, Florence, mid 16th century
Rock crystal, cast gold, niello, enamel
Firenze, Museo delle Cappelle Medicee, Tesoro della basilica di San Lorenzo, inv. n. 1945, n.2

Of cylindrical shape, resting on a circular foot, rising to a tall splayed neck, the body carved with repeating oval medallions with a border with small hexagonal cartouches filled with addressed birds, the shoulder with a band of Kufic inscription:

and joy, and favour, and ease, and wealth, and eternal fame (E.J. Grube in *Eredità dell'Islam*, 1993, p.148).

The top of the neck with a carved decoration of stylised crouched lions, preceded by a pair of circles in relief around the junction of neck and body. Fatimid rock crystals are possibly among the rarest and most skilled artistic achievements of Islamic Art. They are rare not only because of the material used, which had to be imported from Basra, Yemen and certain islands in Eastern Africa, but also because of the difficulties faced when working this hard surface, sanctioning the craftsmen' extraordinary expertise.
A Sh'iah dynasty, the Fatimids were particularly appreciative of the rock crystal quality to capture light – one of the manifestations of Allah – and reflect it. They used to consider rock crystal their "dynastic material" *par excellence* (Shalem 1996, pp.61-62, n. 60).
Selected for their shininess and transparency, rock crystals were often associated to water for its "iced water" effect. In his *Treaty on Precious Stones* (973AH-1048 AD), Al-Biruni, a renowned Arabic scholar, master of several disciplines, attributes to rock crystal healing powers against sore throat and stomach ache and associates it with air, water and Paradise. Even in the Qur'an, the virtuous believers:

will be served on silver trays and with jugs of pure crystal, harmoniously forged' (76:15-16).

Rock crystals were thus once part of the Fatimid caliphs' treasuries, now dispersed through the commercial Mediterranean routes and partly looted in 1068. This jug is one of the 180 examples that survived to this day and are known to us (Contadini 1998, p. 18). Egyptian rock crystal jugs and beakers were very much sought-after in the West too, where the mystical and spiritual inspiration brought about by the material transformed them into desired commodities in the religious panorama. Indeed, these objects started appearing and being collected as reliquaries in the churches and basilicas, as testified by the jug in the Tesoro di Fermo or the two cups preserved at the Treasury of St. Mark, Venice (inv. n. 99 e 73).

Bibliography: Heikamp 1980, n. 21, pl. III, figg. 40-41, pp. 236-238; Gabrieli, Scerrato, 1985, cat. n. 540; *Eredità dell'Islam*, 1993, cat. n. 57, pp. 147-148; A. von Gladiss, in *Islam specchio d'Oriente*, 2002, cat. n. 53, p. 80.; *Islam e Firenze*, 2018 p. 191 n. 6.

I.B.

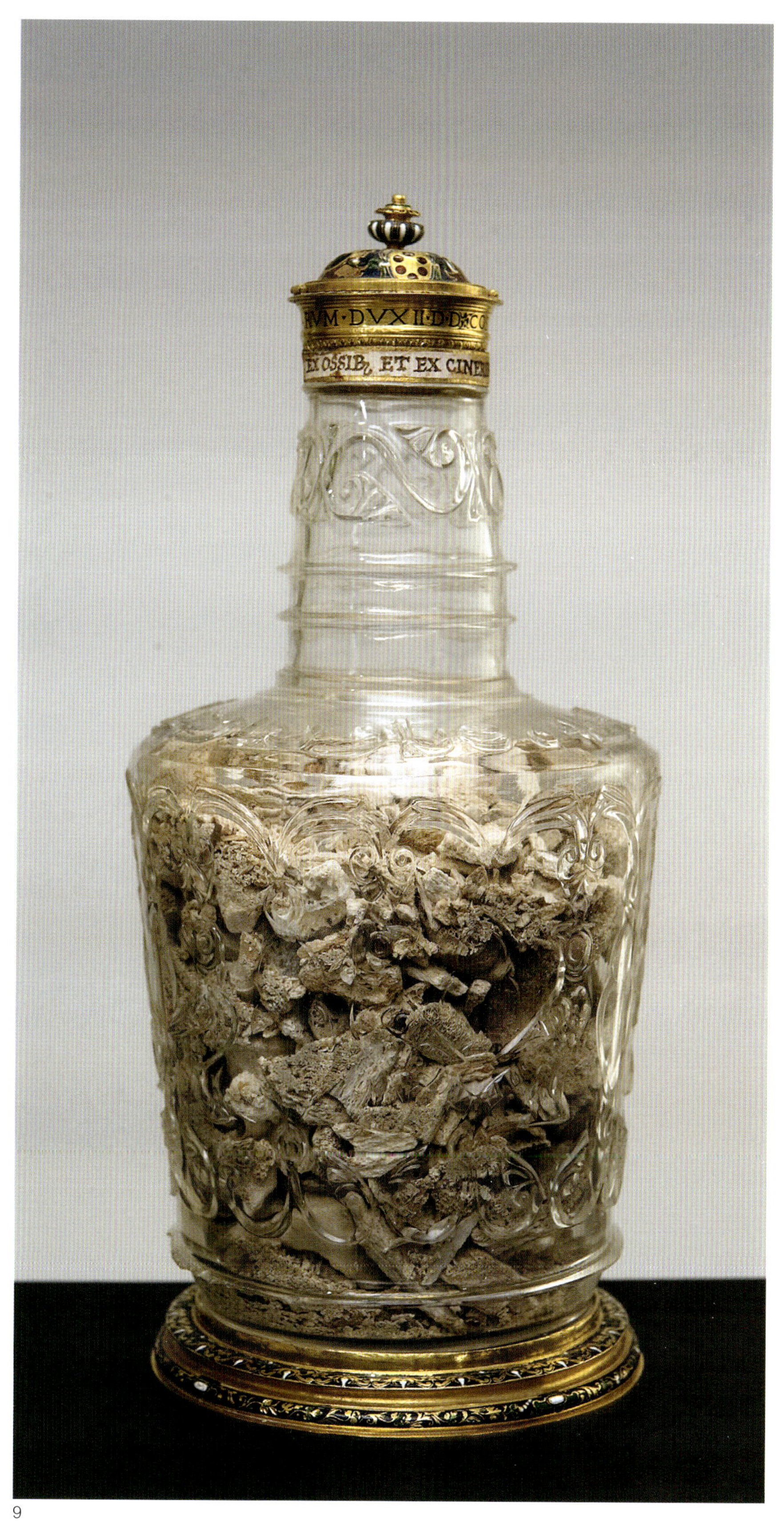

9

10-11-12
Three flasks (*mataras*)

Turkey, 17th century
Leather and velvet brocade with silver embroidery
Fondazione Musei Civici di Venezia, Museo Correr,
inv. n. Cl XIV SN1-1432-1431

Of typical shape, comprising two flasks of pyramidal shape and a third polygonal one with rounded body and cylindrical neck and spout, the decoration on the metal thread embroidered velvet with hyacinths, rosettes and tulips – typical of the *Kara Memi* style, a truly Ottoman naturalistic style invented by Kara Memi in 1545 the then director of the *nakkashane* (Royal workshop). Flasks of this shape tend to be rather common personal objects for everyday use, even among soldiers, but their decoration defines the social status of their owners – from simple leather to encrusted rock crystal and to *tombak* (see cat. n. 14), going through pleasant and refined examples such as these.

As personal accessories, flasks (*mataras*) were proper *status symbols*. During special ceremonies at the Ottoman Court, sultans often gifted his courtiers with either arms or *mataras*. Several miniatures testify this trend and show the ruling sultan followed by an attendant carrying his ceremonial flask. The most famous example is possibly the *matara* of Suleyman I, preserved at the Topkapi Museum in Istanbul (inv n. 2/3825) or the rock crystal flask with gold mounting, exactly in the same shape of these ones, also preserved at the Topkapi Museum (inv. n, 2/474). Among the different types of flasks used in the Islamic lands, one worthy of mention is the so-called pilgrim's flask, specifically used to contain water from a holy source. Pilgrim's flasks share a very similar shape with these *mataras*, though often they were made of very simple, plain leather, without any decoration. Pilgrims would carry such flasks during their pilgrimage to Mecca (*hajj*) for personal use to gather water from the Zamzam well. An example can be found at the British Museum, inv. n. As. 4248 a-b. Bottles filled with holy water (*Zamzamiyas*) used to be packaged, closed with a leather cap, sealed with wax and sold to the pilgrims in Mecca as a souvenir. These are very dear to all Muslim pilgrims to this very day. For another example, see the British Museum, inv. Af.+1756. Analogous flasks to the ones here presented were looted during the siege of Vienna (1683), as part of the Karlsruhe Türkenbeute (Petrasch et al., 1991, n. 256, pp. 295-296, mentioning six examples in total in Central Europe). Another flask with similar decoration is published in Koç and Bilgi, 2005, n.48, pp.118-119; and two more are part of the Furusiyya Art Foudation published in Bashir, 2008, cat. nos. 272-273, pp. 280-281.

Bibliography: *Eredità dell'Islam*, 1993, n. 257, Hocquet and Pyhrr in *Venezia e l'Islam 2007*, pp. 48 and 337, M. Socal in *Venezia e Istanbul*, 2009, p. 208 nos. III.51 a-b-c.

I.B

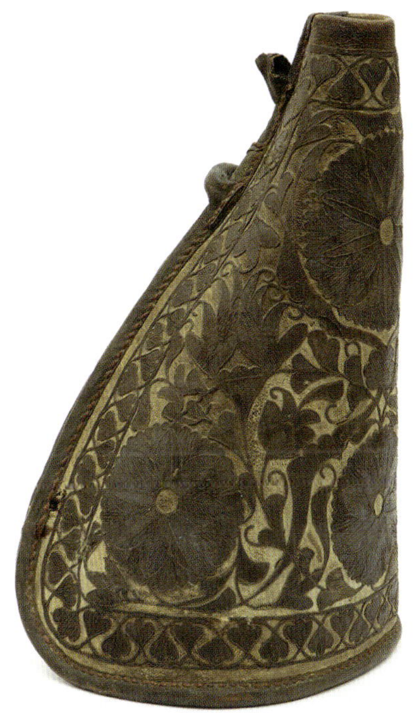
10

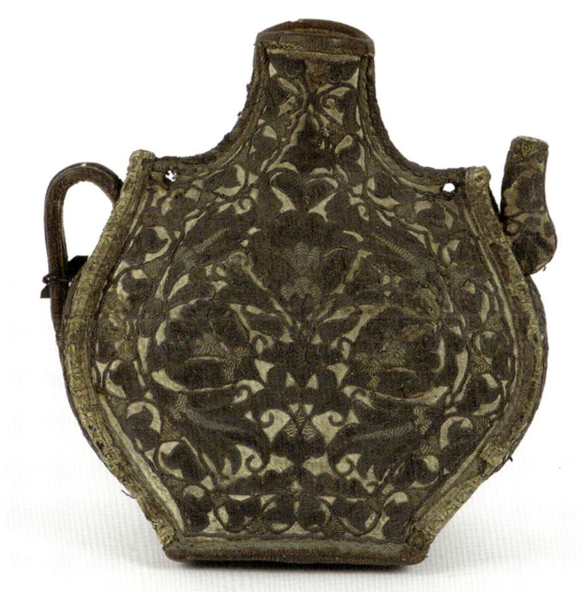
11

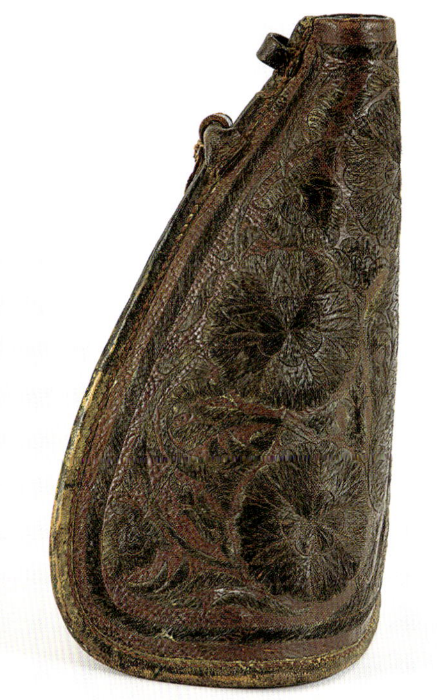
12

13
Achrome pilgrim flask

Iran, 13th-14th century
Earthenware, unglazed with decoration
MAO Museo d'Arte Orientale, Turin, inv. n. ISv/100

Of compressed circular shape, with flattened sides and double handles, with flared shoulder, narrowing neck, straight rim, the sides decorated with concentric circles filled with fretwork, a calligraphic band against a ring-punched ground, baluster-shaped motifs and a subtle disc filled with a crown of pearls, the centre with moulded intertwining split palmette decoration.
I motivi decorativi alludono alla tematica idrica e al fatto che l'oggetto nascesse come contenitore per acqua.

Bibliography: unpublished. For a similar example, see Watson 2004, cat. Ab.13, p. 119.

I.B.

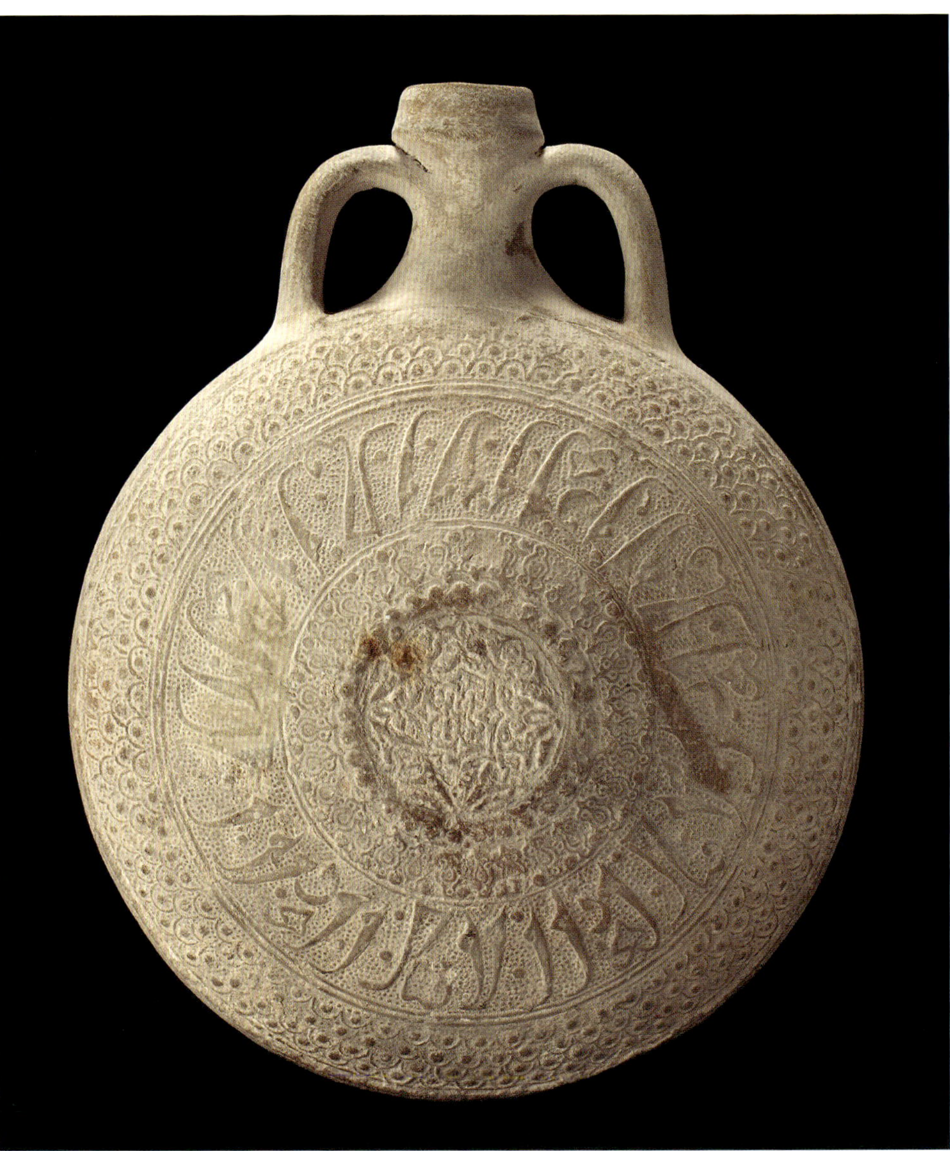

13

14
Flask

Turkey, 17th century
Brass sheet, engraved and molded with traces of gilding
h. 24.5 cm
The Aron Collection, inv. n. 212

Of pyramidal shape, with a wide bottom, a cylindrical neck and a curved handle cast separately, the exterior engraved with a delicate decorative band of floral motifs and split palmettes around the neck and sides, with button-shaped pattern with small discs imitating the seams of the leather prototype joints and leaf-shaped cartouches filled with stylised phytomorphic motifs and vegetal tendrils, the decoration reminiscent of the one present on *tombak* armours of the same period.
The shape of this flask is reminiscent of the typical leather pilgrim's flasks used to pour in the water from the Zamzam well. Its material and decoration though clearly indicates it belongs to an important, member of the social elite. For an in-depth discussion, see cat. n. 10.

Provenance: antique art market.
Bibliographical references: Bilgi 2005, cat. n. 48, pp. 118-119, Sotheby's 2017, lot. 202, Metropolitan Museum of Art, New York (inv. n. 1984.100), Louvre (inv. n. K 3442).

I.B.

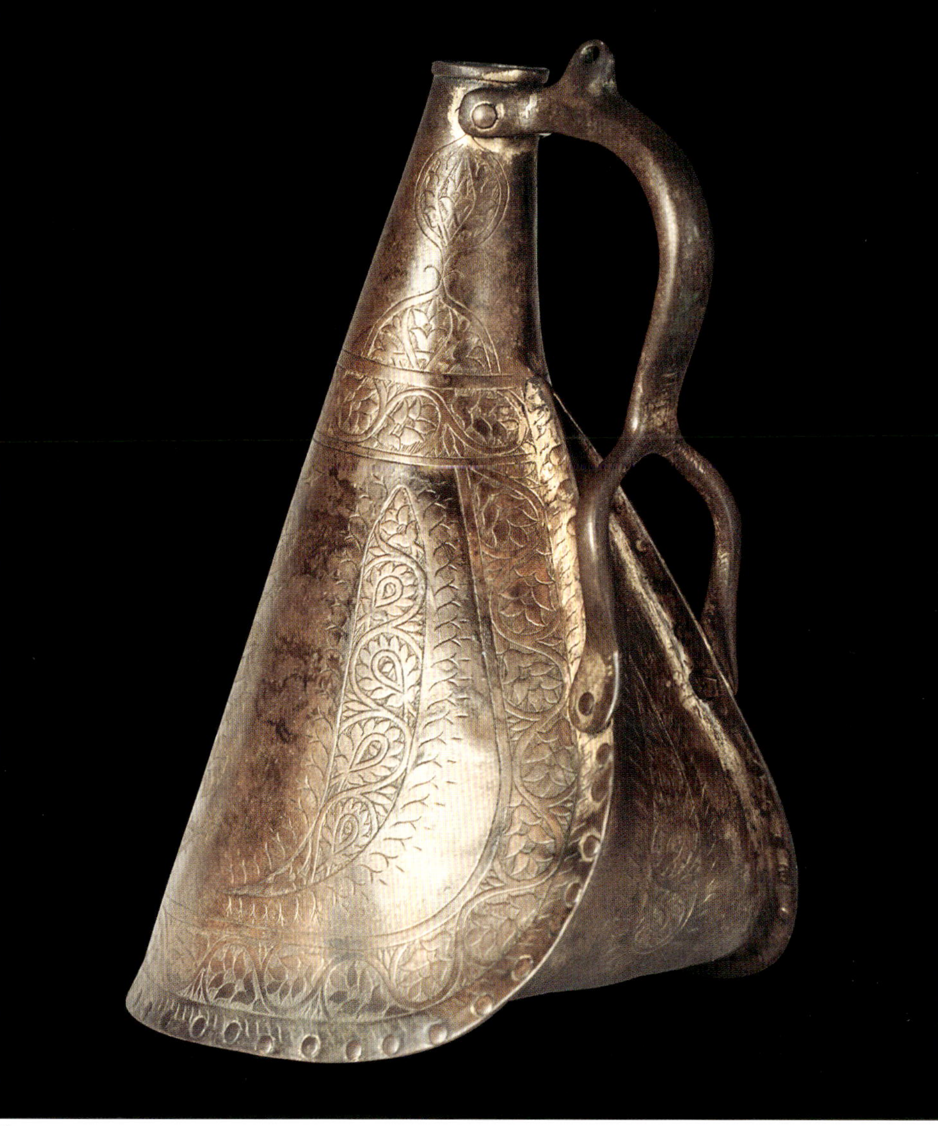

14

15
Magic bowl

Syria, 12th century
Engraved bronze
h. 3 cm, Ø 11 cm
Museo e Real Bosco di Capodimonte, Napoli, inv. n. 112103
(previously Borgia collection)

Of hemispherical shape, on a plain base, with splayed rim, the interior engraved with two divinatory squares, five-pointed stars, several inscriptions in broken script, and zoomorphic astrological symbols including a serpent, a scorpion, an aries, and a two-sided knot, an inscription on the outer rim:

The work of the needy Muhammad b. Yanus, may the Lord have mercy upon him (Scerrato 1967, p. 35).

Similarly to cat. n. 16, the inscription on the interior of the bowl refers most probably to the healing properties of the bowl.

Bibliography: Scerrato 1967, fig. 21 and the there-mentioned bibliographical references.

I.B.

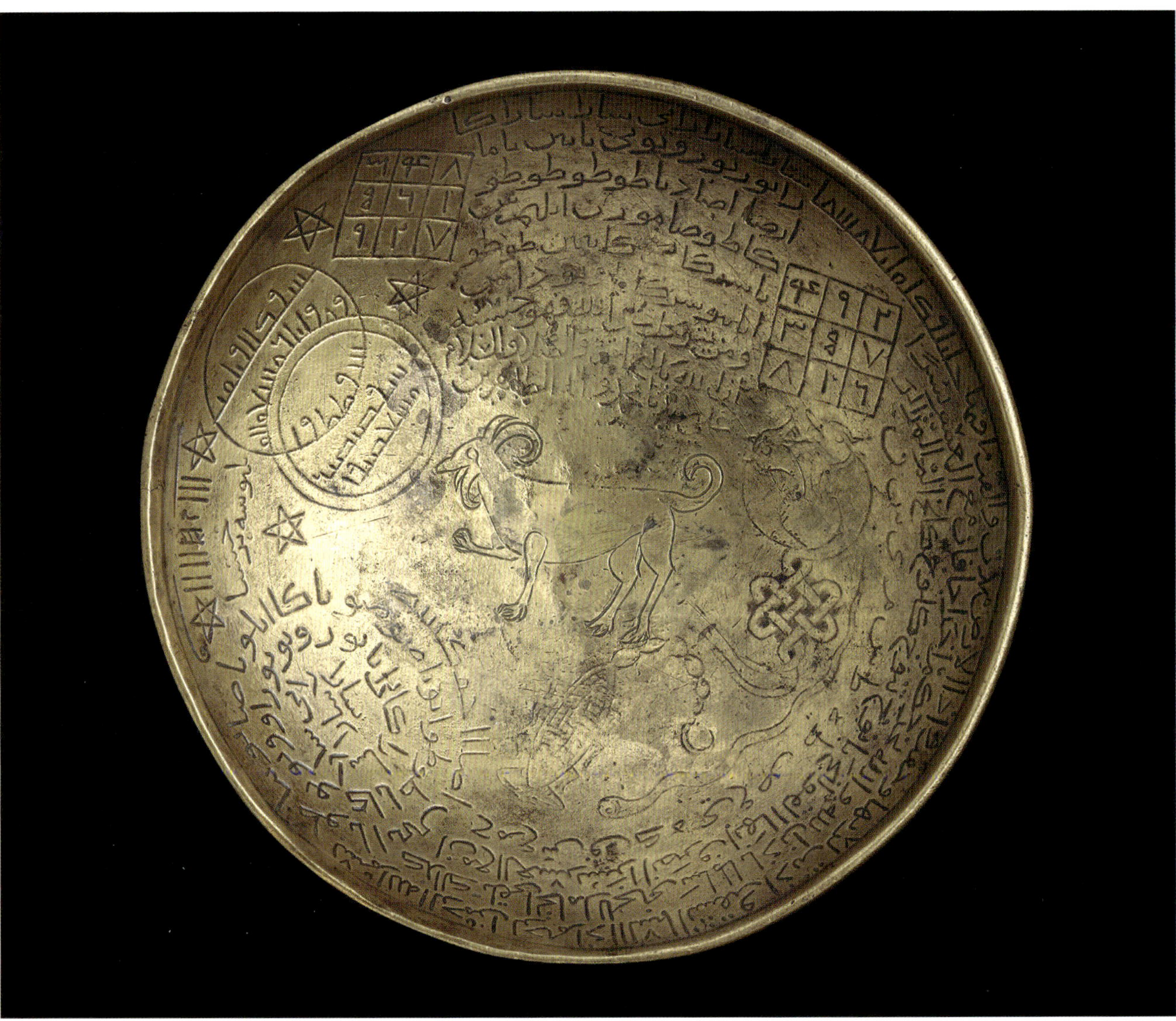

15

16
Magic Bowl

Syria, 12th century
Engraved bronze
h. 2.4 cm, Ø 11.8 cm
The Aron Collection, inv. n. A.162

Of hemispherical shape, on a plain base, with curved cavetto and slightly splayed rim, the interior incised with two magic squares, five-pointed stars, inscriptions, knotwork, and zoomorphic figures such as a scorpion, a snake, a double-headed dragon, and an undefined quadruped in the centre, the exterior with a simple epigraphic band around the upper border.
Among the inscriptions, one can read both invocations to and passages from the Qur'an, but also the instructions for the correct use of this bowl:

This blessed bowl can heal from the bites of snakes, scorpions, dogs with rabies, it can heal fever, it increases milk in the new mothers, it stops bleeding from the nose and internal organs, it helps women giving birth and it calms anxieties (R. Giunta)

The figural depictions on the bowl are thus interconnected with the inscriptions making the function of this bowl clear to even illiterate users.
A similar example can be seen at the David Collection in Copenhagen (inv. n. 36/1995 and cat. n. 15).

Bibliography: Giunta 2018, pp. 21-25.

I.B.

17
Magic bowl

Syria or Jazira, 16th century
Tin-plated, engraved bronze
h. 5 cm, Ø 21 cm
The Aron Collection, inv. n. A.216

Of circular shape, on a plain base, with flattened splayed rim, a central boss with flattened top and decorated with a six-pointed star, the interior engraved with dense concentric calligraphic bands filling oval cartouches in the cavetto, the exterior with further calligraphic inscriptions within roundels and lobed medallions, in the centre a star filled with a magic square.
Inscription: Qur'an 2:255, *ayat al-Kursi*; bismillah; and pseudo-calligraphy.

Provenance: antique art market.

I.B.

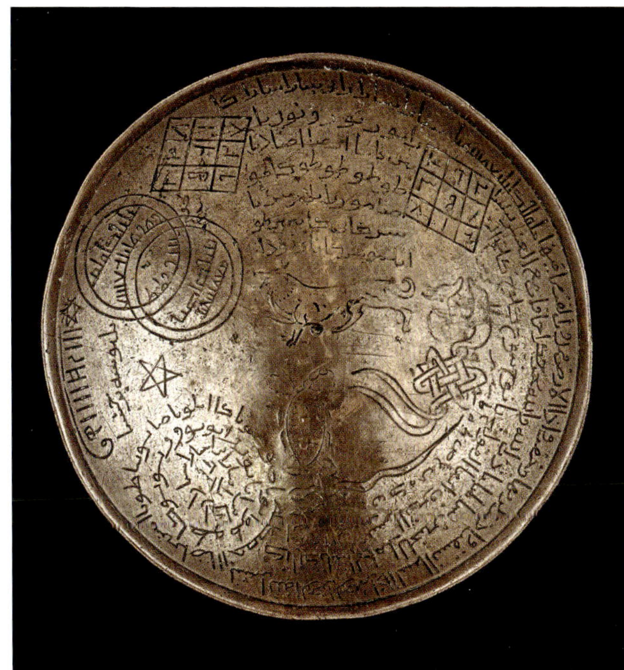

16

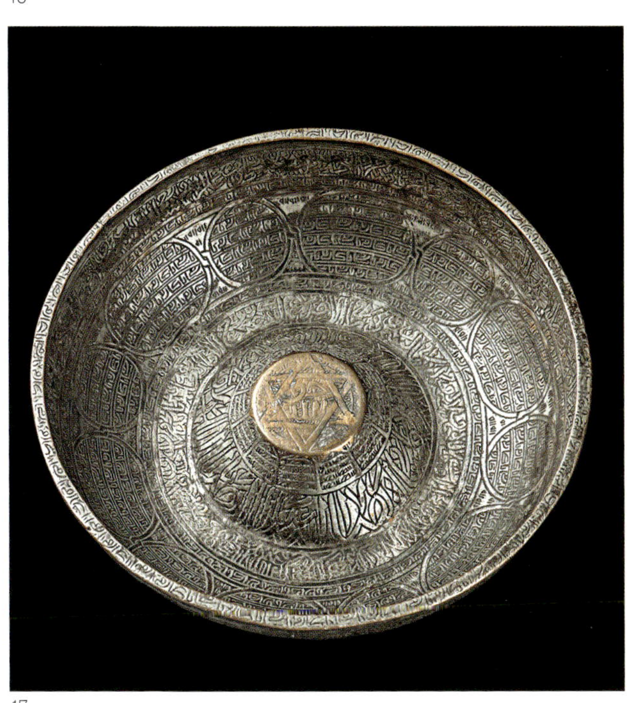

17

18

Magic Bowl

Iran, Shiraz, dated 1655-1656, 1066 AH
Brass, cast with incised and engraved decoration
h. 7.3 cm, Ø 22.3 cm
The Ashmolean Museum, University of Oxford.
Presented by Mrs Johnson, 1992
inv. n. EA1992.51

Of hemispherical shape, on a short circular foot, with a central boss, curved cavetto and slightly splayed rim, the interior decorated with a dense grid of interconnected cusped cartouches filled with Quranic inscriptions, arranged to spread from the centre to the rim, near the rim an epigraphic band and more inscriptions, the central boss engraved with an eight-pointed star within a circle filled with invocations to 'Ali, interspersed with six figural roundels representing planets, the exterior inscribed similarly to the interior with a continuous band creating eight-pointed stars filled with anthropomorphic representations of the twelve Zodiac Signs, the inscriptions all Quranic and in particular referring to 3:25-26, 21:87-88, sura 110 and sura 112.
This object is part of a group of five other divinatory bowls showcasing the same decorative features, with small variants, all clearly commissioned by and produced for a Shi'a audience, as suggested by the invocations to 'Ali and the Twelve Imam, possibly here personified by the Zodiac Signs (E. Savage- Smith, *Hunt for Paradise*, 2004, pp. 241-247).
For an in-depth discussion on magic bowls, see cat. n. 19.

Bibliography: *Hunt for Paradise*, 2004, n. 9.4, p. 244.

I.B.

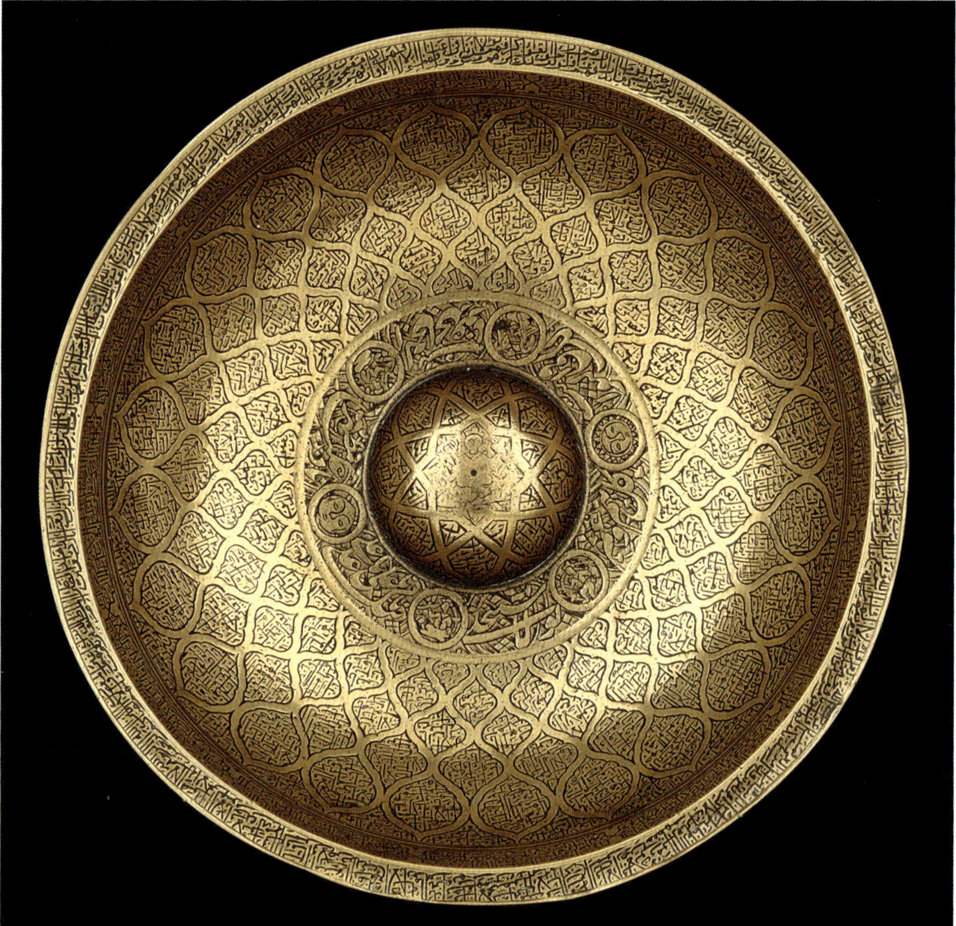

18

19

Large magic bowl

Iran, 17th century, dated [1]185 AH, 1771-1772 AD
Bronze, cast, tin-plated and engraved, filled with a black bituminous substance, h. 7.5 cm, Ø 26 cm
The Aron Collection, inv. n. A.321

Of circular shape, on plain base, the cavetto densely engraved with inscriptions within radial circles around the centre decorated with a seven-lobed flower, epigraphic cartouches all around, the exterior decorated with a calligraphic band next to the upper border, below it a decorative band interrupted by twelve cusped cartouches filled Zodiac signs against a floral ground, the rest of the body densely inscribed.
Inscriptions: Quranic passages, invocations and prayers.

Provenance: antique art market.

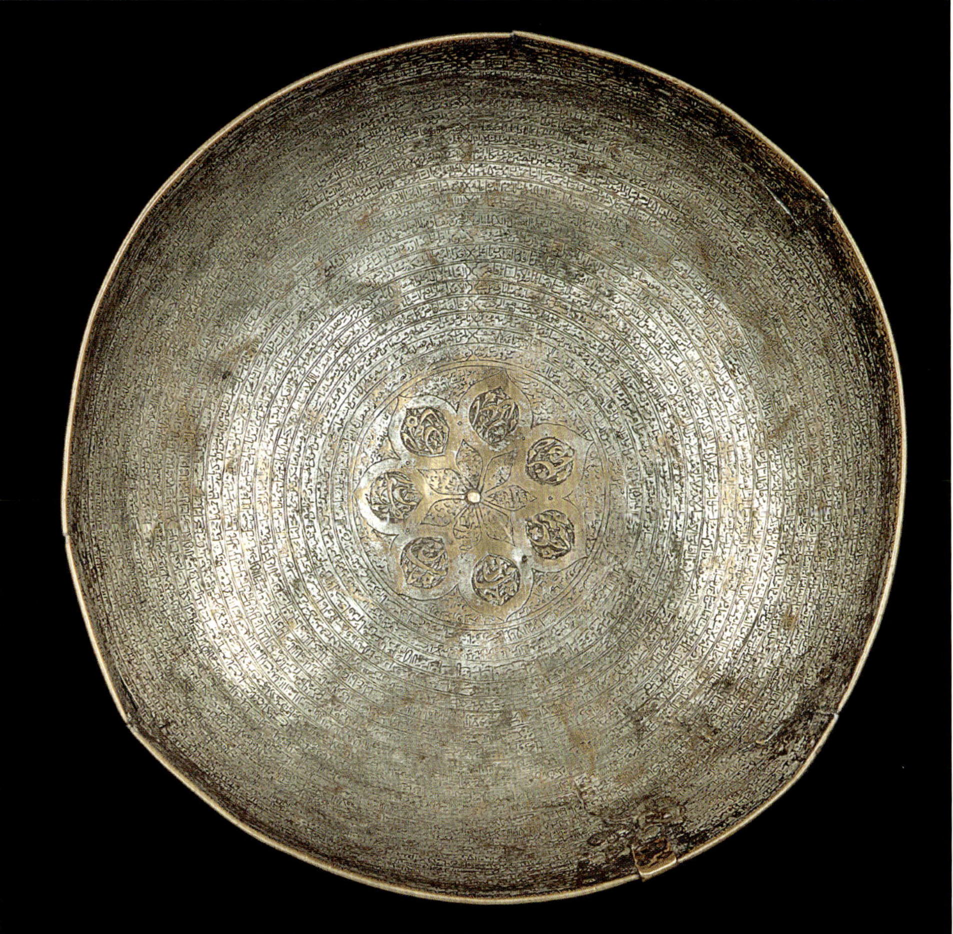

19

Magic bowls

These bowls were used in traditional medicine as remedies. They used to be filled with water, possibly from the Zamzam well; then suspended (most of them still present holes on the rims); and spun around to let the water get imbued with all the beneficial and healing properties the epigraphic inscriptions contained. This healing water was then drunk. Divinatory bowls seem to be present in Islamic art since at least 12th century. Each with different degrees of complexity, the earlier examples show a very simple circular form and often present clear instructions on the beneficial powers of that specific bowl (see cat. nn. 15 and 16). The later examples show more complex shapes, often ornate with a central boss (see cat. n. 17), and later on astral symbolism start appearing on them as well. However, these examples are deprived of the instructional and therapeutic inscriptions. In both cases, they are filled with magical squares, talismanic formulae, Quranic passages and religious invocations. Each epigraphic inscription is imbued with healing powers transferred to the drinker. However, some examples also present numbers and pseudo-inscriptions without an apparent meaning. During the Safavid period (1501-1722), one notices a substantial production of this type of bowls (see cat. nn. 18 and 19). Safavid Magic bowls come in various shapes, forms and with a variety of decorative motifs, but generally they can always be narrowed down to three main categories: bowls with magical inscriptions; with astrological motifs; and with magical squares (E. Savage-Smith, in *Hunt for Paradise*, 2004, pp. 241-247).
The presence of Zodiac signs on both our Safavid bowls leads us to allocate them within the second category.

I.B.

Hammam

To understand *hammams* from an artistic point of view, one has to look at them from an architectural perspective with their fascinating decorative and structural innovations and to study the ancient tradition of which they are part. In this sense, the link to Roman architecture is undoubtable.

Islamic *hammams* have a special relation with figural decorations. Although in the Qur'an a clear ban of figural representation is not to be found (Ghabin 1998), the tone of certain *hadiths* debating this subject is rather different (al-Bukhari 1980, IV, pp. 81-83). Nevertheless, Islamic art witnessed from its very early days a substantial presence of images and its most ancient and, perhaps, most famous example is the desert castle of Qusayr 'Amra, built by the Umayyad caliphs. Every single wall there is decorated with beautiful frescoes, depicting portraits of the Six Kings, hunting and amusement scenes, the arts and crafts of the time, and topless dancers. This tradition was kept alive in the following centuries as well, as figural decorations kept on appearing in the most hidden and intimate areas of Islamic palaces, especially in the baths (Di Branco 2009, pp. 231-254; Fontana and Lavino 2003, pp. 693-699).

But Islamic *hammams* are also filled with a great array of objects like ewers, jugs, ointment containers, brushes, and slippers, mostly used during daily ablution rites and those moments dedicated to the care of the self. These objects linger as the most explicit witnesses of refined aesthetic practices and are partly responsible for the Orientalist lure of the East.

It is essential to point out that the use of *hammams* made in the Islamic world differs considerably from their Western interpretation. Clearly, the sensuality of baths and their erotic component were well-known and understood in the Islamic world too – this can be easily noticed in a few Ottoman and Persian miniatures. However, for the Westerners, *hammams* or Turkish baths, as they are often called, became the embodiment and tangible expression of the Oriental lust and promiscuity. As an example, Nicolas de Nicolay, a 16th century French geographer and traveller, wrote what "dangerous" places Ottomam *hammams* were: gathering such large numbers of women in the privacy and intimacy of a bath would only stir feelings of female lust and Sapphic desires. Since then, most Western visitors would fantasise on lascivious eroticisms, sweaty naked bodies and aroused eunuchs and this type of fanciful fantasy would flow into theatrical works, novels and Orientalist paintings. But those who entered the *hammams* in reality, discovered a different universe. Like Lady Montague, one of the very few travellers gifting us with a female perspective on those lands, who wrote a letter in 1717 attempting to tame European male fantasies:

> *The mistresses sat on the first couches, filled with cushions and precious tapestries; the [female] slaves would sit behind them; but their attire couldn't possibly differentiate them by social status, as they were all as nature created them or, to put it simply, completely naked ... nevertheless, they did not share libertine smiles, nor unchaste, lewd gestures.*

Sadly, these accounts did not suffice to eradicate ideas which had already taken deep roots in the common Western imagination and which had been so powerfully illustrated by the great Orientalist masters of the 19th century, such as Ingres, Delacroix, Gérôme, Sargent. Those images of sweaty bodies and rarefied atmospheres settled deep down in the Western minds and contributed to feeding a profound misunderstanding for centuries.

20
Bucket

Khorasan, present Afghanistan, Herat, 12th-13th century
Bronze, cast, engraved and copper damascene
h. 21.5 cm, Ø 28 cm
The Ashmolean Museum, University of Oxford, Purchased 1969, inv. n. EA1969.8

Possibly a hammam water bucket, of wide globular shape, resting on a tall splayed foot, with a flat everted rim, on the sides two pierced grafts attached to an arcuate tilting handle, the exterior engraved in concentric decorative bands of varying height, two small bands with interlocking floral sprays and another small one with Kufic epigraphic cartouches interspersed with circular rosettes, the large band below the rim filled with an auspicious *naskh* calligraphic inscription interspersed over a scrolling floral ground, the second-largest band with *mihrab*-shaped markers alternating with circular roundels filled with the twelve Zodiac symbols set within star-shaped octagonal medallions, both the calligraphy and the braided medallions inlaid with copper. At the time of this bucket's production, Herat, now Afghanistan, was a metalware centre of primary importance. Indeed, it was in Herat that the craftsmen started moving away from plain casting and started embracing new techniques such as hammering and metal sheet embossing. The decorative motifs typical of the Herat production often involve calligraphic inscriptions and Zodiac signs, as the Bobrinski bucket testifies, now part of St. Petersburg's Hermitage Museum collection.

Bibliography: unpublished. For a similar example, see cat. no. H10.3.

I.B.

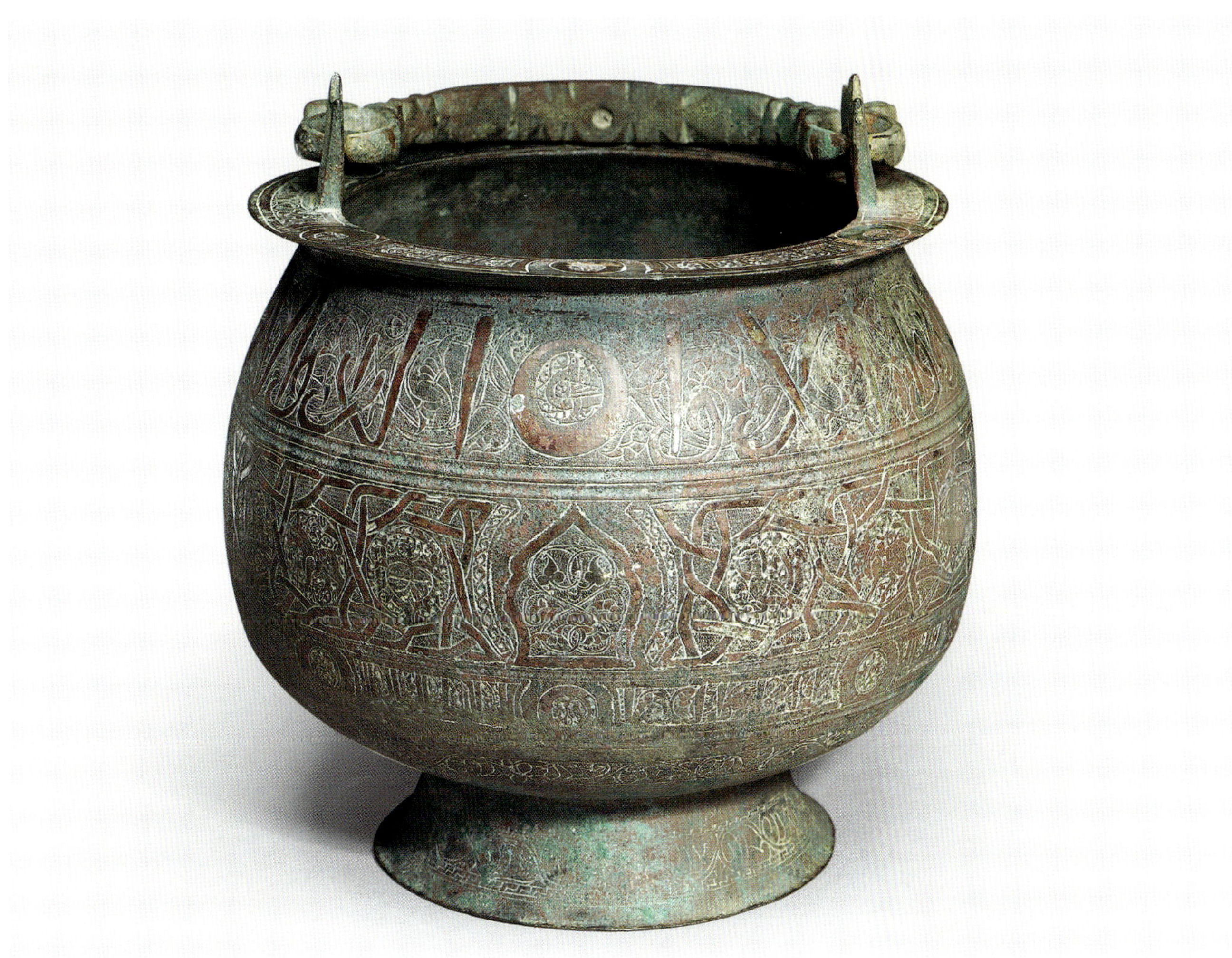

20

21
Bucket

Eastern Iran, late 15th-early 16th century
Brass, cast, engraved and silver damascene
h. 10 cm, Ø 20.4 cm
Courtesy of the L.A. Mayer Museum for Islamic Art, Jerusalem, Israel
inv. n. M 203-72

Of compressed circular shape, resting on a circular base, with slightly flared walls and tilting handle modelled in the shape of two regardant dragons, the body profusely decorated with incised interlocking arabesques and a row of lobed medallions highlighted with silver inlay on the borders, four rectangular cartouches located to the centre of the medallions with inscriptions bearing the name of the maker:

the work of the master Mohammad, son of the master 'Ali, may he be truly forgiven by the Lord (Hasson, 2014, cat. n. 95).

The base of the bucket further embellished with elaborate arabesques surrounding the centre.
The shape of this bucket can be traced back to the first Islamic period with examples produced in Egypt and Iran dating back to 8th-10th century.
A similar shape can also be found in the Persian metalware production of 12th-13th century. It then appears once again during the Timurid / Turcoman period, like in the case of our bucket, as testified by numerous miniatures depicting analogous buckets in the *hammam* scenes.
The shape and decorative programme of our bucket showcase strong analogies with Veneto-Saracenic metals. These are a type of metalware which was originally believed to have been produced by Arabic craftsmen settled in Venice in the 15th century. Scholarship later on disputed this hypothesis and attributed the production to the Mamluk genius, explaining that these motifs were only subsequently copied in Italy (Hans Huth, 1972 in Abouseif, 2005, p.147).
The debate on the attribution and origin of this group of metals has not been exhausted yet and a minor group of scholars, among which R. Ward (1993, pp. 102-103) and S. Auld (2004, pp. 11-35 and Auld in *Venice* 2007, pp. 213-224) ascribes part of this production to North-Western Iran and South-Easter Anatolia, in particular to the workshop of Mahmud al-Kurdi, one of the most prolific masters of Veneto-Saracenic metalware, whose name appears on at least twenty works (Atil et al., 1985, p. 178).
Instead, Allan (in Abouseif, *op. cit.*, p. 148) provides further proofs that link the work of the master Mahmud to the style of the decorative arts produced during the rule of the Mamluk Sultan Qaitbay.

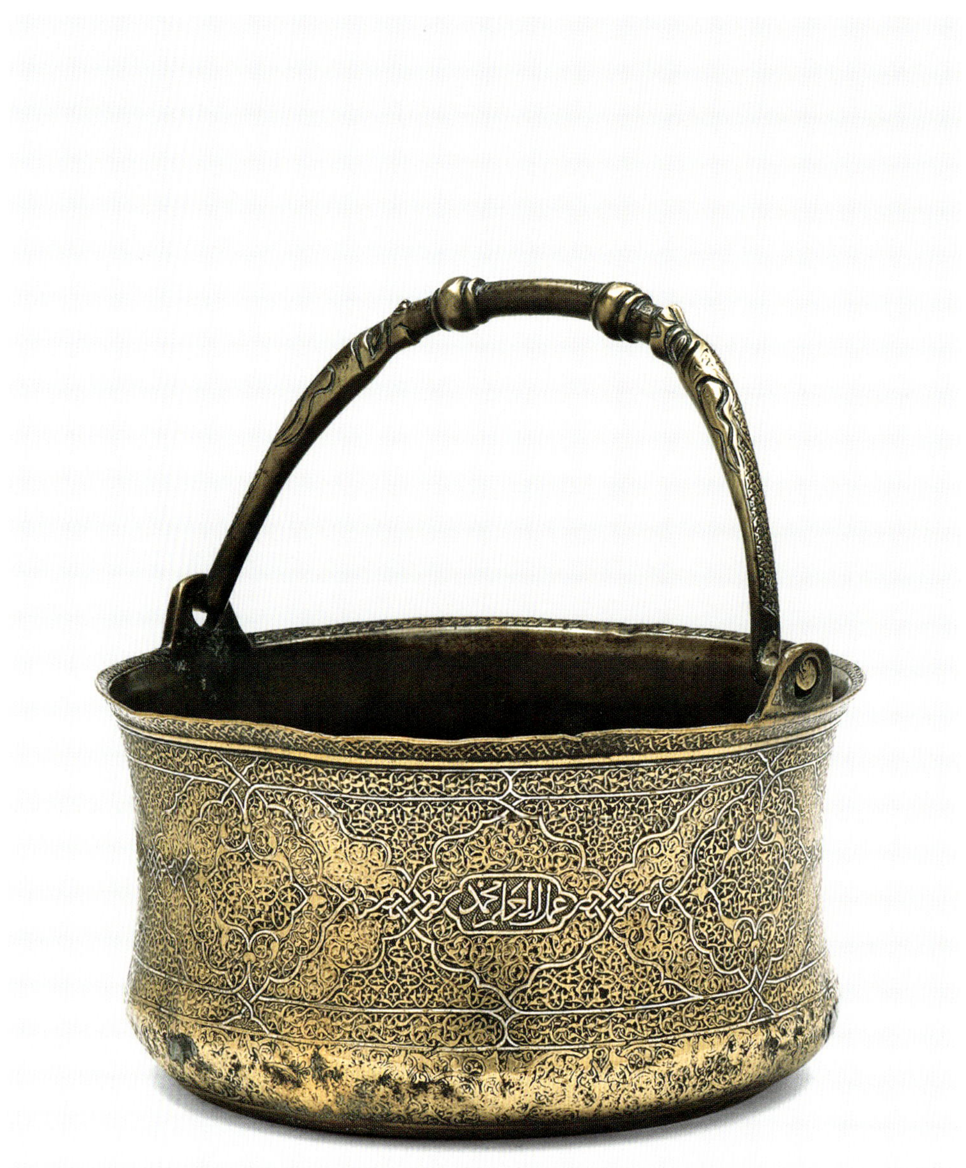

21

Bibliography: Mayer 1959, p. 66; S. Auld in *Venice* 2007, pp. 215-25; Hasson 2014, cat. n. 95.
For similar examples, see: British Museum, inv. n. 1865,1209.1; Atil et al. 1985, cat. n. 24, pp. 176-180; Victoria and Albert Museum, inv. n. 1826-1888.

I.B.

22
Bath bucket

Iran, Afghanistan (Khorasan), Seljuq period, 12th century
Copper alloy, cast with engraved decoration
h. 22.5 × 19.5cm
weight: 2464 g
Museo d'Arte Orientale – MUCIV, inv. n. 20734

Of globular shape, resting on a tall flared foot, with a sharp-edged rim and two perforated pentagonal hinges for the arch-shaped handle, with a rectangular section, modelled with grooves creating alternating geometric motifs (rectangular and diamond-shaped), the body engraved with four overlying horizontal bands filled with good-wishing Arabic inscriptions in cursive Kufic script against a ground of vegetal tendrils; zoomorphic representations (quadrupeds and birds); floral and geometric motifs; and more vegetal motifs, near the foot's graft a horizontal sequence of small interlocking arches with trilobed vegetal elements, on the foot a band of engraved vertical segments at regular distance, a recent cleaning bringing back to light the engravings on the handle showing rhomboidal elements of varying sizes.
This very refined artefact belongs to a group of metal bath pails mostly produced in the Eastern Iranian territories in the 12th century, distinguishing themselves from other examples for their globular and smooth bodies and for the presence of a decoration arranged in horizontal registers (Ivanov 2004, p. 172; Laviola 2016, pp.112, 196-197, 205-283, 310-311). Among the examples already known, recently some other unpublished Ghazni artefacts joined the group, providing new case studies and elements of comparison for this class of objects (Laviola 2016, pp.205-283). The MAO bath

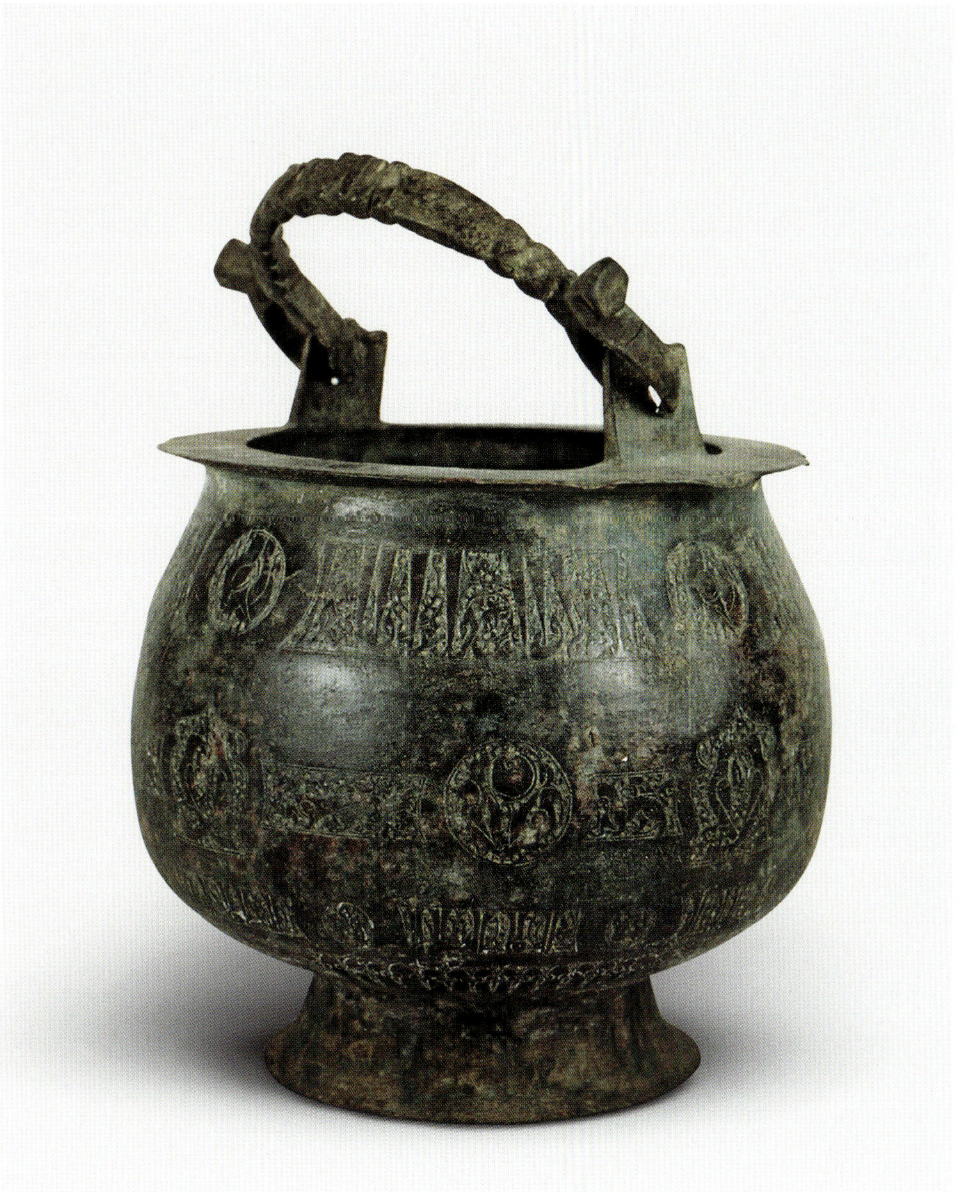
22

pail showcases tight parallels with some examples of metals found in Ghazni, both in decorative and morphological terms (horizontal rim, flared border and often, handles with stylised promotes).

F.M.A.

23
Basin

Spain, Sevilla, late 15th-early 16th century
Glazed majolica
h. 22 cm, Ø 59 cm
Instituto de Valencia De Don Juan, Madrid
inv. n. 1489

A large pottery tub, of oblong hemispherical shape, possibly used in origin as a washbasin, the interior embellished with dense geometric decoration and painted in turquoise, manganese purple, yellow and green, with a large central rosette spreading to an intricate geometric scrollwork, highlighted by a white lath ending in a delicate knotwork, the exterior worked in the shape of floral petals repeating the same colours of the interior.

Bibliography: Martínez Caviro 1978, n. 90, p. 76; Luz, Nur 2013-2014, n. 180-181, pp. 248-249.

This basin and the below-discussed three pottery tiles share the same decorative techniques, stylistic motifs, and use. Their common decoration is the so-called *lazo*, a geometric composition normally based on forms with six, eight or multiples sides, often producing multi-pointed stars. This type of decoration finds its roots in Roman art and it was later favoured in the arts of Islam as supposed to foster and promote meditation. Indeed, perfection, harmony, symmetry and tension to the infinite, all elements to be found in this type of decoration, can also be directly linked to God.
In Nasrid Andalusia, these motifs spread over any surface and media like ceramics, textiles, metalwork, wooden and stucco ceilings and at times, they became a fundamental part of the architectural vocabulary of those lands, as the *mocarabes* (*muqarnas*, honeycomb pattern) testify. The two major decorative techniques used on ceramics of the time are the *cuenca* and the *cuerda seca*, showcased by the examples here presented. Our tiles would have once been part of *alicatados* (large panels of ceramic mosaics, see *Arte Islamico en Granada* 1995, cat. n. 144, p. 381), an easy and cost-effective solution to decorate long floors and large walls. Although the mosaic technique is in origin Byzantine, the Andalusian craftsmen reinvent it and add it to the dado, the lower part of the wall, following a typically Islamic pattern. The *alicatados* were incredibly functional, as they were easy to wash and not subject to great wear. Thus, they became the perfect solution for *hammam* walls.

I.B.

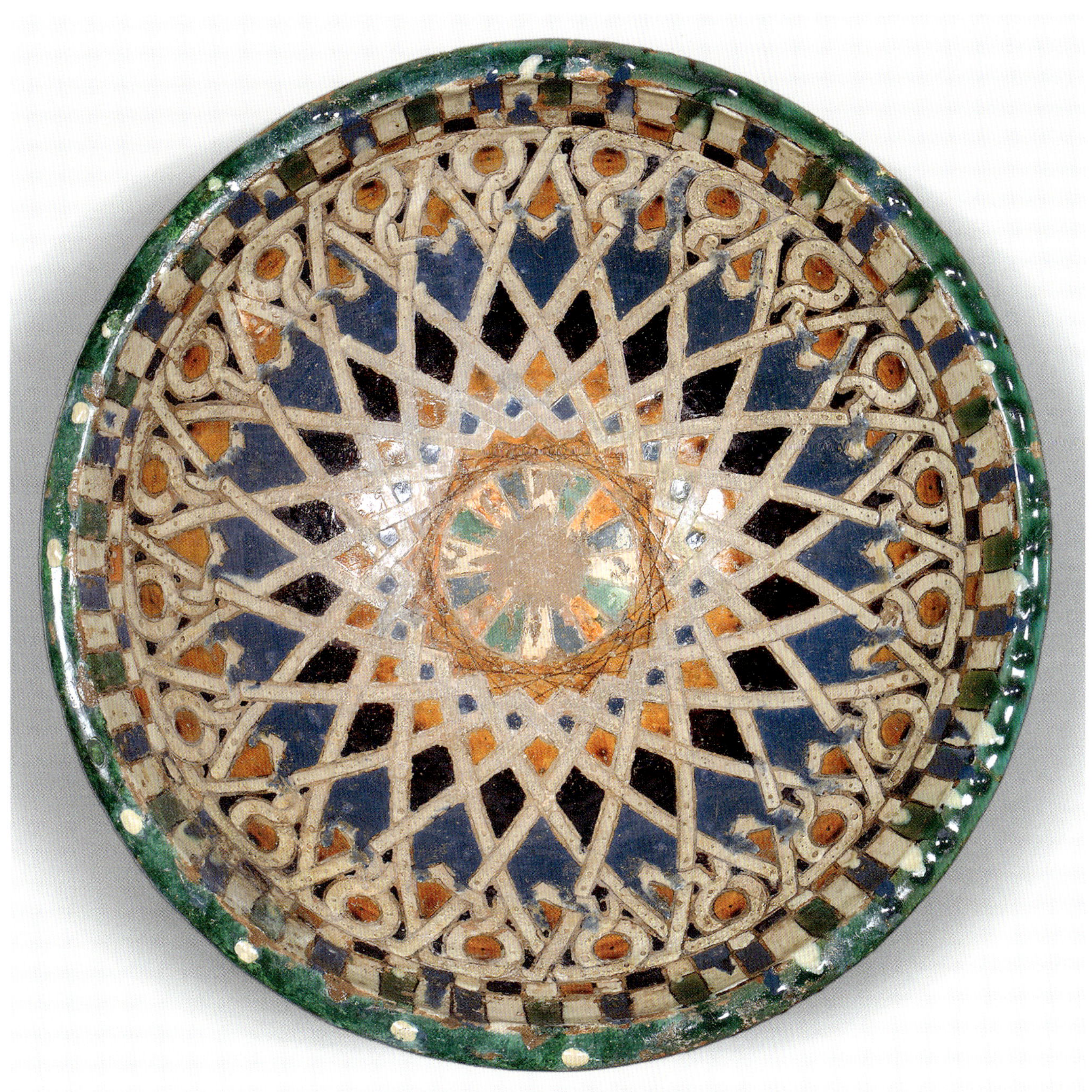

28

24
Tile

Spain, Valencia, 15th century
Glazed polycrome majolica
16.5 × 12.5 × 2 cm
MIC, Museo Internazionale delle Ceramiche in Faenza, inv. n. 10255

Underglaze-painted in turquoise, manganese purple, mustard yellow and green, interstitial spaces filled in with white, the tile fragment decorated with a geometric motif of a multi-pointed star, once part of a larger decorative panel with other stars and rosettes.
This tile is decorated in the typical *cuenca* style. This decorative method involves placing the coloured enamelled pigments into niches carved out from the main body material and raising the walls near each section, to ensure that during the firing process the colours don't mix and corrupt.
The colors used are: turquoise, brown manganese, mustard yellow and green, while the resulting spaces of the decoration are enamelled in milky white.

I.B.

25
Tile

Spain, Valencia, 15th-16th century, 1440-1499
Glazed polycrome majolica
14.5 × 14.5 cm
MIC, Museo Internazionale delle Ceramiche in Faenza, inv. n. 610

Of square shape, decorated in *cuenca* style, with interlocking geometric motifs made of elongated hexagons producing cross-shaped forms and a central dark-coloured eight-pointed star, each figure interconnected and creating a system of orthogonal frames with an open design.
A similar example is preserved at the Galleria di Arte Antica in Rome (see Colonna 2011, p.14).

Bibliography for H11.2-3-4: Scerrato 1967, nn. 278-80, fig. 107, pp. 118-119; Gonzales Marti 1952, Vol. II, pl. 11; *La Céramique* Médiéval 1997, p. 618. For an example of skirting board, please see Dodds, 1992, cat. n. 119, pp. 374-375.

I.B.

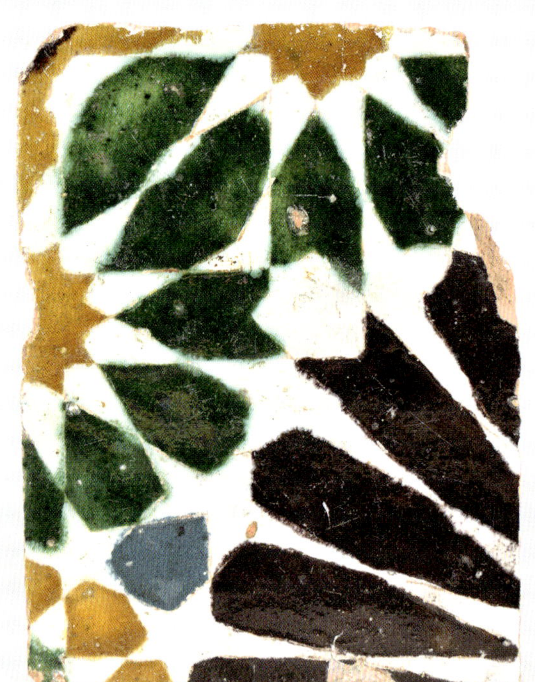

24

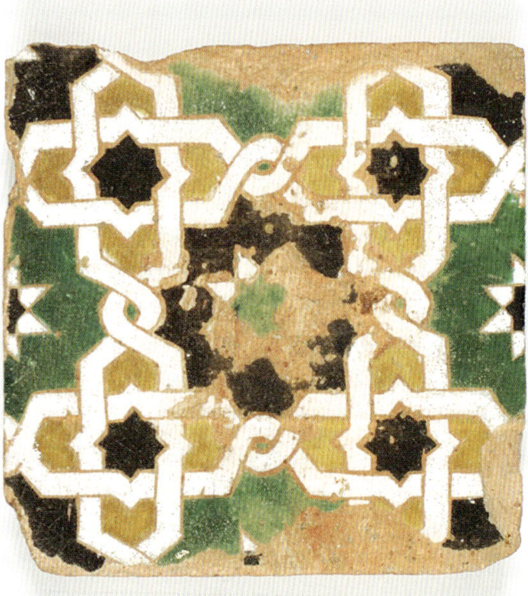

25

26
Tile

Spain Valencia, second half 15th-beginnig 16th century
Glazed polycrome majolica
17 × 16.5 × 2 cm
MIC, Museo Internazionale delle Ceramiche in Faenza, inv. n. 10263

The tile fragment decorated with dense geometric motifs developing into twelve-pointed rosettes, once part of a larger decorative panel with other stars and rosettes, interstitial spaces filled in with white.
The decorative technique here used is called *cuerda seca*. The design would be painted onto the desired tile panel. Then, each section of a different colour would be delimited by a greasy substance, often a cord (*cuerda*) dipped in manganese, which disappeared during the firing process but ensured the colours would not run into each other and mix before the firing was complete. Underglaze-painted in the typical colours of Valencia manufacture such as turquoise, manganese purple, yellow and green.

I.B.

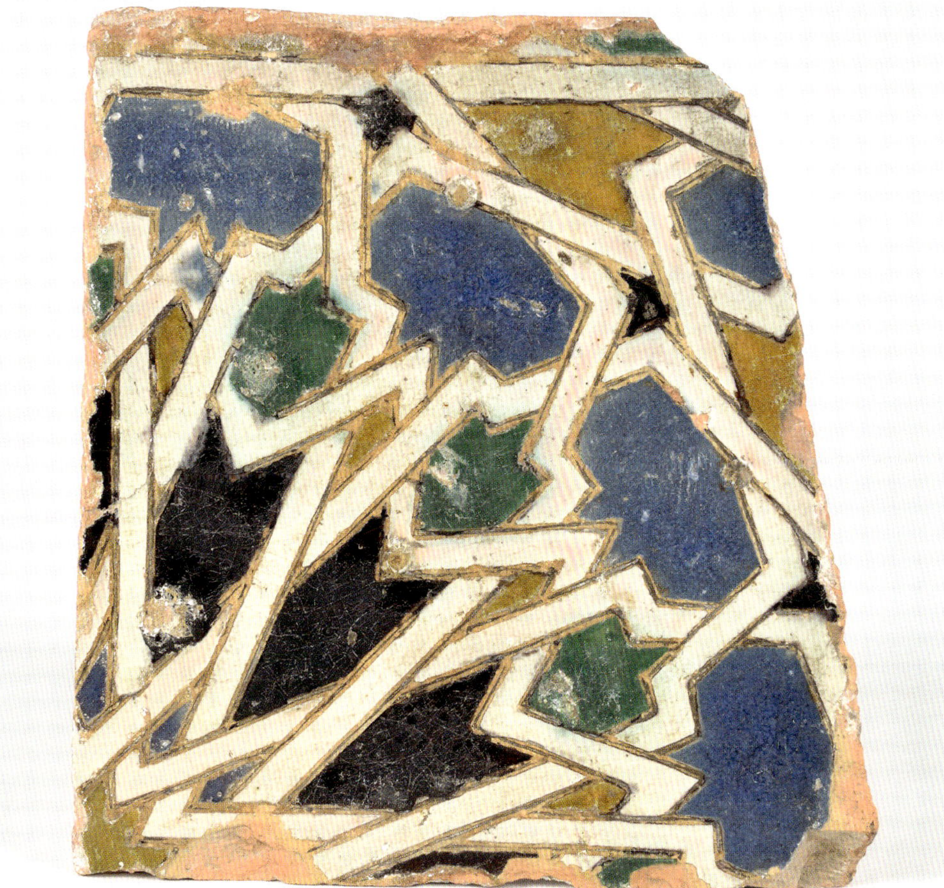

26

27
Blind

Southern Spain, Granada, 14th century
Alhambra, Comares Palace, the Bath of Comares, the Room of the Beds
Inlaid wood
98 × 67.5 × 5.8 cm
Museo de la Alhambra. Patronato de la Alhambra y Generalife, inv. n. 10201

Of rectangular shape, carved with intersecting geometric motifs forming a virtually infinite pattern, bands of rhomboidal designs and cross-shaped cartouches, four diagonal hexagons marking the corners. These panels were built to concurrently shield windows from excessive light and the arrival of birds, and facilitate the ventilation of the interiors. They also played a crucial role as social dividers, to safeguard the privacy and intimacy of the household and to hide female beauties from prying looks in the courtly environment.
The function of the *Sala de las Camas* was to welcome the bathers to undress, get used to the temperature, get treatments or massages by the *tellak* (hammam' servants) and last but not least, relax on couches before and after the bath. Screens similar in function and style to the presented one were a wide-spread element in Islamic architecture. Their names and materials may vary but their presence is recorded in multiple different areas of the Islamic lands, from the Mughal marble *jalis* of India to the wooden *mashrabiyyas* of the Near and Middle East.

Bibliography: unpublished. For a similar example, see *Arte Islamico en Granada* 1995, cat. nn. 110-111, pp. 325-326 and the bibliographical references there mentioned.

I.B.

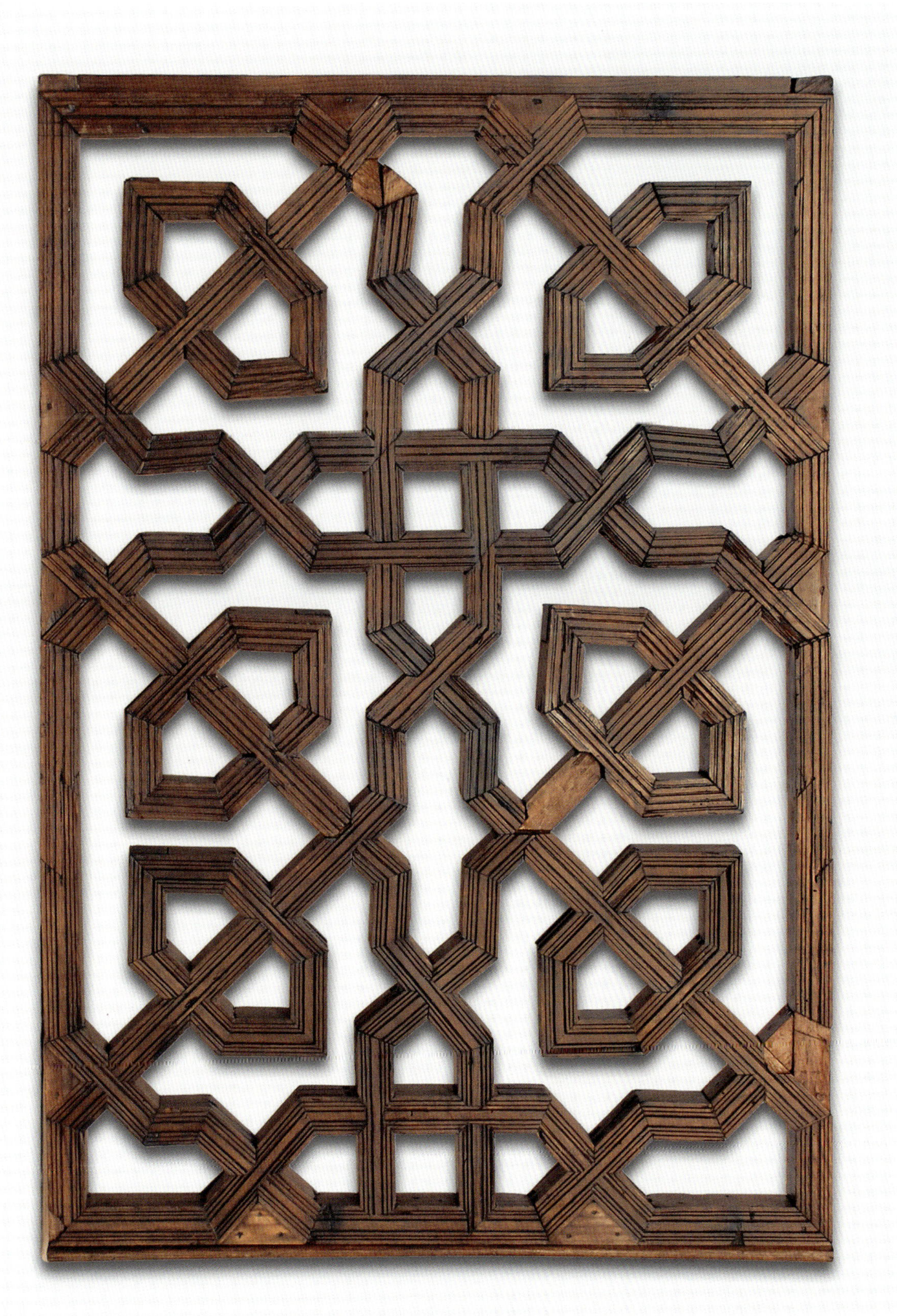

27

28
Fountain

Southern Spain, Granada, 14th-15th century
Sculpted stone, 12.5 × 62.6 cm
Museo de la Alhambra. Patronato de la Alhambra y Generalife, inv. n. 428

Basin with a central hole for the water jet, lobed, with carved and grooved walls reminiscent of a shell.
Similar fountains would have been mass produced to embellish strategic spots inside the Alhambra Palace. Another example, almost identical, is published in *Arte Islamico en Granada*, 1995, cat. n. 97, p. 306.

Bibliographical reference in the cataloguing note.

I.B.

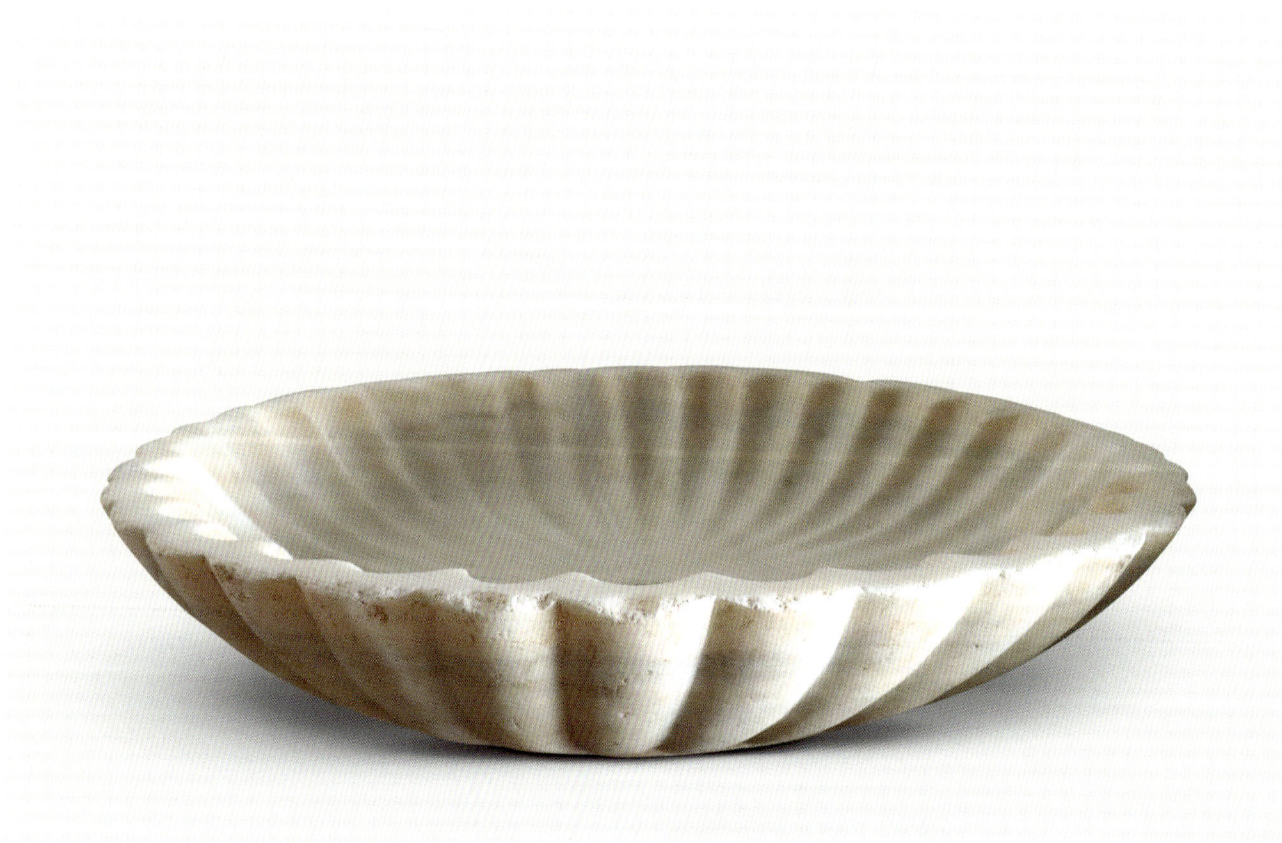

28

29
Basin

Egypt or Syria, late 15th century
Engraved and embossed brass
max. Ø 36.5 cm
Museo Poldi Pezzoli, Milano,
inv. n. 1657

Of circular shape, with straight walls and narrowing shoulders, with a cylindrical rim, the exterior with panels embossed and chased in high relief in the shape of petals filled with dense Veneto-Saracenic scrollwork, interlocking split palmette tendrils, a grid of polylobed and rectangular cartouches, within them wide calligraphic inscriptions and the cup-bearer coat of arms, the base further embossed with swirl beading embellished with interlocking arabesques, peonies, floral sprays and vegetal tendrils, all converging to the centre with a stylised flower with lobed petals surrounding a roundel filled with the cup blazon, the attention to detail almost equivalent to a miniature painting.
The inscription in the cartouches reads some honorific titles:

The Excellent, the Wise, the Master, Emir …

But the inscription is otherwise incomplete. Thus, it is not possible to establish for sure who did it belong to. That said, the cup blazon could be interpreted as a clear reference to the Sultan Qaitbay (r. 1468-1496). It is thus likely to suggest that this basin would have been produced around the time of his rulership (Melikian-Chirvani, 1969, pp. 99-104, figs.1-4).
During his reign, Qaitbay dedicated a lot of his energies in reviving Mamluk metalware and the decorative arts in general, previously ended in decay in the first half of 15th century.
He commissioned some of the most opulent works of this time characterised by the most innovative designs and unusual forms. Among the novelties, one can notice the creation of these large brass basins with articulated base; new epigraphic styles; innovative floral motifs with pointy curved petals.
Several analogous examples can be found in international museums and private collections such as a similar basin in the Metropolitan Museum of Art in New York (inv. n. 91.1.565 in Atil, 1981, pp. 102-103); a silver-inlaid basin in the Museum of Turkish and Islamic Art in Istanbul (inv. n. 2959 in Sahin, 2009, pp. 170-171); a plain basin in a private collection (Melikian-Chirvani, 1969, figs. 5-6); and another embossed basin successfully sold at Sotheby's London recently (20 April 2016, lot 123).

Bibliography: Bertini, *Museum's Inventory*, 1881, cat. n. 15, p. 74; Melikian-Chirvani 1969, pp. 99-104; Poldi Pezzoli catalogue, cat. n. 5, p. 277; Abuseif 2005, pp. 148-149 and fig. 4.

I.B.

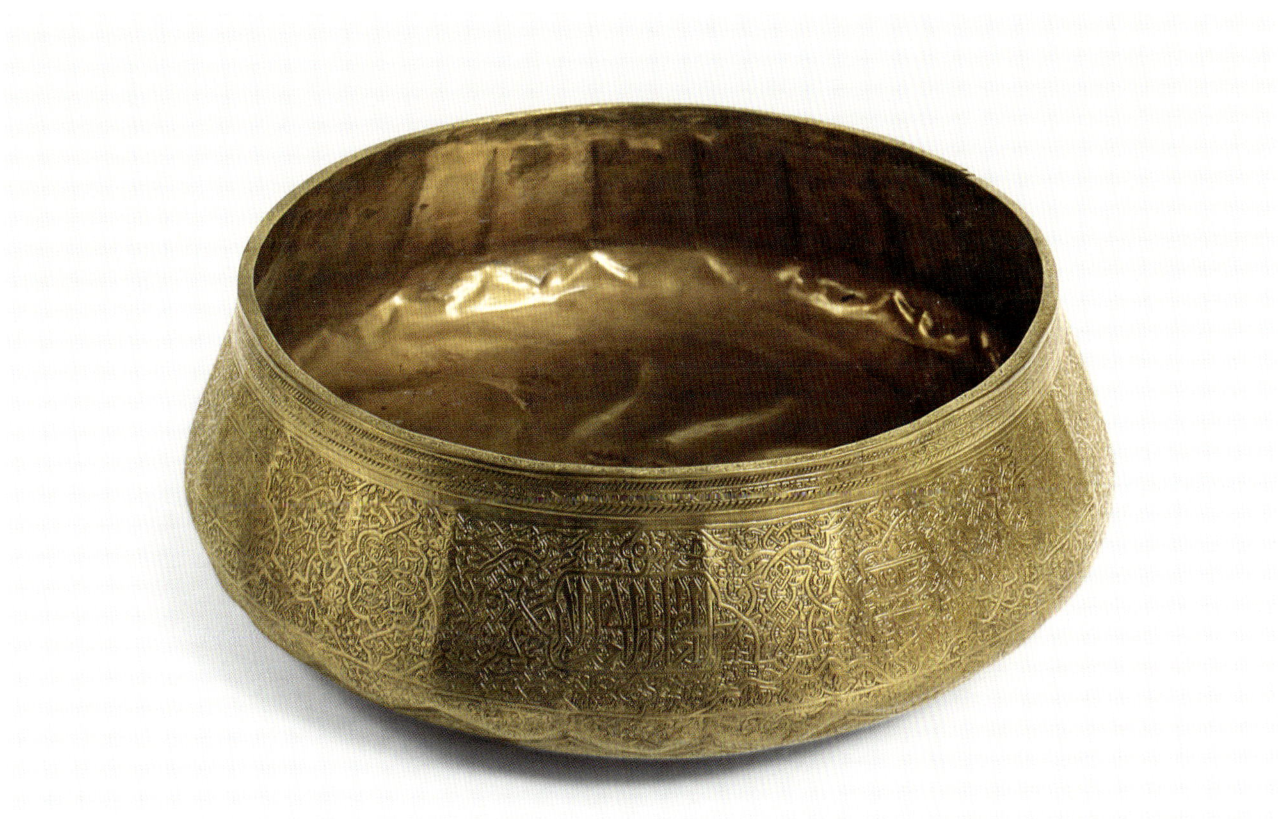

29

30
Bowl

Ottoman Empire, Balkans,
19th century
Embossed silver, burin crafted
Ø 23 cm
Private collection, Milan

Of circular shape, with a central boss and fluted walls, with a dense grid of niches over two concentric orders, the inner band in the shape of petals, fitting in the interstitial spaces created by the oval cartouches of the outer band, the base decorated with a large steamer in the central roundel, chased in high relief from the outside, the cavetto with twelve boats interspersed with floral motifs. The peculiar shape of these bowls is dictated by the fact that the embossed, hollow centre made it easier to grab and hold them. The bowl would then be used like a ladle, filled with water and let the liquid pour over the bather. Besides this main use, such bowls could have also been used as cushions in time of need: if turned upside down, one could rest his/her head against the hollow centre.
When the Ottomans conquered the territory of the Balkans, one of their advantages was the addition of the local silver mines, two in particular Novo Brdo and Srebrenica. Here, they not only conquered the material, but they also acquired new knowledge, styles and skills on how to work silver based on the local craftsmen's knowledge, echoing past traditions from the Byzantine world, Venice and Northern Europe. With the advent of the Ottoman domination of the Balkans, these syncretic traditions and designs all flew into one and led to the rise of a pan-Balkan style. The Balkan silversmith stylistic tradition was indeed kept in high regard by the Ottomans and this is testified by the presence of recurrent Balkan motifs and shapes not only on silverware, but also on Iznik pottery (Carswell, 1998, pp.32-36, see also cat. n. 31). Moreover, several documents of the time confirm that at the Ottoman court there were several high officials of Balkan origin, proving they were perfectly integrated in the Ottoman society.

Provenance: antique art market.
For a similar bowl, please see Koc et al, 2007.

I.B.

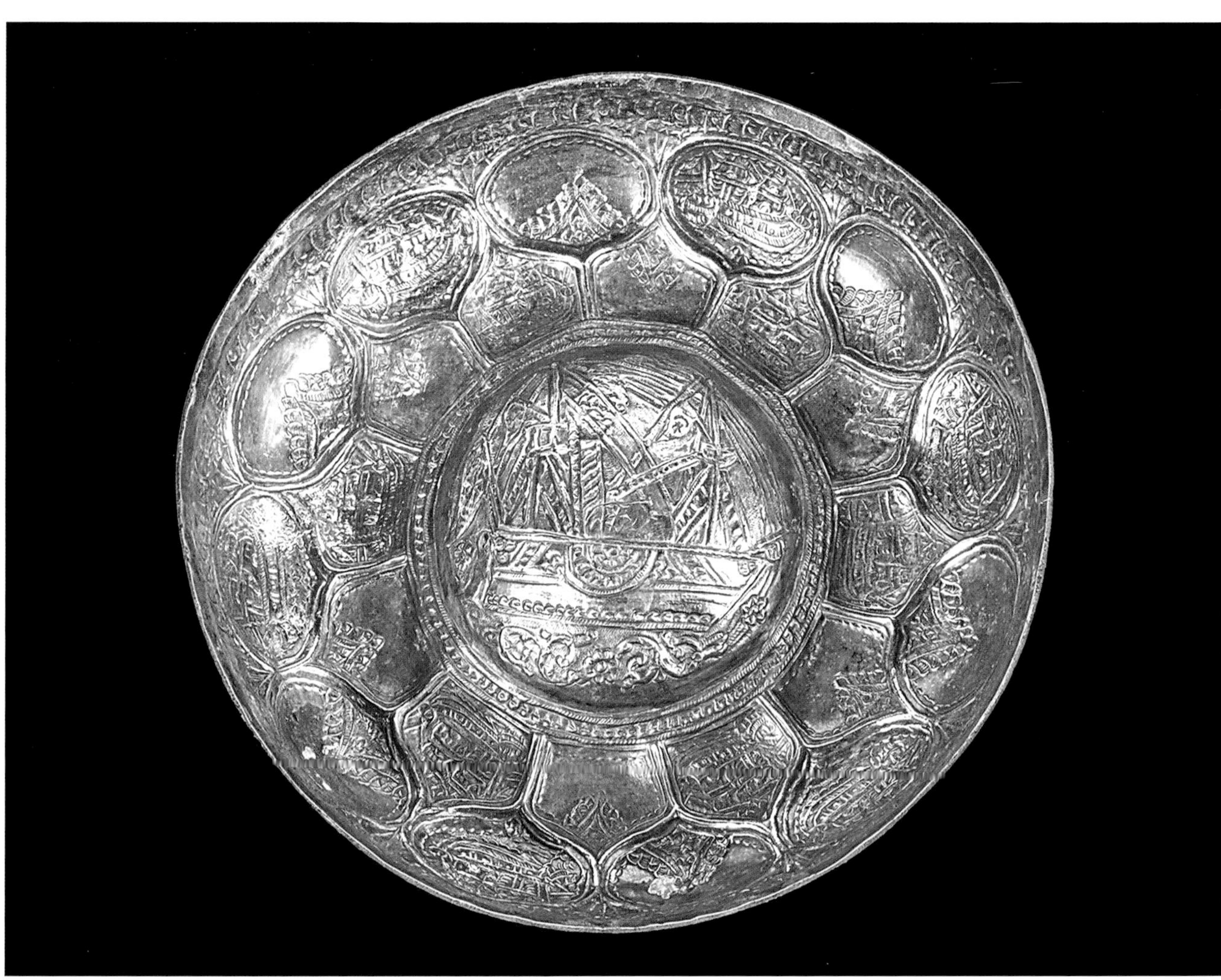

30

31
Cup

Turkey, 17th century
Cast, engraved and parcel gilt silver
Presence of bituminous substance on the inside
h. 3.5 cm, Ø 15 cm
The Aron Collection, inv. n. 199

Of circular shape, resting on a short circular foot, with a small central boss incised with two facing birds against a ground of split palmettes, the incision filled in with a black bituminous substance, the interior decorated with concentric circles incised with floral elements, arabesques, vegetal tendrils, interspersed with three pointy cartouches filled with figural decoration, the cavetto with *tughra* mark.

The decorative motif of the first concentric band is reminiscent of some elements common in the artistic repertoire of Iznik ceramics, showing two tulip buds and the *cintamani* motif in the centre (Atasoy, Raby, 1989, fig. 320 and the ewer cat. n. 81). As a matter of fact, Carswell confirms that Ottoman Balkan metalware and Iznik pottery wares witnessed a fruitful exchange of decorative motifs and designs (Carswell, 1998, pp. 32-36, and for an analogous example *Ibidem*, fig. 13, p. 33). As far as their use is concerned, Allan speculates there could be a possible link between these embossed bowls and the Greek *phialae*, a type of wares connected to water and often used to drink wine and libations, which was very widespread in Graeco-Roman art. It is likely to believe that it was later adopted by the Persians and with time became part of the Turkish and also of the Italian Renaissance traditions, with minor variations (Allan, 1986, pp. 42-47). Differently from the Graeco-Roman tradition though, in Ottoman Turkey these bowls were primarily linked to water, thus their common use in the *hammam*.

Provenance: antique art market
Bibliographical reference in the cataloguing note.

I.B.

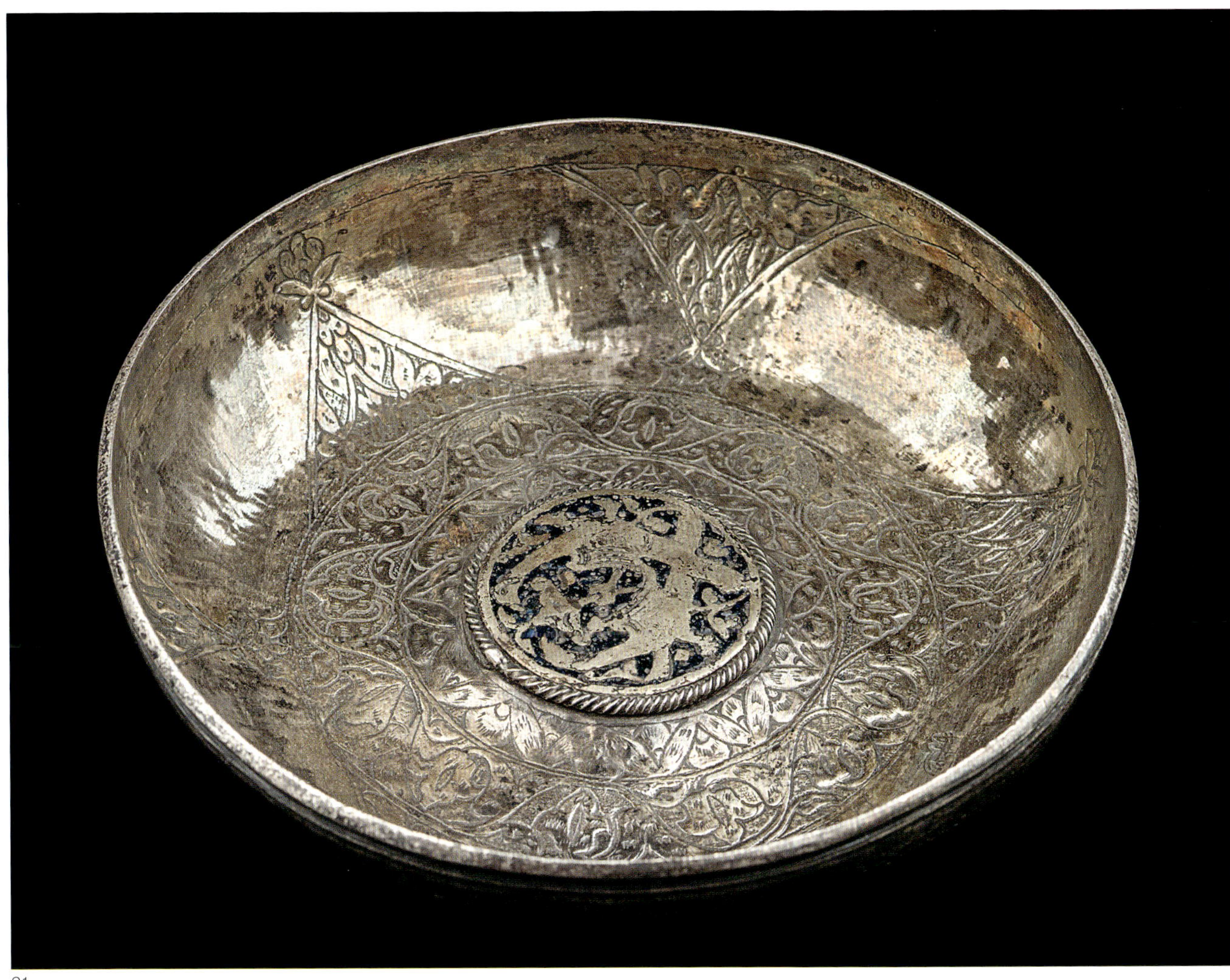

31

32-33

Two rosewater sprinklers

Syria, late 15th-16th century
Engraved brass, silver damascene
Bologna, Museo Civico Medievale
inv. nn. 2117 and 2118

Comprising two very similar sprinklers, of pyriform shape, with a flat plain base, rising to a tall tapering neck with a bulbous disc near the juncture of body and neck, the body profusely inlaid with silver thread, inv. n. 2118 decorated with three concentric bands of varying height, filled with knotwork, complex geometric designs and scrollwork, repeated on the neck as well and framed by a frieze of diamond-shaped motif, inv. no. 2117 with a similar decoration, the body finely engraved with a floral composition consisting of flower heads with four petals within interlocking roundels, against a minute refined vegetal ground heightened in silver. Legati describes them both in the following terms:

Two flasks of similar craftsmanship, that is to say *Zemina*, used by the Turks for odoriferous waters (Legati, 1667, p. 15).

Both sprinklers belong to the so-called *Veneto-Saracenic* production, a manufacture on which academia has been arguing for a long time now. Originally, it was believed that such items would have been produced in Venice and then decorated in Syria, and vice-versa. A recent study however confirms that the vast majority of the Veneto-Saracenic pieces would have been produced in late Mamluk Syria (H. Huth, 1972 in Abouseif, 2005, p. 147). Their uncertain classification was due to the fact that several of these artworks presented typically Western shapes and very often, they were engraved with noble Italian families' coat of arms. This curious syncretism is not hard to explain in the light of the important commercial and diplomatic exchanges taking place between Venice and the Middle East. On those commercial routes, not only goods were travelling and being exchanged, but also styles, designs, craftsmen and decorative patterns.

Bibliography: Legati, 1667, p. 15; Legati, 1677, Book III, chapter 19, p. 260, *Inventario Cospiano*, 1743 (Ms. 273), Gabrieli and Scerrato, 1985, cat. n. 583 (inv. 2118).

I.B.

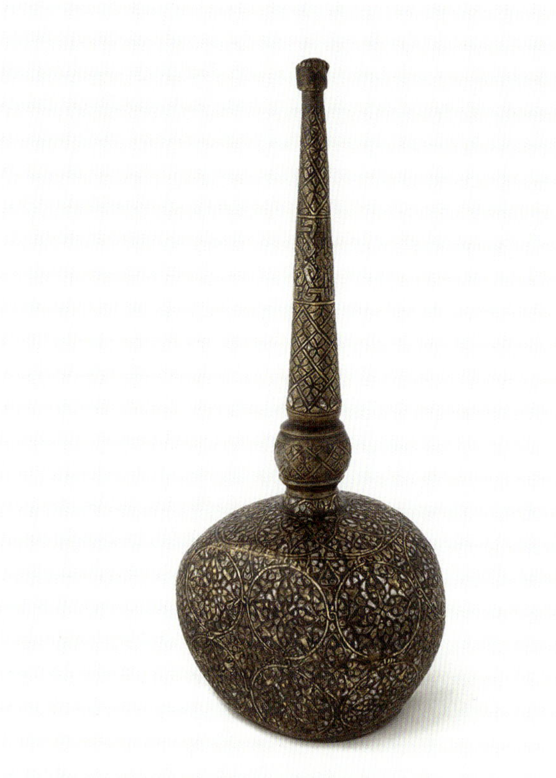

32

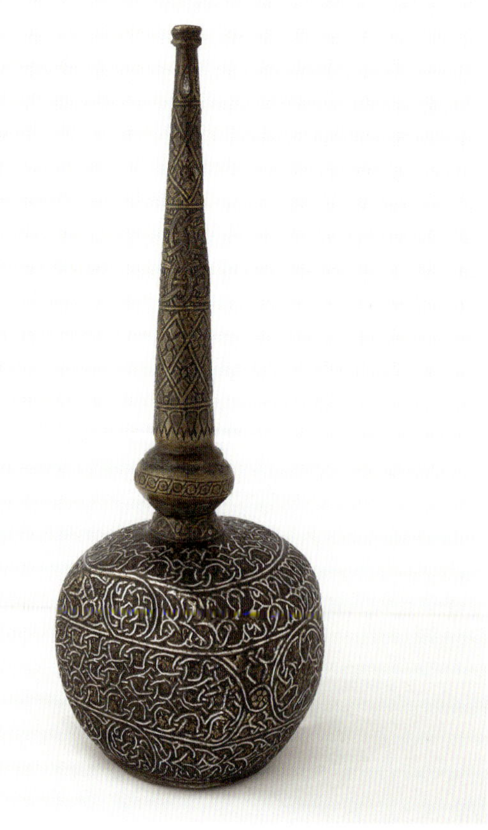

33

34
Rosewater sprinkler

Turkey, Kutahya, first half 18th century
Fritware, with polychrome underglaze painting
h. 16 cm
MIC, Museo Internazionale delle Ceramiche in Faenza, inv. n. 1229

Of globular shape, resting on a short circular foot, rising to a tall cylindrical neck, the main body moulded with lobed cartouches filled with an interlocking composition of small diamond-shaped elements in relief and painted with drooping floral motifs to the centre and interspersed among the medallions, a floral crown embellishing the protruding element on the neck's base, inspired by metalwares, the palette typical of Kutahya wares with yellow, green, blue and red all highlighted in black.
For an in-depth discussion on Kuthaya wares, appendix to cat. n. 55.

Bibliographical references: Carswell et al. 1991, pp. 54-55, 63, nn. K13-K17; Şebnem, Bilgi 1997, cat. n. 21-A, p. 42; Soustiel 2000, cat. 78, pp. 129.

I.B.

35
Rosewater sprinkler

Turkey, Kutahya, first half 18th century
Fritware, with polychrome underglaze painting
h. 13 cm, Ø 9.3 cm
MIC, Museo Internazionale delle Ceramiche in Faenza, inv. n. 1230

Of globular shape, resting on a short circular foot, rising to a cylindrical neck, the decoration highlighted in black and divided in vertical panels alternating dense series of red dots located around a central diamond-shaped motif with fluctuating floral tendrils, the base of the neck and its protruding element embellished with red dots and graphemes matching the colours of the below decoration, the palette typical of the Kutahya production painted in yellow, green, blue and red bole, inherited from the Iznik manufacture.
For an in-depth discussion on Kuthaya wares, appendix to cat. n. 55.

Bibliographical references: Carswell et al. 1991, pp. 54-55, 63, nn. K13-K17.

I.B.

Roses and Islam

Rosewater is a key element in several religious and social rituals in the Islamic lands. Indeed, Zamzam water mixed with roses is used to clean the Ka'ba and the body of a deceased Muslim.
This type of bottles were very much in use for the care of the self and in the social etiquette of Islamic hospitality and welcoming. Upon the entrance of a guest, it is traditional practice to offer them some rosewater to freshen their hands.
Rosewater is also much appreciated in Iran and the Near East in the cosmetics and cooking. Roses are the quintessential symbol of elegance and fineness in Arabic and Persian poetry, especially in love poems:

On the roses of her cheeks, on this velvet, a panacea fallen from the cheekbones, on the red coral mouth opening to a smile of pearls and a beautiful East below the lips. (One Thousand and One Nights)

Lastly, the rose is among the most recurrent flowers in the Islamic decorative vocabulary. As an example, the Ottoman Four Flowers style includes carnations, hyacinths, tulips and roses.

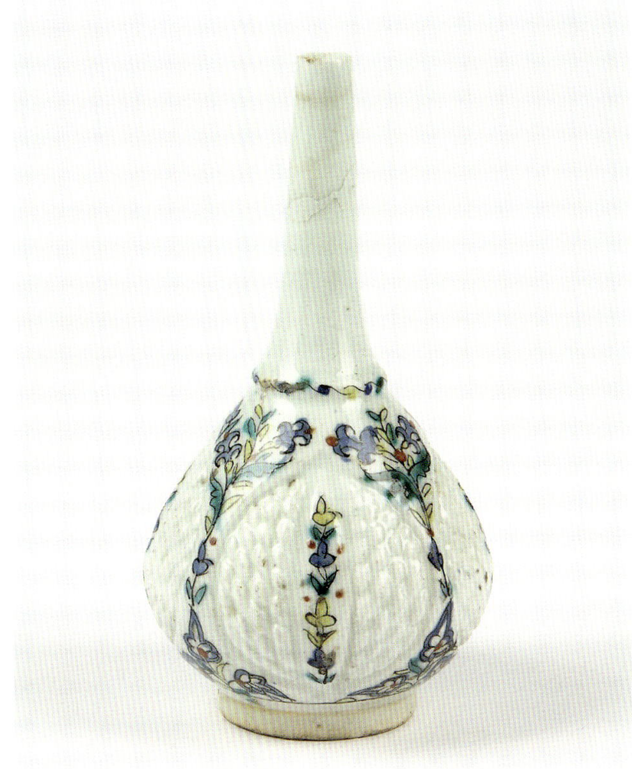

34

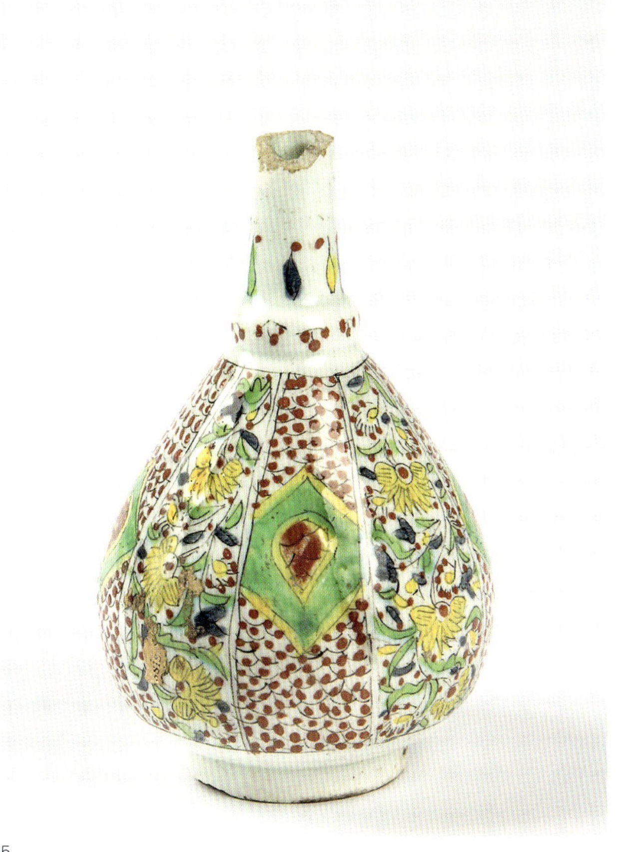

35

36
Cosmetic mortar

Iran, 12th century
Bronze, cast and engraved
h. 3.6 × l. 19 × w. 15 cm
The Aron Collection, inv. n. A.142

A small melting pot, of hemispherical shape, with a long beak-shaped spout, three incised elliptical grips, decorated with intertwined palmettes, the central one larger and the lateral ones smaller, the perimeter with a ridged design.
Originally, these mortars were considered oil lamps and medical tools. However, in 1987, Melikian-Chirvani speculated they could have easily been used as cosmetic mortars and that the long spout worked as a funnel for antimony powder (*kohl*) or indigo, used to dye hair and eyebrows.
The hammam was the primary place where one could spend time looking after and taking care of their body. Often, men would dye their beard and hair with privet there and women would paint their hands and feet with arabesques or put make up on their eyes with *kohl* or *daghba*.

Provenance: antique art market.
Bibliographical references: Allan, 1982, figs. 79 and 82, pp. 74-75; *L'etrange*, 2001, cat. n. 107, p. 145.

I.B.

37
Large mirror with handle

Iran, 15th century
Engraved steel
l. 35 cm, Ø 17.6 cm,
weight: 778 g
The Aron Collection, inv. n. A.347

The mirror of circular shape with a long twisted handle, the front plain and levigated, the rear densely incised and decorated with intertwined palmettes and lotus flowers set around a lobed central cartouche, the external perimeter with a decorative band with a chain motif, an unmissable accessory for the *hammam*.

Provenance: antique art market.
Bibliographical references: Christie's London 2011, lot 203. An analogous mirror was successfully sold at Christie's London 2008, lot 131.

I.B.

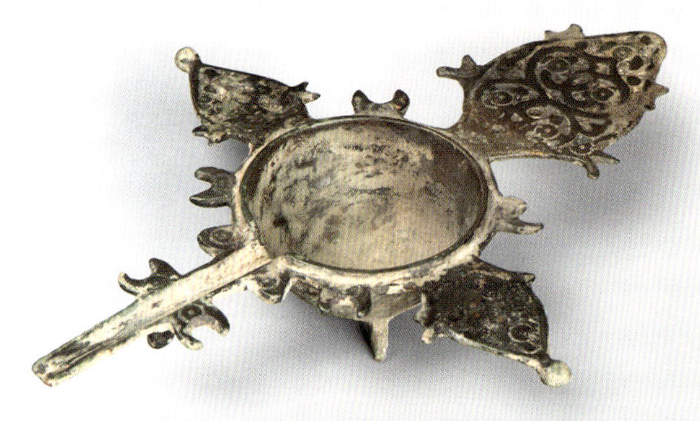

36

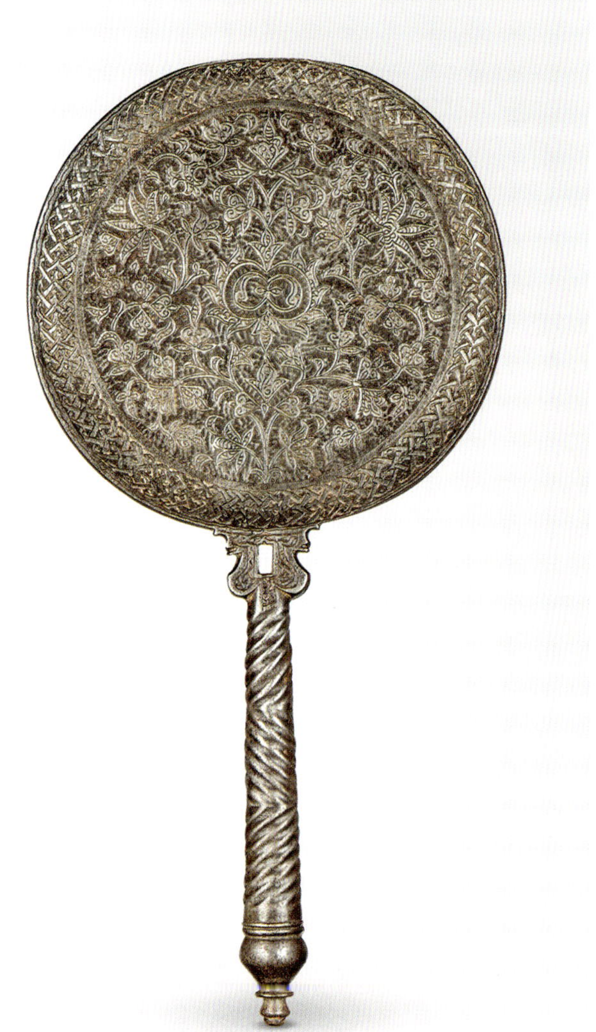

37

38
Clog

Turkey, 18th century
Wood, metal, ivory, fabric
Museo del tessuto e della tappezzeria "Vittorio Zironi", Bologna, inv. n. 757

Female hammam slippers, of typical shape, raised from the floor through two wooden platforms, the sole of square shape at the front and pointy on the heel, inlaid in silver with vegetal scrollwork and flowers, the containment band with gold thread-embroidered chevron. The name for these slippers in Arabic is *qabqab*, an onomatopoeic noun referring to the sound they produce when touching the floor. The height of these slippers allowed women to walk in the *hammam* without touching the floor, and getting in contact with its humidity and filth, but it was also a symbol of their status. The higher the slippers, the more well-off the wearer was, because to walk in such high heels one would need more than one assistant. For a similar example, with mother-of-pearl and silver inlay, please see British Museum, inv. n. As1553.a-b.

I.B.

39
Towel

Middle East, 20th century
Cotton and linen, h. 56 × w. 22 cm
Museo del tessuto e della tappezzeria "Vittorio Zironi", Bologna, inv. n. 2039

A large towel of rectangular format, the white textile ending in tassels, decorated with an embroidered band of elegant flowers and interlocking vegetal sprays.

Bibliography: unpublished.

I.B.

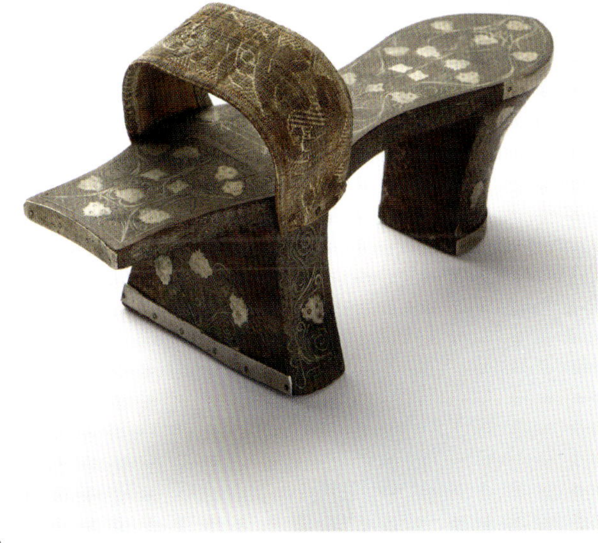

38

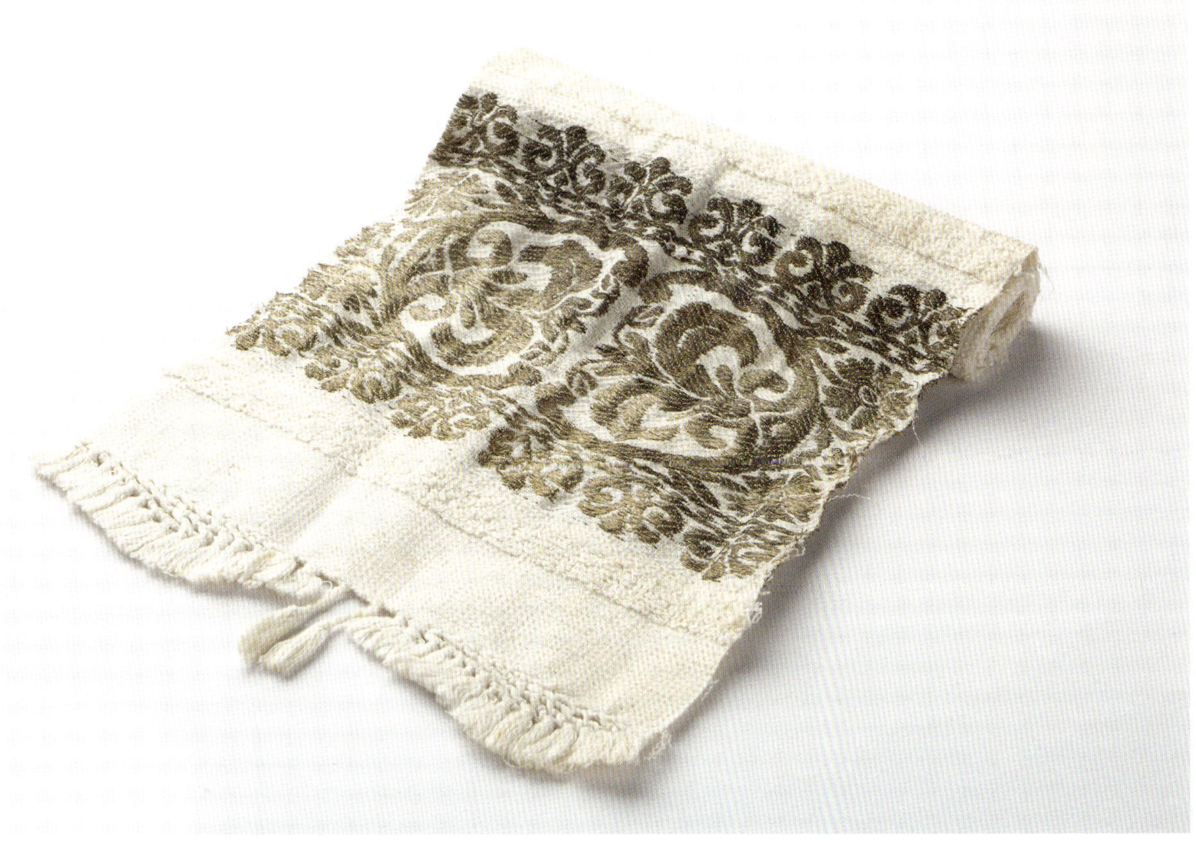

39

40-41
Kaftan

Turkey, 18th century
Purple cotton velvet with silver embroidery
h. 129 × w. 195 cm
Museo del tessuto e della tappezzeria "Vittorio Zironi", Bologna, inv. n. 553

Kaftan

Turkey, 19th century
Crimson cotton velvet with silver embroidery
h. 145 × w. 100 cm
Museo del tessuto e della tappezzeria "Vittorio Zironi", Bologna, inv. n. 554

Comprising two wide and long female caftans, one on a purple ground, the latter on a madder red ground, each embroidered on paper padding with silver metal thread, decorated with full floral bloom and vegetal sprays.
This type of clothes originate most likely in Persia and their use later spread further to the Islamic lands and Arab world. Worn by both men and women, caftans and their precious embroidery were often indicators of the social status and wellbeing of their owners. Especially in female caftans, one can notice the presence of recurrent symbolical decorative motifs in their designs such as special flowers linked to immortality, or symbols of prosperity and fertility. Floral bloom and sprays are the most common decorative element on Ottoman clothings, creating a metaphorical garden from which one steps out the moment they submerge themselves in the purifying water of the *hammam*.

Bibliography: Benevolo in Benevolo et al. 2018, pp. 51-52 (inv. n. 554).

I.B.

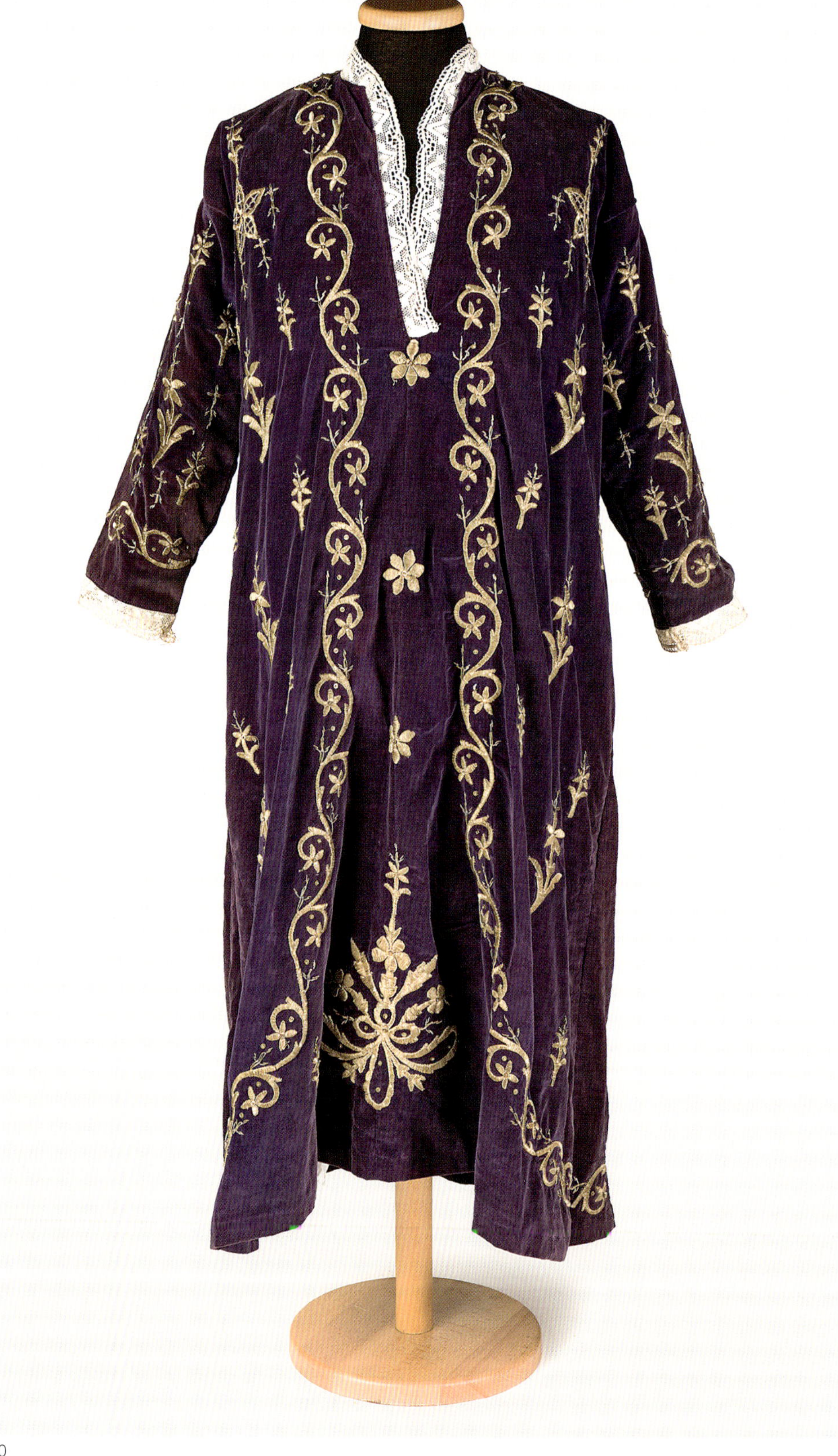

40

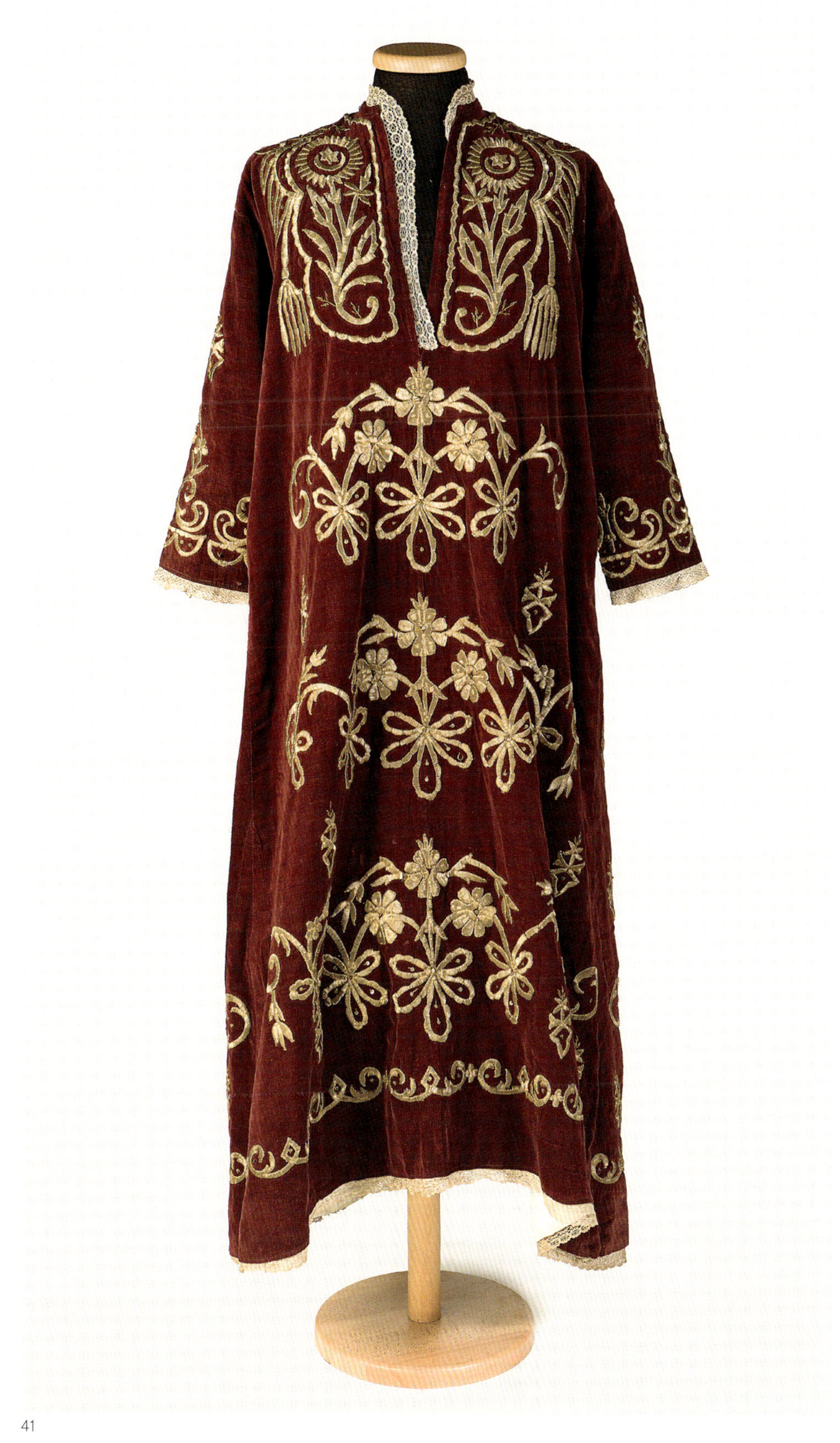

41

42
Ms Vat. Pers. 32, *Hammam scene*

15th century
Manuscript
Opaque polychrome tempera on paper
280 × 195 × 15 mm
Vat.pers.32, © Biblioteca Apostolica Vaticana

A fragment of the renowned *Makhzan al-asrār* by the famous poet Nizami Ganjavi (ca. 1141-1209). This work was produced as the opening to his famous "Five Jewels" (*Khamse*), a collection of epic *mathnavi*, long poems divided in hemistichs. The *Makhzan al-asrar* (the Emporium of Secrets) is written in a mystical-religious style and acts as a form of wise and didactical introduction to the other four poems, which instead belong to the narrative genre. After an initial prayer, the poetic and symbolical description of Muhammad's ascension to the sky follows, and immediately after there are the praises of Bahram Shah, to whom the poem is dedicated.

Bibliography: Browne 1951-1953; Pagliaro, Bausani 1968; Piemontese 2014.

A.V.

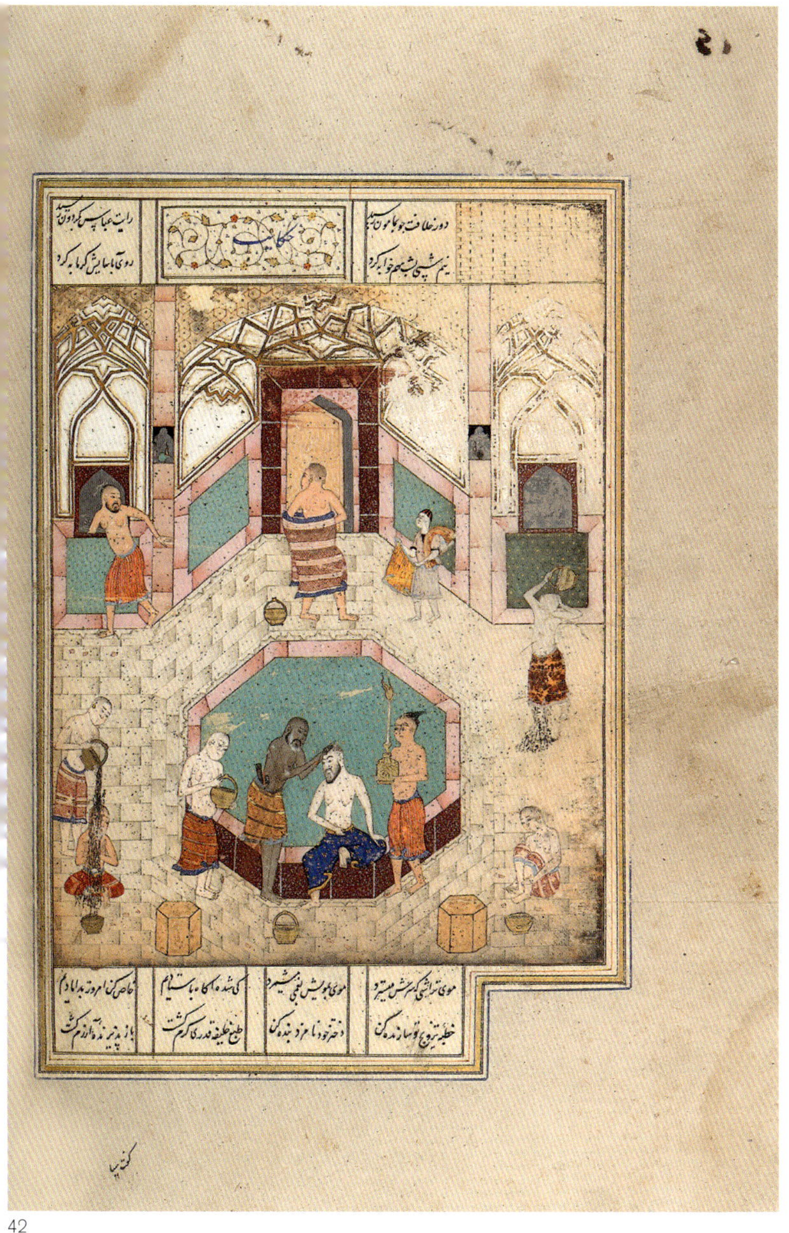

42

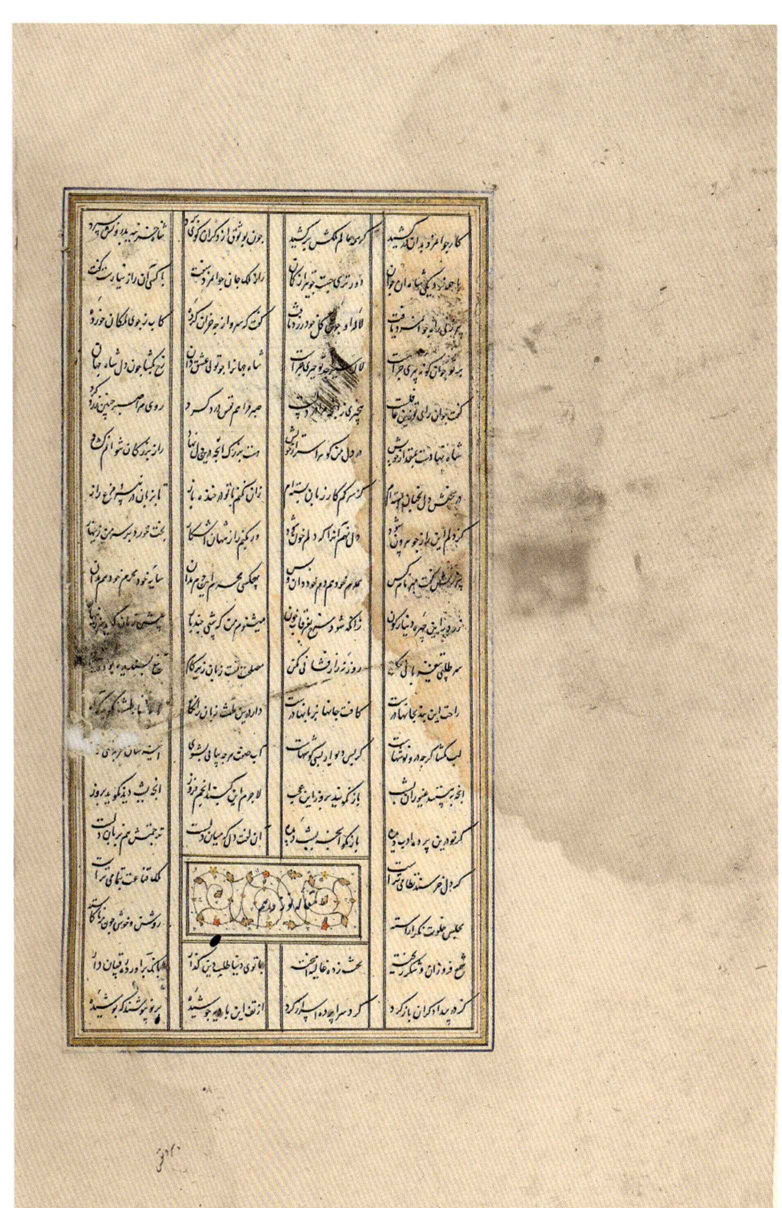

42

43
Oriental costumes

18th century
Manuscript
Pen drawing in black, red, and gray ink and polychrome tempera on ivory calendared paper
Courtesy of Biblioteca dell'Archiginnasio di Bologna

An example of Ottoman *murakka* (from Persian *muraqqa*, "what has been assembled"), a book-shaped album, which starting from 16th century became the main format for miniatures in the Ottoman, Safavid and Mughal lands. These albums were produced for both the autochthonous courtly elite and the Western travellers, merchants and diplomats, as it's the case of the one here exhibited.
The examples present in Western libraries are numerous, from the Venetian *Foggie diverse di vestire de' Turchi* (Wilson, *Turkish Costume Illustration*, cit., p. 125) all the way to the Swedish *Ralamb Codex* (Kungliga Biblioteket, Cod. Ral. 8:o nr 10). In general, the compositional arrangement looks the same. The Ottoman artists were producing individual figures, one per page; then, it was the commissioner's job to join them together in the book format, a process which is confirmed in the notes in Western languages usually located on the margins of the folios.
This specific *murakka* contains 324 Ottoman miniatures, depicting the Sultans and several other social classes, mostly connected to the courtly entourage. Possibly, the majority of these images was accompanied by brief explanatory captions on the upper border, but a later (and inattentive) binding has cropped the vast majority of these writings. It is thus through the Sultans' sequence that one can hypothesise a more specific dating.
Indeed, the last Sultan depicted seems to be Mehmet IV, who started his rulership at the age of seven and ruled from 1648 to 1687. In the two miniatures dedicated to him, he is portrayed with teenager features. If this assumption was correct, one could speculate that the album would have been put together shortly after 1660, an hypothesis that finds solid ground also in the strict stylistic similarities with some miniatures here contained and others more precisely dated like in the *Ralamb Codex*.
The two images here exhibited portray scenes from the *hammam*: in one, a lady is about to approach the bath, followed by an attendant holding the necessary tools; in the latter, a naked woman is caught whilst inside the bath, sitting down on a blue cloth covering her genitals and combing her hair. Next to her, the beholder can see a marble basin (*kurna*) filled with water from two overlying tabs. These compositions showcase renowned and common iconographic models. Similar images were incredibly successful and sought after, not only in Western Orientalist depictions, but also in the Ottoman iconographic tradition.

Bibliography: Schick 1999, pp. 625-628; Schick 2004, pp. 93-102; Ådahl 2006; Artan 2006, pp. 408-480; Firat 2008; Vanoli 2014, pp. 273-288.

A.V.

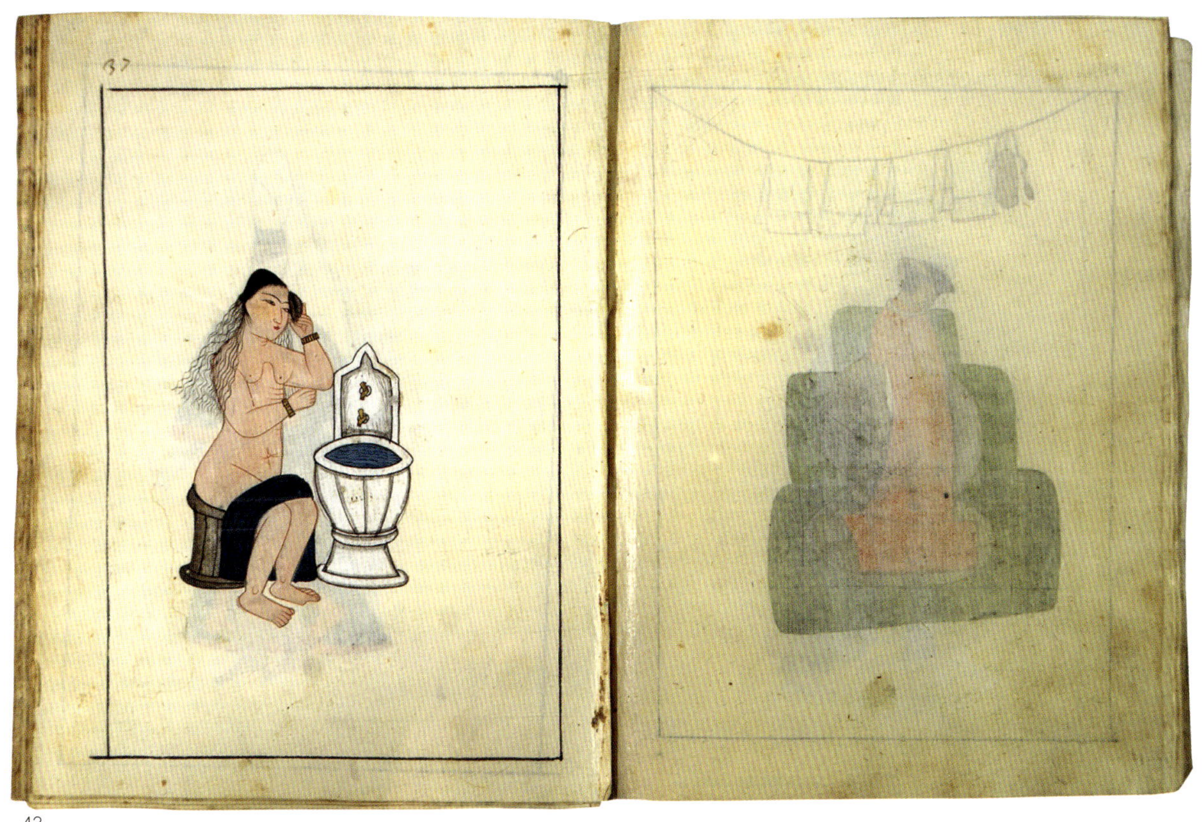

43

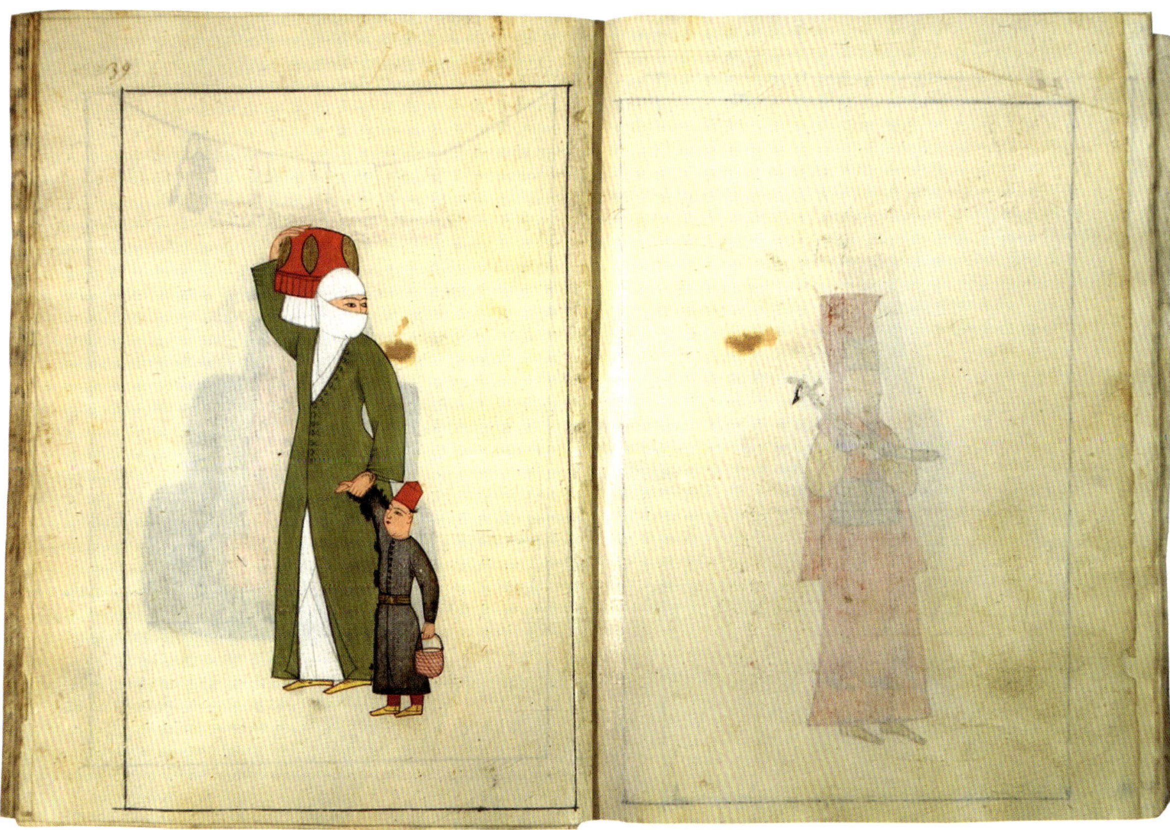

43

44-45
Hammam Scene

Gevork Mehredum
Smirne, 1741
Two paintings, oil on canvas
49 × 62 cm
Private Collection, Brussels

These two interesting paintings can be attributed both stylistically and chronologically to a series of work produced between 17th and 18th century by the Flemish painter Jean Baptiste Van Mour (Valenciennes 1671/Istanbul 1737). Van Mour's works gained recognition and fame at the European courts of the time and they contributed immensely to the Western understanding of the customs and traditions of the Near and Middle East. Invited to Istanbul by the French ambassador Charles De Ferriol for the first time in 1699, Van Mour specialised himself in the depiction of scenes from the courtly life, characterised by a faithful and realistic portrayal of each character. This skill made him become a painter appreciated and sought after by several renowned diplomats of the time who exploited his skills to immortalise crucial historical moments or political encounters, as in the case of the Dutch ambassador Cornelis Calkoen (Rijksmuseum, Amsterdam, Inv.n. SK-A-4078, *The Ambassador Corneliz Calkoen meeting Sultan Ahmed III*). This fostered the spread in the West of lively and realistic scenes from a world yet still not fully known. Having spent a long time in Istanbul with both local and international diplomats, Van Mour started developing a strong familiarity with the methods of conduct and social protocols of the Ottoman court. This guaranteed him a privileged access to the Ottoman palaces, allowing him consequentially to be able to reproduce not only scenes of great political solemnity, but also of everyday life, such as the intimate moments of the female gatherings in the *harem*, or the scenes at the hammam, which to this very day remain a precious testimony of a protected world, hard to access from the outside (Mosland et al., 2015, p. 296). The two works here presented, each characterised by a crowded gathering of figures, can be intended as 'consequential', almost in conversation, and perhaps they were part of a broader cycle related to the theme of the female hammam. Following this assumption, the central female figure in the first painting is shown together with other ladies whilst getting undressed; in the latter painting she is depicted in the centre of the composition, in front of a simple wall with a little fountain, surrounded by attendants washing her, whilst the other characters of

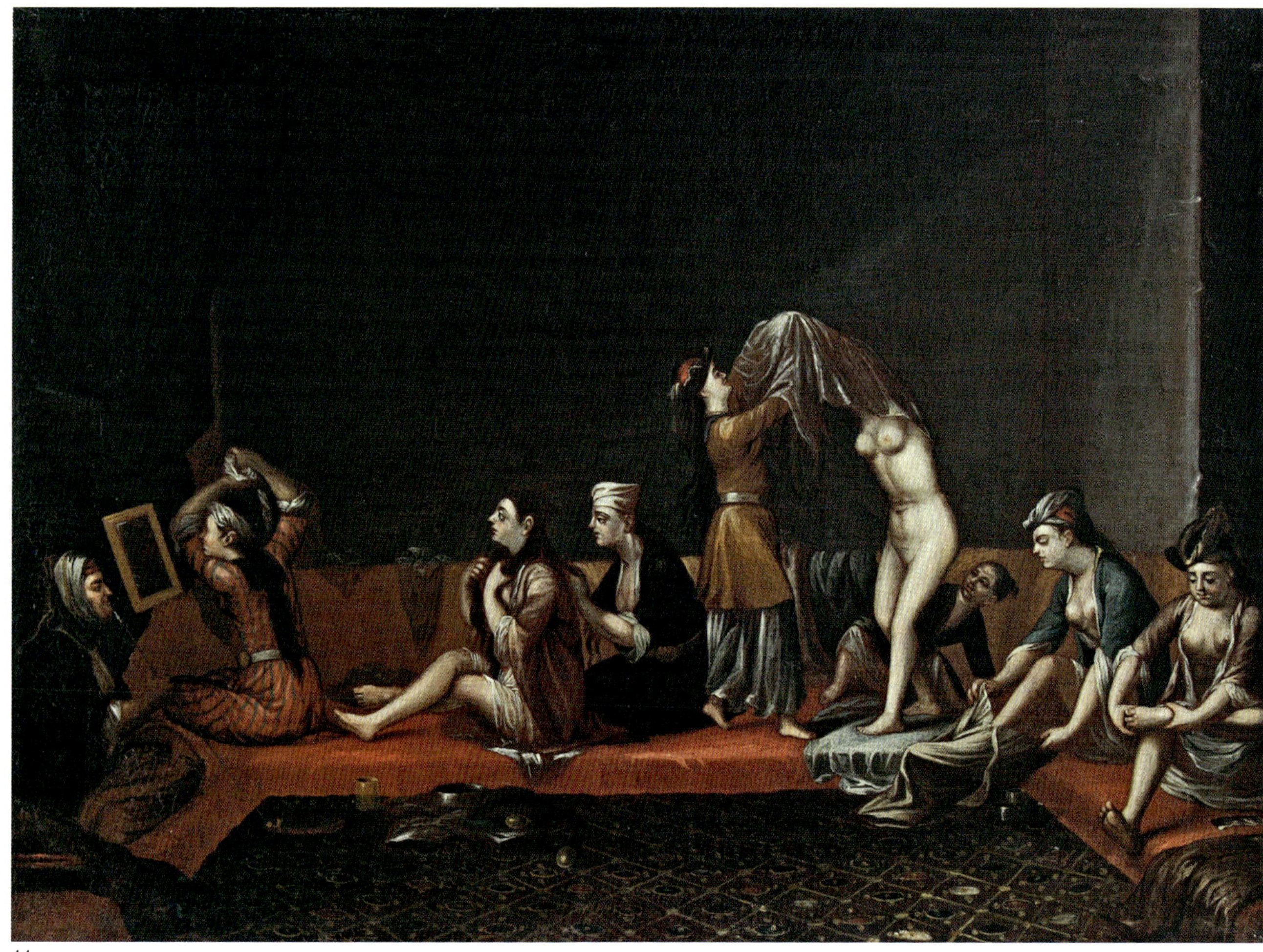

44

the composition attend their personal cleansing routine. However, the signature at the back of each canvas and the use of the specific appellative 'Armenian' lead to speculate that these were not painted by Van Mour but instead by a painter who could have been Armenian and active in Izmir, around the mid of 18th century. The *gavur*, unfaithful, Izmir, as it was often called by the Muslims of the time due to its high numbers of Christian communities there settled, hosted several painting ateliers and a flourishing Armenian community. This hypothesis could be further supported by the writing in Italian, given the tight relationship between Izmir and its Armenian colony with Venice. Indeed, already at the beginning of 1700 Venice had welcomed to San Lazzaro a community of Armenian Mekhitarist fathers, trying to escape persecutions. The evident formal indebtedness to Van Mour's models is in this case justified also by the presence of an important cycle which the Flemish painter dedicated to the Armenian community in Turkey, with lively and truthful scenes captured from daily lives, ceremonies and celebrations typical of this culture (see the Rijksmuseum for the full 'Armeniam' cycle).

Bibliographical reference in the cataloguing note.

I.B.

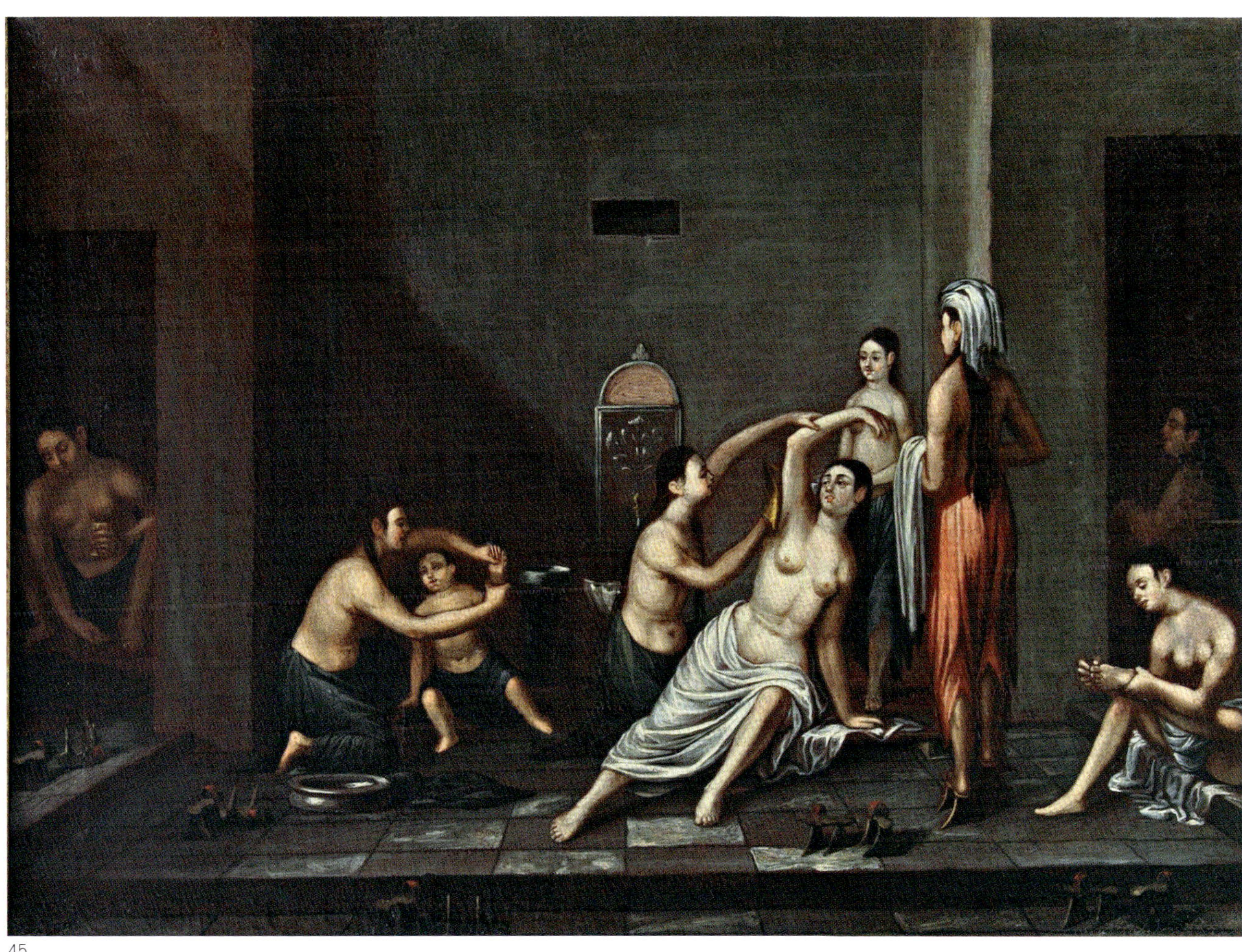

45

46
Granata or perfume bottle

Afghanistan, Kabul area, 11th-13th century
Earthenware, vitrified with decorations in relief
h. 11.5 × l. 10.4 cm
MIC, Museo Internazionale delle Ceramiche in Faenza, inv. n. 23356

Of sphere-conical shape, the moulded body decorated with concentric decorative bands showcasing lobed ovules in relief.

Bibliography: Guida, 2014, p. 31 fig 1. For a similar example, see: Burzacchini et al., 2015, figs. G112-G113, p. 220.

Similar objects have been excavated in several different areas of the Islamic lands from Egypt to Iran and Afghanistan. Their use and function are to this day debated. There are several different theories. Some scholars suggested they were used as grenades (*qawarir*). However, this hypothesis doesn't find a common ground in the military treaties of the time. Other scholars suggested they could have been used as special containers for mercury. But this substance was rather rare and instead many examples of these objects have been unearthed (Gouchani, 1992, p. 72).
Some of them bear epigraphic inscriptions which led some scholars to speculate whether they were instead used as perfume and essential oil containers. Ettinghausen (1965, p. 224) supported this theory, drawing as a reference to two stucco fragments from Qasr al-Hayr al-Gharbi, on which a female figure holds similar sphere-conical vessels in her hands. Other epigraphic inscriptions together with archaeological, literary and technical evidences led some other scholars to believe that these objects were used as beer containers (*fuqa'*). Lastly, the hypothesis that these were used as aeolipile, vapour containers already in use during the Roman times, is embraced by some scholars (Rogers 1969 - Savage-Smith et al., 1997, p. 325) and discarded by others (Ettinghausen 1965, pp. 224-225). Fonatana (1999, p. 8) believes that the truth lies in the middle: it is plausible to believe that these objects may have been used in different contexts for different functions.

I.B.

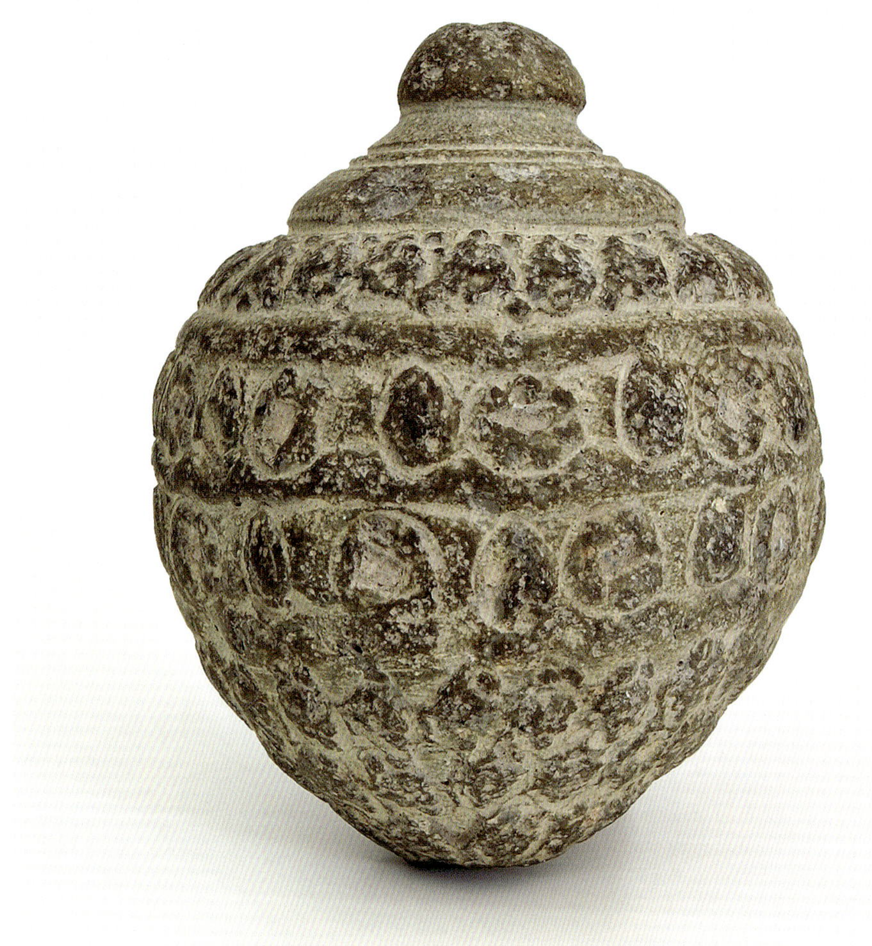

46

47

Granata or perfume bottle

Egypt, al-Fustat production, 10th-13th century
Earthenware, vitrified
MIC, Museo Internazionale delle Ceramiche in Faenza, inv. n. AB3864

Of sphere-conical shape, with a stopper, the moulded body decorated with vertical panels defined by deep grooves filled with fish scale and stylised flower motifs.

Bibliographical references: Burzacchini et al. 2015, figs. G112-G113, p. 220; Watson, 2004, cat. n. Ad.3 p. 131; Soustiel, 1985, cat. n. 143, p. 132.

I.B.

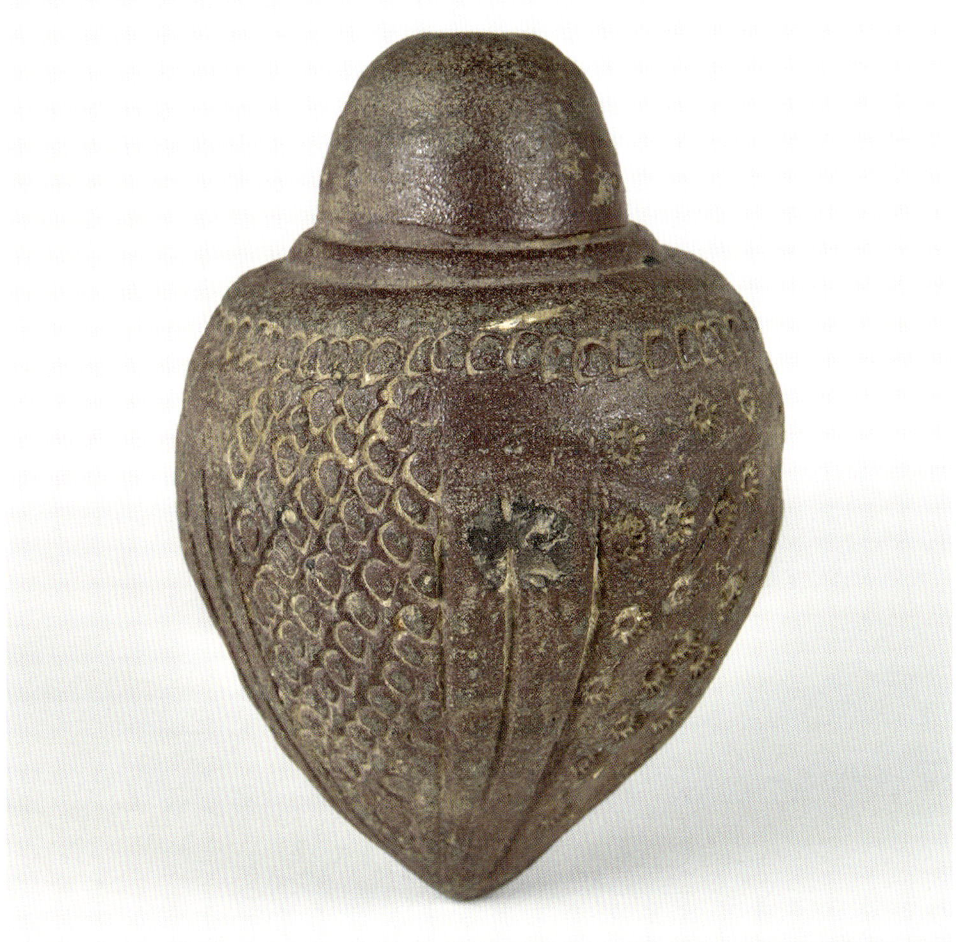

47

48
Base of water pipe

Iran, 17th century
Fritware, with polychrome underglaze painting
h. 17.8 cm, Ø 18 cm
The Ashmolean Museum, University of Oxford. Gift of Gerald Reitlinger, 1978, inv. n. EA1978.1712

Of globular shape, resting on a small circular foot, on the sides with the two typical holes to accommodate the pipe tubes, underglaze-painted in blue, green and red, the decoration consisting of two bands of red lobed cartouches and drooping medallions filled with floral bloom and green vegetal sprays, against a ground of scrolling blue vegetal tendrils, the base with stylised blue rocks against a white ground.
The technique and the colours of this *qalyan* base are typical of the Kerman kiln (southern Iran), a very important centre of ceramic production during the Safavid period. The most common shapes of Kerman ceramic *qalyans* were *kendis*, pyriform vases, and spherical vessels. The first example drew its inspiration from the typical Chinese porcelain pouring vessels, similar to tea pots, (*kendi*, see also cat. n. 51); the second from the local bottles (Watson 2004, cat. U.26, p. 472); and the last is the one analysed here.
The blue vegetal tendrils in the background seem to have been painted rather in free hands, differently from the red cartouches and inner floral bloom, which showcase talented draughtsmanship skills, almost up to a miniaturist's level.

Bibliography: Deborah Willis in *Eastern Ceramics*, 1981, n. 353, p. 123; Allan, 1991, n. 39, p. 62, illus. p. 63. For analogous examples, please see the Al-Sabah Collection (LNS 130) and Soustiel J., 1985, cat.n. 308, p. 281.

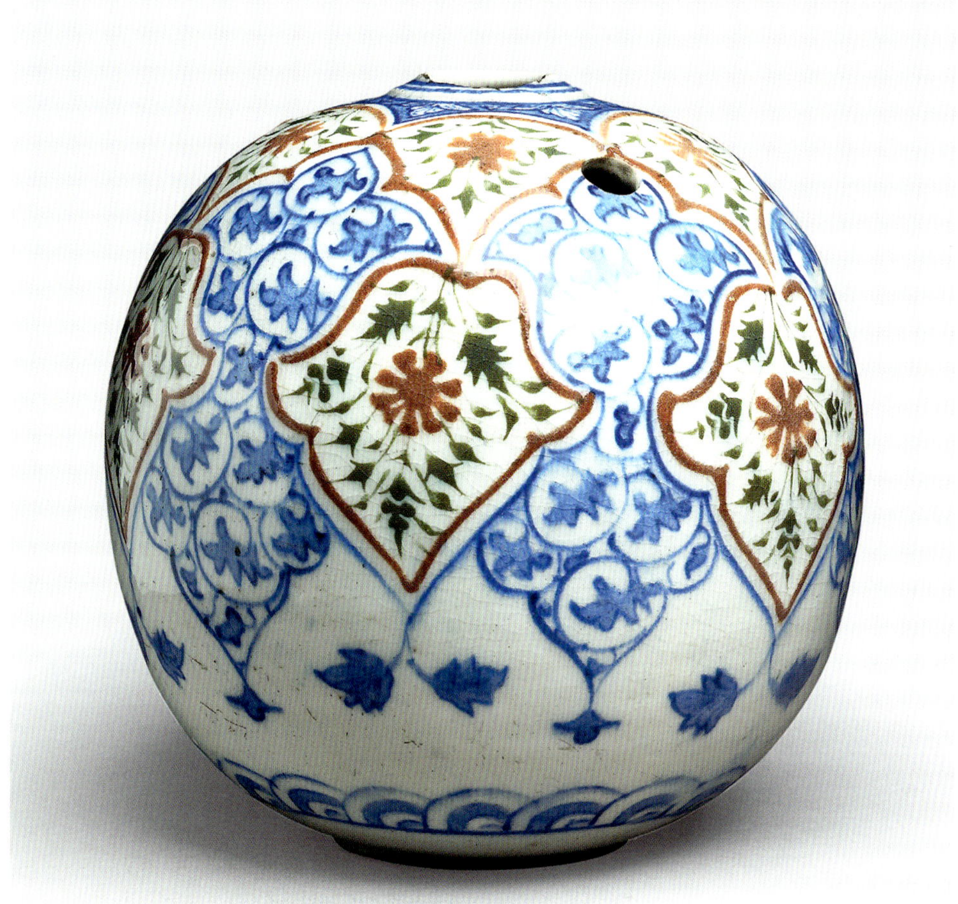

48

Water Pipes

Water pipes had been first introduced to the Islamic lands by the Westerners, who imported tobacco from the Americas,. However, their use method developed in a surprisingly different way. Indeed, in the Middle East water pipes (*huqqa* in India and *qalyan* in Iran) normally had pipe tubes attached to a pottery or metal container of different shapes. Tobacco was burnt on the brazier above the vase and the smoke would be breathed in through the pipe attached to the shoulder. Rosewater was often used to sweeten the flavour.

Smoking *huqqa* was considered a noble pastime and numerous miniatures with rulers or noblemen were produced with this subject, especially at the Mughal and Rajput courts. Of those days, a few bejewelled *huqqas* survived, made of precious metals and encrusted with gemstones, symbolising their belonging to a royal or imperial entourage.

Smoking was also among the favoured recreational activities allowed at the *hammam*. Often an attendant would pass by the bathers and offer them water pipes, so that they could smoke and relax in between baths. Water pipes played and play to this very day a crucial role in the context of social rituals. Still today, Middle Eastern men meet and gather at coffee shops to smoke together and discuss.

I.B.

49

Base of water pipe

Iran, Mashhad, 17th century
Fritware, opaque white slipware, blue and black underglaze painting
Courtesy of the L.A. Mayer Museum for Islamic Art, Jerusalem, Israel, inv. n. C 420 - 73

Of typical *kendi*-shape, with compressed globular body, resting on a circular foot, with straight narrow shoulders, flared neck and onion-shaped spout, the decoration on the body highlighted in black and arranged in subtle floral bands, one large band embellished with flowers and long-tailed birds, the neck and spout painted with vegetal motifs, the base with a pseudo-Chinese mark within a square frame.
Since the 1620s, Persian potters started copying the shapes, the colours, and the design of Chinese porcelains. This is a perfect example of that time, whereby a *kendi*, a typically Far Eastern pouring vessel, has here been readapted to be used as a water pipe. The decorative and chromatic vocabularies here used, such as the long-tailed birds and the Chinese cloud bands crown (*ruyi*) around the neck, are heavily rooted in the Chinese tradition. This is also confirmed by the presence of a pseudo-Chinese mark on the base. Differently from Chinese porcelains though, the decoration is here delineated in manganese black, a solution which allowed to enhance depth and volume in the composition and to maintain the colour stable during the firing process.
On the function of water pipes, appendix to cat. n. 48.

Bibliography: Soustiel, 1985, cat. n. 321, p. 302 and 276; Hasson, 2014, cat. n. 98, Baily, 1996. To compare the mark on the base, please see Lane, 1957, p. 117. A similar *kendi* can also be found in Carswell, 1985, cat.54, p. 112.

I.B.

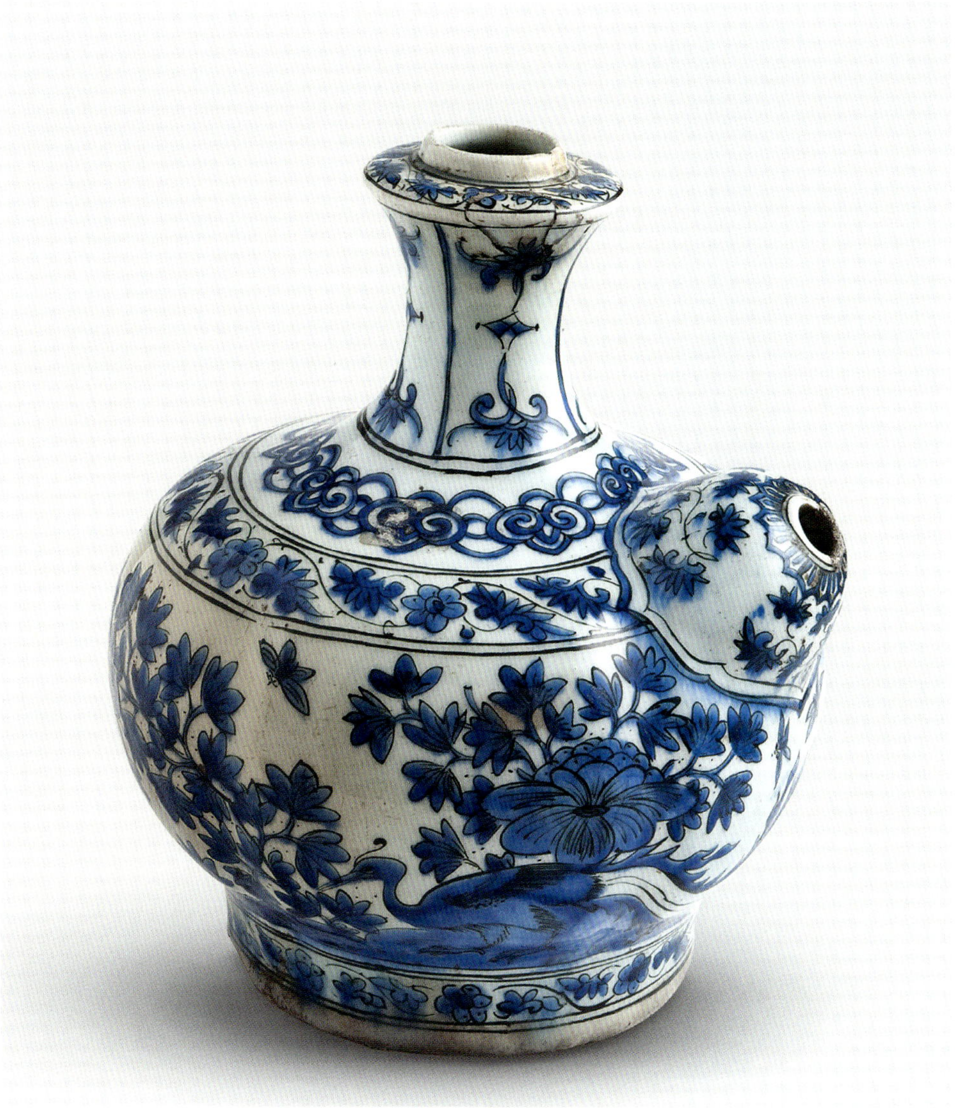

49

50
Ewer

China, Jingdezhen, 18th century
Porcelain, with cobalt blue underglaze painting
h. 26 cm
MIC, Museo Internazionale delle Ceramiche in Faenza, inv. n. 13660

Of pyriform shape, resting on a circular foot, rising to a short neck and everted mouth, with a sinuous handle on the side and a long bent beak-shaped spout joint to the body through a chain-modelled bracket, the decoration of the base with a subtle band of spirals followed by a crown of lobed flower petals against a blue ground, the decoration of the rest of the body against white ground and consisting of different registers, one with peonies tendrils and other flowers interspersed with polylobed medallions filled with peach blossoms, with stylised vegetal tendrils to the spout, the neck painted with a crown of lanceolate leaves, the handle with a little hoop, possible once used to tie a stopper, now gone, the base with Qianlong mark with six characters.
The decorative style of this ewer, which is dated to the Qianlong period, is reminiscent of the Yongle production (1403-1425). Its peculiar shape (*zhihu*) is already in use during the Yuan period (see inv. n. 52.132 at the Brooklyn Museum) and it originally derived from Islamic metalware.

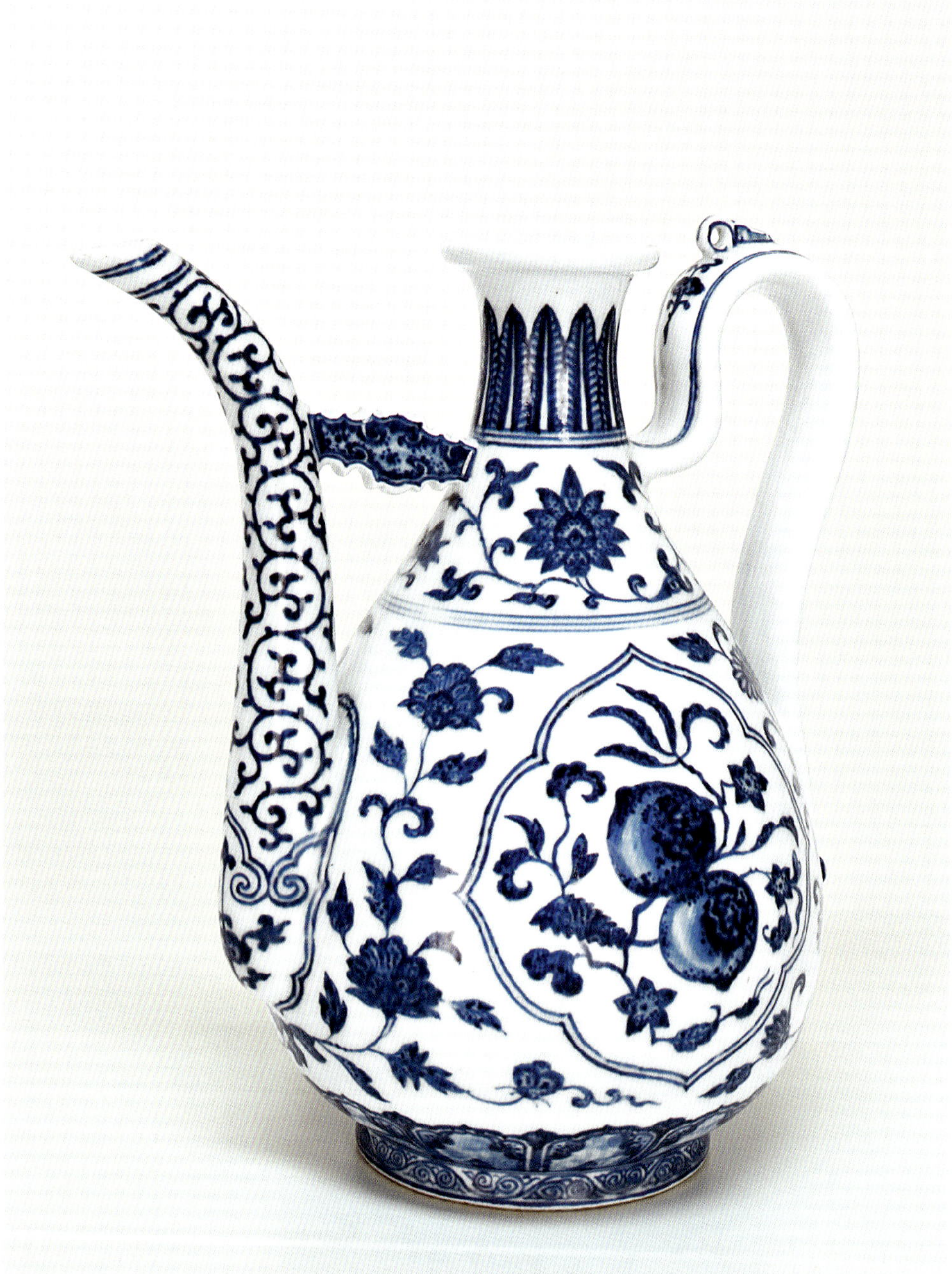

50

In the 13th-14th centuries, China and Persia were both under the control of Mongol rulers, the Yuan in China and the Ilkhanids in Persia. This communal link , fostered by the historical period of the so-called *Pax Mongolica*, favoured intense commercial exchanges and the transfer of decorative motifs and artistic skills. Several Arab merchants settled down in strategic locations along the Chinese commercial routes and Muslim officials started holding high-rank posts at the Mongol court. These special historical-economical circumstances led to fruitful artistic exchanges between the two lands: Chinese potters started experimenting Islamic metalware shapes, often adding pseudo-calligraphic inscriptions, and Persian potters tried to develop new materials to equal Chinese porcelains. Chinese productions were very sought after in the Islamic lands and were constantly in demand as precious luxury goods, to be preserved in the *Chini Khane* and used at court, as testified by several miniatures of the time (see the Cleveland museum example).
Evidences of influences between China and the Middle East in terms of shapes and decorative elements can be observed even before the Mongol conquest, going back all the way to the relations between Sassanid Iran and the Tang dynasty.

Bibliography: Pope, 1953, n. 29.427, Tab. 54; British Museum Inv. n. A.696.

I.B.

51
Kendi

China, Jingdezhen, late 16th century
Porcelain, with modelled decoration and underglaze painting in cobalt-blue
h. 22 cm, w. 15.5 cm
The Ashmolean Museum, University of Oxford. Gift of Gerald Reitlinger, 1978, inv. n. EA1978.1936

Of globular shape, resting on a flat base, with a tall straight neck with everted disc just before the rim, the spout shaped as a crayfish, its moulded body stretching diagonally around the neck and body of the ewer, the underglaze cobalt blue painted decoration following a marine theme, the base decorated as a seabed with waves, the body painted with fishes among seaweeds, the neck with cartouches filled with heads of *ruyi* (a sort of scepter with polylobate ends) and blue fish scale motifs.
This type of *kendi* was produced in China to then be exported to South East Asia, where they were very sought after, and to Persia, where they were readapted as water pipe bases (see cat. nn. 49 and 48). For an in-depth discussion on the exchanges between China and the Islamic world, see the appendix to cat. n. 50, and on the function of water pipes, appendix to cat. n. 48.

Bibliography: *Eastern Ceramics*, 1981, n. 33, p. 29.

I.B.

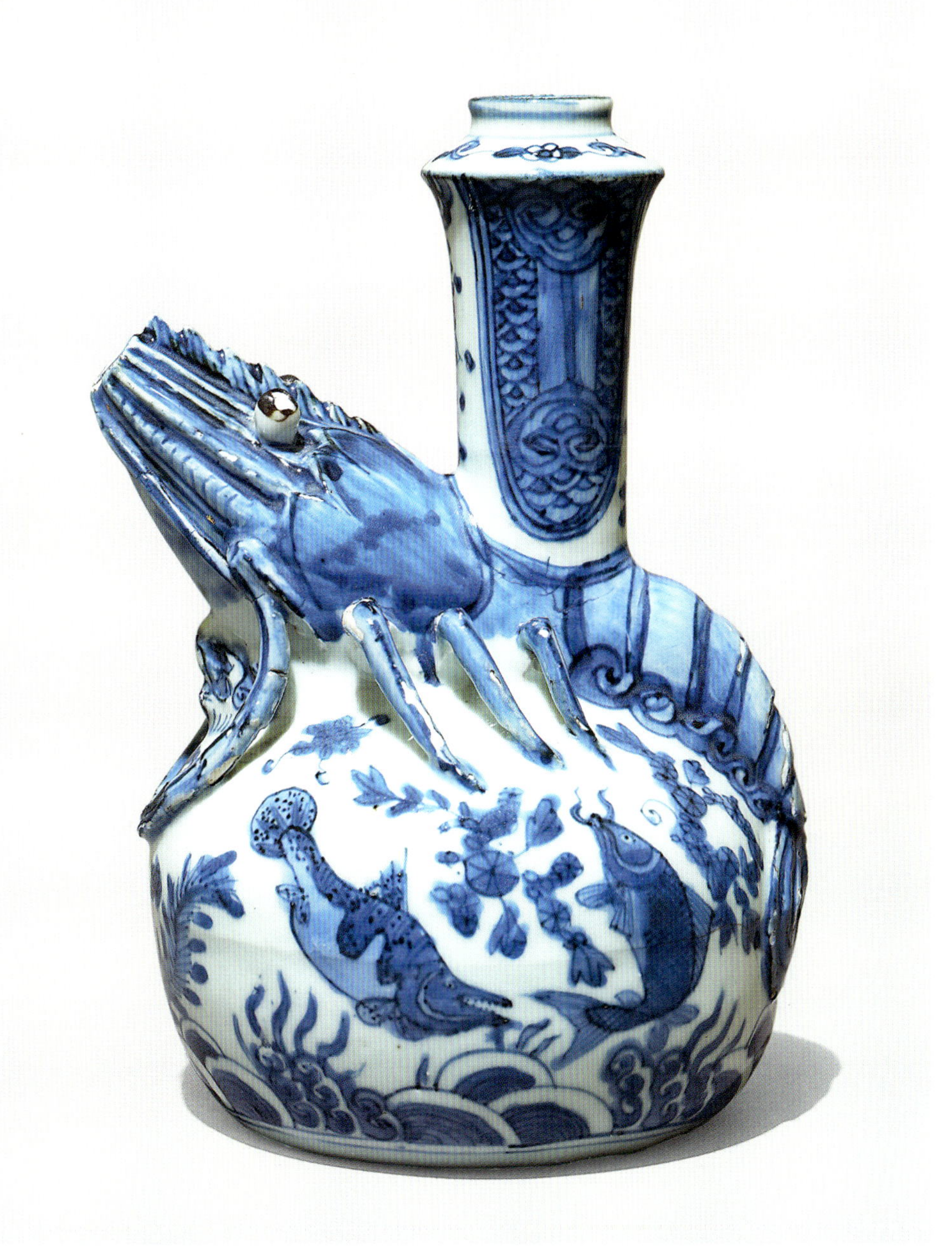

51

Drinking Water

Water is normally drunk fresh. Thus, the need to preserve that freshness through large clay containers, often covered by cloths or natural elements, such as tree leaves, palm branches or stones.

In several areas, however, water was often polluted and unclean. So the community needed firstly to boil it, then to filter it.

The importance of water was confirmed by medical literature, where detailed descriptions of its precious properties and its different varieties were provided, making a clear distinction between water from wellsprings, canals, or rivers.

The wealthy would clearly not be satisfied by regular water. Not only were they ready to offer more for good quality water, they also had the means to maintain its freshness. Indeed, the richest members of society would have both sophisticated clay jugs, which helped lowering the water temperature of a few degrees, and the possibility to buy snow even in summer, a lavish commodity back in those days. The founder of the Fatimid dynasty, 'Ubayd Allah al-Mahdi (10th century), is known to have ordered that a spare stock of snow would be taken with him on his pilgrimage to Mecca. In Baghdad, snow sellers (*thallajun*) used to fill entire stores with snow that travelled from far away. It is said that water mixed with a small amount of snow (*ma' muthallaj*) was such a rare beverage that it was preferred to lemonade; it was such a lavish drink to the point that one *qadi* (Islamic judge) wrote a treaty on whether the poorer members of the community should be allowed to drink it.

Water was also the basic liquid ingredient for a multitude of fruit beverages clearly listed in most Islamic culinary treaties. Indeed, drinks like lemonade, ginger tea, apple, orange, and pomegranate juice, water with floral essences such as violets, herbs, vegetables, and spices such as turmeric were all very sought after. The combination with one of these flavoured waters with snow was a real lavish drink.

Some of these beverages were believed to have medical properties and to work as tonics of the body and spirit, and in medical treaties one can often find them mentioned in chapters dedicated to *ashriba* (drinks).

Several of these drinks became very popular and carried on being served over the centuries, to the point of being still very much present in today's consumption: tamarind (*tamr hindi*), liquorice (*sus*) or dried grape (*zabib*) juices are still sold by street vendors in most Islamic cities nowadays.

In Islam, following the tradition of those cultures which developed near deserts and semi-arid regions, the offer of water to someone thirsty is considered an important moral duty, almost a religious one.

The value of hospitality was cherished in these countries way before Islam and is deeply rooted in the social structure of Arabic society. Indeed, the very sense of male honour (*muruwwa*) was built through a list of values including generosity and hospitality. The desert's dryness and the lack of safety during travels led to the social necessity of offering hospitality to any traveller for at least three days. The Qur'an highlights in several passages how sinful it is to ignore the needs of the less well off (69:34; 74:44; 89:18; 107:1-7) and how pious it is to be generous and charitable (2:215, 274, 280; 13:22; 22:35; 35:29; 57:7; 58:12; 76:8; 90:14-16).

The subject of hospitality is also dealt with particular depth in the *hadiths*. To the question "what is the best part of Islam?", the Prophet replied: "to offer food and to greet everyone you know and everyone you do not know". And every offer of hospitality in Islam would start with the offer of water.

52-53
Base (Kilga) and Jar

Egypt, 12th century
Marble base or kilga and marble jar
Base/Kilga: h. 33 × l. 48 × w. 32 cm
Jar: h. 55 cm
Benaki Museum, Athens,
inv. nn. 10833, 10834

A water dispenser, of typical shape, with a marble base, surmounted by a marble jar, the four feet forming cusped arches, each side carved with niches (*muqarnas*) and seated figures, around the rim of the basin a Kufic epigraphic band with auspicious and good-wishing blessings to the owner:

Perfect blessings, eternal grace, glory, infinite happiness and luck.

Its typical shape with a protruding open tray was dictated by its function: the surmounting jar would filter the water, which was then made available to drink in the lower basin. The jars were normally made in unglazed earthenware to allow evaporation and therefore to maintain the freshness of the water. Once filtered, water would freely flow to the protruding lower basin and poured through a ladle. Whilst the Fatimid marble *kilgas* survived, their accompanying jars haven't reached us due to their fragility and dimensions.

Bibliography: Ballian, Moraitou, 2006, p. 85. For similar artworks, see The British Museum, inv. n. 1988,1107.1; Piotrovsky, 1999, p. 148. For an in-depth discussion on the marble bases, see Knauer, 1979, pp.67-101.

I.B.

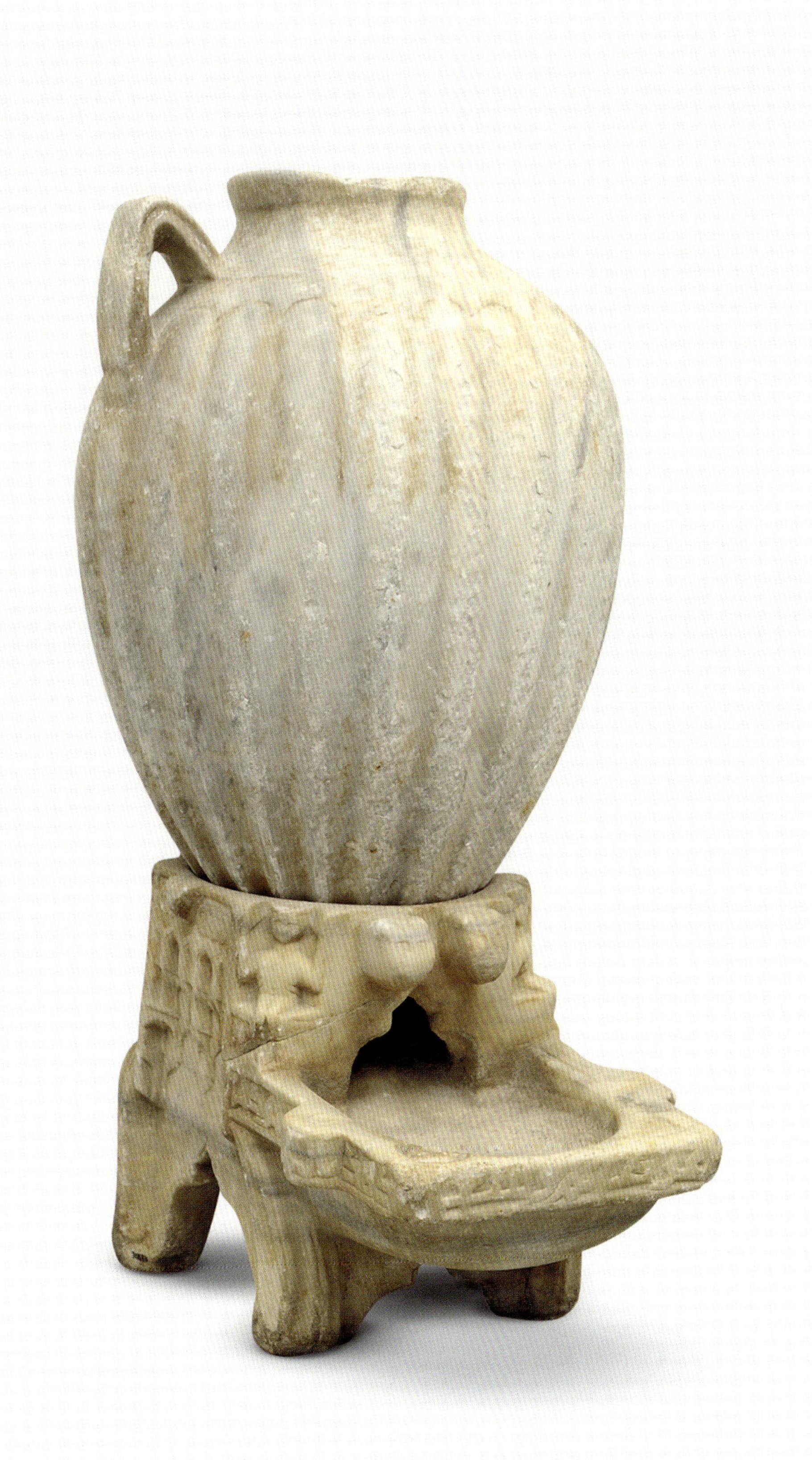

52-53

54
Ceramic flask with floral designs

Kutahya, 18th century
Fritware, with polychrome floral underglaze painting
h. 17 cm, Ø 14,5 cm
Benaki Museum, Athens, inv. n. 175

A pilgrim's flask, of circular shape, with flattened sides, a short cylindrical neck and an everted rim, the decoration on the body consisting of concentric bands leading to a central roundel with a yellow, red and blue painted rosette, around it cusped lollipop-shaped trees interspersed with red-painted flower heads all against a stylised vegetal ground. The other side constituted by the very rib of the object determining its depth, polychrome-painted with alternating vegetal motifs.

Bibliography: unpublished.

I.B.

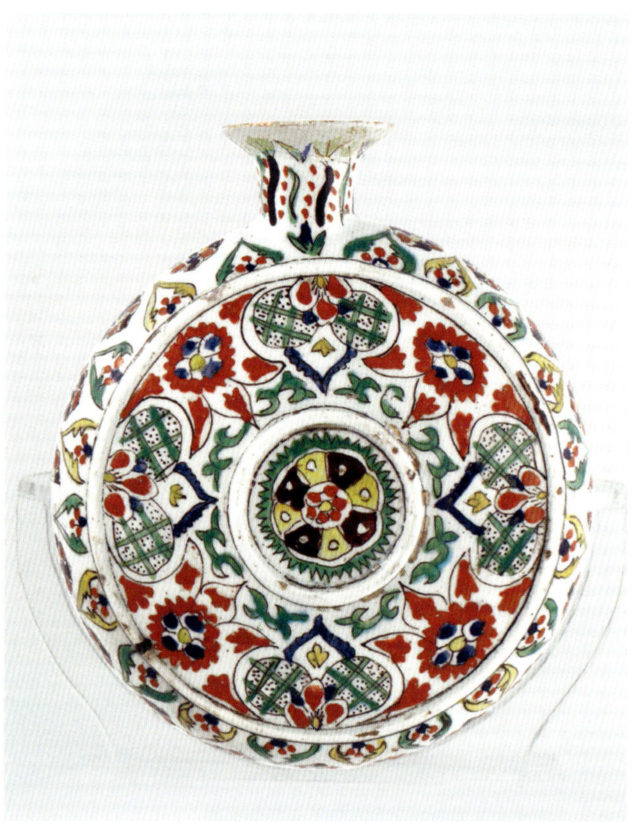

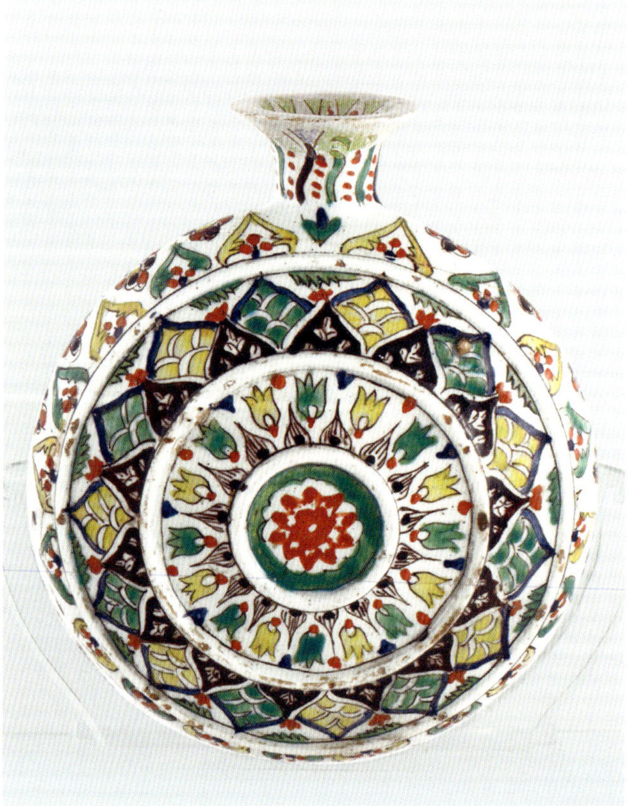

54

55

Ceramic flask with figurative design

Turkey, Kutahya, late 18th-early 19th century
Fritware, with polychrome figurative underglaze painting
h. 24 cm, Ø 22 cm
Benaki Museum, Athens, inv. n. 159

A pilgrim's flask, of circular shape, with flattened sides, a short cylindrical neck with slightly everted rim, small protruding elements on the sides for the suspension, the decoration similarly to cat. n. 54 consisting of concentric bands, the central roundels the rear and front central roundels surrounded by a frame of repeated ovoid patterns, with male and female characters. The largest roundel filled with a floral and vegetal crown designed and painted in the typical Kutahya style with ochre yellow, red, manganese purple and green palette.

Bibliography: Ballian, Moraitou, 2006, p. 192. For similar examples, see Watson 2004, cat. n. T.24, p. 445; Pasinli, Balaman, 1991, p. 109; Victoria and Albert Museum, Londra, inv. n. 777-1892 and C.2035-1910.

Kutahya wares:

Following the decline of the production of Iznik wares in the late 17th century, the kiln of Kutahya became the new heir of the Ottoman ceramics tradition. The first vessels belonging to this new production were created at the same time of Iznik wares (the so-called *Abraham wares*). Scholars struggle to exactly establish which wares were produced where, but it is likely to suggest that the two kilns were concurrently active and that only after the 18th century Kutahya wares stopped being subordinate to Iznik (Carswell 1998, p. 48). Given the huge success of Iznik wares, Kutahya vessels adopted similar shapes, designs and colours, especially the bole red.
Nevertheless, Kutahya wares also introduced a variety of novelties: new colours such as yellow and aubergine purple started appearing; old shapes were reinterpreted and readapted; and from a stylistic point of view, the decoration became very dense and packed, blooming into a folk and colourful *horror vacui* considerably distant from the fluctuating elegance of Iznik wares. Furthermore, Kutahya vessels were often decorated with Christian motifs and symbols due to the local flourishing Armenian community.
Carswell (1972, vol. II, pp. 25-36) links the chromatic palette change of Kutahya wares concurrently to the Chinese porcelain *famille verte* one, establishing thus a connection between the early 18th century introduction of the pink *falangcai* in China and of the purple at Kutahya before 1740. As far as the shape is concerned, it seems that the vast majority of the Kutahya production focused on tiles, hanging ornaments, sprinklers, cups, dishes and bottles (see cat. n. H17.3-4), and more rarely citrus squeezers or pilgrim's flasks such as the ones here showcased, indicating that most of the Kutahya vessels production was thus devoted to the containment of liquids and the consumption of beverages.

I.B.

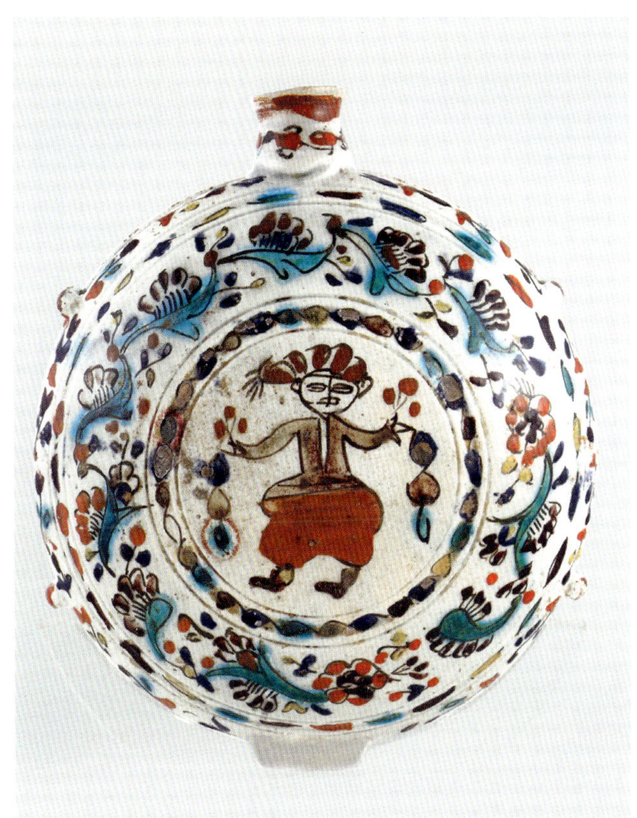

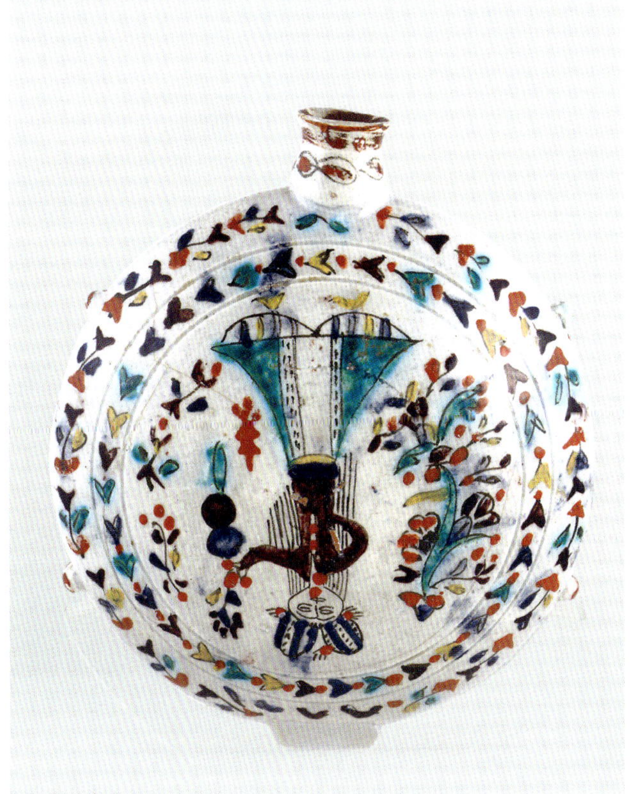

55

56 (1-10)
Ten water filters

Egypt, 10th-12th century
Unglazed filtered achrome earthenware
MIC, Museo Internazionale delle Ceramiche in Faenza

Of circular shape, unglazed and colourless, with pierced decoration, usually set on water jugs and bottles of common use, specifically on their necks. The pierced decoration had the function of filtering the water and ensuring that no dirt or insects would infiltrate; the unglazed porous material instead allowed evaporation and kept the water fresh. These filters are surviving fragments of more complex ewers, of which they often retain parts of their bodies and necks. Their shape is mostly standardised and easy to replicate. That said, two main styles can be distinguished: the convex filters, made at the time of the ewer's making; and concave filters, added onto the ewer at a later stage by pressing them and causing them to adhere on the main body material. The vast majority of the filters shown here belong to the first category. Filters can also be classified in chronological order and through decorative motifs. The earliest examples would be the pre-Fatimid ones, followed by the Fatimid, Ayyubid and Mamluk ones. Each period shows a preference for one motif or the other, assisting scholars in the dating. All the filters here shown belong to the Egyptian Fatimid production and their decoration is mostly geometric, floral, zoomorphic, epigraphic or figural, usually framed within an incised frame with chevrons.

More specifically:

- filter decorated with ship on rhomboid-perforated background, inv. n. AB 5038; h. 3.8 cm, inner Ø 4.5 cm;
- filter decorated with running hares on rhomboid-perforated background, inv. n. AB 5044; h. 2.3 cm, Ø 7.6 cm;
- filter decorated with a hare in profile on rhomboid-perforated background, inv. n. AB 5046; h. 2 cm, Ø 5.5 cm;
- filter with cursive Arabic inscription. The inscription reads: "Anyone who picks up this jug will find it overflowing!", inv. n. AB 5049; h. 2.8 cm, Ø 6.3 cm;
- filter decorated with cursive Arabic inscription. The inscription reads: "Anyone who picks up this jug will find it overflowing!", inv. n. AB 5053; h. 1.7 cm, Ø 6.2 cm;
- filter with mirroring floral decoration, inv. n. AB 5083; h. 3.5 cm, inner Ø 4.8 cm;
- filter geometrically decorated with a triangle engraved with a zigzag line on triangle-perforated background, inv. n. AB 5148; h. 3.5 cm, inner Ø 6.6 cm;
- filter engraved with floral element similar to the soul star, deriving from intersecting semi-circles, inv. n. AB 5168; h. 5.6 cm, inner Ø 3.4 cm;
- filter with perforated geometric decoration that creates a central six-pointed rose, where each petal is interspersed by another smaller circle, inv. n. AB 5171; h. 3.8 cm, Ø 3.4 cm;
- filter decorated with engraved fish on rhomboid-perforated background, inv. n. AB 5176; h. 4.5 cm, Ø 7.3 cm, inner Ø 4.5 cm.

The primary centres of production for this type of filters were Al-Fustat and Qena-Ballas, both located in modern-day Cairo. The period in which the biggest production is recorded, in terms of both quantity and artistic repertoire, is during the Fatimid dynasty. The time preceding and following this dynasty shows a narrower repertoire of motifs and the pierced decoration is mostly geometric.

Bibliography: Olmer 1932, pl. Figs. LVI, a, b, c, d; Barrucand 1998, p. 182; Casalini 2016, pp. 21- 35. For analogous examples, see Watson, 2004, p. 133.

I.B.

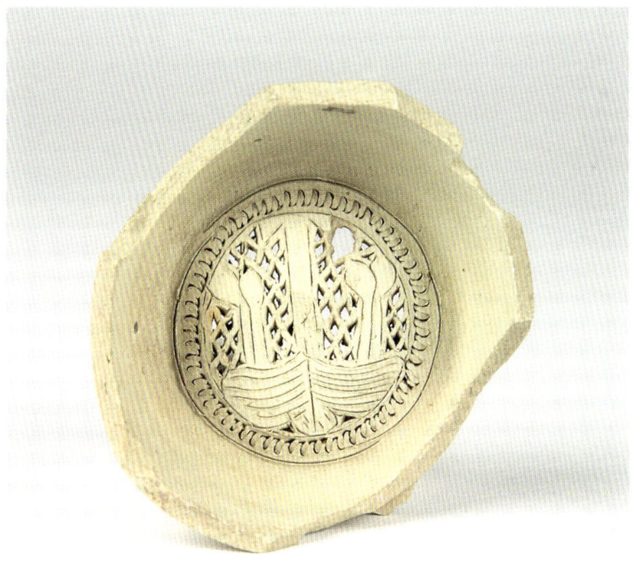

56.1

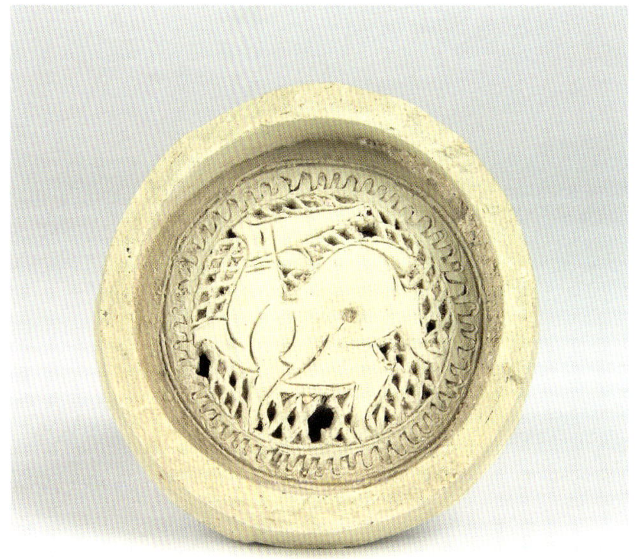

56.2

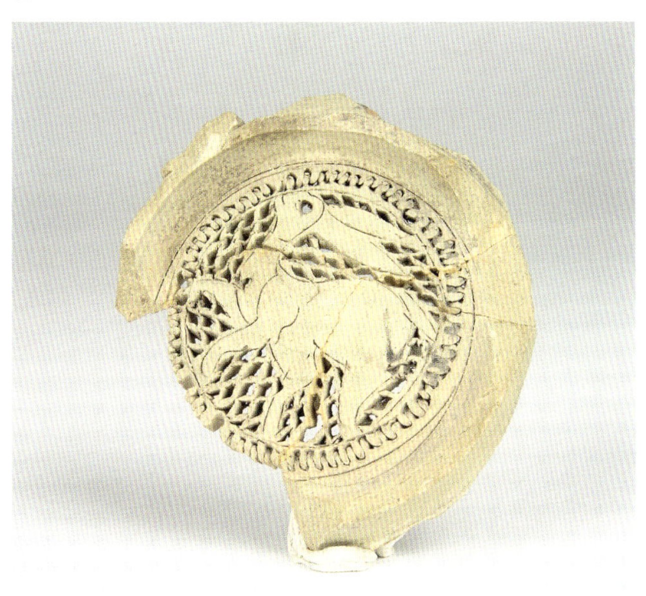

56.3

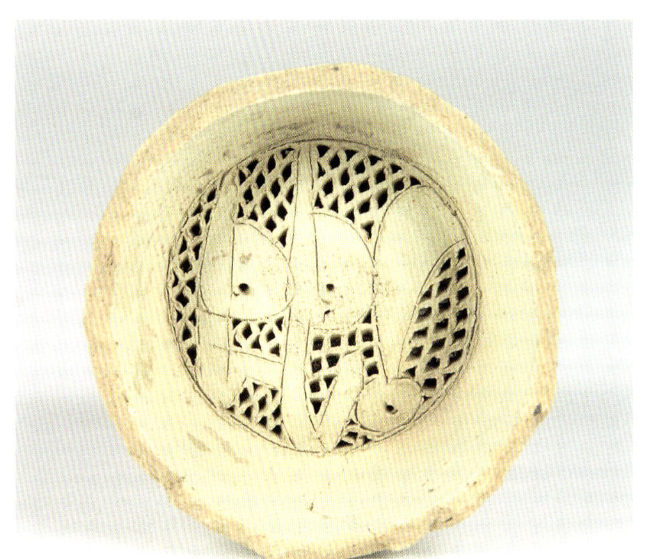

56.4

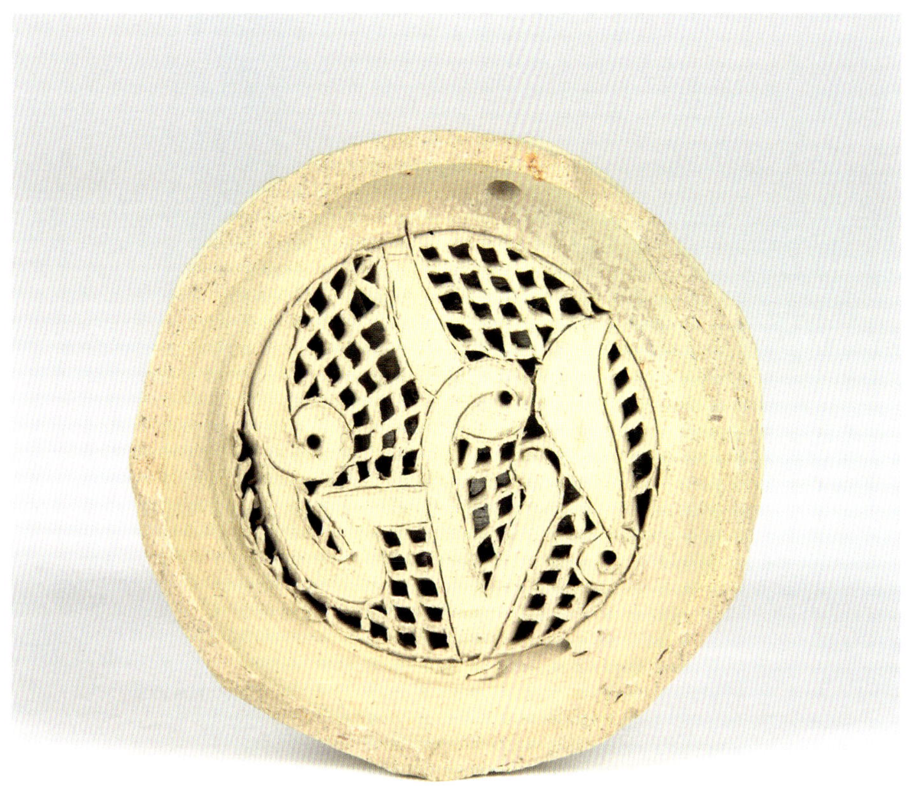

56.5

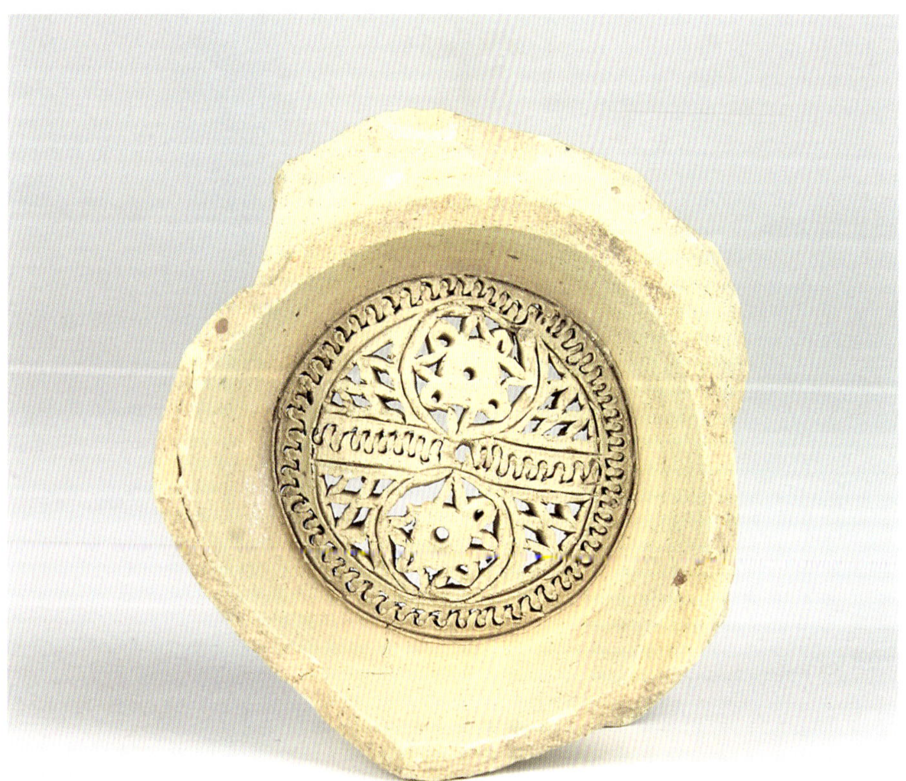

56.6

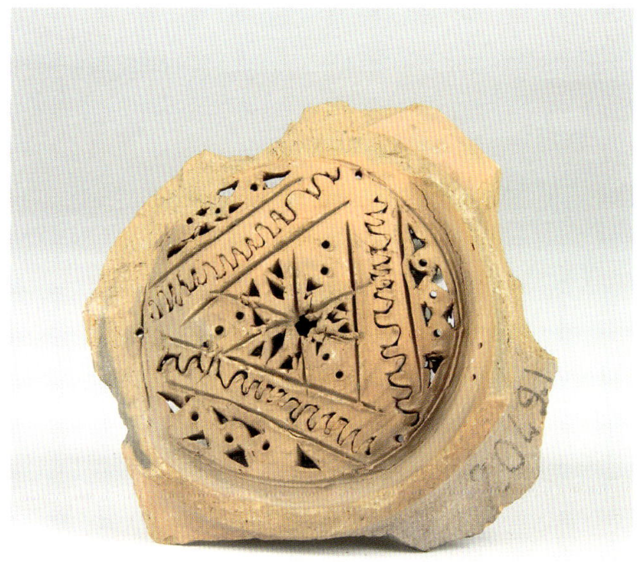

56.7

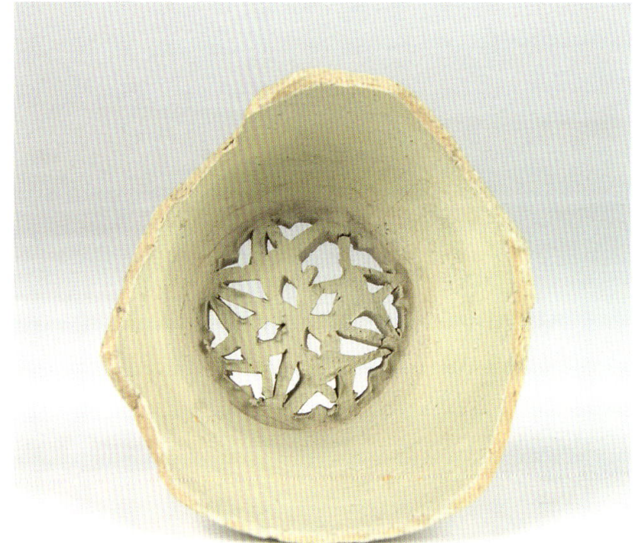

56.8

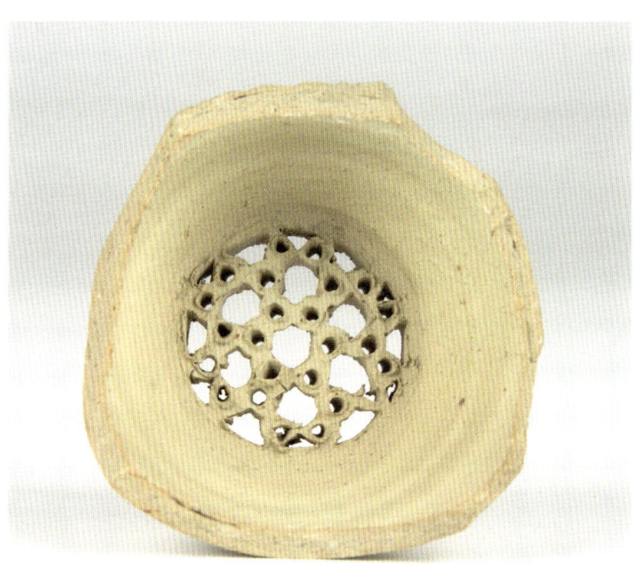

56.9

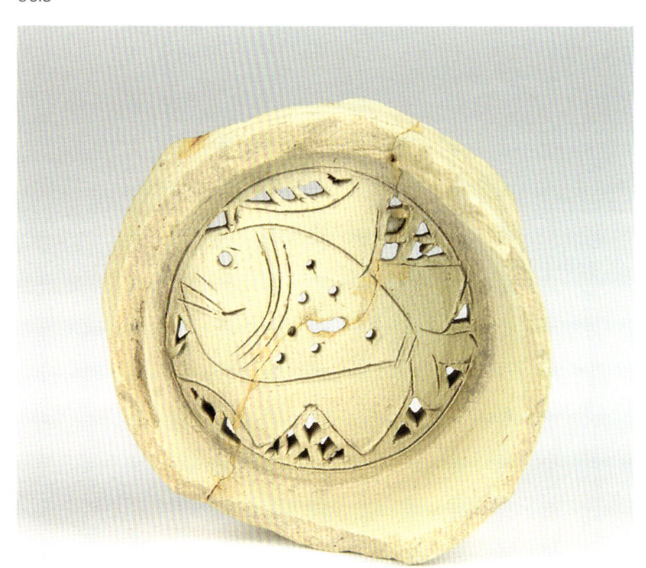

56.10

57
Unglazed jug

Syria or Iran, 12th-13th century
Unglazed earthenware, engraved and mold decoration
h. 32.8 cm, max. Ø 22 cm, foot Ø 11 cm
MAO Museo d'Arte Orientale, Torino
inv. n. ISv/99

Of globular shape, almost conical to the base, resting on a flat circular foot, with narrowing shoulders and a long flared neck with three bulging discs, with a single handle on the side connecting shoulders and neck. The body, to the base, the body decorated with alternating panels filled with meanderings, circles and diamond-shaped geometric motifs, interspersed with a subtle vertical band of vegetal tendrils, the shoulder with a decorative frieze filled with rampaging quadrupeds, each framed within lush greeneries.
The shoulders with a decorative frieze with rampaging quadrupeds, each framed by lush greenery.
The decorative motif on the shoulder is reminiscent of Sassanid art in both its subject and compositional arrangement. However, some of these motifs migrated further West from Iran into the Middle Eastern and Mediterranean regions, so it is hard to establish the precise origin of this object.

Bibliography: unpublished.

I.B.

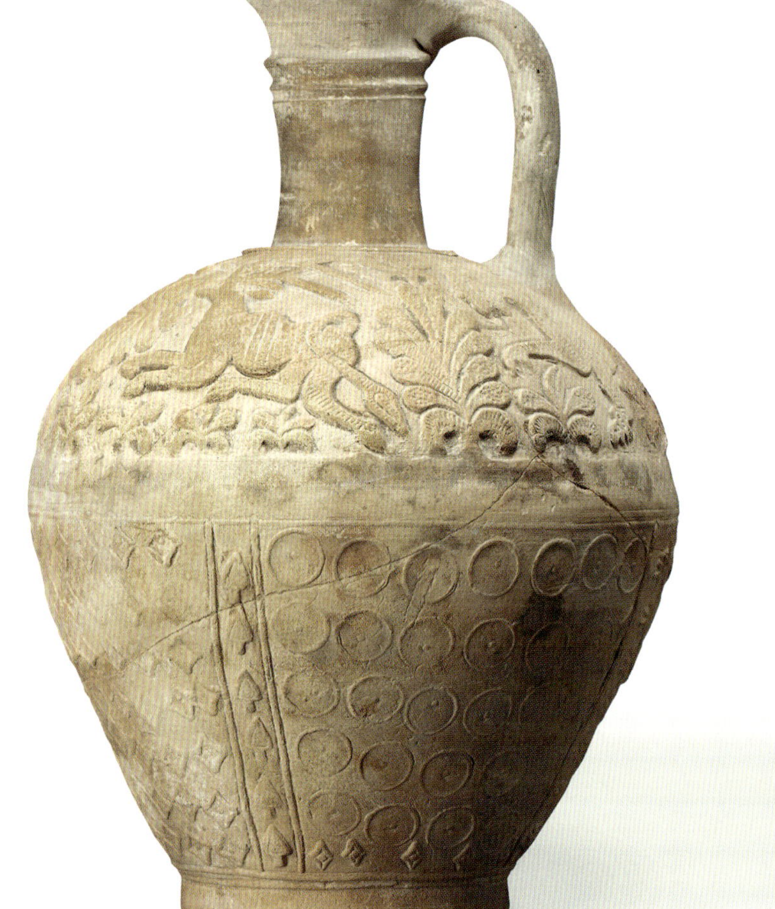

57

58

Jug flask

Iran, Gurgan, 11th-12th century
Unglazed earthenware, cast in a mold
h. 36 cm, Ø 22 cm
Courtesy of the L.A. Mayer Museum
for Islamic Art, Jerusalem, Israel
inv. n. C 40-69

Of circular shape, on a tall circular foot, with flattened sides, cast in two parts and joint, on the shoulder a thumb rest handle and a tall spout with beak-shaped mouth and two bulging elements at the top and end. According to Komaroff, the shape of this jug is dictated by the attempt to prevent spreading germs and illness in case it was used by different people, (L. Komaroff, in Blair, Bloom, 2009, p. 116).
The dense decoration on both sides consisting of concentric bands filled with roundels, dotted meanderings and a Kufic inscription in the recessed area harking to the central roundel:

Blessings and prosperity to the owner of this jug. May he drink a righteous, invigorating beverage with pleasure and health. The work of Khidash in Gurgan.

The shape is also reminiscent of the pilgrim's flasks and its signature makes it one of the most ancient signed pieces of Islamic art.

Bibliography: Baer E., 1989, figs. 4-5-17, pp. 85-89; Hasson 2014, cat. n. 34. For similar examples, read J. Sauvaget 1932; Pope 1938-1939, V. IV, pl. 195 A.

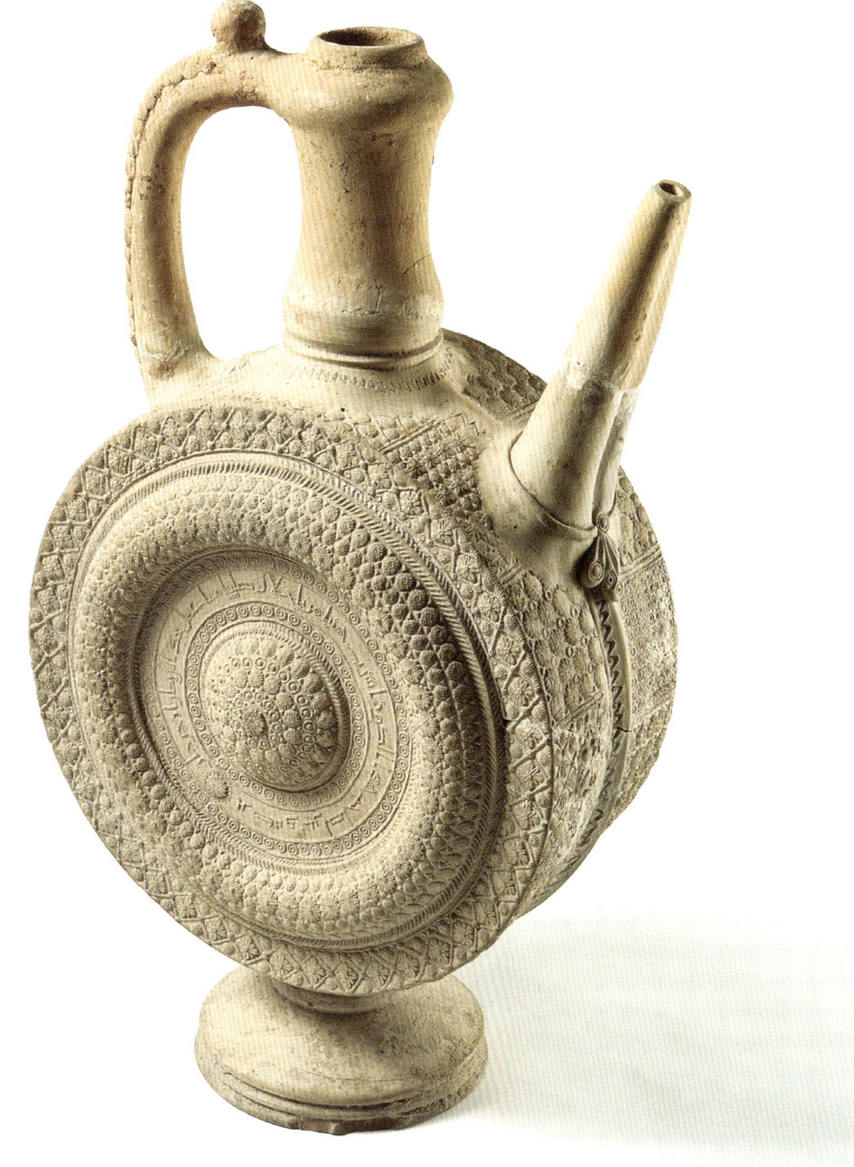

58

Unglazed earthenware

Jugs, ewers, containers and flasks made of unglazed and colourless earthenware were typically linked to water consumption, as given the porous body material, water could evaporate and keep fresh.
This expedient led them to be very much in use, not only in the Islamic age but also before Islam. A more specific attribution is hard to establish, unless corroborated by archaeological evidences, as the production of similar artworks was repeated over time in several different geographic areas.
Several examples do not present any decoration, as their role was mostly functional. However, some other examples, such as the one here exhibited, present inscriptions and moulded decorations in relief.
These jugs would have met likely had filters as the ones cat. n. 56 (1-10).

I.B.

59
Bottle

Iran, 17th century
Turquoise glazed stonepaste with applied brass elements
h. 33 cm
Courtesy of the L.A. Mayer Museum for Islamic Art, Jerusalem, Israel, inv. n. C 406-88

Drop-shaped, resting on a circular brass foot, with tapering neck, the pinched mouth with brass fitting, the turquoise-glazed body with moulded decoration with clover or *hamsa* and an oval cartouche embellished with braided borders and pierced brass fitting plaques ornate with interlocking vegetal motifs.
Among the most refined Safavid wares, the monochrome ceramics, mostly produced in Kerman or from the imperial atelier, deserve a special mention. Within this group one can find a wide repertoire of shapes and of colours such as white, celadon, different shades of blue, ochre yellow, shades of green and of manganese purple. To enhance the brilliance of the colour, these wares were usually glazed twice, the first time with a coloured glaze and the second with transparent glaze only.

Bibliographical references: Soustiel, 1985, cat. n. 313, p. 289, Watson 2004, cat. n. U.31, p. 476.

I.B.

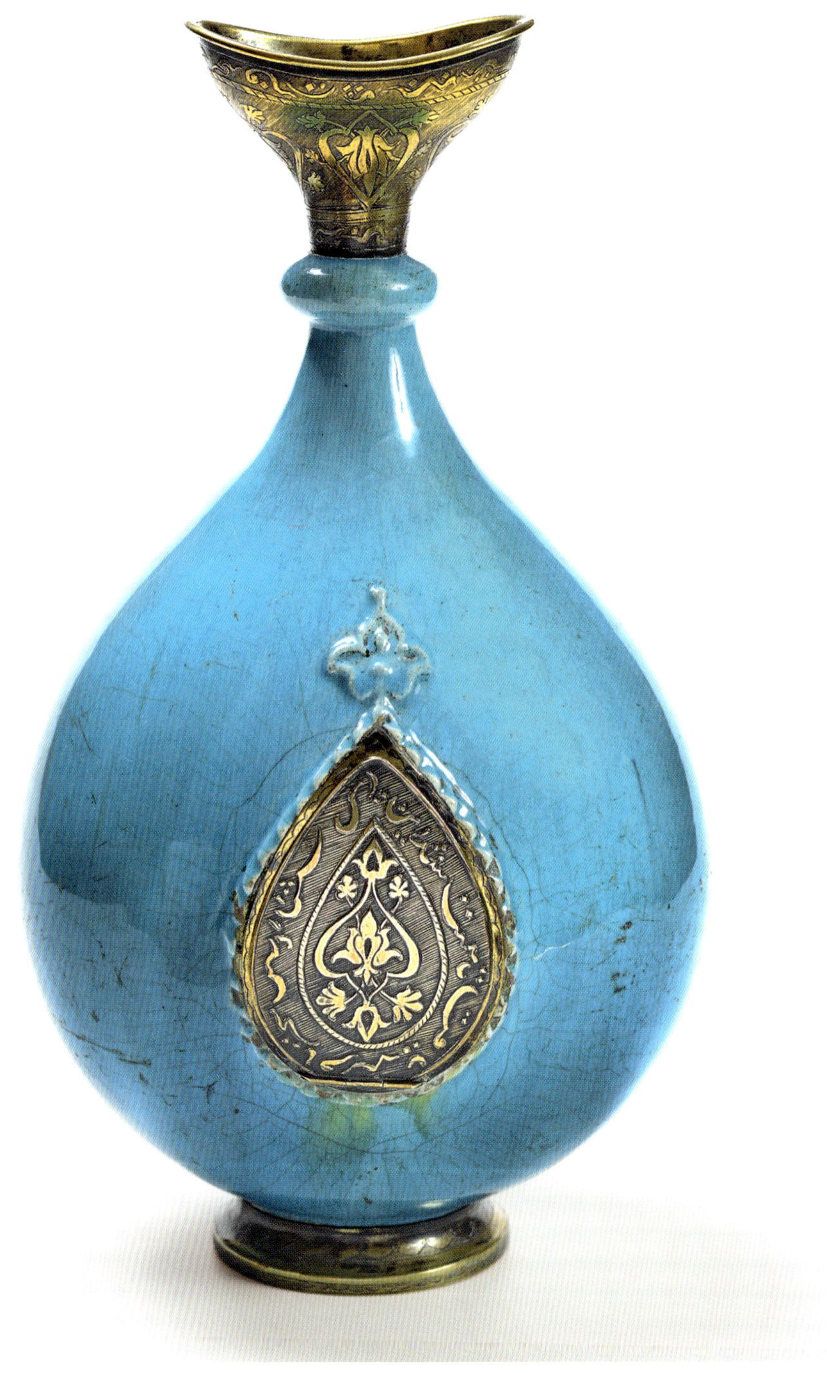

59

60
Bottle

Iran, 17th century
Fritware with blue underglaze painting
h. 27.5 cm
Courtesy of the L.A. Mayer Museum for Islamic Art, Jerusalem, Israel, inv. n. C 93-69

Of pyriform shape, resting on a short circular foot, rising to a cylindrical neck, the body decorated with superimposed horizontal bands, filled with floral motifs and vegetal sprays against a dotted ground.

Bibliographical references: Crowe, 2002, cat. n. 375, p. 217.

I.B.

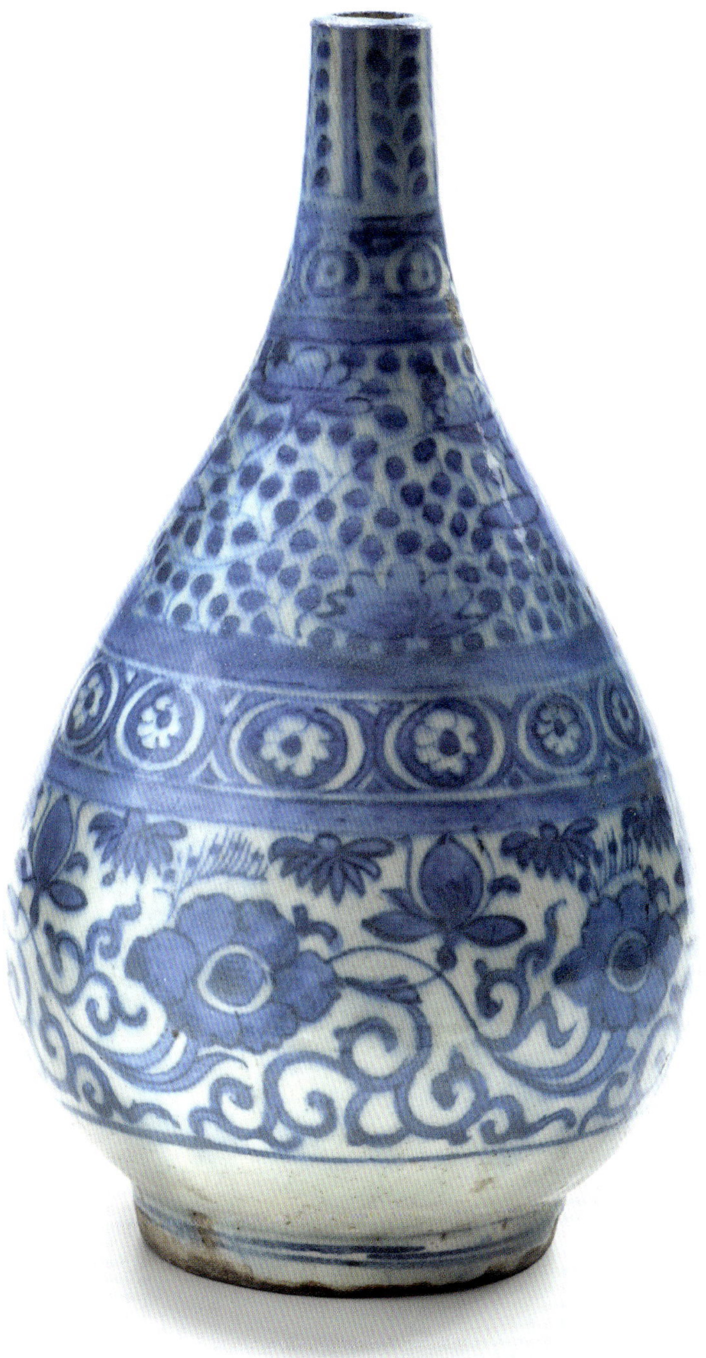

60

61
Bidriware water pipe base

India, Deccan, late 18th-19th century
Bronze, silver damascene
h. 19.1 cm, Ø 16.2 cm
Courtesy of the L.A. Mayer Museum for Islamic Art, Jerusalem, Israel, inv. n. 296-84

Water container for smoking tobacco, bell-shaped, with wide splayed foot, the body decorated with subtle bands at the top and bottom filled with floral festoons, the main decoration with equidistant bloomed branches.
The decorative style of this huqqa base is reminiscent of *pieta dura* inlays, typical of the Mughal architectural production.
The term *Bidri* originates from the city of origin of this manufacture, Bidar, in central India. This production consists in producing metalwares made of a blackened alloy of copper and zinc inlaid with silver and rarely with brass.

Bibliographical references:
Ashmolean Museum, inv. n. 1993-14 in Zebrowski M., fig. 399, p. 237.

I.B.

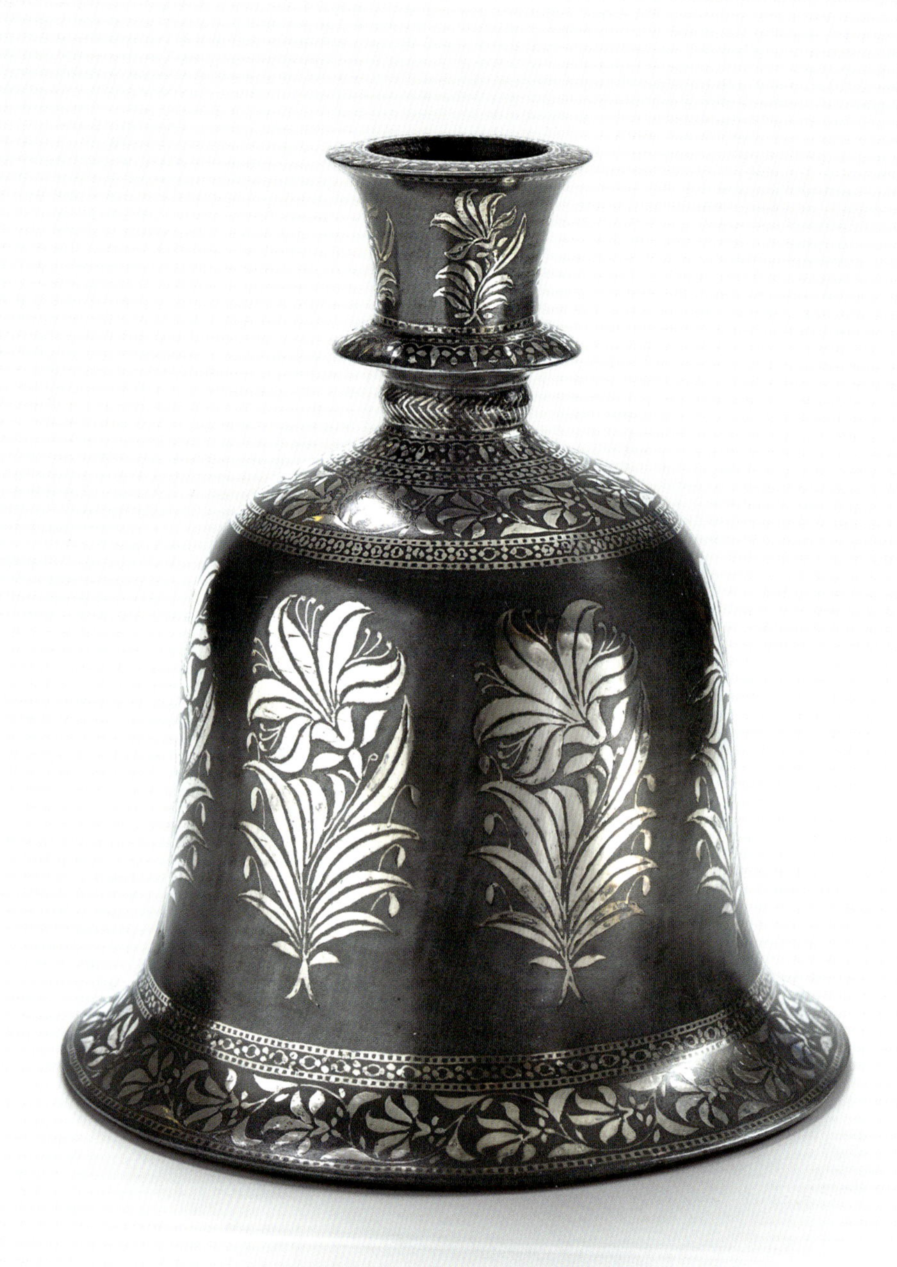

61

62
Goblet

Iran, 9th-10th century
Cut glass
h. 11 cm
Courtesy of the L.A. Mayer Museum for Islamic Art, Jerusalem,
inv. n. G 85-73

Beaker of conical shape, resting on a tall circular foot, with flat walls embellished with a decorative frieze with oval medallions filled with birds. The shape of this beaker is one of the most common in the 9th-10th century Iranian glass production. Similar beakers without decoration or simply decorated with a disc half way through the stem tend to be rather common. Among the decorated examples, birds seem to be a recurrent motif.

Bibliography: Prudence 1961, pp. 9-29. For a similar example, see Carboni, 2001, pp. 86-89.

I.B.

63
Beaker

Syria, Aleppo or Damascus,
14th century
Blown enameled glass
h. 18 cm, Ø 5.3 cm
Courtesy of the L.A. Mayer Museum for Islamic Art, Jerusalem,
inv. n. G 58-71

Of cylindrical shape, with flat walls, the flared mouth bending inwards, the base with a circular disc, the blown-glass body decorated with concentric bands with red-enamelled pseudo-Kufic inscription and floral motifs.
In the Islamic lands, the technique for enamelling glass was developed in Syria and Egypt between 12th-15th century. The reasons behind its creation and decline are yet to be established. The technique was possibly first experimented in Syria, but its development and common use started in Fustat, when Cairo became the official capital of the Mamluk empire. From the material evidence, one can notice an evolution from small and colourful examples to larger ones (see Mamluk mosque lamps) with a much stiffer decoration and standardised chromatic palette involving red in the borders, blu as background, and gold for relevant details.
Among the most recurrent decorative themes, one can see animals, floral and vegetal motifs and stylised figurines, matching the artistic vocabulary present in other media of the time such as manuscripts and metalware.

Bibliographical references: Ward 1998, pl. I, cat. nn. 12.5-12.6; Carboni 2001, cat. 85a, p.326.

I.B.

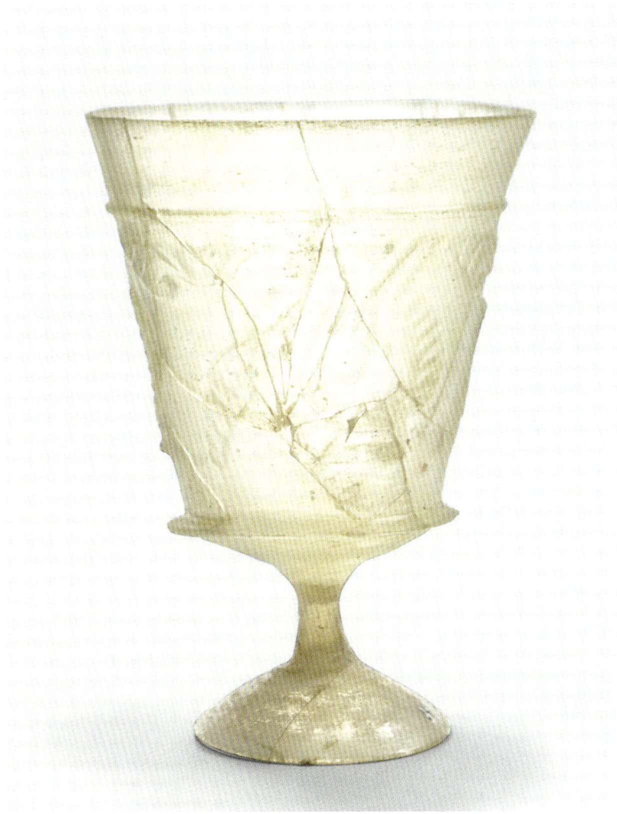

62

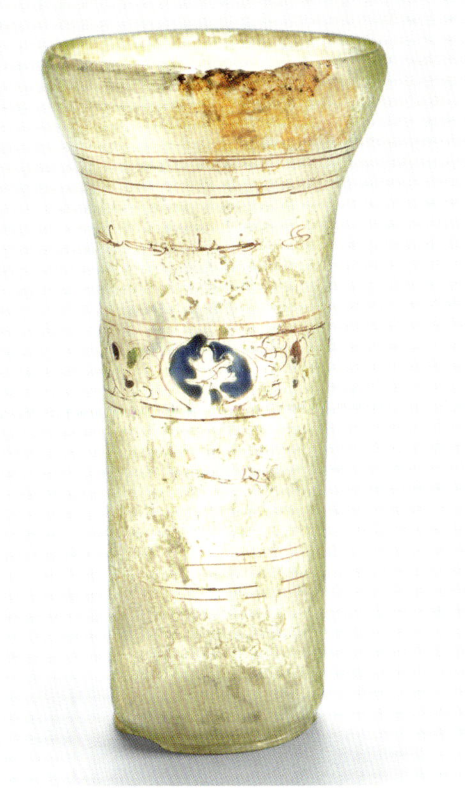

63

64
Peacock-shaped ewer

Spain, 10th-11th century
Lost-wax cast bronze with engraved chiselers decorations
Base in green marble
h. 31.5 cm, l. 26.7 cm, w. 12.50 cm
base: h. 5 cm, l. 16.80 cm, w. 17 cm
Polo museale della Sardegna
Pinacoteca nazionale di Cagliari, inv. n. SC13

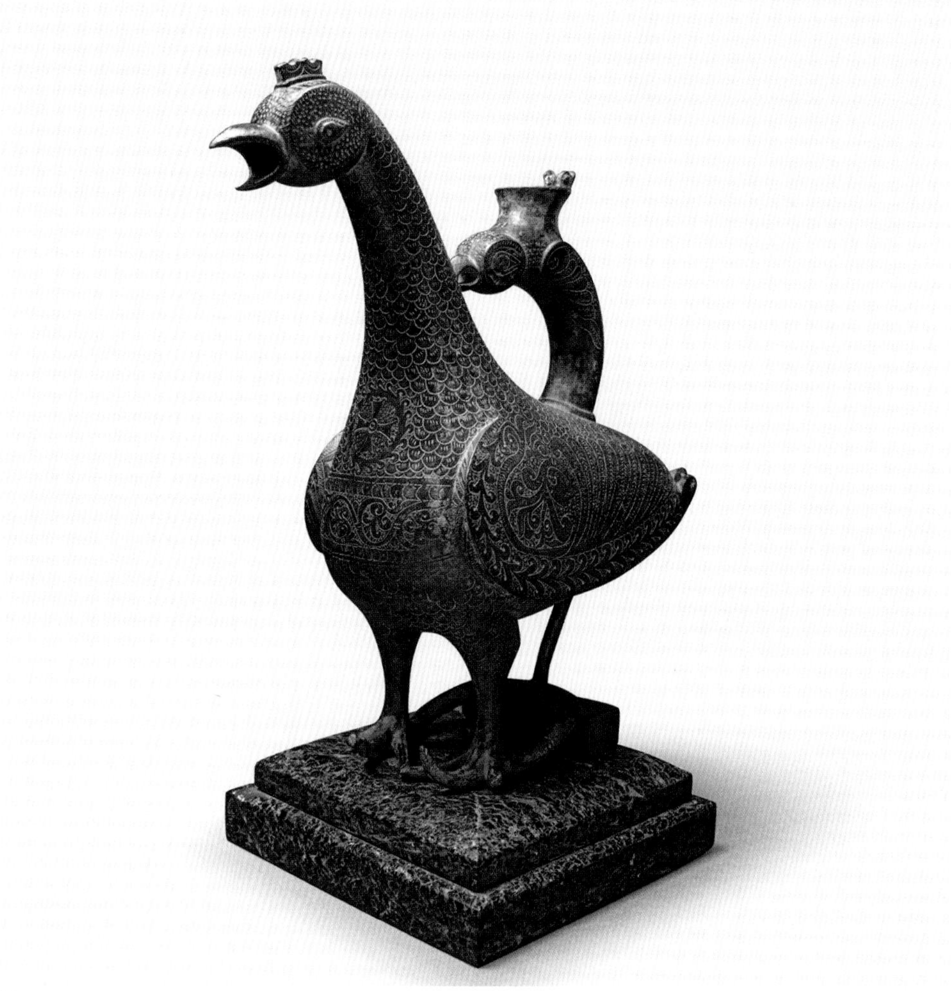
64

A bird-shaped ewer, realistically portrayed, the feathers stylised as fish-scales, the wings ornate with long feathers worked in a fish-bone pattern, on the bird's chest a decorative band with spiralling and interlocking vegetal tendrils, above it a cross patty, repeated on the handle made from the head and neck of another bird, the handle pierced to let the water flow in, the beak pierced to let the water out, the lid now missing.
The earliest evidences of similar bronze ewers used in the West in a liturgical context date back to the 8th century. The exact time is still debated. The most likely source of their inspiration seems to be rooted in the Islamic models, primarily Sassanid, which were sought-after and collected in great quantities in the West. It is also possible that in the Middle East and Muslim Spain, these zoomorphic bronzes were used as fountains' accessories rather than ewers to wash one's hands. These objects reached the Western shores in several different ways and were often kept as treasures in churches. Shalem suggests that exotica objects made of non-precious materials, such as bronze, were accepted by churches and used as liturgical tools only if their making technique was superior to the ones available on the local markets (Shalem 1998, p. 99). This specific ewer was indeed found in a religious context in San Salvatore, near Mores (Sassari, Sardinia). Bought in 1919, it was later donated to the Pinacoteca Nazionale in Cagliari. Scholars such as Scerrato and Contadini believe the ewer to come from Muslim Spain and to have been produced around 11th-13th century, given its similarities with other peacock-shaped ewers parts of the Louvre collection (inv. n. MR 1569) in Paris and David Collection (inv. n. 5/1990) in Copenhagen. Indeed, the three objects share the same stylistic features of eyes, beaks, crests and the same sense of stiff monumentality (A. Contadini in *Eredità dell'Islam*, 1993, pp. 125-126).
Similar features can also be seen on the famous Pisa griffin and the Bargello quadruped (cat. n. 101), attributed also to Umayyad Spain, and on an analogous ewer now part of the Furusiyya Arts Foundation in Vaduz (*Les Andalousie* 2000, fig. 88).
Three of the examples here discussed (Cagliari, Louvre and Vaduz) show an engraved cross on the birds' chest, which might indicate either a Christian manufacture or most likely their secondary use in a Christian context. Indeed, the bilingual inscription on the Louvre ewer bears the title "the Christian", a superfluous clarification if the ewer had been produced in a Christian context. Bautier thus supports the Umayyad Spain attribution and the later use in a Western liturgical context. (Bautier, 1977, p. 98).

Bibliography: Scerrato 1966, fig. 34; Gabrieli, Scerrato 1985, n. 651; Concas 1988, p. 129; *Eredità dell'Islam* 1993, cat. n. 42, pp. 125-126; *Moriscos* 1993, cat. n. 49, p. 45; Anedda, Pala 2014, pp. 689-731.

I.B.

65
Bird-shaped pitcher

Afghanistan, Ghaznavid period, 11th-12th century
Unglazed earthenware, engraved and cast in a mold
22 cm × 15.5 cm
Museo d'Arte Orientale - MUCIV, inv. n. 8403

Of zoomorphic shape, with a cylindrical neck ending in a small beaker diagonally set on the body, rebuilt from three fragments, representing a headless bird, the body cast in two parts and joint together, the wings decorated with triangular punching and enhanced with parallel diagonal lines meeting at the top and forming a fish-bone design, among the wings a Tree of Life with sinuous leaves, the tail decorated with two rampaging regardant lions, their interlocking tails forming a five-lobed palmette, on the lower area of the body near the legs a protruding diagonal element. The bird's position and plumage's rendering find a similar counterpart in a duck-shaped ewer made in Palestine and dating 9th-11th century published on the Barakat Gallery catalogue. However, this doesn't have a resting tray and is pierced on the back to let the water flow in.
The exhibited ewer presents a few puzzling elements such as the absence of a homogeneous proportion between the body of the bird and the upper part of the vessel, and the bold red slip, entirely covering the clay body. In absence of more thorough analysis, these elements, together with the fact that the bird hasn't been brought to light through excavations, lead to believe that this object is the result of a profound and complex modern remaking.

G.M.

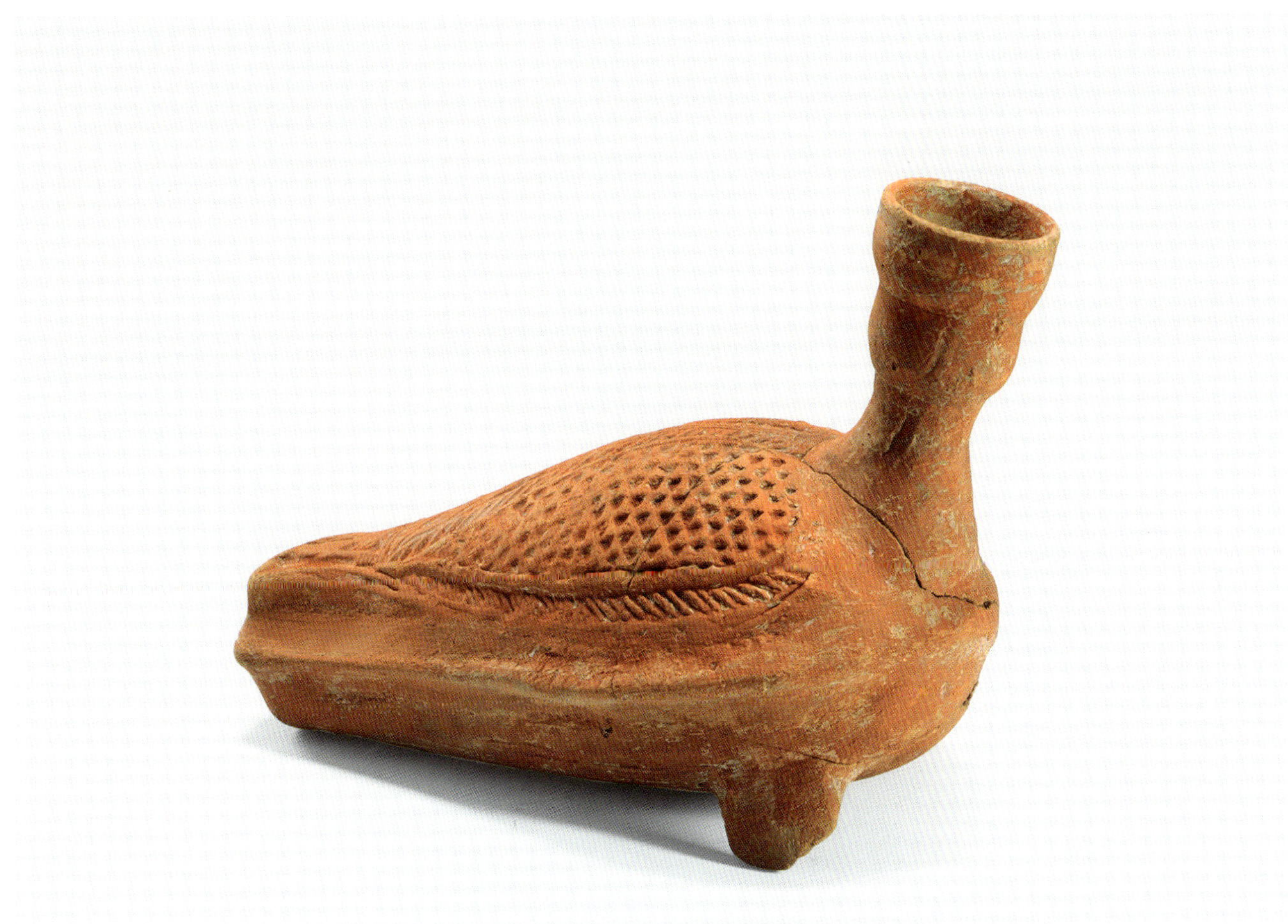

65

66
Bowl with figures of knights, dancers, and musicians

Western Iran, Ilkhanat dynasty, late 13th-early 14th century
Pounded sheet, copper alloy, engraved, gold and silver damascene on black ground
h. 13.5 cm, max. Ø 28 cm, rim Ø 19.4 cm
Museo d'Arte Orientale - MUCIV, inv. n. 6034

Of compressed globular shape, on a plain rounded base, with a flat rim and a wide mouth, the exterior decorated with overlying horizontal bands from the bottom to the top consisting of interlocking arches with cusped palmettes below them, the centre with a large band narrowly framed by meandering motifs and decorated with ten epigraphic cartouches with Arabic auspicious inscriptions, above and below each cartouche two medallions filled with swastika motifs among vegetal sprays, interspersed among the cartouches hunters on horse-back facing the left side, each with their swords, mace, bow, spear and falcon, and couples of musicians and dancers; above this composition another band filled with animals such as hares, felines, sphinxes, goats and dogs against a spiralling vegetal ground, also facing the left side and set in couples divided by medallions with swastika motifs; two narrower bands alternating vegetal tendrils, knot work and more swastika medallions, these medallions inlaid in gold whilst the animals inlaid in silver, engraved and incised to highlight their naturalistic details; the interior with a central radial motif symbolising the sun, surrounded by harpies, fishes and ducks, the overall composition framed within a band with triangular motifs.
Inscription in the ten exterior *naskh* cartouches:

Glory, eternity, fortune, fame, desire [...] generosity, prosperity, prestige, praise, affection [...] eternal life, beauty, health, spiritual integrity, happiness, joy to the owner.

The scope of this bowl is to contain water, as indicated by the decorative motif engraved on the interior. The iconographic repertoire consists of courtly scenes, good-wishing inscriptions, solar motifs such as the swastika, water motifs such as the fishes, all symbolising an auspicious blessing of eternal life to the owner (Baer 1968, pp.14-28). This type of bowls was very much sought-after during the Ilkhanid period in Iran (1256 - 1353), as documented by the fabulous examples preserved in important collections like at the Freer Gallery of Art in Washington (Atil et al. 1985, pp. 155-161) and the Gallerie Estensi in Modena, (Scerrato 1966, pp. 102, 106, fig. 47). The model spread further into the Middle East and Egypt with the Mamluk dynasty (1250 - 1517), but the decorative vocabulary became primarily epigraphic, followed at times by figural decorations, mostly peonies, animals and flying phoenixes. These themes, clearly presenting a Far Eastern origin, were transmitted to Mamluk craftsmen by Ilkhanid Iran.

Bibliography: Di Flumeri Vatielli 2010, pp. 35-45, figg. 34 e 36b; Di Flumeri Vatielli, in *Orienti* 2018, pp. 85-91, esp. p. 85, fig. 1, p. 90.

G.D.F.

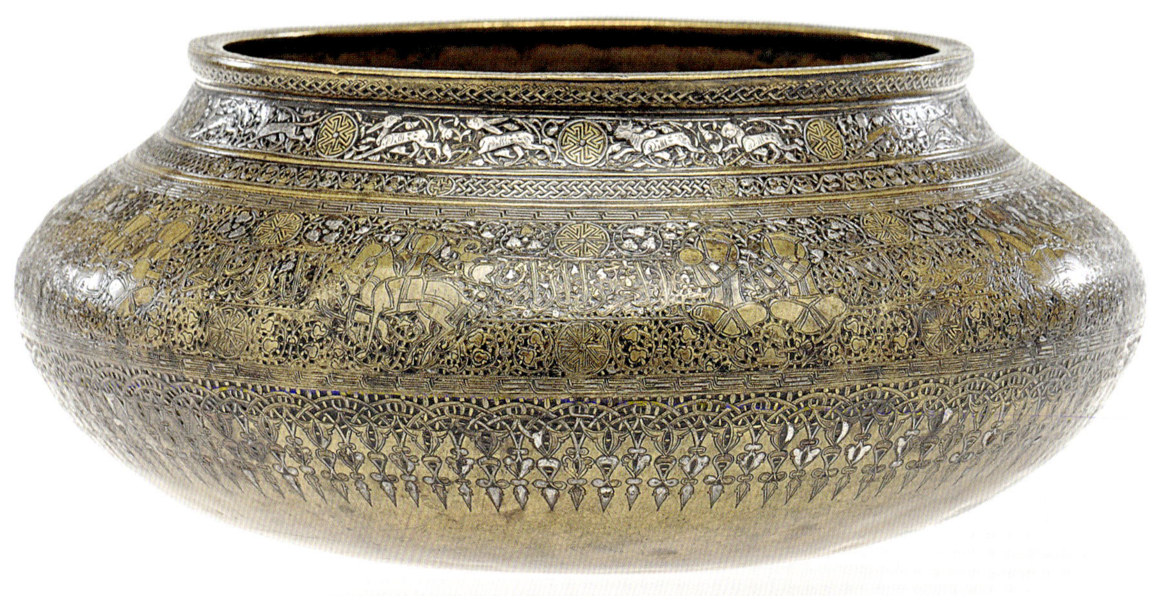

66

67
Cup

Egypt or Syria, mid-14th century
Brass, silver and gold damascene
h. 8.3 cm, base Ø 11.1 cm
MAO Museo d'Arte Orientale, Torino,
inv. n. ISb/22 733

Of hemispherical shape, resting on a flat base, with narrowing shoulders, splayed neck and a straight circular mouth, the engraved and inlaid exterior presenting two decorative registers, the first located towards the base and decorated with subtle almond-shaped medallions with drooping arabesques and narrow bands of quadrupeds against a floral ground, the latter located around the shoulders and with a *thuluth* inscription against minute floral ground interspersed with circular medallions filled with regardant ducks on an arabesque ground, the quadrupeds on the lower register present on a decorative frieze on the flat area of the mouth, the central roundel engraved with a group of silver-inlaid fishes, a water symbol indicating the function of the cup as water container (Baer 1998, fig. 119, p. 105. See also cat. nn. 66 and 71).

Inscription on the shoulder:

Oh thou drinking this fresh water,
This you ought to state assertively.
Drink and shout: may be cursed those who moved by evil intentions deprived Hosseyn of water,
May thou receive water from the hand of his father the day you'll be thirsty
Don't you know that Hosseyn had the best among the fathers and the best among the mothers?
His glory should be passed on to future generations, as he belongs to the noblest descent.

This inscription clearly refers to the battle of Kerbela (Iraq), in 680, when the third Shi'a Imam, Hosseyn died, and his followers were tortured to thirst and killed by the Umayyad troops, who blocked their access to the river Euphrates. This was a crucial moment for Islam as it led to the still-standing division of the community between Sunni and Shi'a believers. Indeed, according to traditional sources, denying water supply to thirsty men, even in a war context, is considered a preposterous action. To this very day, during Ashura and the commemorations of the battle of Kerbela, Shi'a believers go to Hosseyn's tomb and offer water to the thirsty pilgrims and visitors, trying to enact a symbolical remedy to an unkind and cruel action of the past.

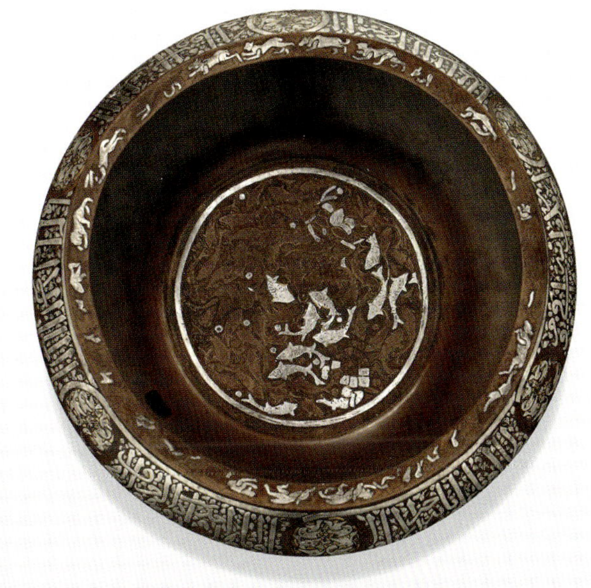

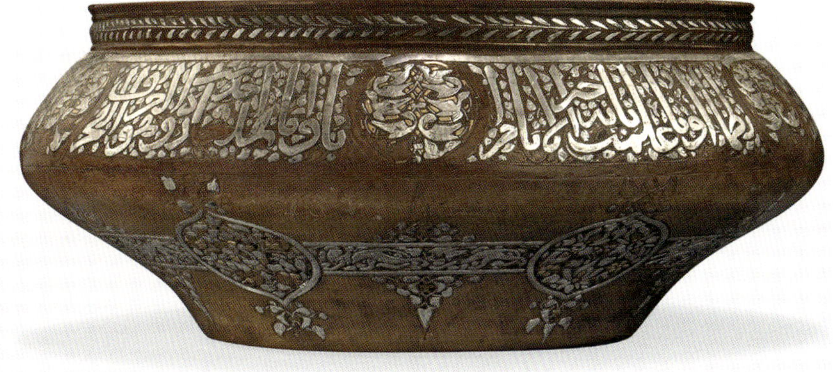

67

Bibliography: Gabrieli, Scerrato 1985, cat. n. 644; *Eredità dell'Islam* 1993, cat. 176, p. 309, Spallanzani 2010, pl. 13, p. 134. For an analogous example, see the cup at the Bargello Museum, Florence, inv. n. 364 C, also published in *Islam e Firenze* 2018 cat. 38, p. 215.

I.B.

68
Ewer

Mamluk Egypt, first half 14th century
Brass, engraved and silver damascene
h. 43.7 cm
Benaki Museum, Athens, inv. n. 13128

Of sphero-conical shape, resting on a splayed foot, with a tall cylindrical neck and flat rim, with a long tapering spout and a curved handle, the engraved body decorated with several horizontal registers filled with interlocking meanderings and geometric motifs on handle, neck, spout and between the main decoration. The main decoration consisting of a band of interlocking split palmettes within circular roundels, a long *thuluth* epigraphic band against floral ground, interspersed with circular medallions filled with palmettes and Y-shaped motif, the junction between neck and body ornate with lobed floral collar with further inscriptions, the decoration with evident traces of silver inlay and the use of a black bituminous substance. The inscriptions refer to an anonymous official of the Mamluk Sultan al-Malik al-Nasir al-Din Muhammad (1293-1341 and see cat. n. 71 and 3). Ewers such as our had several functions: they were used to wash hands, to pour water in the bath, for ritual ablutions or simply to embellish the houses and rooms of viziers, officials and sultans.

Bibliography: Ballian, Moraitou, 2006, p. 192. For a comparative example also made for an official of Ibn Qalawun, see the collection of the Islamic Art Museum in Cairo, inv. n. 24084.

I.B.

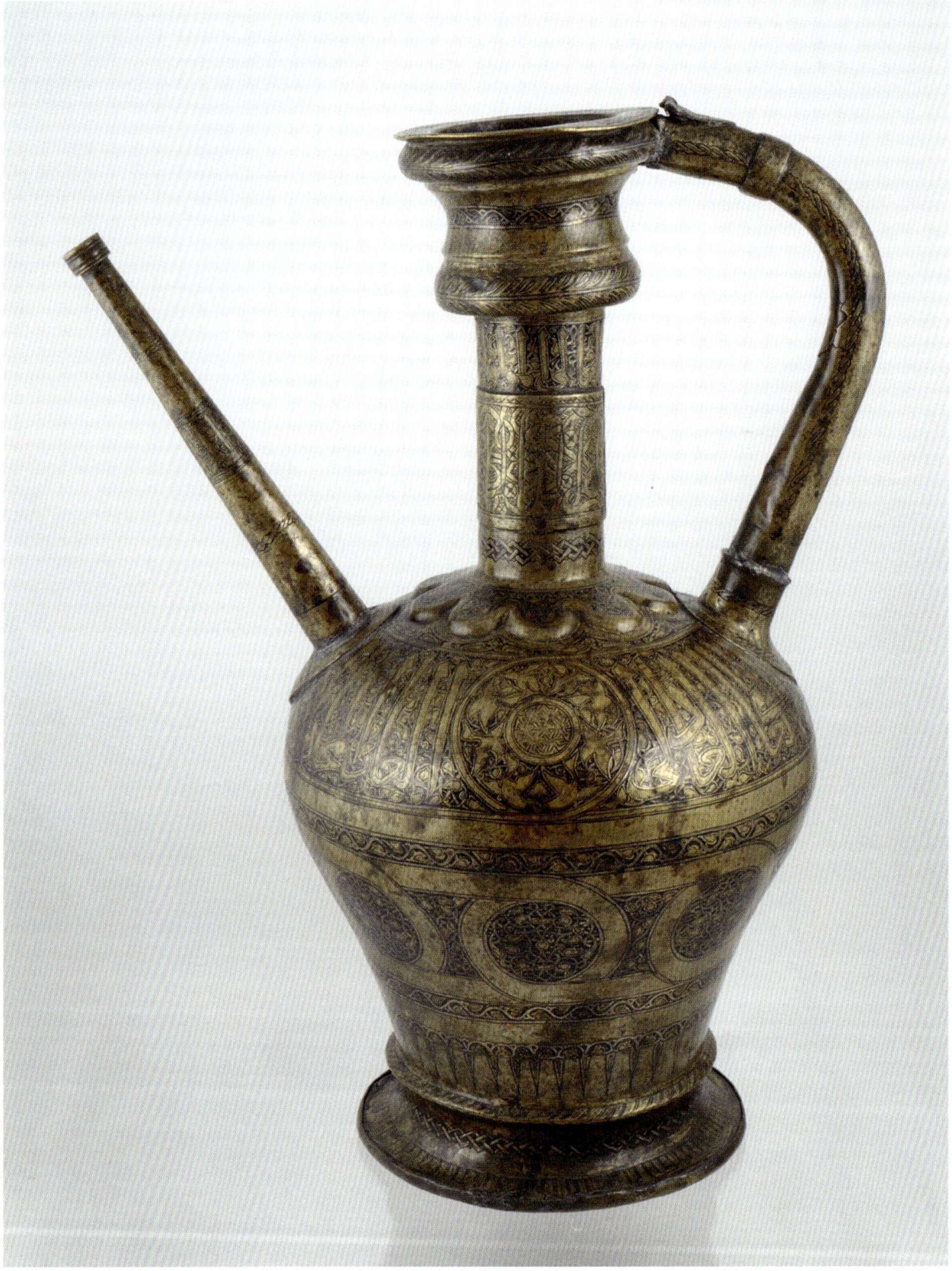

68

69
Ewer

Northern Mesopotamia, 14th century
Brass, engraved and silver damascene
h. 32.5 cm, base Ø 14.5 cm
Weight: 1470 g
Museo Poldi Pezzoli, Milano,
inv. n. 1654

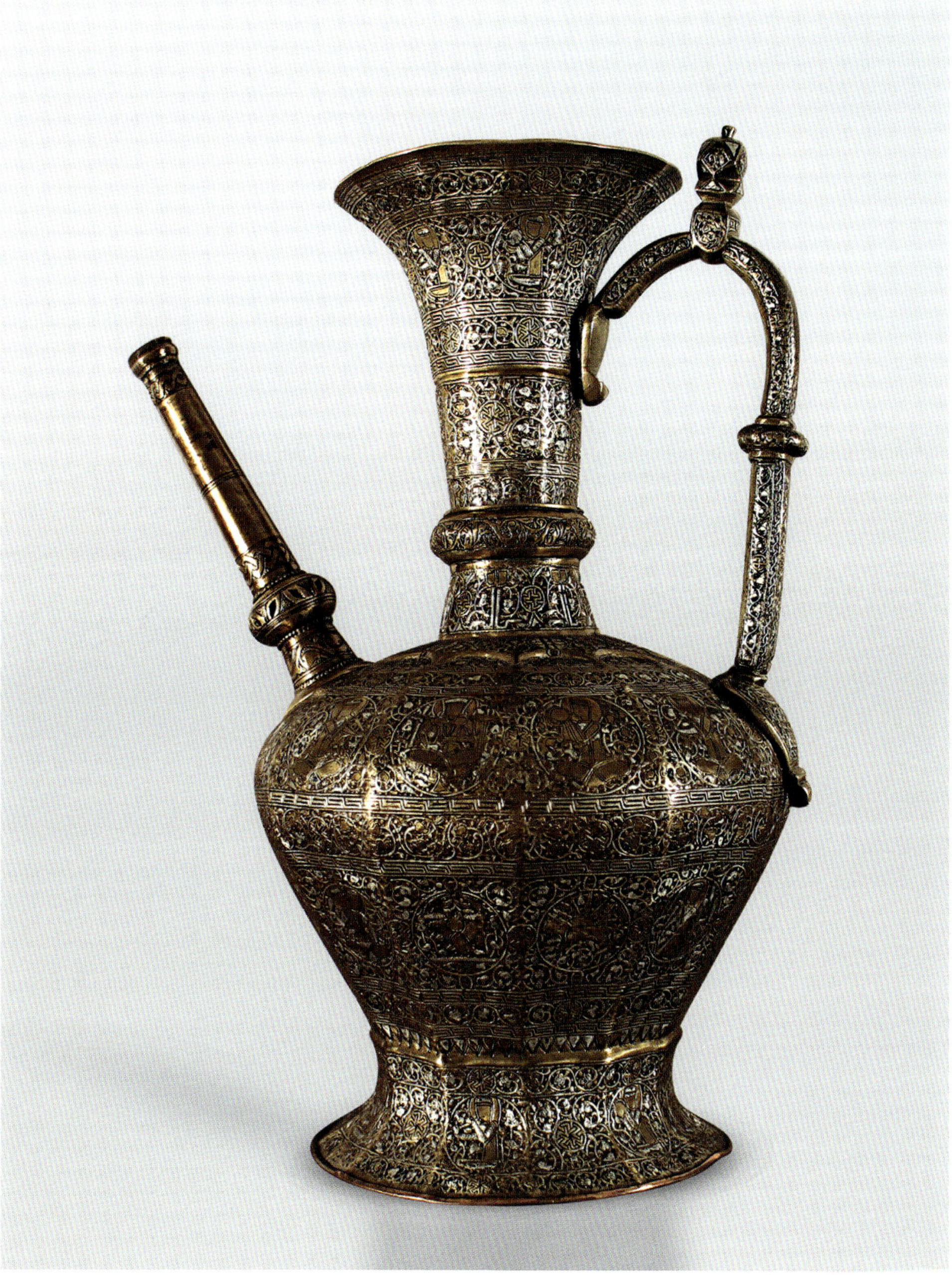

Of faceted globular shape, resting on a large splayed foot, rising to a tall flared neck, with a flat circular mouth, on the sides a tapering spout and a curved handle with thumb rest, possibly a later addition given the stylistic incongruence, the densely engraved and inlaid exterior arranged in a series of horizontal decorative bands filled with the typical repertoire of metalwares from Mesopotamia, indebted to the Khorasanic school in Herat. The main decorative repertoire presented here is the cycle of the prince with his courtiers combined with the Zodiac signs cycle, characteristic of the Herat school and here reinterpreted by Iraqi craftsmen. Another feature adopted from the Khorasanic tradition is the use of the so-called *animated script*, in which the shafts of the long letters end in figural decorations, mostly human heads. An animated calligraphic band is indeed evident on the neck base. Among the most famous comparative examples, see: the Blacas Ewer, at the British Museum in London (inv. n. 1866,1229.61, in Ward 1993, fig. 59, pp. 80-81) and the Keir Collection ewer (inv. n. K.1.2014.82).

69

The decoration on this ewer has been ascribed to the school of Mosul, a very active centre of production in the 13th century. Material evidence enumerates 35 objects signed by 27 craftsmen identified by the epithet *Al-Mawsili* (from Mosul).
The Andalusian historian Ibn Sa'id, who visited Mosul in 1250, wrote:

there are a lot of crafts here, especially inlaid brass vessels, which are given to rulers, near and far, and special embroidered silk garments" (J. Raby in Porter, R.Owen1988, p. 22).

This comment testifies the high quality of the artworks produced in Mosul at the time. Around the second half 13th century however, two more centres were producing sublime examples of metalware, i.e. Damascus and Cairo. Thus, in absence of signatures with Mosuli epithets or clear indications, one prefers to attribute this production to Mesopotamia in general. Some of the decorative motifs and shapes present in these artworks will then influence and filter in the Mamluk metalware production, as evident in the cat. n. 68.

Bibliography: *Inventario*, Bertini, 1881, p. 75; Scerrato 1966, fig. 50; Poldi Pezzoli catalogue, cat. n. 1, pp. 280-281; *Eredità dell'Islam*, 1993, cat. n. 154, pp. 268-269.

I.B.

70
Khorasan cup

Iran, Khorasan, 12th-13th century
Bronze, cast, engraved and silver damascene
h. 13.3 cm, Ø 17.4 cm
Museo e Real Bosco di Capodimonte, Napoli, inv. AM n. 112114 (previously Borgia collection)

Of hemispherical shape, resting on a tall splayed foot with bulging disc to the middle, the exterior engraved with large medallions filled with arabesques and small rosettes decorated with geometric knotworks and stylised eight-lobed flowers, the upper border with a long calligraphic *naskh* inscription with silver inlay, the long shafts in the typical animated script, the lower parts of the letters with minute birds against a scrolling vegetal ground.

Inscription:

Eternal glory, healthy life, tranquil time, wholesome prosperity, fulfilling success, rising fortune, favourable destiny, infinite delight, happiness, health, prosperity, generosity, peace, may the owner live long (transl. in Scerrato, 1967, pp.2-3).

Below this dense calligraphic band, there is another inscription, a later addition, mentioning the name of a late owner, Khalif ibn al-Julaki (Rice, 1955, p. 14).
The use of the animated script attributes this metal production most likely to the Khorasanic area, which possibly drew its original source of inspiration from the bird-shaped inscriptions of the Samanid wares (Nishapur, Iran, 10th century).
Rice (1955, p.12) attributes this shape, which can be distinguished only by the different varieties of feet, to the new tendencies introduced by the Seljuq rulers, taking over at first the ceramic production and later radically influencing Islamic metalwares. The cup in Naples shares several similarities with another cup preserved at the National Museum in Florence (Rice, 1955, p.12, tab. 13) and with the Fano cup part of the National Library Collection in Paris (Ibid. tab 15).

Bibliography: Rice 1995, pp. 14-20 and tab. XII, Lettieri, 1839, pp. 1-8; Ettinghausen, 1957, pp. 356-358; Scerrato, 1966, fig. 19, Scerrato, 1967, cat.n. 2, p. 2.

I.B.

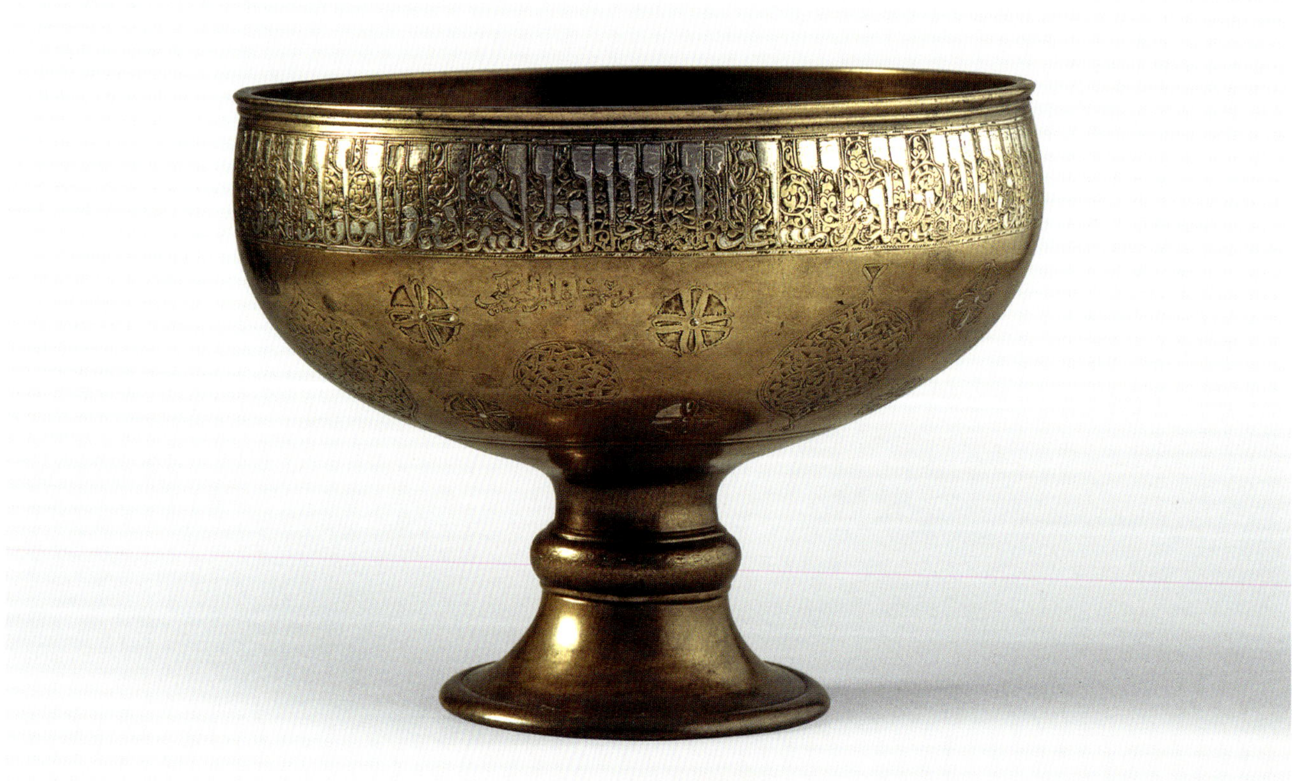

70

71
Bowl

Syria or Egypt, first half 14th century
Brass with silver and gold damascene decoration
h. 9 cm, Ø 13.6 cm
Museo e Real Bosco di Capodimonte, Napoli, inv. n. De Ciccio 779 (inv. DC 779)

Of circular shape, on a plain base, the exterior decorated with dense vegetal scrolls, with a large rosette to the centre, a subtle band with scrolling tendrils and a larger band filled with wide inscriptions in *thuluth* against a leafy ground, interspersed with large peonies within circular medallions, the interior engraved with a group of fishes (see cat. nn. 66 and 67) and embellished with a cross potent, possibly a later Western addition, added once the cup arrived to the Western countries.

Inscription:

the High Excellency, the noble, kingly, wise, active, fair, authoritative, zealous, treasure, help, support, assistant of Al-Malik an Nasir,, may his victory be glorious (transl. Scerrato 1967, p. 21).

The epigraphic band, following the typical Mamluk artistic protocol reserved to high rank members of society, mentions that the bowl's owner was an anonymous official of the Sultan al-Malik al-Nasir al-Din Muhammad ibn Qalāwūn (r. 1293-1341, see cat. n. 68). This bowls should thus be contextualised in the same grouping of another basin exhibited here (cat. n. 3), sharing the same style and decorative fineness.

The shape is quintessential of the Mamluk metalware production, only imitated by a few Fars examples produced in Iran around the same time (see 66). Fars productions always favoured figural decorations and poetical inscriptions, adding more variety to the standardised Mamluk panegyric repertoire.

For analogous examples, see a cup preserved at the Gallerie Estensi in Modena (inv. n. 2062 in *Eredità dell'Islam*, cat. n. 175, p. 308); another one in the Aron collection (in Allan, 1986, cat. n. 9, pp. 86-87); and lastly, the one at the Cairo Museum of Islamic Art (inv. n. 15131 in Atil 1981, n. 29).

Bibliography: Scerrato 1967, cat.n. 13, fig. 15; *Eredità dell'Islam*, cat. n. 178, pp. 310-311.

I.B.

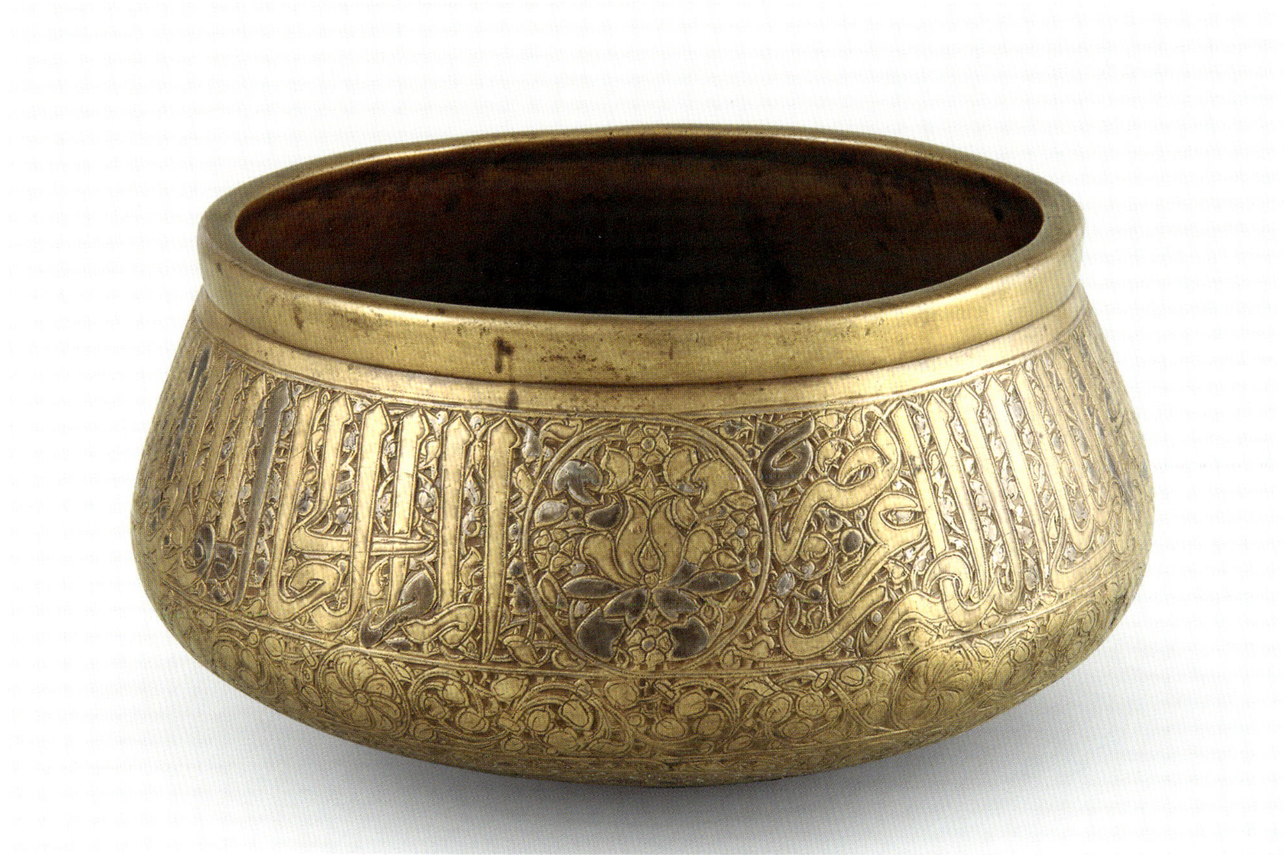

71

72
Ewer

Eastern Iran, Khorasan, 12th-13th century
Bronze, cast and engraved with silver damascene traces
h. 19 cm, max. Ø 9.4 cm
The Aron Collection, inv. n. A.148

Of pyriform shape, resting on a wide splayed foot, rising to a flaring neck, with lid, curved handle and thumb rest, all cast separately, on the body the area of the widest diameter engraved with an epigraphic band in Kufic script, set within four rectangular cartouches interspersed with roundels against vegetal tendrils. Inscription:

al-baraka wa al-salama (Blessing and Well Being)

This type of objects embodies the Khorasani craftsmen's first approach to inlay, whose development would have started shortly after in the area of Herat. On this example, the areas originally inlaid are interspersed with wide undecorated areas. The nature of the inscriptions is usually auspicious and good wishing to the owner, as in this example, and at times they bear the name of the craftsman, as in the example of the Louvre (inv. n. MAO 428). The inlay work, now lost on our example, is at times in silver and more often in copper, highlighting the destination of this type of work to the middle class.

Bibliographical references: for an analogous example, see a jug of the same collection in Allan 1989, cat. n. 32, pp. 126-127.

I.B.

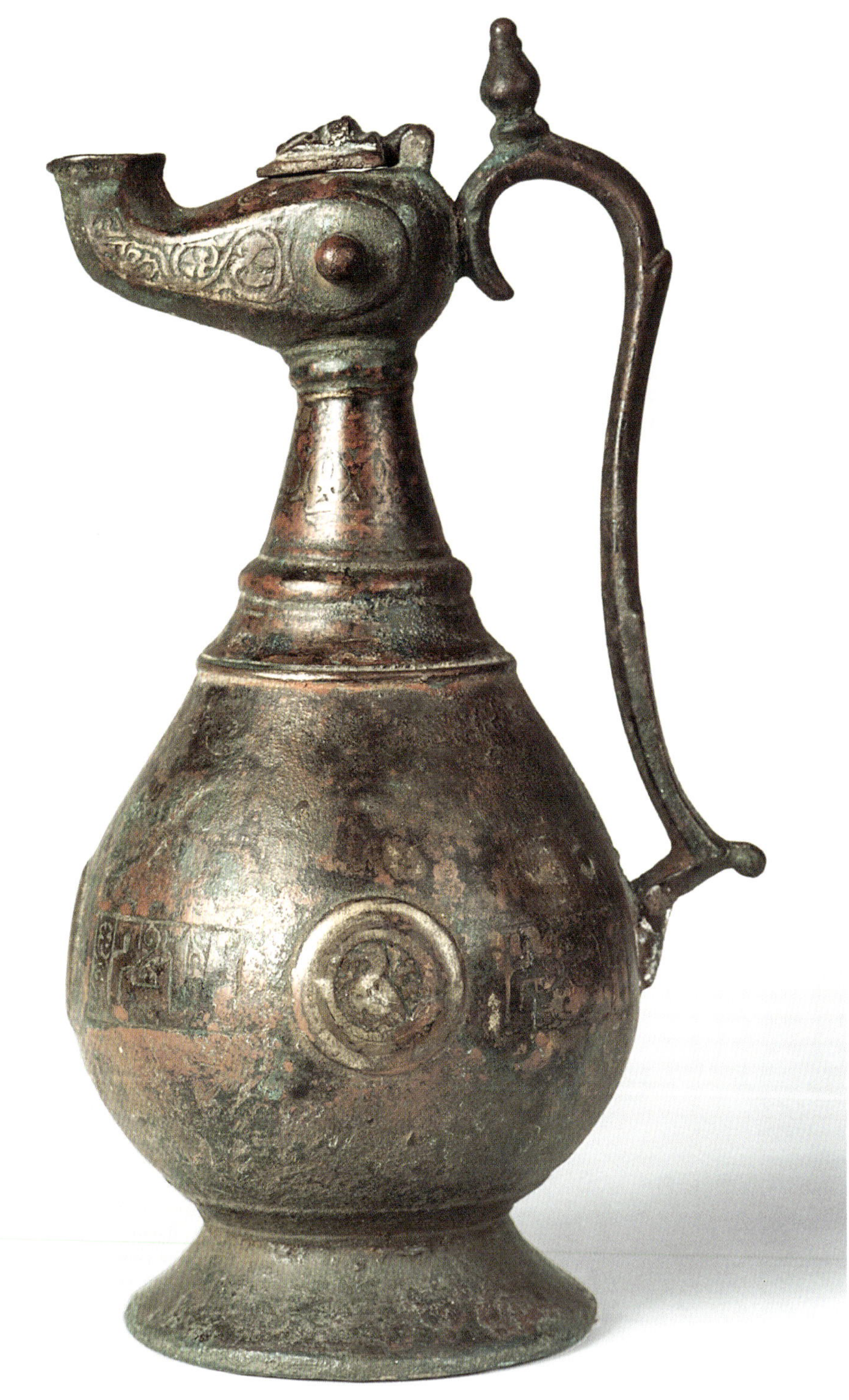

72

73

Fragrance sprinkler

Eastern Iran, Khorasan, 12th-13th century
Bronze, cast, engraved, and silver damascene, h. 18.8 cm, base Ø 6.7 cm
The Aron Collection, inv. n. A.370

Of globular shape, resting on a tall conical foot with flat base, rising to a tapering neck, with a flared mouth embellished with splayed semi-circles, the decoration consisting of several bands highlighted by copper-inlaid lines, the smaller ones filled with inscriptions in animated Kufic and cursive script against scrolling sprays, the primary band with circular figural medallions filled with the characters of the prince cycle against a dense animated ground of interlocking vegetal motifs, bearing five auspicious and good-wishing inscriptions to the owner, repeated with different lengths.

Inscriptions:

Glory, success, luck, wellbeing, prosperity, long live the owner!

Glory, success, luck, wellbeing, prosperity, divine favour, prestige, vitality and prophetic intercession to the owner (transl. Roberta Giunta)

The quality of the engraving and the profusion of silver inlay are indicative of the high social rank of the owner of this object. Objects shaped in the same fashion were often used as rosewater sprinklers (for an in-depth discussion, see appendix to cat. 34).

Provenance: antique art market.
Bibliographical references: a very similar example is present in the same collection (Allan, 1989, cat. n. 28, pp. 120-121); another one can be seen at the David Collection, Copenhagen (Inv. n. 65/1998); and a third example is with the Al-Sabah Collection (Inv. n. LNS539), see in *Civiltà islamica* 2010, cat. n. 33.

I.B.

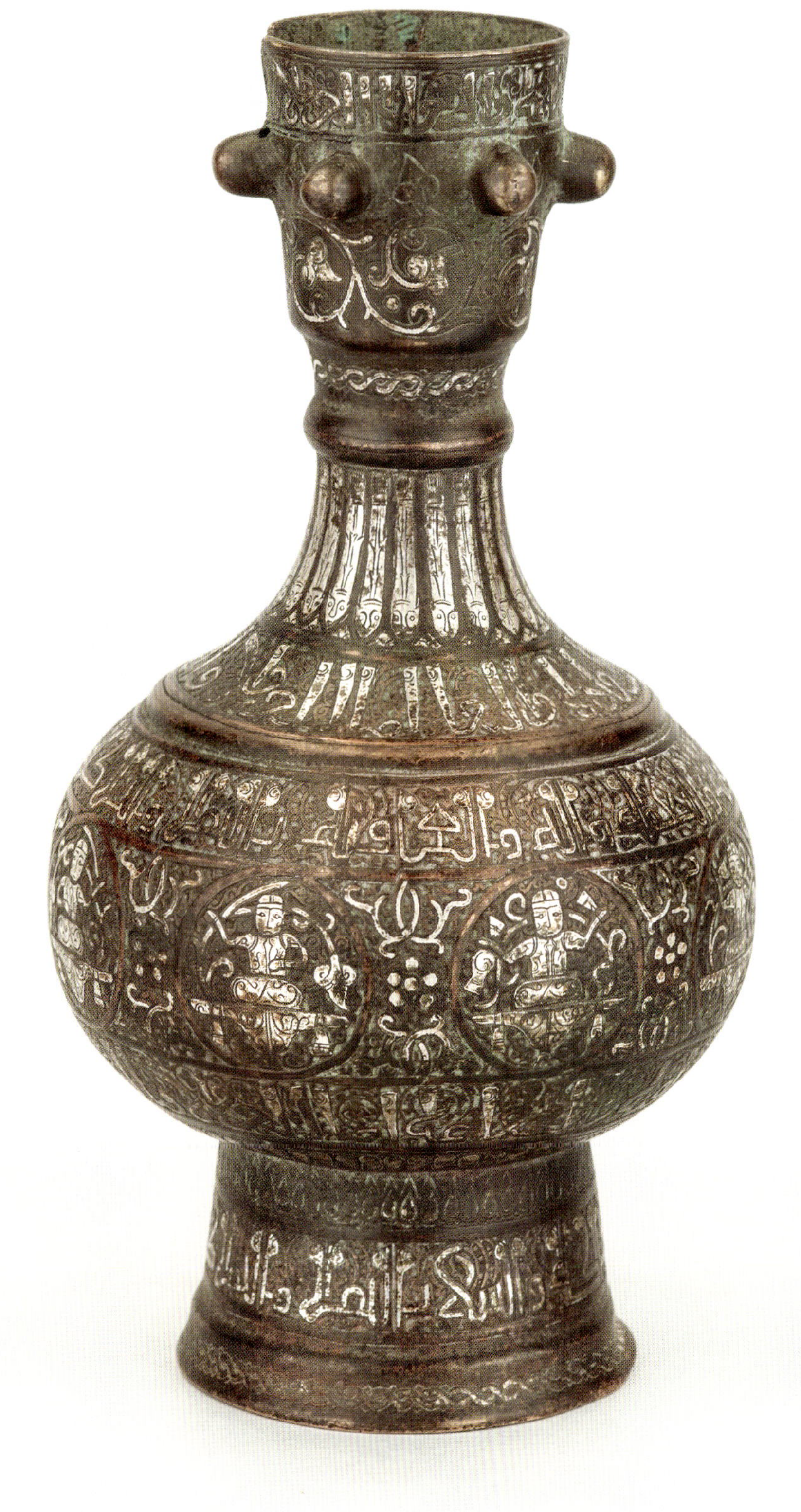

73

74
Tray (Gulla)

Egypt or Syria, ca. 1320-1330
Brass, pounded and engraved
Ø 45.9 cm
Private collection, Genoa

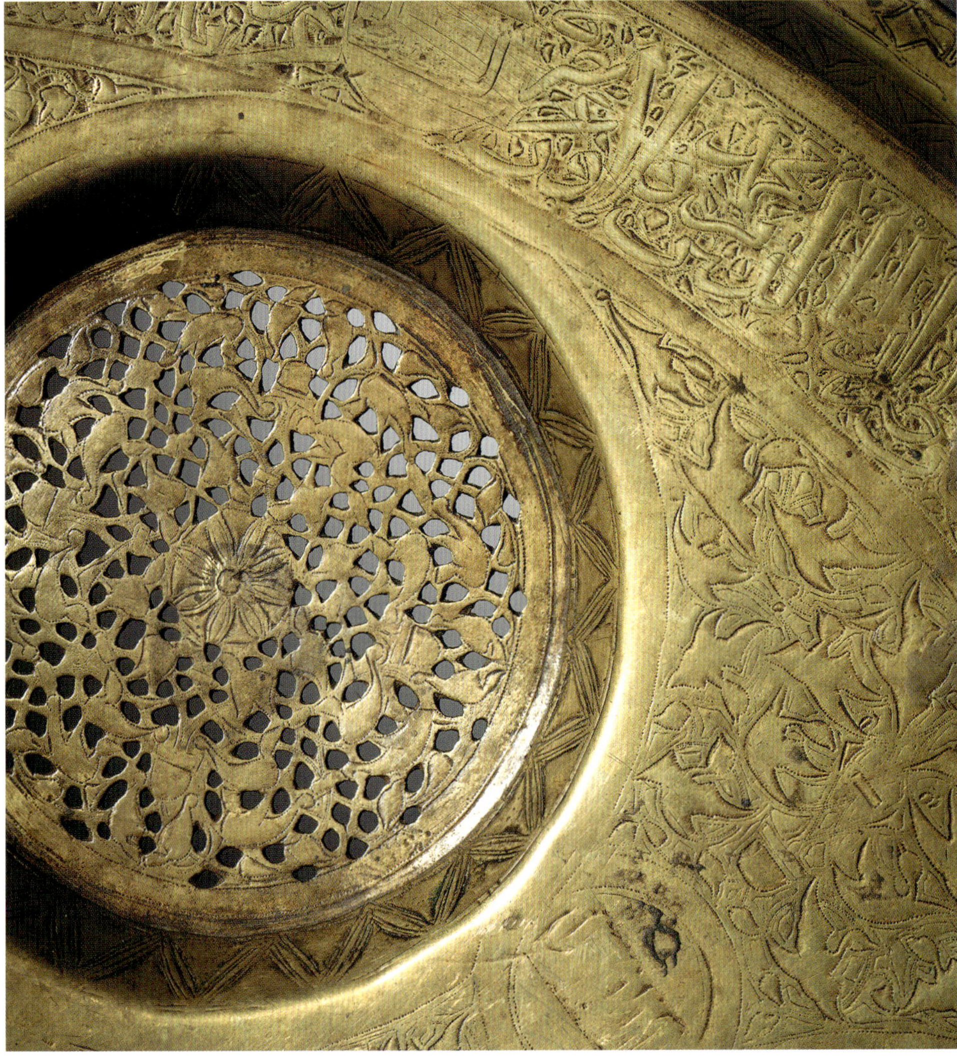

Of circular shape with a reinforced rim, the interior densely and finely decorated with chased in relief borders, with seven circular reentrant medallions with pierced base, inside each roundel and in the area surrounding it engraved lotus flowers, rosettes and birds forming a dense interlacement, along the border and in the centre two concentric bands filled with two epigraphic inscriptions in *thuluth*, dividing the composition harmoniously. The owner of such a precious object, as indicated by the inscriptions, was the Mamluk sultan al-Malik al-Nasir al-Din Muhammad ibn Qalawun, son of one of the most important sultans of the Bahri dynasty, al-Mansur Qalawun. During his reign, the Mamluk lands witnessed a period of economic prosperity and artistic flourishing. Originally inlaid in silver and still presenting traces of the black compound used on the ground to enhance the shininess of the inlay work, the object here presented showcases analogous features to other very refined metalwares attributable to the Mamluk period. The style and dimensions of the epigraphic inscriptions and the abstract and stylised interpretation of the standard decorative repertoire, with the addition of motifs of clear Chinese flare, all suggest a 14th-century Mamluk attribution. The morphology of this object, with the central pierced roundel which at one point in time would have been used to carry small ceramic or metal cups filled with water, was not very common. The pierced bases were possibly designed with the intention of letting the air flow in and out, guaranteeing to keep the beverages cool. Three similar trays with the same shape and decorative programme of our tray are known. Two were commissioned for the same illustrious owner, the sultan al-Malik al-Nasir, and are currently preserved at the Benaki Museum in Athens (inv. 13126; M. Ballian in *Ibn Jaldun*, 2006, pp. 252-253) and at the Archaeology and Islamic Art Museum in Jerusalem (inv. B. 69.0711). The third one, now at the Museum of Islamic Art in Cairo (Wiet, 1932, n. 7278, p. 130) was commissioned for the emir Saif al-Din Taibugha Ahmadi and presents minor differences in the decorative arrangement. Indeed, the epigraphic inscription is here not included in the long band on the border, but only in the central roundel and in six small circular cartouches among the hollowed medallions, overall looking more compressed and less spacious. Moreover, compared to the *gulla* here exhibited, the fitomorphic elements of the Cairo tray, creating a dense decorative scrollwork on the surface of the object, appear less defined and more approximately carried out. On our example, notwithstanding the passing of time, the quality of the decoration draughtsmanship is evident and attributable to its important owner.

Provenance: Sotheby's London, 16 April 1985, lot 109;
Christie's London, 27 April 2017, lot 10.

Bibliography: *Il Montefeltro e l'Oriente islamico. Urbino 1430-1550. Il Palazzo Ducale tra Occidente e Oriente*, exhibition catalogue by A. Bruschettini, Urbino, 23 June - 30 September 2018, Genoa 2018.
Ibn Jaldùn. El Mediterráneo en el siglo XIV. Auge y declino de los Imperios, exhibition catalogue by J. Páez López, Real Alcázar, Sevilla, 2006.
G. Wiet, *Catalogue général du Musée Arabe du Caire. Objets en cuivre*, Cairo, 1932.

Lo.P.

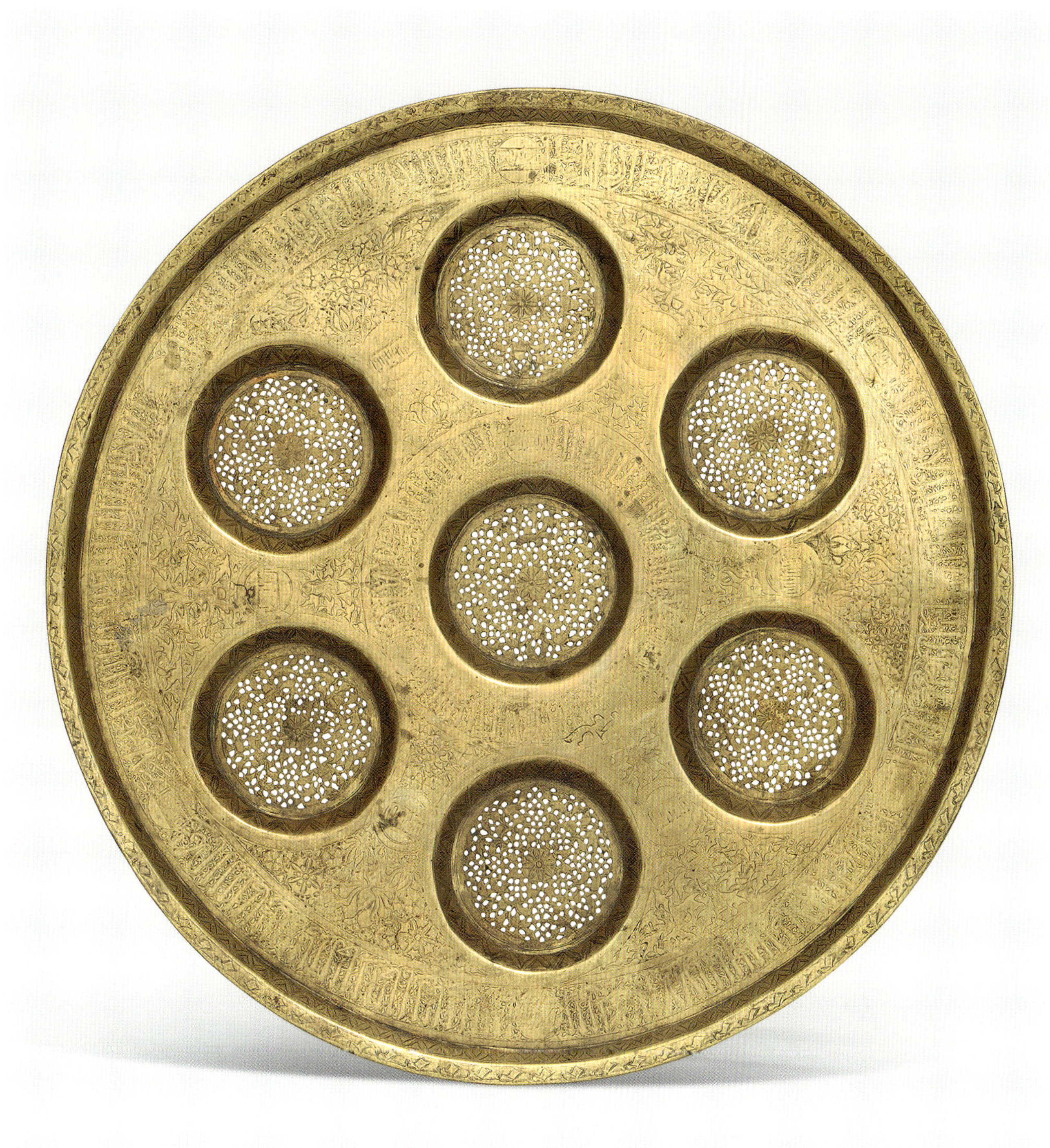

74

75

"Alhambra" vase specimen

Glazed majolica decorated with blue underglaze painting and metallic lusterware
h. 110 cm, Ø 52 cm
Private collection, Sanremo

Of typical shape, resting on a narrow circular base, with wide conical body, narrowing shoulders, a cylindrical flared neck and two handles worked in a style reminiscent of birds' wings, supported by a bronze tripod holding it in place, the body primarily painted in copper-lustre with dense *ataurique* (arabesques) and inscriptions, some areas highlighted with underglaze cobalt blue such as oval medallions filled with arabesques, lobed cartouches with inscriptions and a large reserve near the shoulder decorated with two regardant quadrupeds against vegetal sprays painted in copper-lustre and against cobalt-blue ground, the handles ornate with inscriptions in blue on a copper-lustre ground.

This vase is here exhibited to showcase its aesthetic qualities, as an example of the refined and renowned type of ceramic vases typical of the Nasrid period. Similar vases would have most likely been produced in Malaga around the 14th century and they are very rare; to this day only eight examples are known and they are all in museums' collections.

The function of these jars is still debated. It has been suggested that they may have been used to contain oil, perfumed water or wine, but their shapes and size seem impractical to these scopes. In the Alhambra Palace, they were probably placed on metallic bases attached inside wall niches, above which there were continuous calligraphic bands with inscriptions connected to water. Thus, the most likely use was as water containers.

The decoration would often be imbued with apotropaic and symbolical meanings such as the *khamsa* (holy hand), suggesting that the content had to be guarded and protected, whilst the inscriptions tend to be of good-wishing, auspicious nature (Hillenbrand, 1999, pp. 192). In the specific case of the Gazelles Vase (Soustiel, 1985, cat. n.221, p.186), a prototype of the one here exhibited, the stylised Tree of Life with regardant animals below it is supposed to represent Paradise and its symbols. The peculiar shape of these vases imitates the *tinajas*, moulded lead green-glazed jars produced in the 10th-11th century and spread all across Andalusia and Western Africa (Soustiel, 1985, cat. n. 197, p. 172). The beauty and characteristic features of these jars have inspired a prolific Orientalist reproduction in the 19th century, especially from the Deck (Victoria and Albert Museum Inv. n. 18-1865) and Pio Fabri (MIC Faenza, Inv. No. 9715) manufactures.

Provenance: antique art market.
Bibliographical reference in the cataloguing note.

I.B.

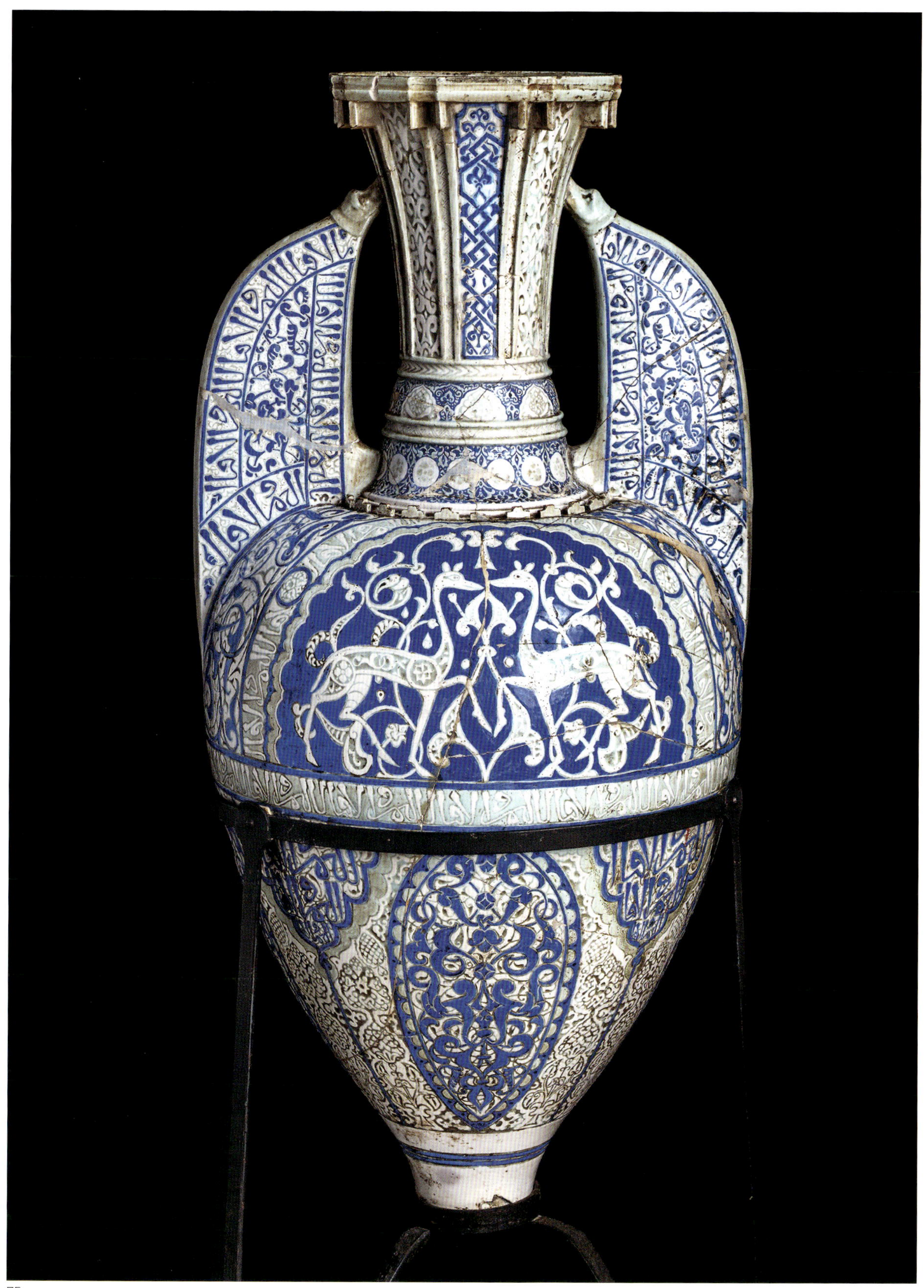

75

76
Jug

Turkey, Iznik, ca. 1545
Glazed ceramic with blue, green, and turquoise underglaze painting
h. 27.6 cm, w. 9.5 cm
Bologna, Museo Civico Medievale, inv. n. 1303

With wide sphere-conical body, resting on a circular foot, rising to a large cylindrical neck, with pinched mouth and S-shaped handle, the exterior underglaze-painted in blue with minute floral spirals, the juncture areas between the neck and base embellished with a turquoise-glazed vegetal crown, the base and mouth with two subtle decorative bands filled with fret- and knotwork motifs.

This jug belongs to a rare category of the Iznik ceramic production, usually dated around the mid of the 16th century and called *Golden Horn* or *Tugrakes* (see appendix to cat. n. 83 for an in-depth discussion).
The first fragments with this design had been found at the beginning of 20th century in Sirkeci during excavations to build a new post office (Carswell 1998, p. 50). Later on, the attribution of this production to the kiln of Istanbul was contested and scholars started believing this design was instead produced in Iznik or Kutahya (Atasoy and Raby, 1989, pp. 108-114), given that the minute and fine motifs seem to have been inspired by miniature paintings and in particular, *tughras*, the sultans' monograms. The style and design of Suleyman I's *tughra*, in particular, could be a direct link to the development of this decorative motif. This analogy would also explain the strict control carried out by the court over the Iznik manufacture in this period.
The *Tugrakes* style was particularly popular and sought-after in Italy, as attested by the numerous examples with Italian provenance, now in foreign museums' collections, (cat n. 81)

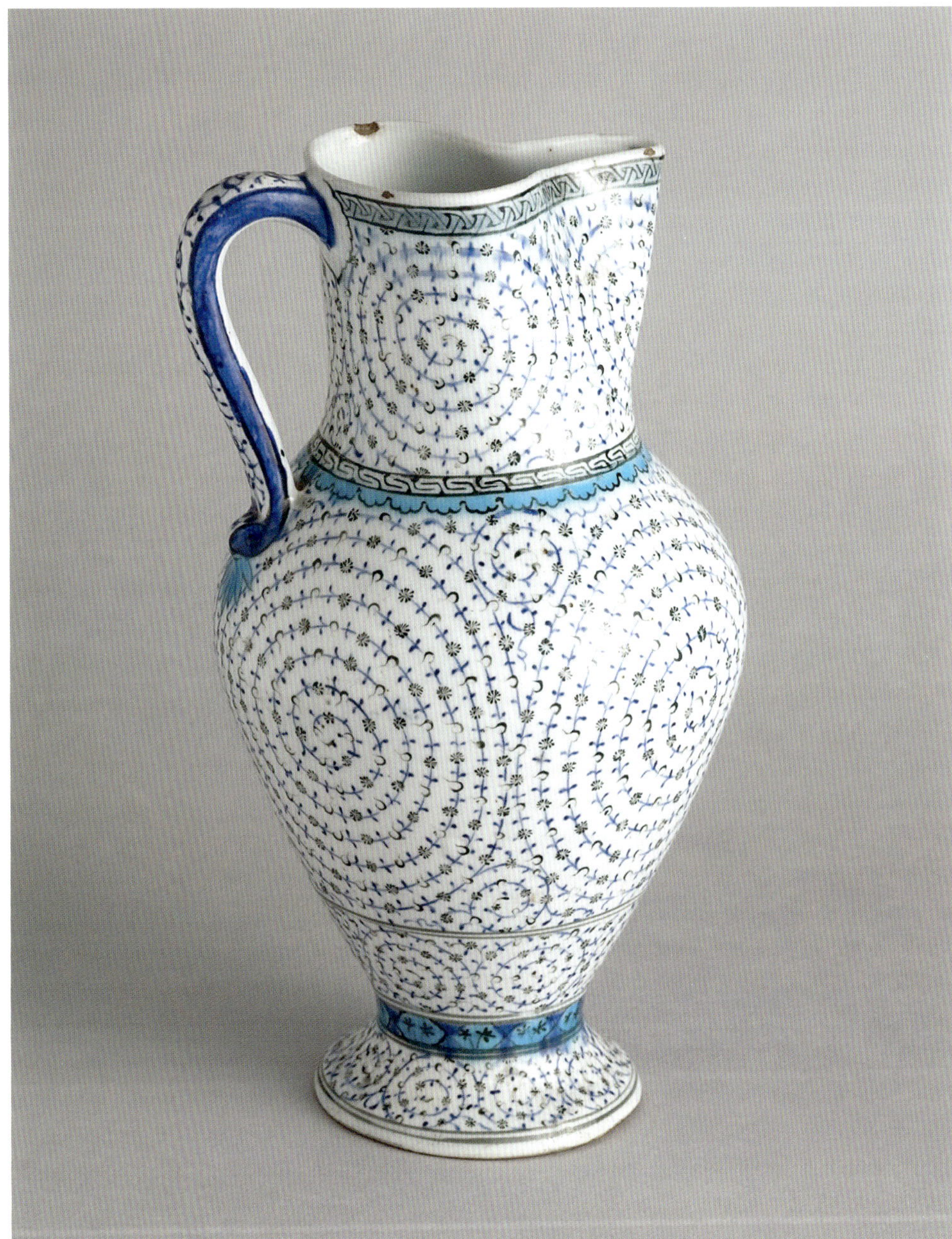

76

and also by the large presence of Italian copies inspired from this manufacture, such as the albarello here exhibited, made from a kiln in Liguria (cat. n. 77).

Bibliography: Atasoy and Raby, 1989, cat. n. 347, p. 110; *Le Mille*, 1990, n. 983; *Eredità dell'islam*, 1993, cat. n. 228, p. 383; Spallanzani, 1994, pp. 102-103; *L'Islam e Firenze*, 2018, cat. n. 95, p. 251.

I.B.

77

Albarello jar with Goden Horn decoration

Liguria, late 16th century
Polychrome majolica
h. 19 cm, Ø 12.2 cm
MIC, Museo Internazionale delle Ceramiche in Faenza, inv. n. 7567

Container for medical herbs, of cylindrical shape, with a tapering foot and mouth, the decoration consisting of a colourless band filled with the inscription *Benedicta S*, perhaps indicating that the content was *Benedicta sylvestris*, a term now no longer used but present in several 18th-century botanical treaties, the inscription surmounted by a painted medallion with Cupid with its bow and quiver, the background painted with subtle turquoise floral and vegetal spirals in the *Golden Horn* style, typical of the first Iznik production (see the jug cat. n. 76).

Bibliography: Guida 2014, fig.2, p. 76; Carswell, 1998, fig. 83, p. 103.

I.B.

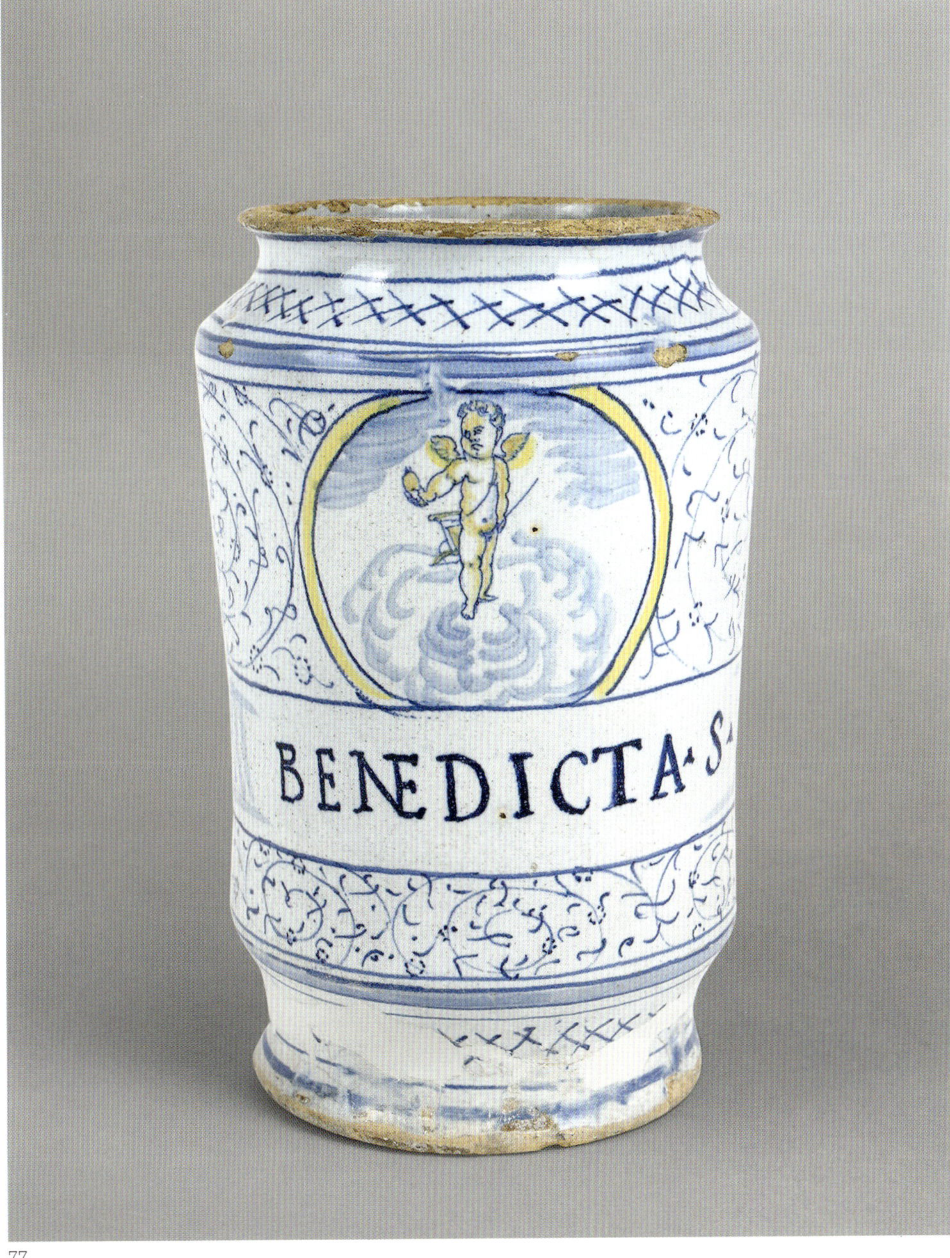

77

78

Barber's Basin

Veneto manufacture, probably from Candiana (Padua), 18th century
Polychrome majolica with underglaze painting
h. 15 cm, Ø 37 cm
Fondazione Musei Civici di Venezia, Museo Correr, inv. n. Cl IV, n 180

Of traditional shape, resting on a circular foot, with wide shaped brim and a recessed area to accommodate the neck, the decoration to the interior and exterior imitating Iznik manufacture style with typical Ottoman motifs such as tulips, carnations, peonies, *saz* leaves and vegetal tendrils, dividing the surface in two halves, the composition painted in manganese purple, yellow, blue against a white ground, the yellow substituting the bole red typical of the Kara Memi style in Turkish ceramics.
Western Iznik reproductions of this type are often attributed to the so-called *Candian* production. Similar examples can be found at the International Museum of Ceramics; at the Sevres Museum; at the Sforzesco Castle in Milan; and in several private collections. Basins like this used to gather the water for functional purposes and testify the great success that the Turkish Iznik manufacture had in Italy.

Bibliography: Fontana, in *Eredità dell'Islam*, 1993, cat. n. 301, pp. 483-484; Fontana e Kennedy in *Venezia e l'Islam*, 2007, pp. 311 e 359; *Venezia e Istanbul*, 2010, cat. n. III 52, p. 209; Atasoy and Uluc, 2012, cat. n. 101, p. 145.

I.B.

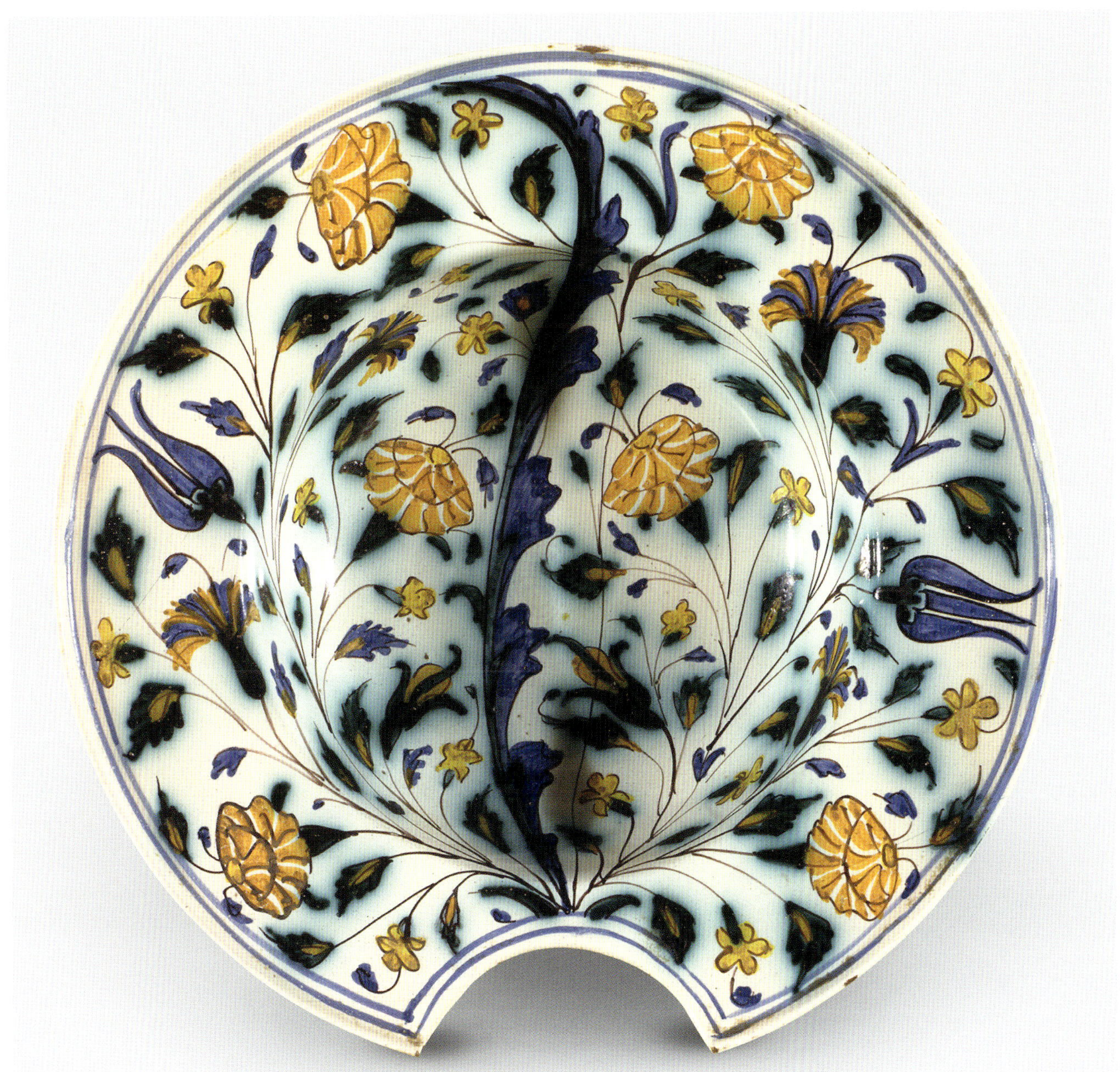

78

79

Ablution basin

Cantagalli manufacture, Florence, first half 20th century
Faenza, underglaze painting
h. 16.5 cm, Ø 24.4 cm
MIC, Museo Internazionale delle Ceramiche in Faenza, inv. n. 18102

Of circular shape, resting on a tall foot, the exterior in the typical Iznik-style with several different flowers painted in white and green over a blue ground, the interior with a central rosette surrounded by fruits with vegetal reliefs, a large band of *saz* leaves and flowers immediately below the upper border, the base marked with a cockerel, the symbol of this manufacture, and the country of origin 'Italy'.

Bibliography: *Verso Oriente* 2012, p. 178.

I.B.

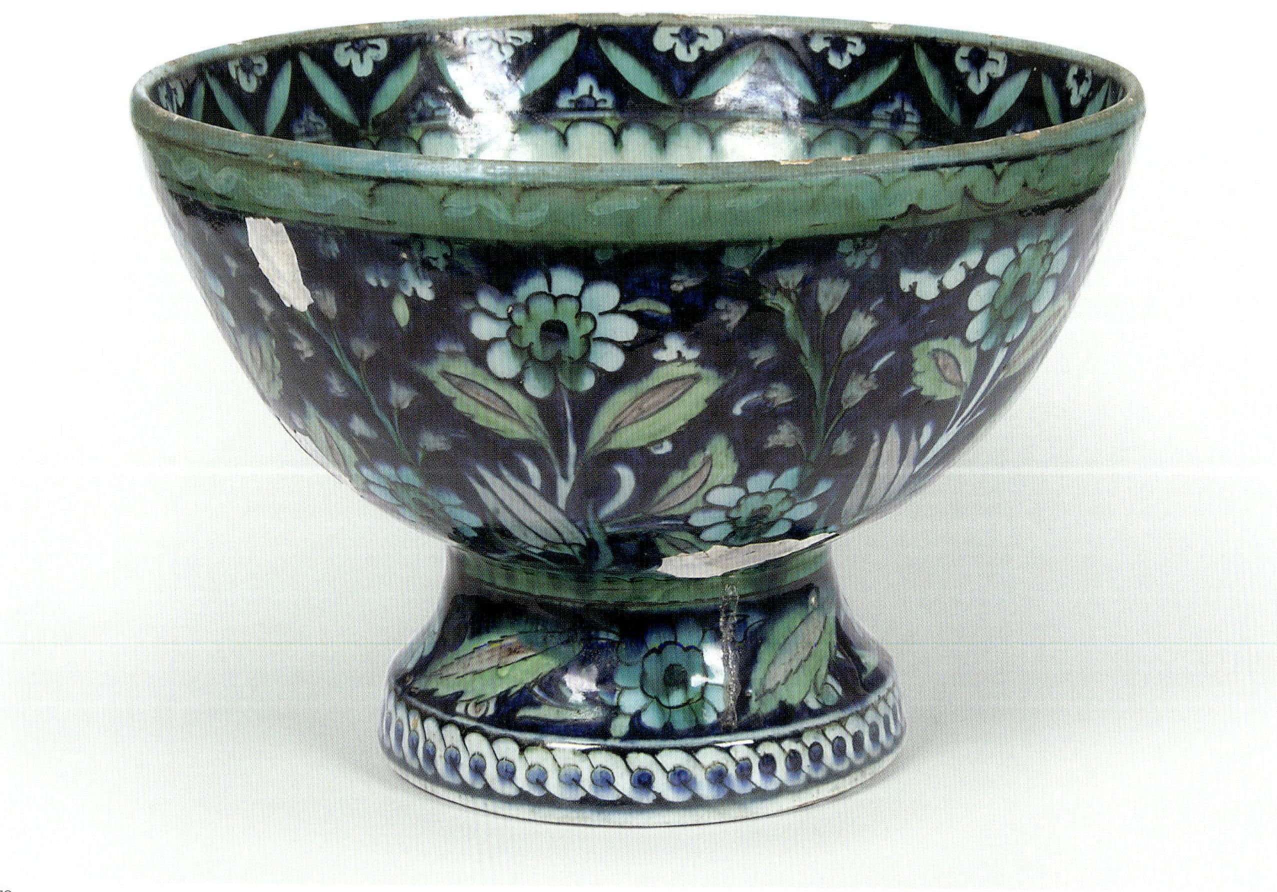

79

80

Cantagalli Tile

Cantagalli manufacture, Florence, Italy, first half 20th century
Faenza ceramic, polychrome decoration and underglaze painting
h. 23.8 cm × w. 23.8 cm
MIC, Museo Internazionale delle Ceramiche in Faenza, inv. n. 3507

Of square shape, underglaze-painted in blue and turquoise with a vase of carnations and tulips, a crown of prunus blossoms branches and two large halves of *saz* leaves, once united horizontally with other tiles sharing the same design, the back with the Cantagalli mark. The flower vase, as a symbol of the reviving water, is a very common decorative motif on Iznik ceramics, often flanked by tall cypresses around the end of the 17th century. Similar tiles come from the Esref Zade Rumi mosque in Iznik (Scerrato 1967, p. 70); other tiles with analogous subjects, but heightened by the presence of the bole red, can be found in the Blue Mosque in Istanbul and in the harem of the Topkapi Palace in Istanbul.

Bibliography: Scerrato, 1967, cat.124, fig. 69a; Museo Bardini, Firenze, inv. 873 in *Islam Specchio d'Oriente*, 2002, cat.n. 133, p. 164. A similar panel can be seen at the Victoria and Albert Museum, in Oney, 1987, cat.n. 95, pp. 94-95.

I.B.

The European copies

Objects and Islamic ceramics always exerted a special charm to the Western minds. Already in the 8th century, through Spain, the West and the Middle East were intricately connected by a dense series of fruitful commercial and diplomatic relations, which were to only grow further in the period of the Maritime Republics in the 12th century.
Together with the goods, the flavours, and the flares of the East, several decorative motifs and craftsmen were travelling on these commercial routes, contributing to the spread of stylistic analogies, syncretism and an aesthetic feeling overcoming geographic borders. In the Middle Ages, owning an Islamic artwork was a way to testify its appreciation, decontextualised as a matter of fact. That's why one often finds Islamic ceramic roundels decorating the façades of the churches in Pisa or Fatimid rock crystals as reliquaries in all the major European cathedrals (see cat. n. 9).
Around the 15th century, the next step was for the craftsmen to try and replicate the same techniques. It is in this way that the Veneto-Saracenic metals come to light (cat. nn. 32-33), and brocaded textiles and carpets rise to a specific place of honour in the Western altarpieces and in the paintings of the greatest masters of the Renaissance period, not to mention the Venetian and Florentine textiles imitating so well the Ottoman ones to be mistaken for them, and at times even produced for the Turkish market.
The barter of the arts between West and East thus has ancient roots, but with the rise of Iznik ceramics the interest becomes two-sided: the Turkish potters start borrowing European shapes , and the Italian manufactures start copying the Ottoman decorative motifs (cat. nn. 77 and 78). The fortune of Iznik ceramics among the Western crowd lasted through the centuries (they are still very much sought after today) and the fashion of Iznik-style artworks rose yet again in the 19th and 20th century. Indeed, around this time, several European ceramic manufactures such as Cantagalli (Italy), Deck and Samson (France) started designing lines in the

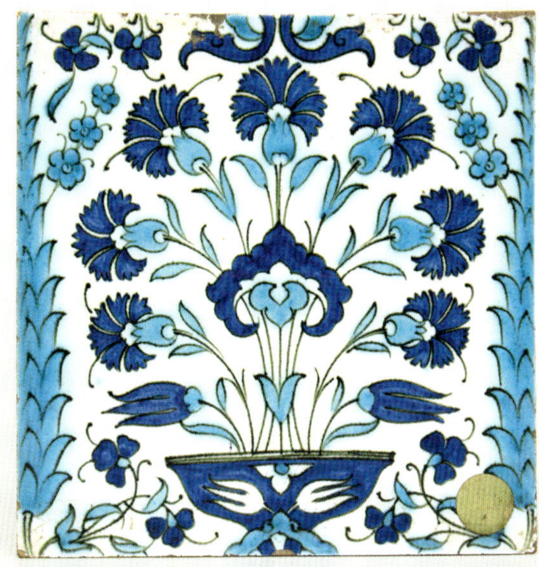

80

so-called *Iznik style*, moved also by the lure of the east and the new orientalist tendencies with Turkish and Japanese flares typical of the *fin du siecle*. The Hispano-Moresque style broadened the horizon and started developing a slavish imitation of the copper-lustre ceramics and the shapes of the Alhambra vases (see cat. n. 75).

I.B.

81
Jug

Turkey, Iznik, 1530-1550
Fritware, with polychrome underglaze painting
25 × 14.5 × 17 cm
The Ashmolean Museum, University of Oxford. Bequeathed by C. D. E. Fortnum, 1899, inv. n. EAX.3272

Of globular shape, resting on a circular slightly splayed foot, with narrowing shoulders, large straight neck with pinched mouth near the spout, a curved handle on the side, three narrow decorative bands filled with geometric motifs and fretwork, segmenting the body in three parts, the rest of the decoration consisting of tulips and roses against a dense blue fish-scale designed ground, each scale highlighted in black, the decoration painted in mauve, sage green, cobalt blue and deep turquoise typical of the Iznik manufacture of 1530s-1560s, preceding the introduction of the bole red.
These colour palette has often been called *Damascus* or *lyrical*, as it was earlier attributed to Syria and only later on to the Iznik kilns. Cecutti (2013, tab. 25) mentions a Florentine provenance; the vase then left Italy to go to the UK.
For an in-depth discussion on Iznik wares, see the appendix to cat. n. 83.

Bibliography: Atasoy and Raby, 1989, no. 348; Allan, 1991, no. 45; *Tresor: Antiquities*, 2008, n. 222, p. 79, illus. p. 79. For similar examples, see Atasoy and Raby, 1989, cat. n. 349-350 e 370.

I.B.

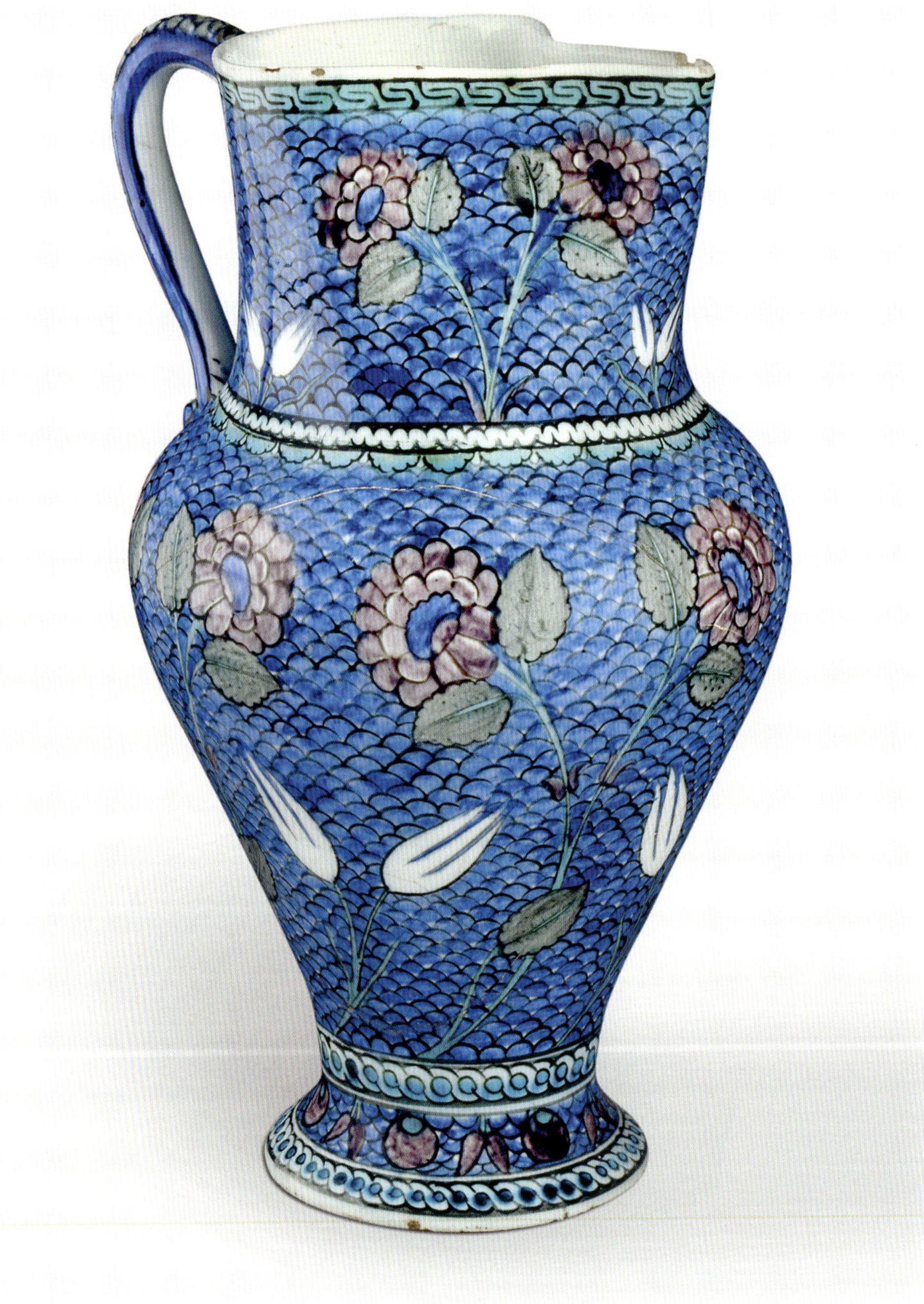

81

82
Jug

Turkey, Iznik, ca. 1535-1550
Fritware, with polychrome underglaze painting
h. 19.7 cm
MAO Museo d'Arte Orientale, Torino, inv. n. ISv/87

Of globular shape, resting on a short circular foot, with a wide tall cylindrical neck and a handle on the side, the body with a floral decoration painted in white and turquoise against a blue ground, three narrow bands with geometric motifs and meanderings highlighting the base, the juncture of the neck and the mouth, the flowers depicted daisies, plants and tulip buds.
This jug is decorated in the so-called *Ceramists style*, a design dating to the end of the 20s of the 16th century and characterised by a freer, more fluid arrangement of the decoration compared to the contemporary *Tugrakes*. In both styles, the colours used are primarily blue and turquoise, but the design on our jug uses a blue ground and simple, aerie compositions.
The rise of this style may be linked to a sink of the courtly demand for local ceramics, due to the growing fascination of Chinese porcelains, which arrived in Turkey through the military campaigns of the sultan Selim I. To respond to this circumstance, the Iznik potters created a simpler, more popular style, making their products accessible even to the less well-off social classes.
For an in-depth discussion on Iznık wares, see the appendix to cat. n. 83.

Bibliography: unpublished. For reference, see Atasoy and Raby, 1989, cat. n. 156 - 266.

I.B.

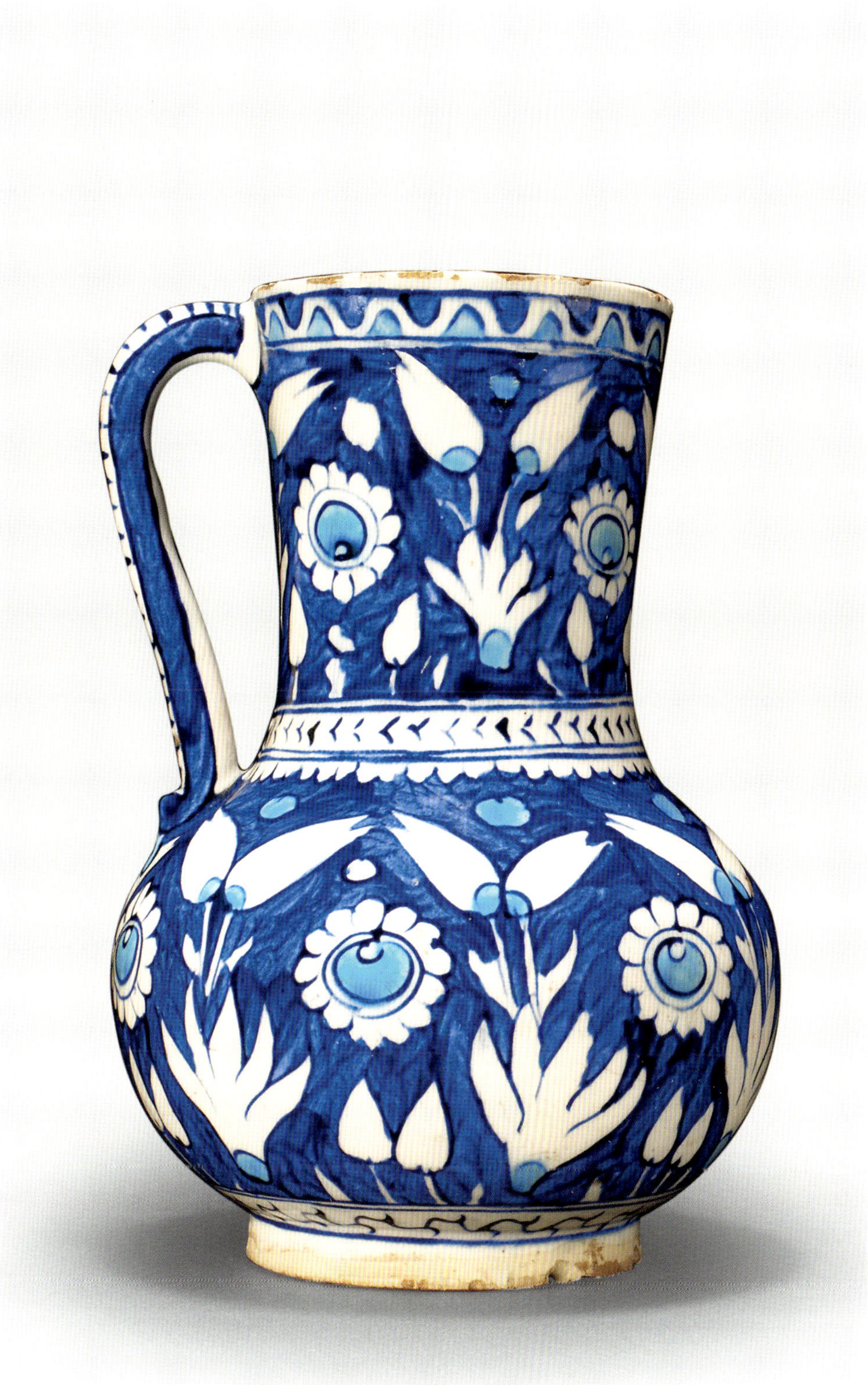

82

83

Tankard (tankard-hanap)

Turkey, Iznik, last quarter 16th century-early 17th century
Fritware, with polychrome underglaze painting
h. 21 cm, w. 14 cm
MIC, Museo Internazionale delle Ceramiche in Faenza, inv. n. 6322

Of cylindrical shape, on plain circular base, with a squared handle, the exterior painted in a vertical composition of *saz* leaves, vegetal sprays, carnations and tulips in the typical colours of Iznik such as bole red, green and blue, the mouth and base ornate with a horizontal band with stylised flowers over a blue ground.
This tankard can be dated to the second half of the 16th century due to the presence of the bole red-painted decoration, a colour introduced to the Iznik ceramic palette only around 1545. This new colour will lead to the spread and development of the *Four Flowers style*, characterised by a combination of tulips, roses, hyacinths and carnations.

Bibliography: Ravanelli Guidotti C., 1987, cat. n. 190, p. 301; Guida 2014, pag. 74, fig.4.

Iznik wares

Iznik (ex Nicea) is a city in Anatolia, located south west of Istanbul. The city is known as one of the greatest centres of ceramic production in the Ottoman Empire and it gets generally acknowledged as the main centres of production of courtly ceramics. The considerable number of Iznik wares that reached us, together with documentary evidences and accounts constitute a substantial organic body through which it is possible to study and understand the stylistic and technical evolution of these ceramics.
Iznik wares' fame is due to its high level of craftsmanship, achieved thanks to local and independent technical and stylistic innovations. Among the major technical innovations, the primary one is the adoption of a siliceous alkaline and lead-based paste for the body rather than regular clay, used in other productions in the Islamic lands. This new paste was discovered at the beginning of the 16th century and it gives to Iznik ceramics a different composition compared to the traditional fritware used since Fatimid Egypt (Henderson e Raby 1989, pp. 115-130). Stylistically speaking, one can notice the progressive departure from Chinese and Timurid models towards a more uniquely and exquisite Ottoman style.
Initially, Iznik wares used to show a strong influence from blue and white Chinese porcelains, considered lavish commodities at the time (see cat. n. 123). Turkish potters were able to reinterpret Chinese wares creating a new unique style, called *Baba Nakkas*, where the *hatayi* (floral chinoiserie) confronted the *rumi* (Seljuq-style arabesques). In short, decorative motifs of the Far East had been put side to side with autochthonous Western motifs, thus redesigning Chinese blue and white on an ideal level rather than in the details.
Another type of blue and white was the so-called *Tugrakes* (or *Golden Horn*), a spiralling style inspired by Suleyman I's *tughra* (see cat. n. 76).
Among the various stylistic innovations, an increment in the chromatic palette is worth noting. From around 1530 new colours were introduced such as turquoise, mauve, sage green; the use of the black line to highlight decorations started approximately in the 1540s (cat. nn. 82 and 81); the red bole around 1550 (cat. nn. 5 and 83-84) and the emerald green in the decade of 1560. The special red colour known also as *Armenian bole* is mentioned in the contemporary treaty by Piccolpasso, confirming the dating of its introduction (*Li tre libri dell'arte del Vasaio, nei quali si tratta non solo la pratica ma brevemente tutti gli secreti di essa cosa che persino al dì d'oggi è sempre stata tenuta nascosta.* Del Cavaliere Cipriano Piccolpasso Durantino 1548).
Colours and designs were dictated and spread by the *nakkashane* (imperial atelier), the creative mind ideating all the decorative motifs for each vessel. Two specific decorative trends which started from here were Shah Kulu's *saz* leaves design, when he was the head of the *nakkashane* in 1526; and his successor Kara Memi's *Four Flowers* pattern with the adoption of a naturalistic rendering of carnations, tulips, roses and hyacinths (see cat. nn. 83, 105, 107, 109).
Although the request of specific decorative motifs was coming directly from Istanbul, it is likely to believe that Iznik wares were not used primarily at court, but rather in the kitchens and barracks of the janissaries. Several wares and fragments that reached us show strong and heavy marks of wear; a large portion of vessels instead went lost forever with the great fire that hit the kitchens of the Topkapi in 1574.
Iznik kilns were not only producing vessels, but also the renowned tiles. The new *Four Flowers* style gave a great contribution to the development of the Iznik tile production, as the colour red served well in intertwined and scrolling compositions, repeated almost endlessly, providing a perfect decorative arrangement to be seen at distance (cat. nn. 115-116). One of the key factors that favoured the development of Iznik tiles and their vast spread was the lucky meeting between Suleyman I and Sinan, the official imperial architect since 1538. It was Sinan who encouraged their use, firstly to highlight the most important areas of a building, then with time to dress up entirely every Ottoman wall, empowering the tiles to express the intrinsic aesthetic value of the architecture.

I.B.

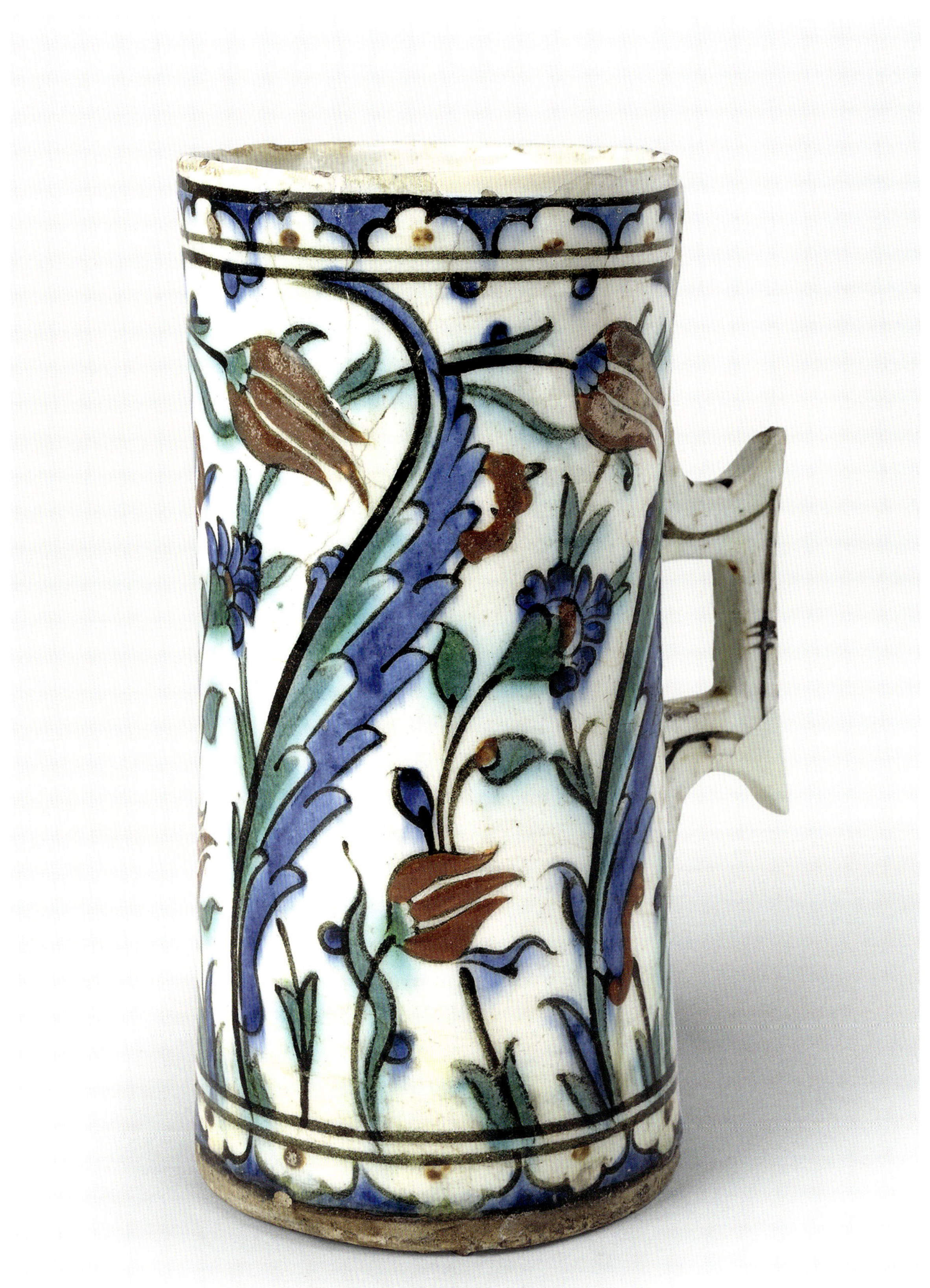

83

84
Tankard

Turkey, Iznik, last quarter 16th century
Fritware, with polychrome underglaze painting
h. 19 cm, w. 17 cm
MIC, Museo Internazionale delle Ceramiche in Faenza, inv. n. 6323

Of cylindrical shape, on plain circular base, with a squared handle, the body decorated with vessels with large Latin sails against blue ground enhanced by small red bole marks evoking streams and reefs, the upper and lower border painted in white against narrow green bands, the handle with short irregular horizontal strokes in blue, the base marked with a small black clover.
Among the known examples of Iznik wares, the first vessel showing a decoration with vessels is a dish dating 1535-45 (Victoria and Albert Museum, Londra, Inv. n. 713-1902). A predilection for figural motifs seems to have been rather common during the reign of Sultan Murad III (1574-1595), a great collector and patron of manuscripts and works on paper, explaining possibly why he was so inclined to appreciate figural themes on different media (another recurrent subject, apart from vessels, is animals).
This type of boats was very well-known to the Ottoman harbours in the 16th century. Normally, the decoration of the sails excludes the one on the background and vice-versa: the sails are often painted with stripes when there is a plain background or white when there is a coloured background, as in this case.

Bibliography: Ravanelli Guidotti C., 1987, cat. n. 192, p. 302. For similar examples, see Atasoy and Raby, 1989, cat. n. 528-529, p. 253; Atil 1973, cat. n. 86; Petsopoulos, 1982, cat. n. 102; Scerrato 1967, fig. 56, cat. 84.

I.B.

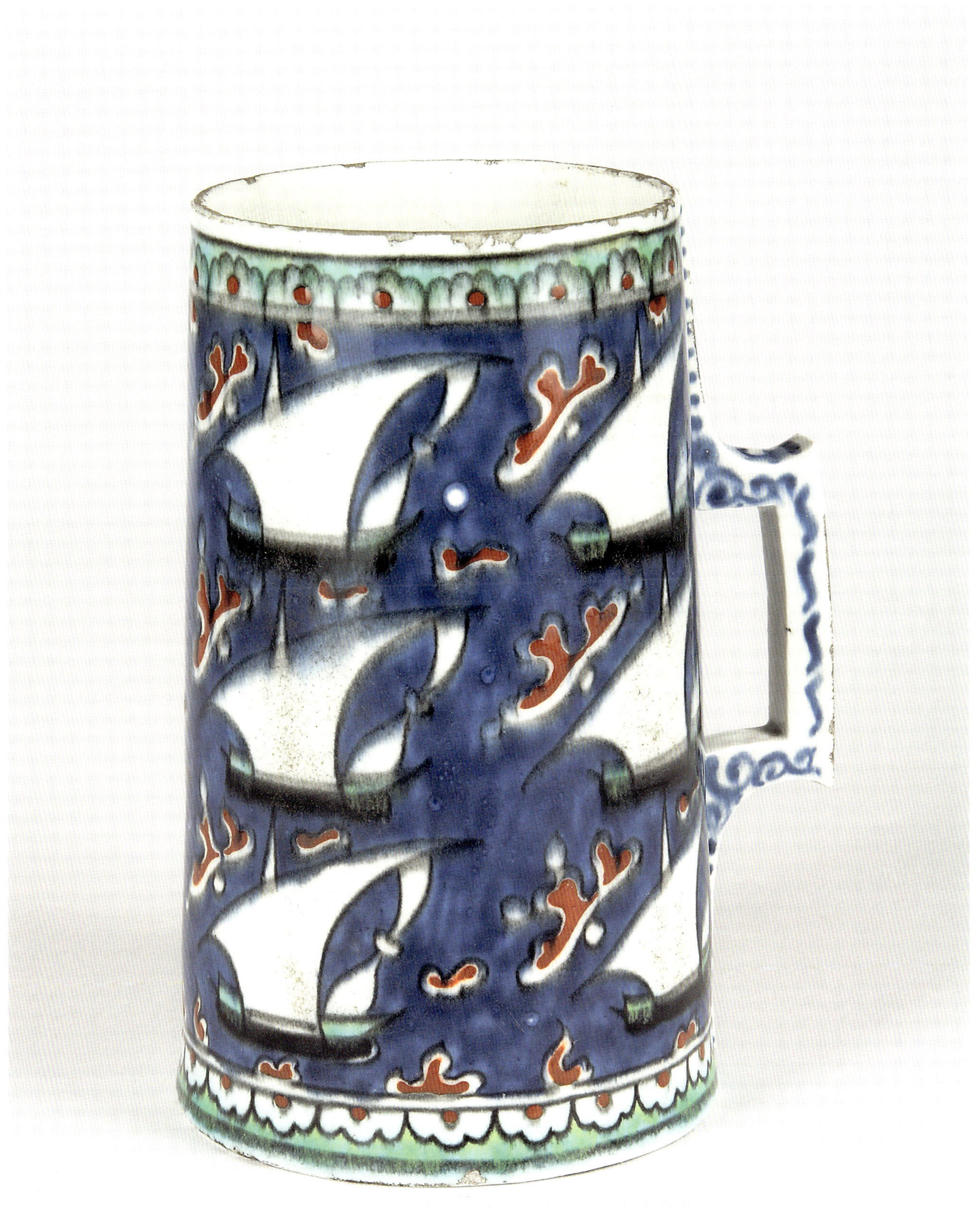

84

85
Amphora

Spain, Valencia, Manises, 15th-16th century
Lusterware enameled majolica
h. 45.5 cm, w. 32 cm
MIC, Museo Internazionale delle Ceramiche in Faenza, inv. n. 21510

Of ovoid shape, resting on a flat base, with double handles enamelled in ivory white and embellished with copper-lustre, the body painted with copper-lustre decoration consisting of bands of petal-shaped panels filled with short strokes and dots, similar to musical notes, and stylised thistle flowers (or pomegranate), the background with similar motifs.
This type of minute decoration tends to involve often shingling motifs, musical notes, thistle flowers, rosettes and copper-lustre wheels (Forthingham, 1952, figs. 110-119, 148-149, 154-156). Its origin can be dated to the 1470s, thanks to some dishes with noble coat of arms (Ibidem, pp. 149-151).

Bibliography: Cora, 1985, cat. 841, p.325; *Sucre e Borja*, 2001, cat. n. 147, p. 413.

I.B.

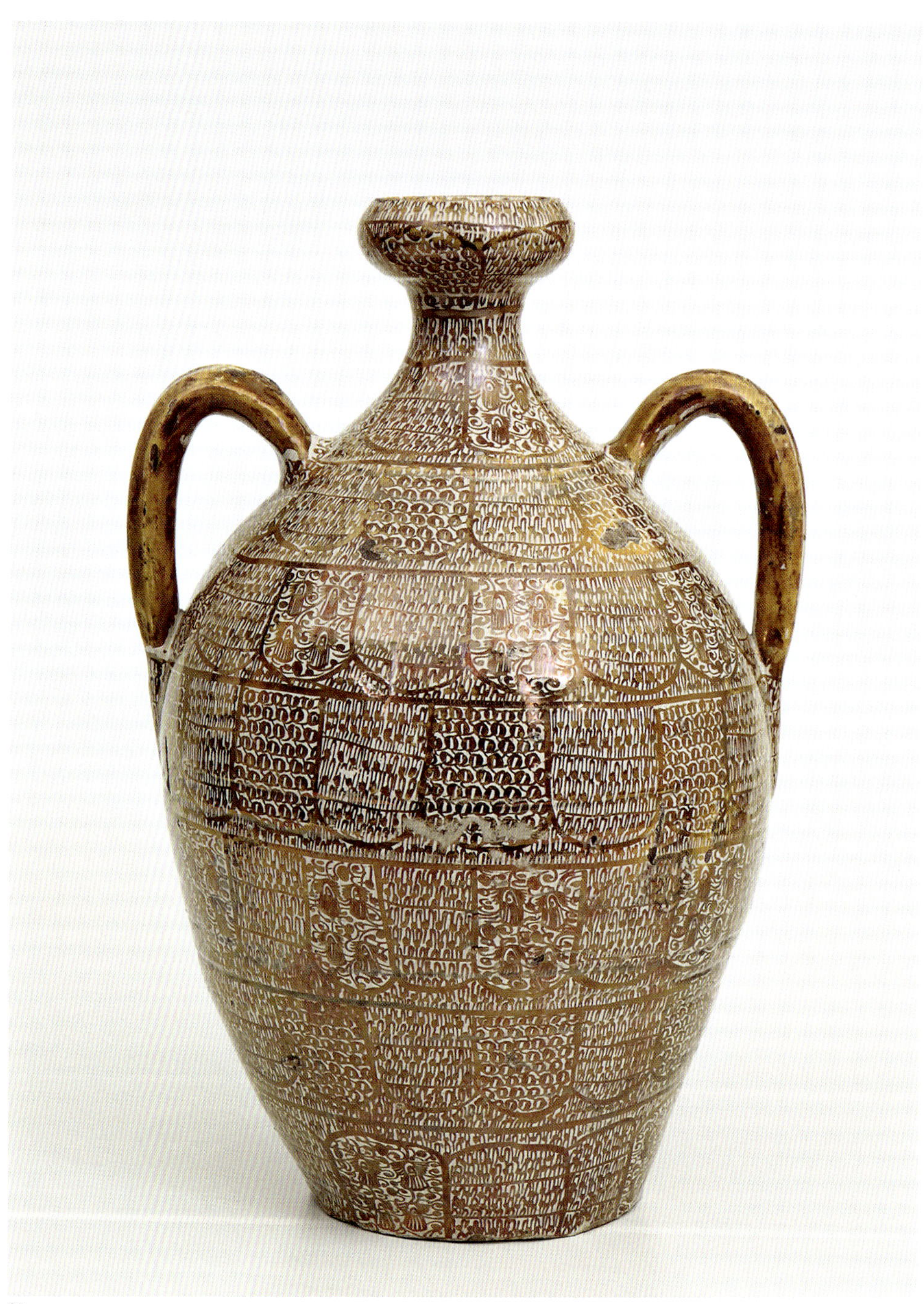

85

86
Two-handled amphora

Spain, Valencia, Manises, second half 15th century
Lusterware majolica with with blue underglaze painting
h. 44.9 cm
Bologna, Museo Civico Medievale, inv. n. 2784

Of globular shape, resting on a wide splayed foot connected to the body through a compressed ring, with a moulded tall conical neck with roundels in relief, ending with a straight mouth, with two large pierced handles with lobed borders on the sides, characterising the object as a "winged vase" due to their shape, the exterior painted in copper-lustre on a white ground with a reinterpretation of Islamic arabesques and fleshy palmettes (Rose-Albrecht, *Le calife* 2002, p. 106), enhanced with some underglaze cobalt blue elements, the overall composition, style and decoration inspired by the "Alhambra vases" with two handles (cat. n. 75).

Bibliography: Ravanelli Giudotti 1985, p. 304-306; *Le calife* 2002, p. 106. For similar examples, see *Eredità dell'Islam*, 1993, cat. n. 203, p. 343; *Beyond* 2006, pp. 99-103, Spallanzani 2006, pp. 301-303.

I.B.

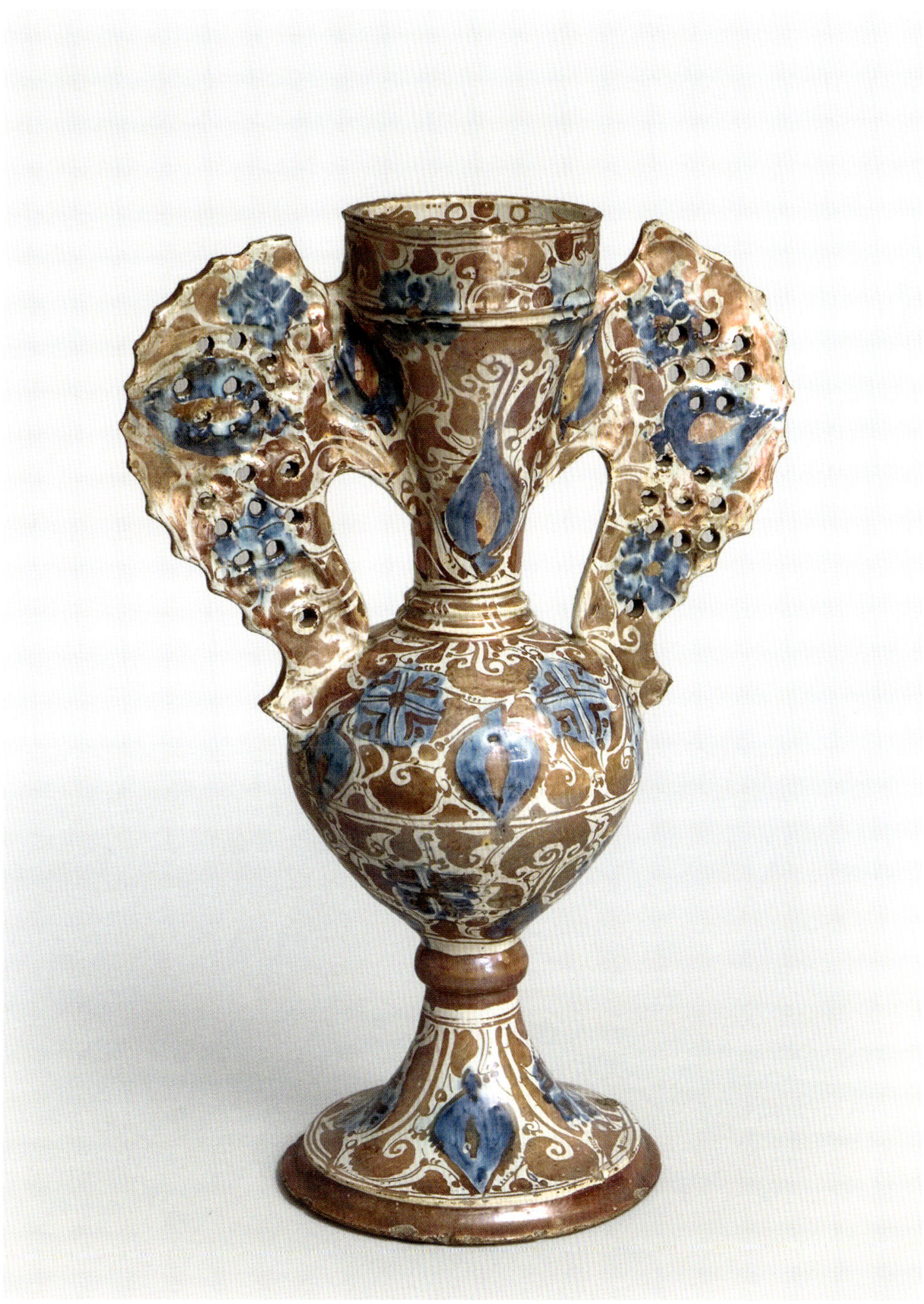

86

87

Single-handled ewer

Spain, Valencia, Manises, last quarter 15th century
Majolica with metallic lusterware
h. 28.5 cm, foot Ø 10.4 cm
Bologna, Museo Civico Medievale, inv. n. 2793

Of globular shape, resting on a tall splayed foot connected to the body through a compressed ring, rising to a tall flared neck, with S-shaped spout and a handle on the side, the exterior painted with copper-lustre decoration consisting of horizontal bands filled with crown of ivy and vegetal tendrils, the spout and handle painted in full.

Bibliography: Ravanelli Giudotti 1985, cat. n. 274, pp. 305-306 and its bibliographic references.

I.B.

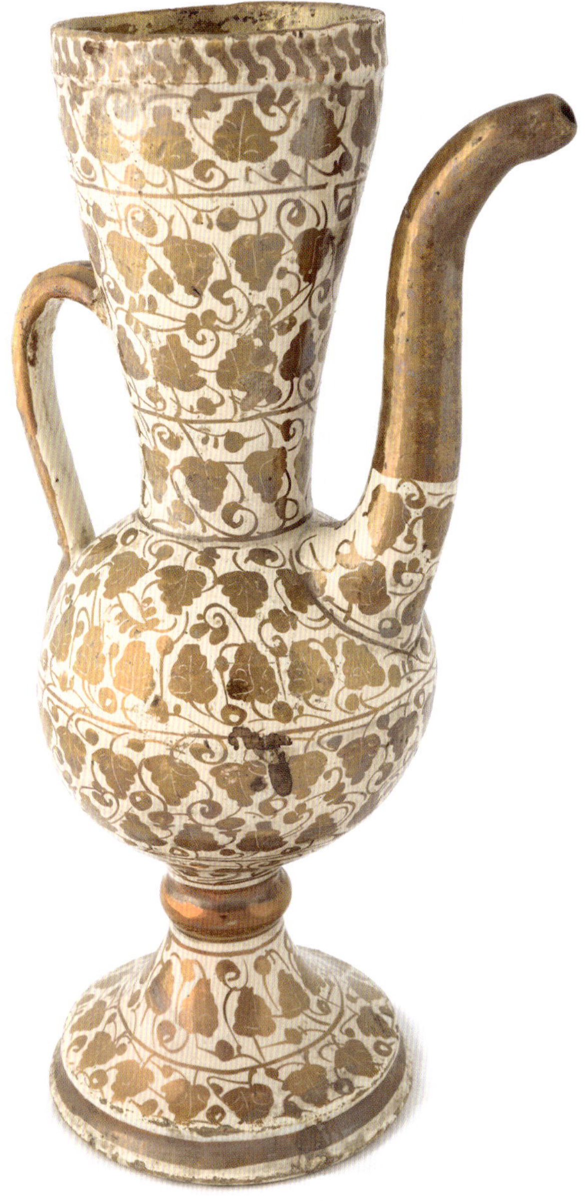

87

88
Bottle

Iran, 12th-13th century
Fritware with metallic lusterware
h. 21 cm
Courtesy of the L.A. Mayer Museum for Islamic Art, Jerusalem, Israel, inv. n. C 82-69

Of globular shape, resting on a circular foot, rising to a tall cylindrical neck, bending towards the interior, ending with a circular ring near the mouth, the exterior painted with copper-lustre decoration in the miniature style with camels among dotted vegetal tendrils, the register flanked by tall chequered trees, the decorative band near the base painted with palmettes and vegetal motifs, the juncture between body and neck decorated with a pseudo-calligraphic inscription embellished with simple strokes and dots.
For an in-depth discussion on the techniques to make copper-lustre ceramics, read the notes of cat. n. 90.

I.B.

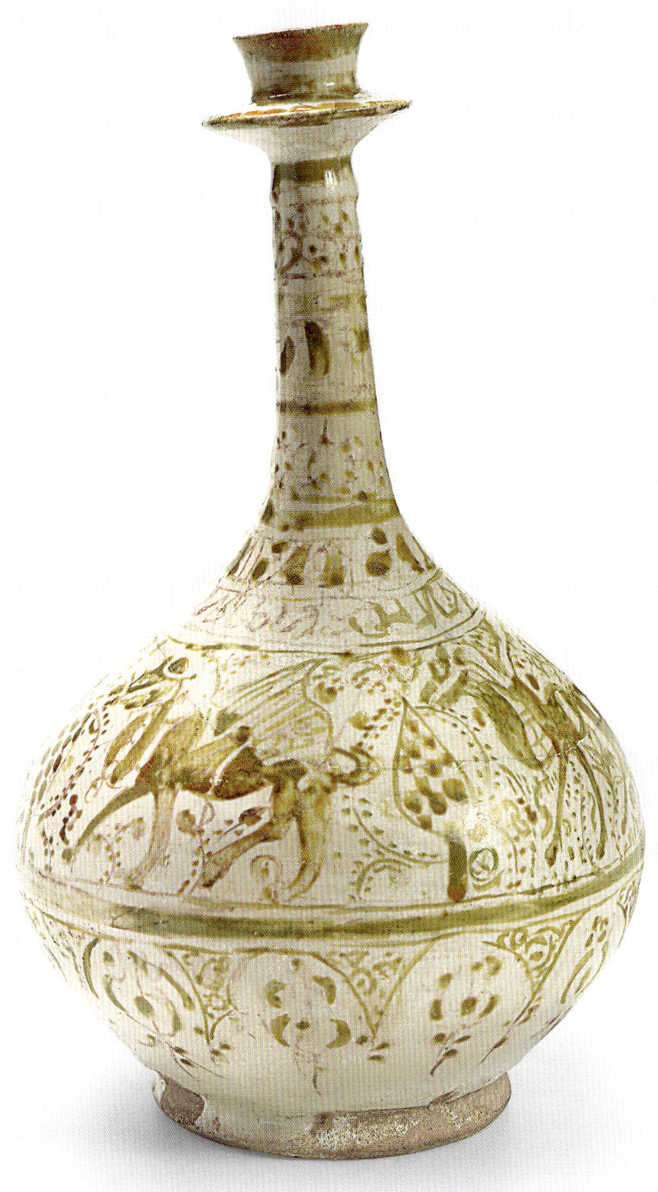

88

89
Jug with cock's head

Persia, Kashan, early 13th century
Pierced fritware, perforated decoration, black motifs with turquoise underglaze painting
h. 29 cm
MAO Museo d'Arte Orientale, Torino, inv. ISv/51 1132

Of cylindrical shape, resting on a flat base, with narrowing shoulders and a long tapering neck ending in a cockerel head-shaped spout, the crest coinciding with the mouth of the object, two epigraphic bands against black ground on the neck and near the base, the body worked with the technique of the double shell, having an internal container and and an external pierced casing, covered in turquoise glaze, inspired by the contemporary models of metalware to ensure to keep the liquid fresh.
A work of this sort requires a high level of craftsmanship and sophistication, as the risk that the double shell gets damaged in the making or during the firing process is very high. These ewers were extremely rare. Grube (1976, n. 137, pp.187-188) counted a group of nineteen then, to which one should add the four examples sold on the antique art market in the following years, as in this case. These ewers come in three main shapes: globular, whose main and most relevant example, dated to 612 AH / 1215 AD, is at the Metropolitan Museum in New York (inv. n.32.52.1); pyriform ending in a cockerel head-shaped spout, examples of which are at the Louvre Museum in Paris (inv. n. MAO 442) and at the Victoria and Albert Museum in London (C.1701977); and bell-shaped with straight walls, the major examples being the one exhibited here, an ewer at the Khalili Collection (POT 773) and another at the Al-Sabah Collection (LNS 185 C).

Bibliography: unpublished.
Bibliographical reference in the cataloguing note.

I.B.

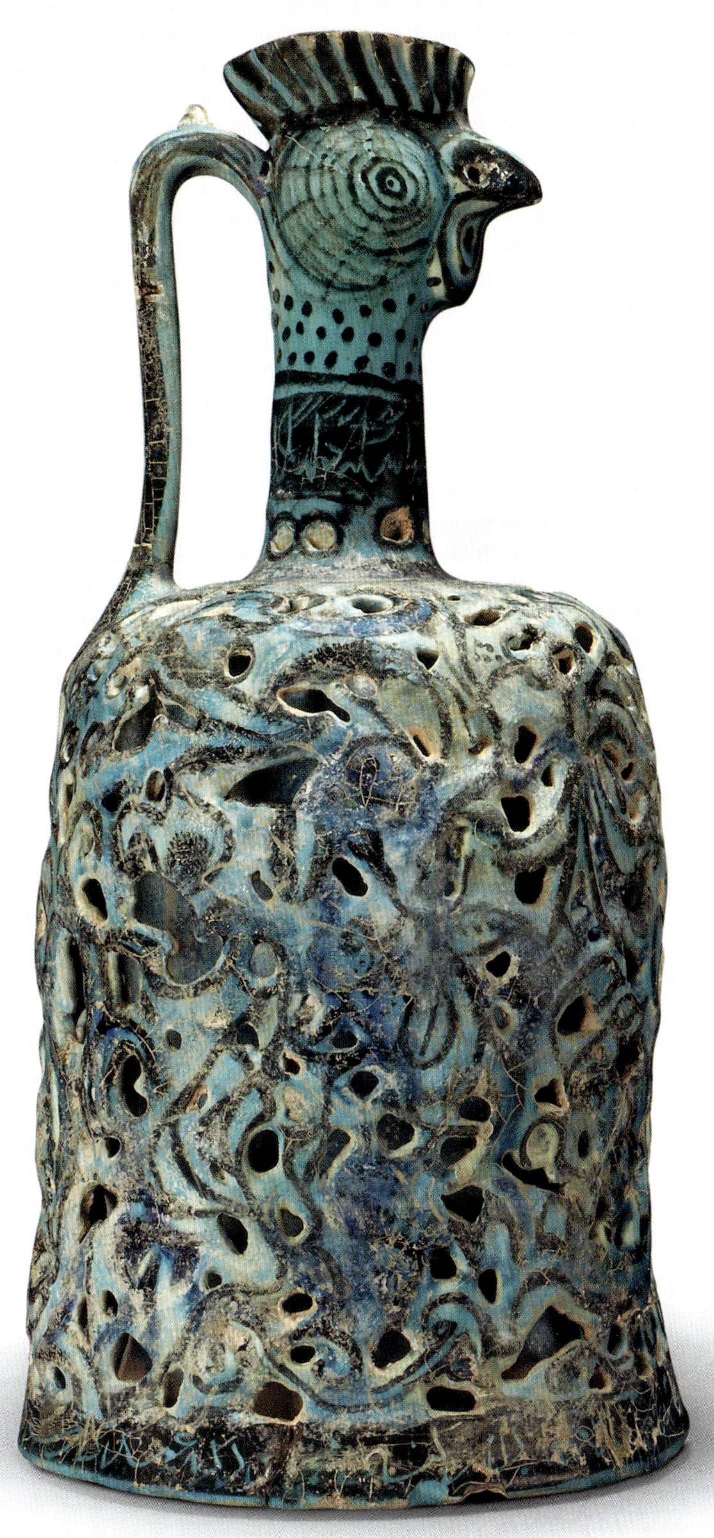

89

90
Lusterware jug

Persia, Kashan, late 12th-early 13th century
Fritware, glazed with metallic lusterware
h. 13 cm, Ø 15.5 cm
MIC, Museo Internazionale delle Ceramiche in Faenza, inv. n. 4892

Of globular shape with a broken profile, resting on a tall circular foot, with a wide shoulder on a flat side bending to the interior, rising to a short cylindrical neck, with a single handle, the decoration divided in three registers: on the lowest, stylised floral elements in radial composition drooping towards the base; the shoulder decorated with circular medallions filled with copper-lustre-painted arabesques painted over a white ground, the composition set within a decorative band with white split palmettes against a copper-lustre ground; and the neck with a Kufic epigraphic inscription with the word *Al-d[awlah]* "abundance", repeated throughout the circumference, the shape of the ewer reminiscent of contemporary Mina'i ware vessels, also produced in Kashan.
For a comparative example in miniature style, see *Splendori a Corte*, 2007, cat. n. 116, p. 148.

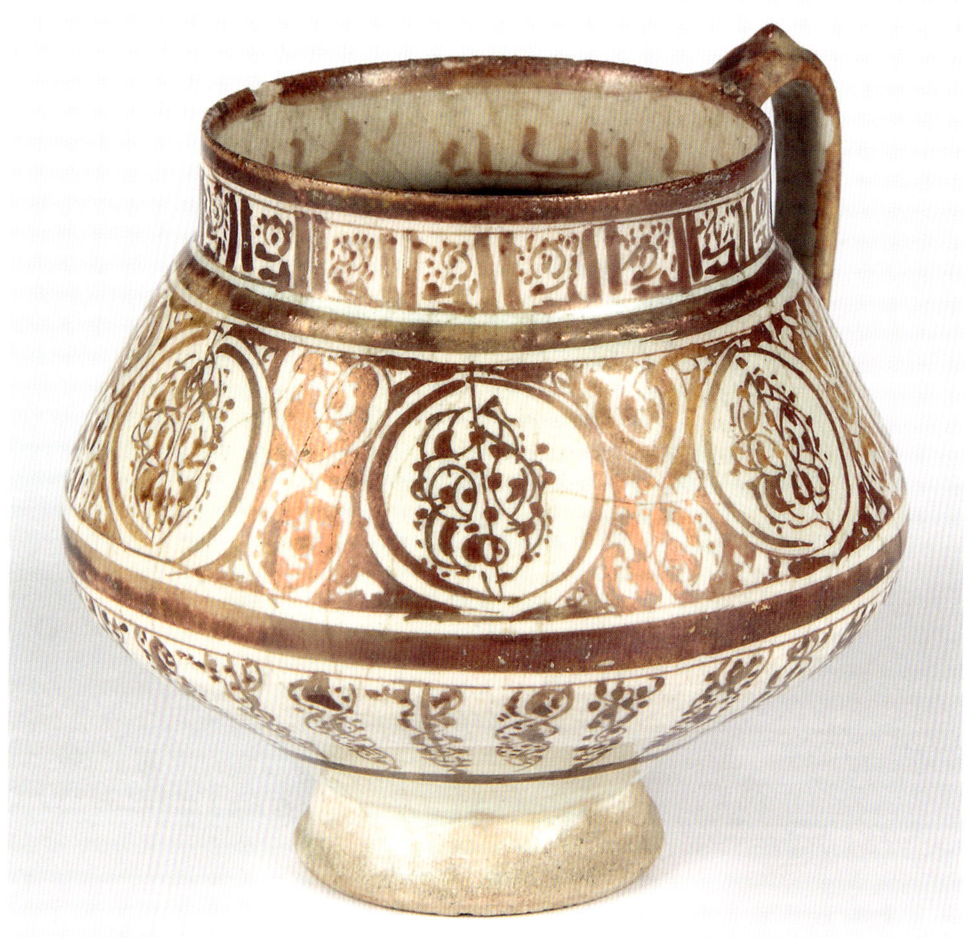

90

Copper-lustre painting was a widely spread technique in 12th-13th century Iran. The original inspiration must have derived from the lustre ceramics produced in the Abbasid and Fatimid period; it is likely to believe that as a consequence of the fall of the Fatimids, Egyptian potters had to migrate eastward to find new patrons and some of them reached Iran and taught the technique to the locals.
This technique involves the use of copper oxides which during the firing process penetrate the stone paste body and once cooked in an oxide-reduced kiln, they come out with a metallic finishing. The colours vary from red, brown to sand, as the one here exhibited.
As far as the decoration is concerned, Watson (2004, p. 60) divides 12th-13th century Kashani copper-lustre wares in three main categories: monumental, miniature and Kashan, a hybrid between the first two style, and also the category for our ewer.

Bibliography: Scavizzi 1966, p. 46, fig. 18; Watson 1985, p.60, fig. 26; *Le mille*, 1990, cat. n. 48, p. 85; *Eredità dell'Islam*, 1993, cat. n. 120, p. 231.

I.B.

91
Lusterware jug

Iran, Kashan, 12th-13th century
Fritware, glazed with lusterware
h. 22.3 cm, max. Ø 19.2 cm
MAO Museo d'Arte Orientale, Torino.
inv. n. ISv/66

Of globular shape, resting on a tall circular foot, rising to a tall cylindrical neck, with a slightly splayed rim and handle on the side, the body with copper-lustre-painted miniature style decoration consisting of a dense grid of Y-shaped cartouches and six-pointed stars filled mostly with minute arabesques, two stars with white figural decoration against a copper-lustre ground, the design inspired by contemporary manuscripts and reproduced in Mina'i wares as well, on the neck elongated hexagons alternating in vertical and horizontal order, creating four-pointed stars in the interstitial spaces, the mouth embellished with a simple weave pattern, the foot unglazed and retaining drooping blue glaze drops, the handle with remains of a thumbrest, possibly originally in the shape of a pomegranate or knot, inferring to a metalware inspiration in regards to the shape of this ewer. Soustiel (1985, p. 104) points out that similar examples were excavated in different centres of production, such as Kashan, Gorgan, Rey and Saveh among others, and that their attribution is often dictated by the location where in was unearthed. The decoration with polygonal compartments and stars seems to be rather typical of the ceramics found in Gorgan. Further motifs appearing here, contemporary to the metalware production, are the minute scrolling floral sprays, the typical background to Khorasani metals.

Bibliography: unpublished. Reference: Bahrami, 1949, pl. XLIV; Soustiel J., 1985, Cat. 111, p. 104; Watson, 1985, cat. n. 81.

I.B.

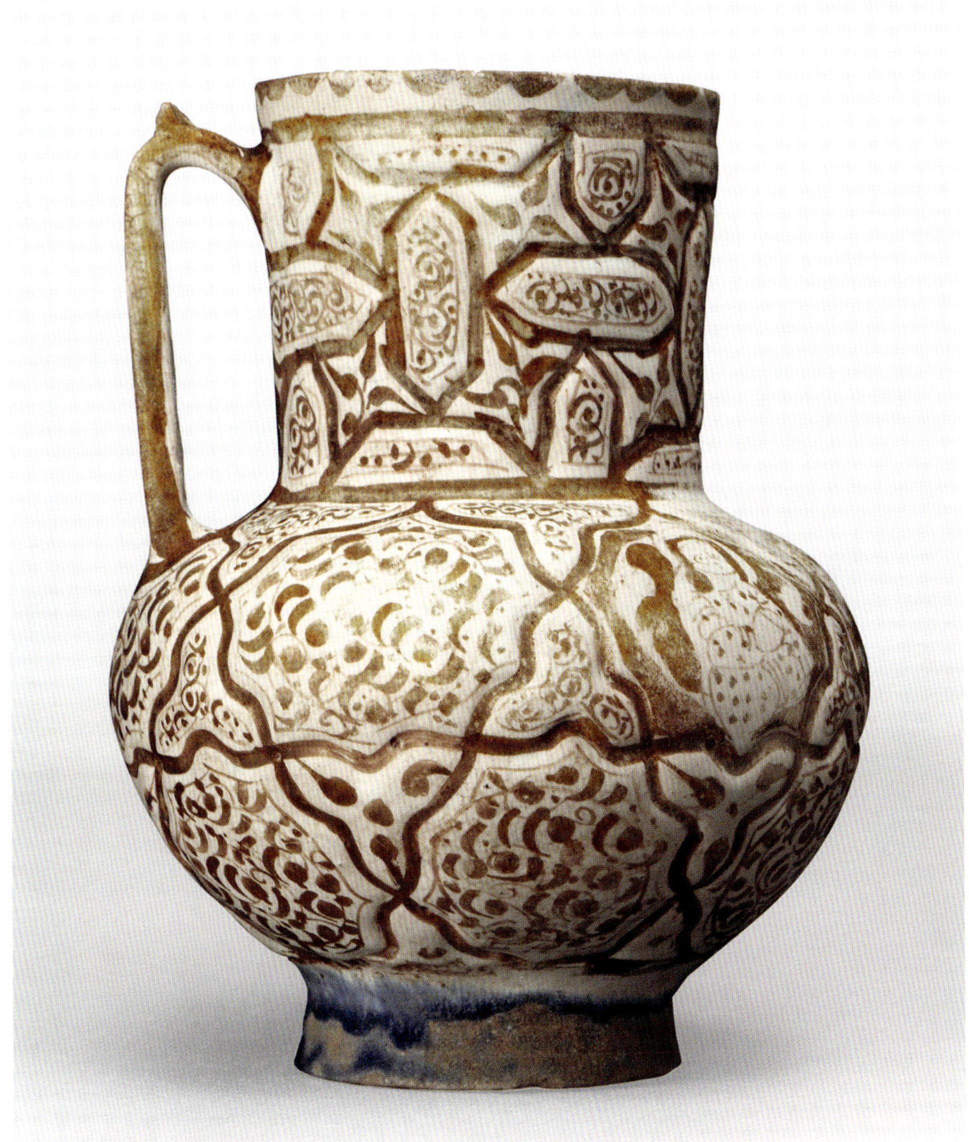

91

92
Star-shaped tile

Iran, Kashan, 13th-14th century
Fritware, enameled, metallic lusterware
h. 31 cm, l. 31 cm, w. 2.3 cm
MIC, Museo Internazionale delle Ceramiche in Faenza, inv. n. 6932

An eight-pointed star-shaped tile, the shape produced from the overlap of two squares, the outer border decorated with a narrow band filled with *naskh* calligraphy, painted in copper-lustre against a white ground, the inscriptions possibly of Quranic nature, the rest of the surface decorated with two large interlocking white arabesques against a copper-lustre ground enhanced by small spirals, repeated in copper-lustre as ornament of the very same arabesque motif.

Bibliography: for similar examples, see the British Museum Inv. n. 1896,0201.103 and G.468; Museo di Capodimonte, Napoli, Inv. n. D.C. 162 in Scerrato 1967, cat. n. 50, fig. 38.

I.B.

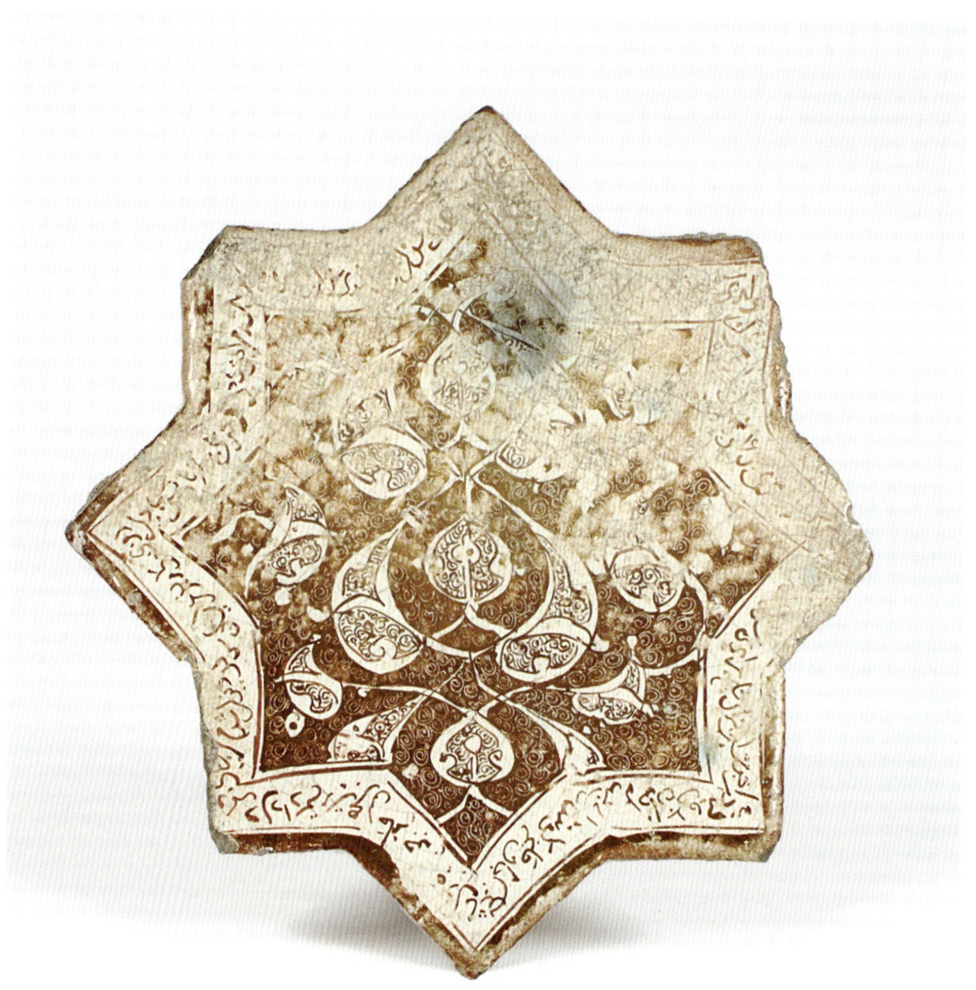

92

93
Star-shaped tile

Iran, Kashan, late 13th century
Fritware, enameled, metallic lusterware
h. 21 cm, l. 21 cm, w. 1.8 cm
MIC, Museo Internazionale delle Ceramiche in Faenza, inv. n. 22014

An eight-pointed star-shaped tile, the shape produced from the overlap of two squares, the outer border decorated with a calligraphic band against blue ground, among the inscriptions the date of production 681 AH (1282-83 AD),
the rest of the surface embellished with an animal flanked by two blossoming trees against a lustre ground, the details of the animal and the trees such as its hairs and the petals of the flowers painted with lustre.

Bibliography: Cora, 1985, p. 329, n. 852, *Le mille*, 1990, p. 97, n. 62, *Eredità dell'Islam*, 1993, pp. 260-261, n. 146; *Matisse Arabesque*, Roma, 2015, pp. 99, 243, n. 89. For a comparative example, see Watson, 1985, pp. 122, 146, pp. 133-134, tab. M, fig. 110.

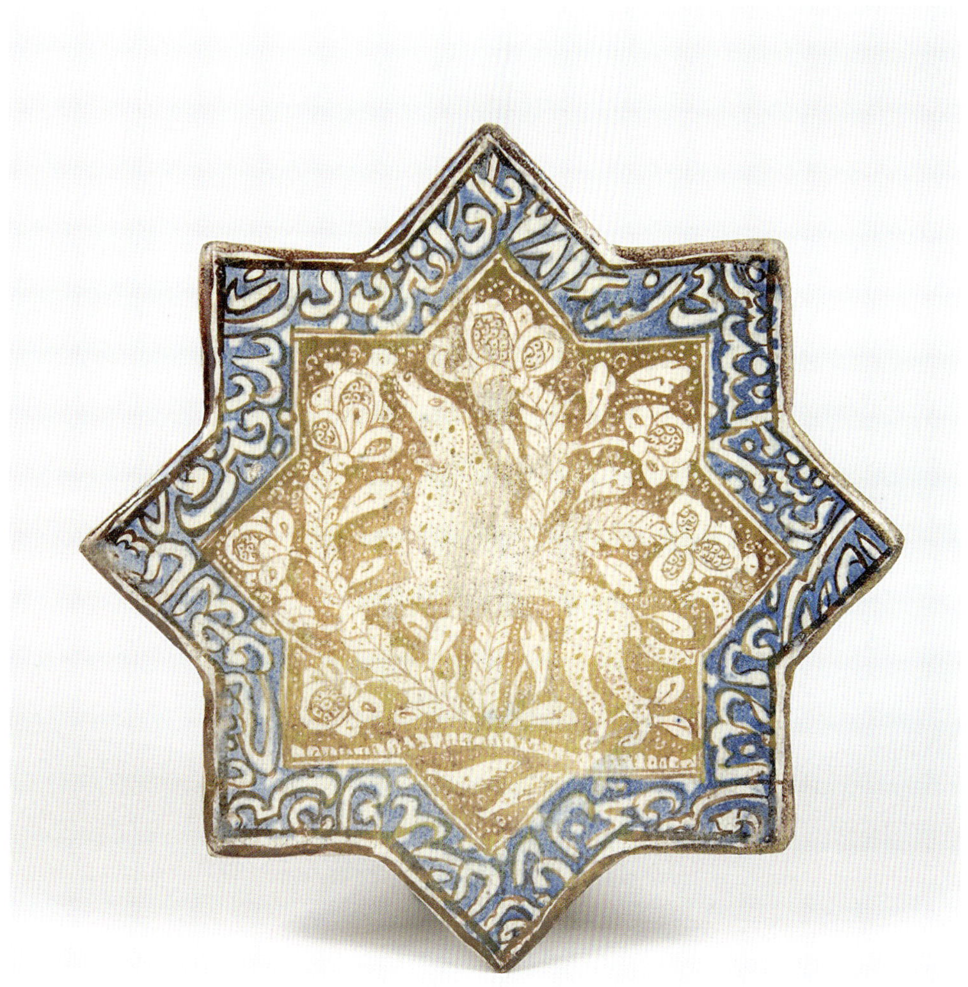

93

Patrons and the religious elite of the Seljuq and Ilkhanid period boosted the tile manufacture to a unprecedented extent in Iran, mostly commissioned to decorate the walls of mausoleums and religious buildings. The more lavish ones were indeed clad in copper-lustre tiles. The primary centre of production was Kashan, a city in central Iran, whose name later became the noun for the tiles, called *kashi* in Persian. Several tiles bear dates (cat. n. 93) and inscriptions. The nature of these inscriptions varies from religious/Quranic for those tiles created to adorn religious buildings, to poetic, often associated with zoomorphic decorations, if commissioned for lay buildings, given that the figural representation of humans and animals is discouraged in a religious context.
However, taking into consideration the concurrent rising supremacy of the Sufi doctrine and its beliefs, it is plausible to suggest that some of the poetic tiles could have also been used in a religious context, due to the fact that love poems could have been interpreted as directed to God rather than peers. This type of tiles would have been united in long panels formed by the alternating combination of eight-pointed with cross-shaped tiles in the interstitial spaces (Daim, 2012, cat. n. XV.2, p. 351).

I.B.

94
Fountain at the Entrance of the Topkapi Palace (Istanbul)

Thomas Hope
ca. 1790
Watercolour on paper
h. cm 28, w. 44.5 cm
Benaki Museum, Athens,
inv. n. ΓΕ 27354

Bibliography: Tsigakou, Moraitou 2016, p. 144.

A.V.

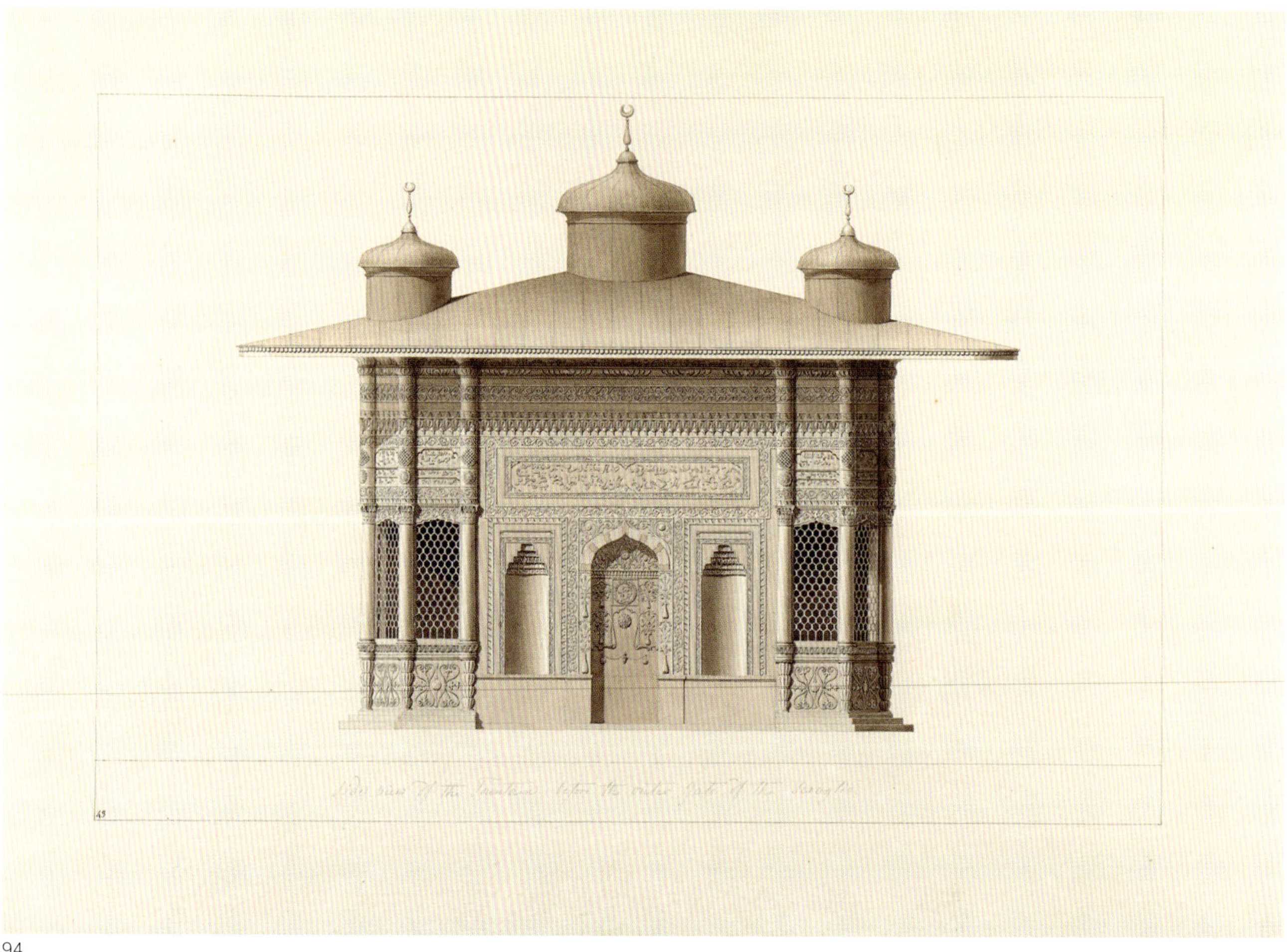

94

95
View of a Fountain in Galata (Istanbul)

Thomas Hope
ca. 1790
Watercolour on paper
h. 29 cm, w. 44.5 cm
Benaki Museum, Athens,
inv. n. ΓΕ 27357

Bibliography: Tsigakou, Moraitou 2016, p. 154.

A.V.

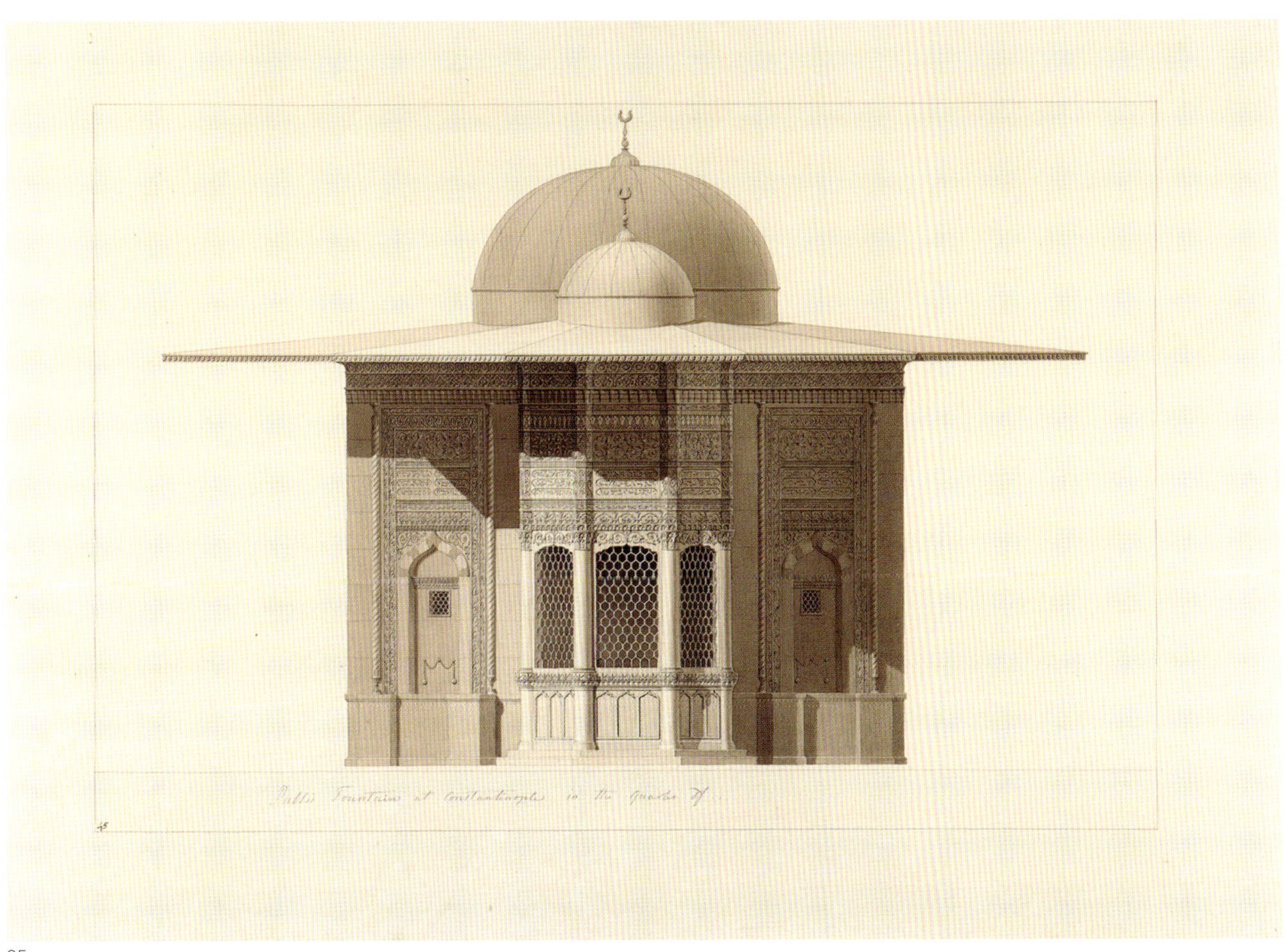

95

96
View of Fountains in Istanbul

Thomas Hope
ca. 1790
Watercolour on paper
h. 29 cm, w. 44.5 cm
Benaki Museum, Athens,
inv. n. ΓΕ 27365, 27366

Bibliography: Tsigakou, Moraitou 2016, p. 150.

A.V.

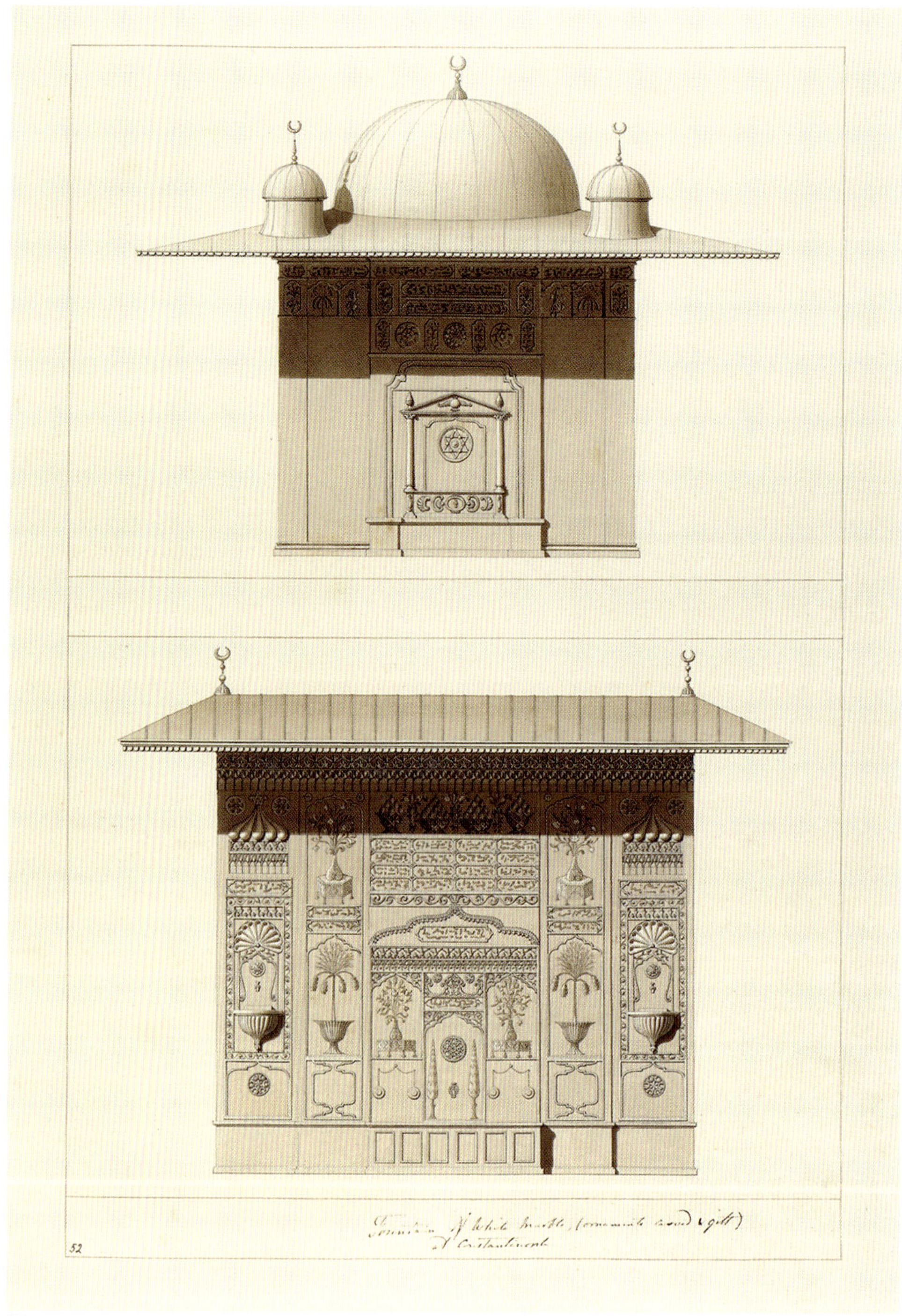

96

97

View of the Sweet Waters of Europe in Istanbul

Thomas Hope
ca. 1790
Watercolour on paper
h. 41 cm, w. 60.5 cm
Benaki Museum, Athens,
inv. ΓΕ 27362

Thomas Hope (1769-1831) was a wealthy collector, traveller, and Anglo-Dutch writer (his main novel is *Anastasius*). Towards the end of the 18th century, similarly to many other Northern European young educated men, he set on a *Gran Tour* across Egypt, Greece and Turkey. What the artist left us of this journey is not a travel diary, but rather a collection of watercolours and drawings. The watercolours here exhibited present different views of the city of Istanbul, where Hope spent a whole year, sketching and reproducing several views, palaces, moments from daily life for a total of 350 drawings. The works here selected show some of the famous monumental fountains in Istanbul, such as the main fountain preceding the entrance to the Topkapi Palace, built by Sultan Ahmed III in 1728; another located in Galata. The last watercolour depicts a view of the *Sweet Waters of Europe*, an area where one of the primary torrents was flowing into the Golden Horn.

Bibliography: Tsigakou, Moraitou 2016, p. 130.

A.V.

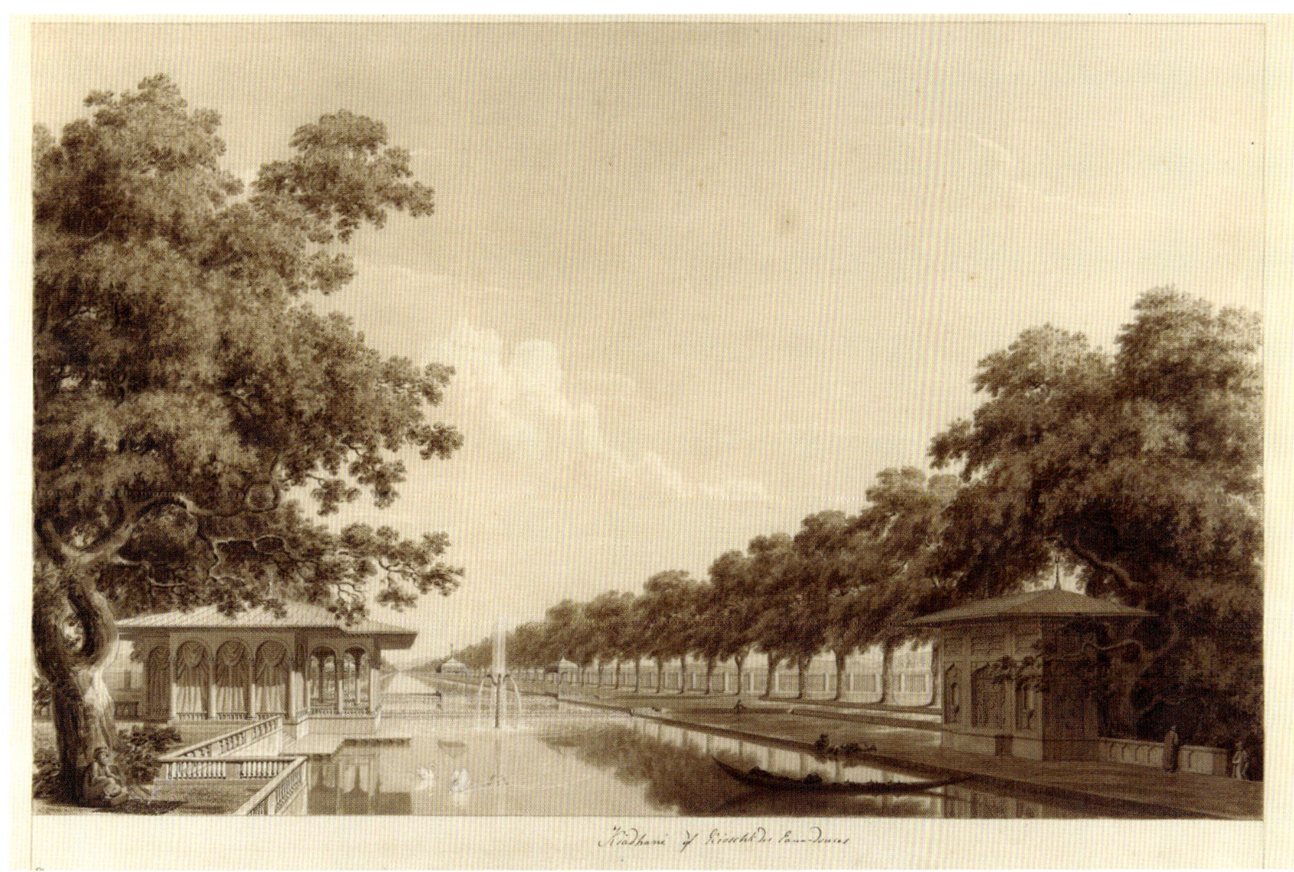

97

98
Arab woman

Alberto Pasini
1855-1856
Sketchbook
Pencil and charcoal on paper
9 × 15 cm, open 8 × 31 cm
Private collection, Turin

From the travel diary of Alberto Pasini (1826-1899) in the years 1855-1856, one of the major exponents of Orientalist Paintings in Italy.
In March 1855, Pasini was appointed as official painter of a French diplomatic mission to Persia, Turkey, Syria, Arabia and Egypt. During that journey he produced approximately sixty studies and several drawings, laying the ground for some of his Verism works with an exotic flare at the core of his success first in France and then in Italy. The Arab woman holding an earthenware jar on her head represents a particularly dear theme, widely exploited in both Orientalist paintings and literature. This is evident as well in the Egyptian travel accounts of Maxime Du Campi in 1849 (1889, 7) and of Gustave Flaubert (1910, IV, 94).

Bibliography: Du Camp 1889; Flaubert 1910.

A.V.

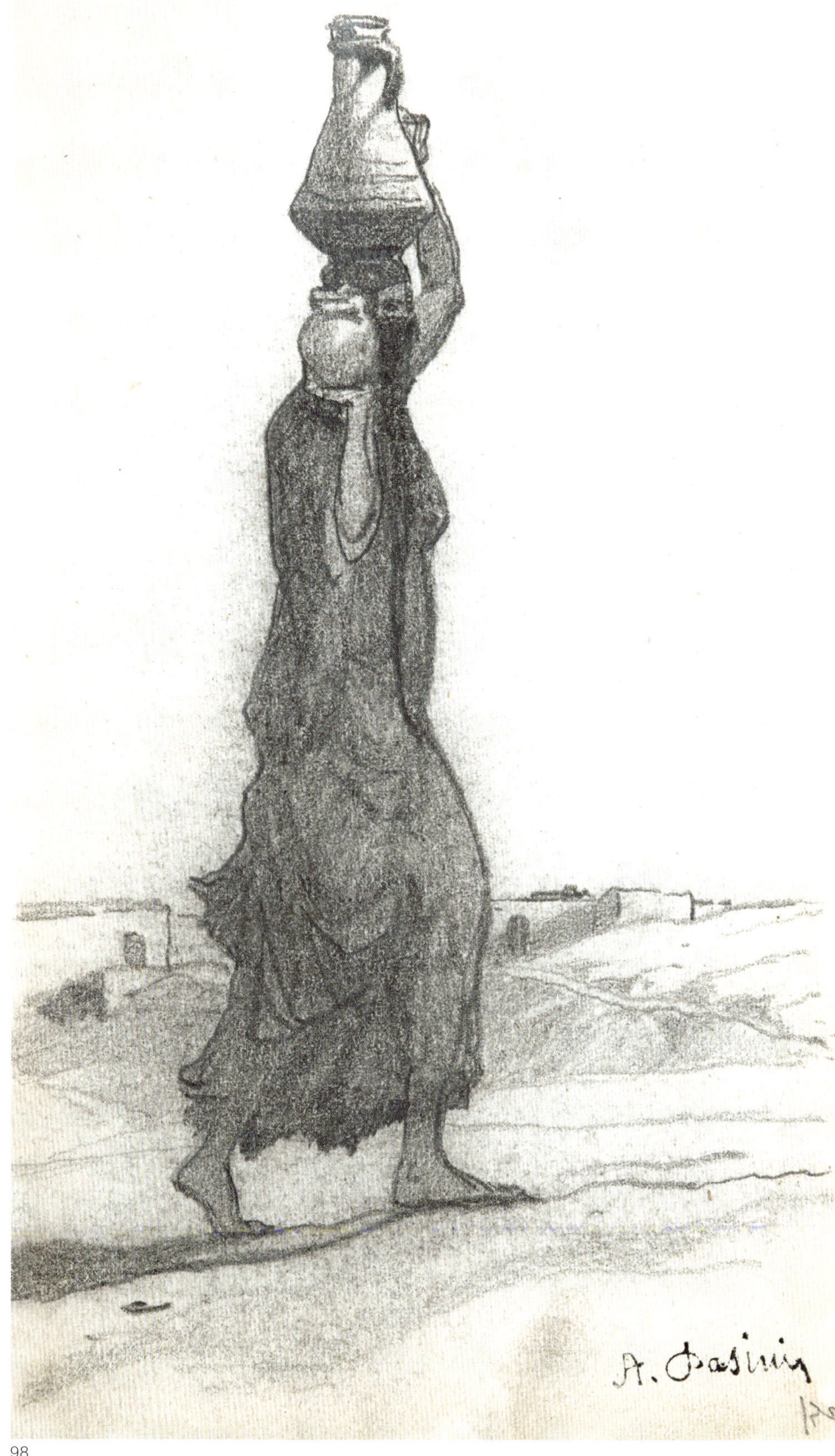

98

99
Pitcher

India, 16th century
Cast bronze, partially gilt on the zoomorphic finials
h. 34.8 cm, base Ø 9 cm
The Aron Collection, inv. n. A.257

Of globular shape, resting on a circular slightly splayed foot, incised with meanderings, the body with streaks reminiscent of the folds of a turban, rising to a tall hourglass-shaped neck decorated with concentric bands and a compressed ring in the centre, the tapering curved handle designed as the body of a dragon, its head holding the dome-shaped lid, the dragon motif repeated on the spout, modelled similarly to the body with several diagonal folds but in inverted order and terminating with a dragon head with open fangs to the let the water flow out.
This ewer shows several analogies with another ewer (cat. n. 122) in this exhibition, both sharing the zoomorphic decorative motifs and the design of the body and foot with meanderings, in one case engraved, pierced in the latter, but always deriving from the Indian water vessels called *lotas*.

Provenance: antique art market.
Bibliographical reference: find a similar example in Zebrowski, 1997, figs. 178 and 523, p. 144.

I.B.

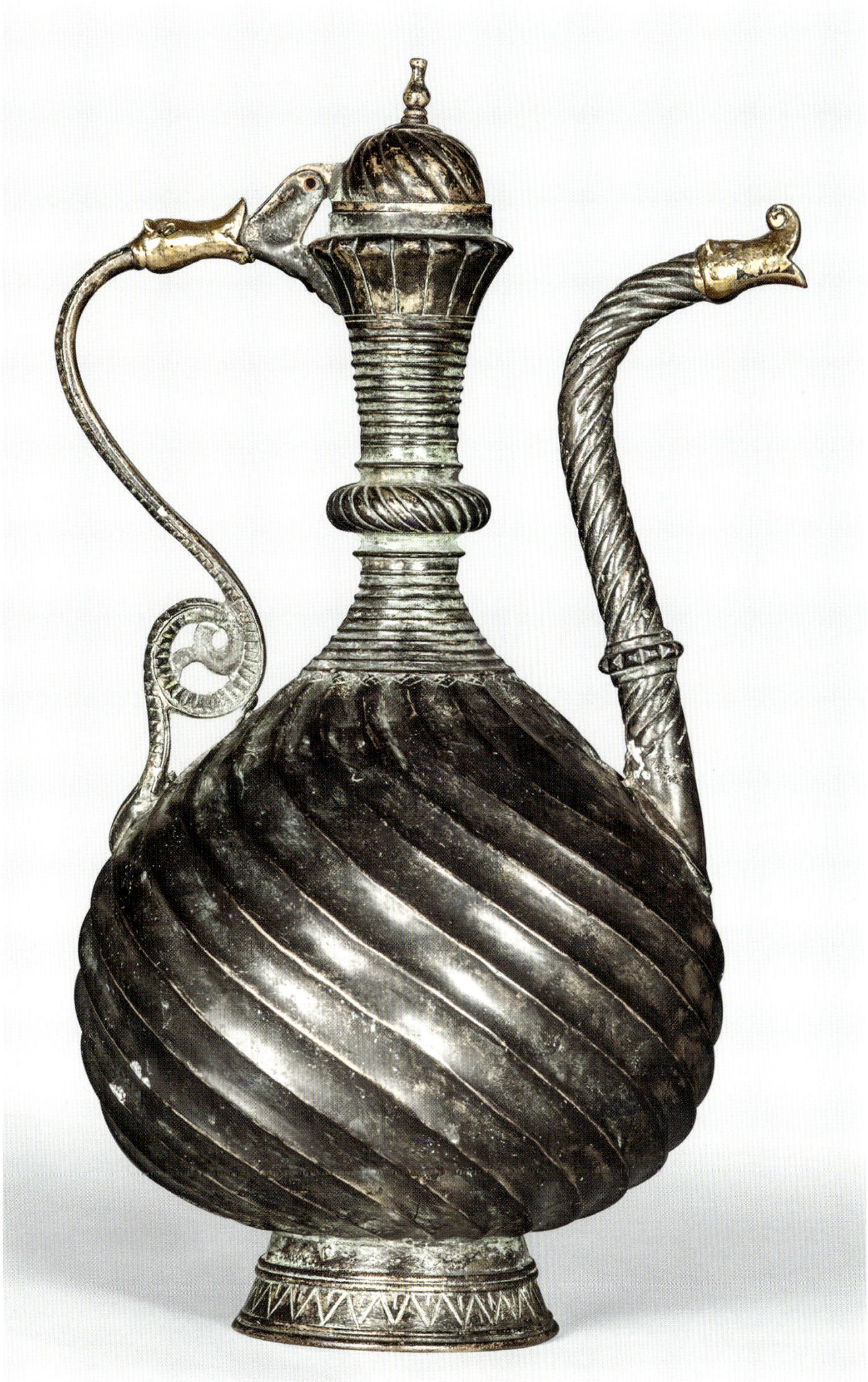

99

100 (1-7)
Seven fountain spouts

Syria, 15th-19th century
Bronze or brass
Private collection

100.1
Dolphin-shaped fountain spout

18 × 16 cm, Ø 3 cm
inv. ME-FO-1

Naturalistic and lively with its dolphin shape with dorsal fin, the tail and mouth open to let the outflow of the water, the body engraved with a dense fish-scale motif, the eyes almond-shaped, on the belly an infinite knot.

100.2
Snake-shaped fountain spout

25 × 19 cm, Ø 6 cm
inv. ME-FO-3

The body engraved with roundels reducing progressively towards the reptile's head, with an open mouth to let the outflow of the water.

100.3
Dragon-shaped fountain spout

17 × 16 cm, Ø 3.2 cm
inv. ME-FO-4

This object showcases all the main features of zoomorphic fountain spouts: such as double fin, twisted tail, open fangs and crest. The only two anomalies are the two parallel lines to suggest the teeth and the engraved eyes, rather than bulging out as usual.

100.4
Bird-shaped fountain spout

17 × 13 cm, Ø 2.5 cm
inv. ME-FO-5

Of unusual shape, with tubular body bent to form the head and tail of a stylised animal, possibly a bird or a stylised dragon. The head characterised by bulging eyes and open beak.

100.5
Bronze fountain spout

17 × 13 cm, Ø 2.5 cm
inv. ME-FO-16

Typical of its category, with S-shaped body, curly tail, elaborate dorsal and frontal fins, bulging eyes and open fangs.

100.6
A fountain spout with crescent moon

18 × 14 cm, Ø 3 cm
inv. ME-FO-21

The body made out of a cylindrical element combined with a ribbed wall tank and a flared spout, surmounted by a crescent moon, a typical Turkish symbol.

100.7
Dragon-shaped fountain spout

17 × 16 cm, Ø 3.2 cm
inv. ME-FO-25

Heavy bronze-cast example, with all the features typical of its category such as dorsal and frontal fins, three parallel lines as a collar, crest and sharp fangs open.

The dragon takes on a morphology, iconography and symbolism peculiar to the civilisations it is representing at that specific moment. In the Islamic lands, the motif of the dragon was inherited from the Chinese Far East, where it has a benevolent nature. It firstly reached during the time of the invasion of the Turkish Seljuqs in the 11th century; and then used more prominently during the period of the Mongol invasions and subsequent ruling dynasties in Iran in the 13th century. From Persia, the dragon motif spread further into all the Islamic lands, together with the lotus flower and the phoenix (*simurgh*) motifs, all designs that were very much present on Chinese silks, a lavish commodity always present on the commercial routes.
Since this moment, the dragon became a widespread, common element in the decorative vocabulary of Islam, often used on its own or more recurrently as a stylised handle to jars and ewers (cat. n. 99). Similar spouts would adorn the fountains of gardens and palaces. Located around the upper border, these fountain spouts would have incessantly let the water flow freely, not only to refresh visitors or the environment, but also to produce a relaxing celestial guttering in the background. Fountains and their accessories would have not only been placed in gardens, but also in strategic locations around the city like in front of mosques, to facilitate the believers with their daily ablution rites.

Provenance: antique art market.

I.B.

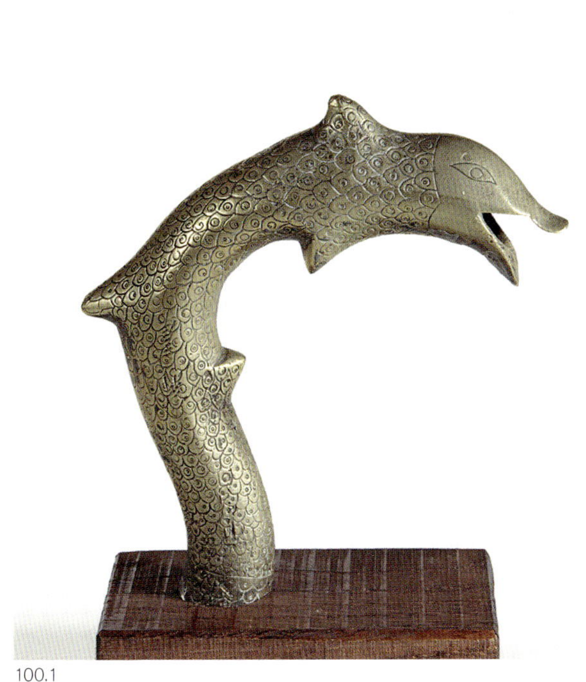
100.1

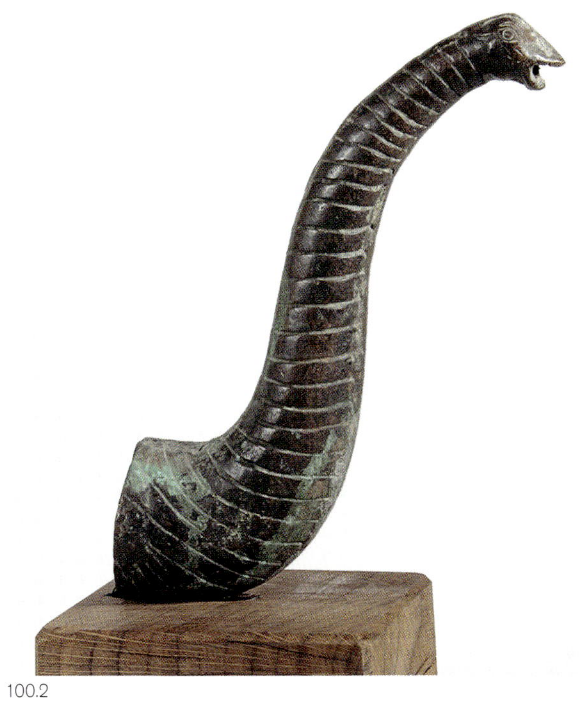
100.2

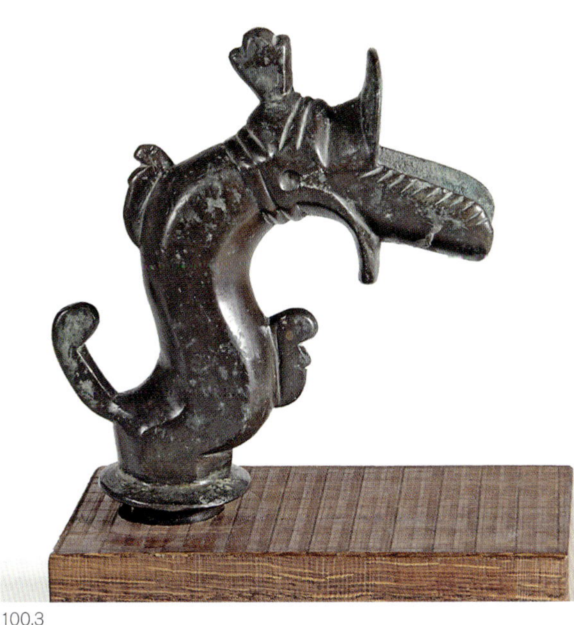
100.3

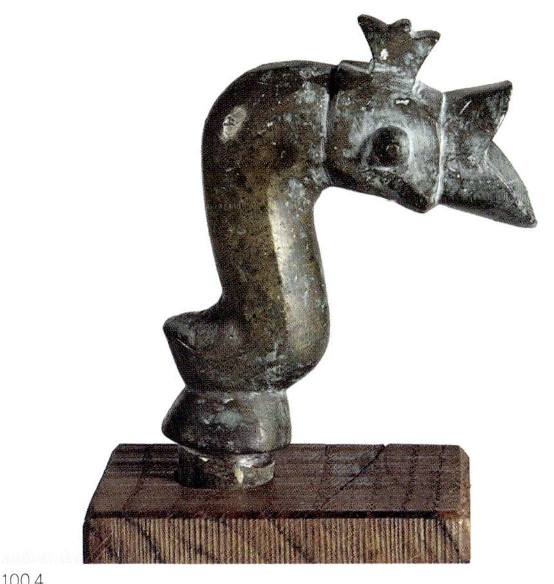
100.4

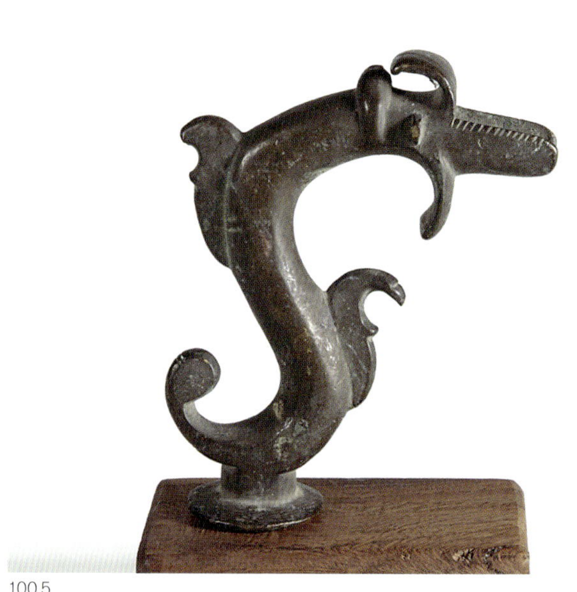
100.5

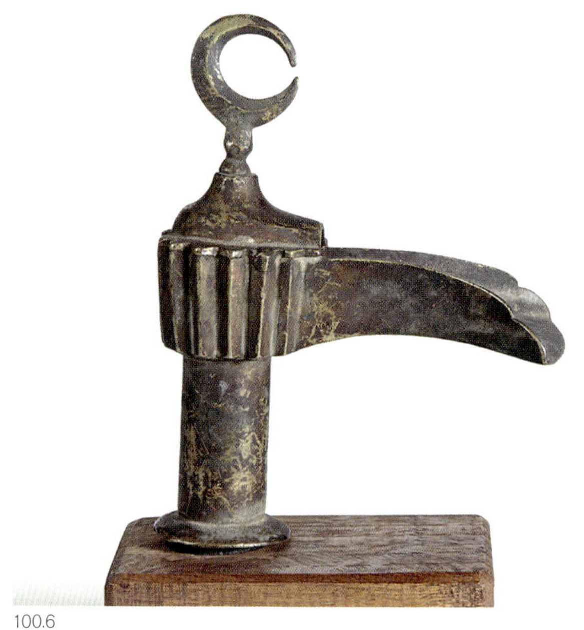
100.6

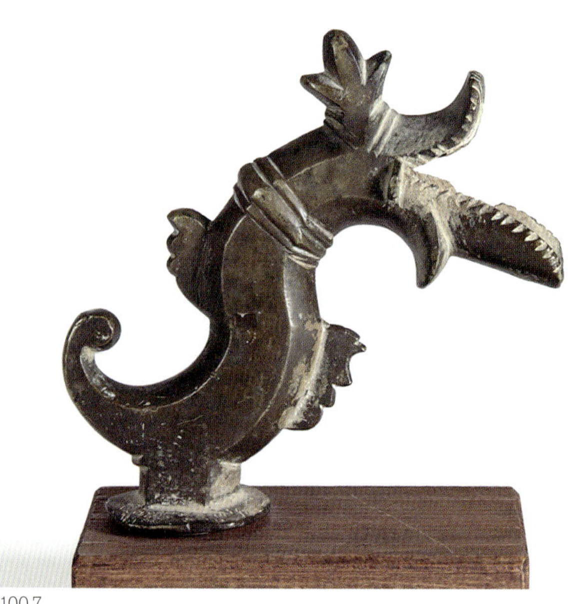
100.7

101
Four-legged animal

Spain, 11th century
Bronze, engraved
(modern base in wood)
h. 12.4 cm
Museo Nazionale del Bargello,
Gabinetto Fotografico delle Gallerie
degli Uffizi, inv. 326 C

The cast zoomorphic body with a hollow interior and a hole in the centre of the belly, two more holes on the head, possibly once accommodating a pair of horns, a fourth opening by the fangs suggesting its use as fountain spout, the body engraved with concentric circles by the saddle, highlighted by a Kufic epigraphic band, the area around the paws highlighted by a cusped cartouche surmounted by a circular medallion filled with vegetal motifs, the rear right paw damaged.

Inscription:

Perfect blessing

The race of this quadruped is still debated. The snout resembles a lion, but the paws do not look like felines' ones and the holes near the ears suggest a missing platform. Contadini compares this quadruped with a deer now part of the Cordoba Archaeological Museum collection (inv. n. 500 in Dodds, 1992, cat. n. 10, pp. 210-211); with another deer now at the National Archaeological Museum of Madrid (inv. n. 51.856); and lastly, with a lion now part of the Louvre collection in Paris (inv. 7883), all examples attributed to the Andalusian production of 10th-11th century (Contadini in *Eredità dell'Islam*, 1993, pp. 124-125).
The four animals share the same rendering of circular engravings, reminiscent of some textiles of the time, and further analogies in their shapes, styles and overall decorative programme, typical of Umayyad Spanish works such as the Pisa griffin, or the Cagliari ewer (see cat. n. 64). As far as the function is concerned, it is worth noting that Ibn Bashkuwal, a scholar living in 12th-century Cordoba, mentions that in the palaces of the city water used to outflow from the mouth of several animals, made of stone, marble and metal (Torres Balbas, 1987, p. 747).

Bibliography: Migeon, 1907, I, fig. 186, p. 374; Gomez Moreno, 1951, fig. 397d; Scerrato 1966, fig. 30, *Eredità dell'Islam*, 1993, cat. n. 41, pp. 124-125, *Islam e Firenze*, 2018, cat. n. 215, p. 319. For a similar example, please also check the collection of the Museum of Islamic Art in Doha (inv. n. MW.7.1997) in Watson, 2008, p.112.

I.B.

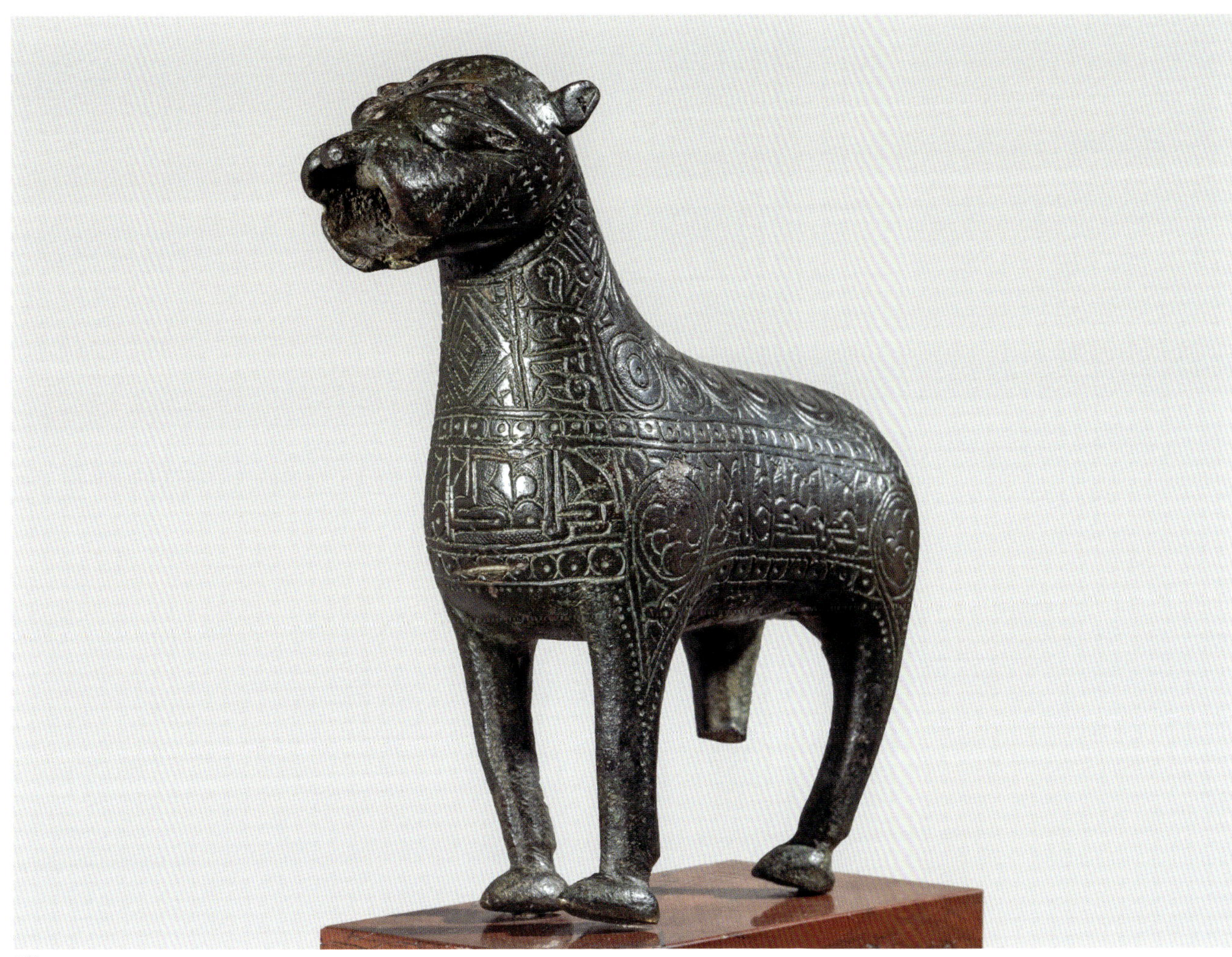

101

Gardens

The garden intended as a direct representation of Paradise deeply influenced Islamic aesthetics. Indeed, the Qur'an refers to Paradise as lush green gardens, where the believers are clad with beautiful garments and adorned with precious jewellery; they rest on luxurious green cloths – this being the quintessential colour of Islam. Young and beautiful servants greet them upon their arrival and never leave their sides. These paradisiacal gardens are eternally blossoming and offer pleasant shade (13:35); and their trees bear ripe and juicy fruits on the lower branches, to make it easier to pick them (69:21-23). The Qur'an even mentions the specific type of trees the believers can find there like palms and pomegranate (55:68), lotus flowers and lush acacia trees (56:28-29). In those immense gardens (3:133), surrounded by fortified walls with several entrances (38:49-50; 57:13), the believers can find fresh water fountains (55:46-50), streams, (2:25; 3:15,136,195,198) and a multitude of milk, wine and honey rivers (47:15). The Holy Book also describes the rooms (*ghurufat*) where the believers safely dwell (34:37), decorated with comfortable cushions and beautiful carpets – a truly mesmerising encampment where the *huris* live in their tents (55:72).

These images permeate every form of art in Islam, from funerary architecture to the real gardens of royal palatial complexes, not to mention the rich natural symbolism of carpets. It is undeniable that the Quranic Paradise yields a model, but one should refrain from assuming that all references in Islam hark back to this. Every architectural structure and artistic expression in the Islamic lands is blooming from a more complex social history, from a mixture between its daily fruition and the cultural habits of the time of its formation – and not all structures reached the heights of Paradise either. As an example, the cruciform scheme present in most Islamic gardens - adopted in the decorative pattern and design of several carpets – was inspired by Pre-Islamic Persian parks, which were considered the most prestigious example of imperial architecture by the first caliphs. It is not a coincidence thus that the name of this scheme, *chaharbagh* – literally the quadripartite garden – comes from Persian.

This scheme proved to be incredibly successful in practice. All of its elements came from rigid geometric structures: the quadripartite plan; the arms of the cross filled by large pathways and canals; the centre characterised by a fountain or a raised platform with a pavilion (another term borrowed from Persian, *kushk*, which then entered the lexicon of Western garden); the surrounding fortified walls with monumental doors and turrets. And yet, all of these strictly geometric elements evoked a long-lasting vision of the delights of Paradise.

102
Chaharbagh garden rug

Northwest Persia, early 18th century
236 × 218 cm
Cotton warp, wool and cotton weft, asymmetric knot
Moshe Tabibnia collection, inv. n. 154021

The following entry also refers to cat. n. 2
Chaharbagh garden carpet
Northwest Persia, 17th century
Zaleski collection, Courtesy Galleria Moshe Tabibnia, inv. n. 156809
see page 38

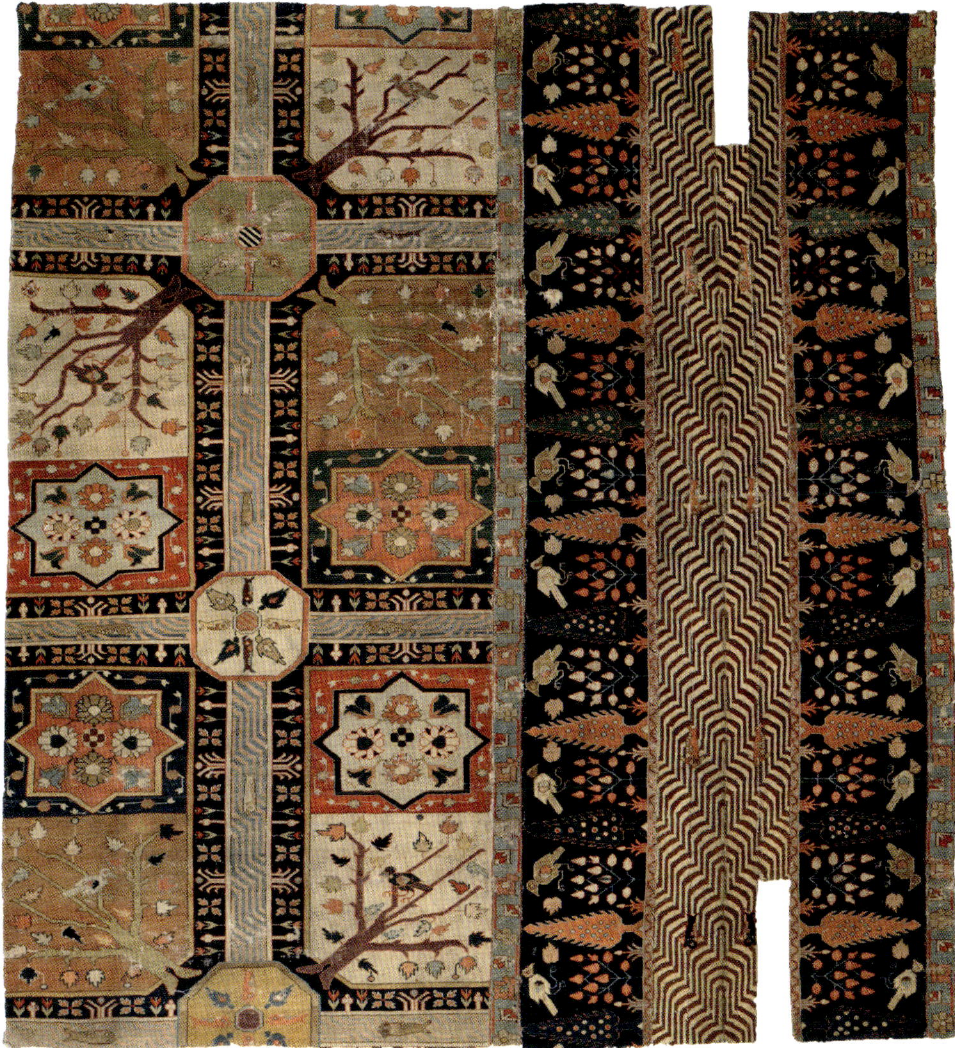

102

Large carpet fragments (the dimensions of one single carpet can reach even 10 meters). The quadripartite garden can also be read as a sheer allegory of Paradise, as it is described in the Qur'an:

... herein there are rivers of unaltered water, and rivers of milk the taste of which never changes, and rivers of wine delicious to those who drink, and rivers of purified honey, and they will enjoy every [kinds of] fruits and forgiveness from their Lord (Surah Muhammad, 47:15).

But for he who has feared the position of his Lord are two gardens (Surah al-Rahman, 55:46).
And below them there will be two [other] gardens (Surah al-Rahman, 55:62).

In the above passages, the Qur'an speaks of four rivers (water, milk, honey and wine) and of four lush and blossoming gardens.
These carpets, together with the very structure of some Islamic gardens (first among all the Mughal Indian ones), could be interpreted as a replica and a "domestication" of the Paradise gardens.
In the Qur'an, the terms used to refer to these gardens are either *chahar bagh* or *jannat al-Janna*, which in its singular form indeed means paradise. The connection between Paradise and gardens doesn't end here though. The Old Persian term *pairidaeza* (fenced garden, royal hunting reserve) entered with time into several Western languages with the meaning of Paradise (the garden of Eden). Thus, the two words, Paradise and garden, are almost interchangeable in certain traditions.
The water element, here portrayed with little stylised waves, serves a vivifying function in the Qur'an; an element thus that cannot miss in the gardens of Paradise.

... and the water that Allah has sent down from heaven, giving life thereby to the lifeless earth [...] between the heaven and the earth there are signs [of his Mercy] for those with intellect (Surah al-Baqarah, 2:164).

By virtue of the artistic and religious symbolism just described, examples of chahar bagh carpets fit well in both the religious and the garden-oriented sections of this catalogue.

Bibliography: 156809 in Burns, 2002, pp. 144-145. For a better preserved example, refer to *Civiltà islamica*, 2015, cat. 141, pp. 168-169.

I.B.

103
Yahya Barmaki Summoning His Children

Mogul Empire (Lahore?), ca. 1585-1595
Opaque watercolor on paper
Folio: 39.8 × 27.7 cm
Miniature: (recto) 24.7 × 14.3 cm; (verso) 19.6 × 10.3 cm
Private collection, Genoa

This illustration comes from the *Akhbar-i Barmakiyan* (History of the Barmakids), the Persian translation of an Arabic text of the 10th-11th century telling the story of a family of Central Asian officials who played an instrumental role during the Abbasid caliphate in the 8th century. This miniature was produced at the Emperor Akbar's court (r. 1556-1605), possibly in Lahore. The artist is likely to be a member of Basawan's workshop, an Indian miniature painter interested in and inspired by European techniques and styles, as his use of chiaroscuro and the three-dimensional rendering of draperies testify. In 803, the Barmakids were imprisoned by the Abbasid caliph Harun al-Rashid, who started fearing their increasing power. Whilst Yahya is informing his sons of the looming disgrace, a guardian speaks to the stable boy looking after the horses. The characters in the composition wear long tunics, rounded turbans and pointy beards in the typical Arab fashion. The setting instead is clearly in 16th century Northern India, as the red sandstone buildings with stucco coatings, the flower carpet and the accessories testify. Among those objects, an ewer (aftaba) and a basin for ablutions (*lagan, chilanchi*), possibly made of brass, are of particular interest. The fountain with the ducks, conventionally associated with Persian miniatures, is rendered here in a much more naturalistic way. The verso shows verses from *Yusuf va Zulaykha* by Abd al-Rahman Jami, which leads to believe that the original context of this miniature must have been different.

Bibliography: other folios of the same manuscript seem to have belonged to John Montagu, Earl of Sandwich (1718-92), British Postmaster General, First Lord of the Admiralty, and Secretary of State for the Northern Department in England. At least two of these were part of the Warren Hastings Album (today known as Philipps MS.14170). Approximately twenty other examples have been offered at auctions at Sotheby's, Christie's and other major auction houses since 1968. Some are still available on the market this very day. Among the published examples, please note Welch and Welch 1982, cat. n. 53; Canby 1998, cat. n. 87-88.

L.P.

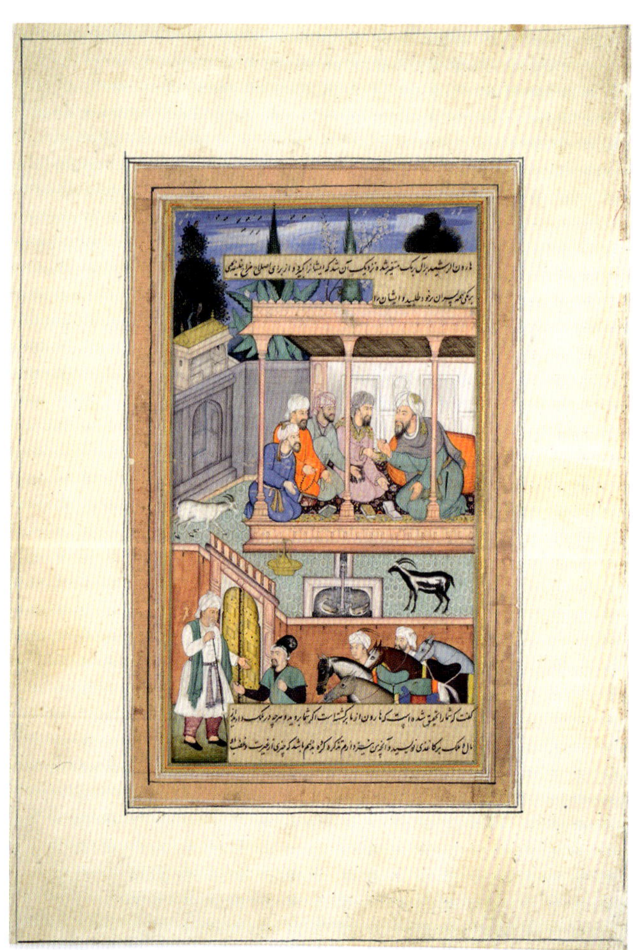

103

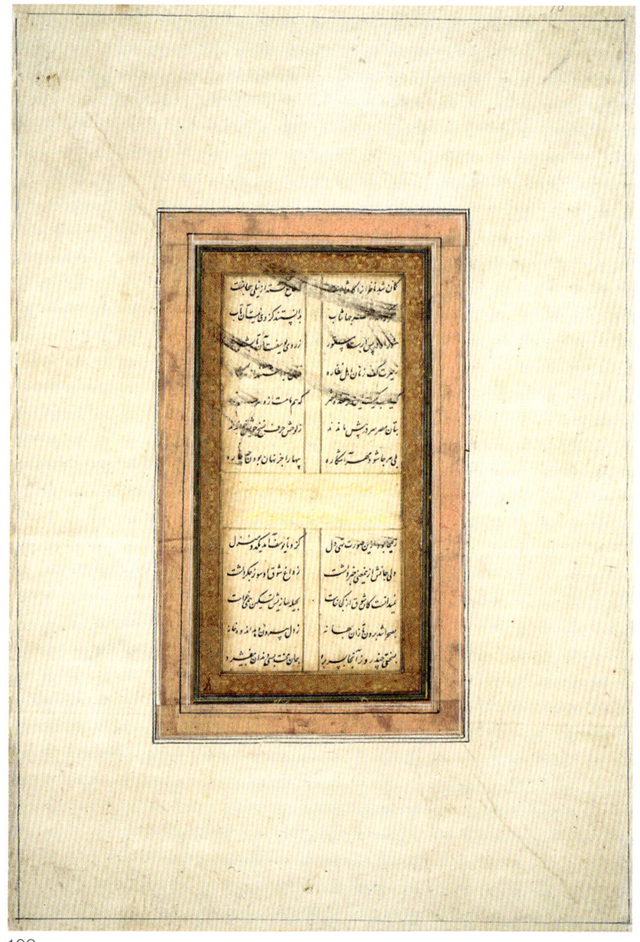

103

104
Miniature

India, ca. 1680
Opaque watercolor and gold on paper
30 × 21cm
Courtesy of the L.A. Mayer Museum for Islamic Art, Jerusalem, Israel, inv. n. MS 136-70

The painting depicting young female bathers in the *zenana*, relaxing in a pool filled with water and lotus flowers, two ladies on the edge of the pool, one smoking a *huqqa* (water pipe).
In Mughal India, the *zenana* (Persian: of the women) was a specific palace area reserved to the women. At the Mughal court, these accommodations were often very lavish, with their own courtyards, lakes, fountains and gardens.

Bibliography: Misra 1967; Hambly 1998, pp. 429–467.

A.V.

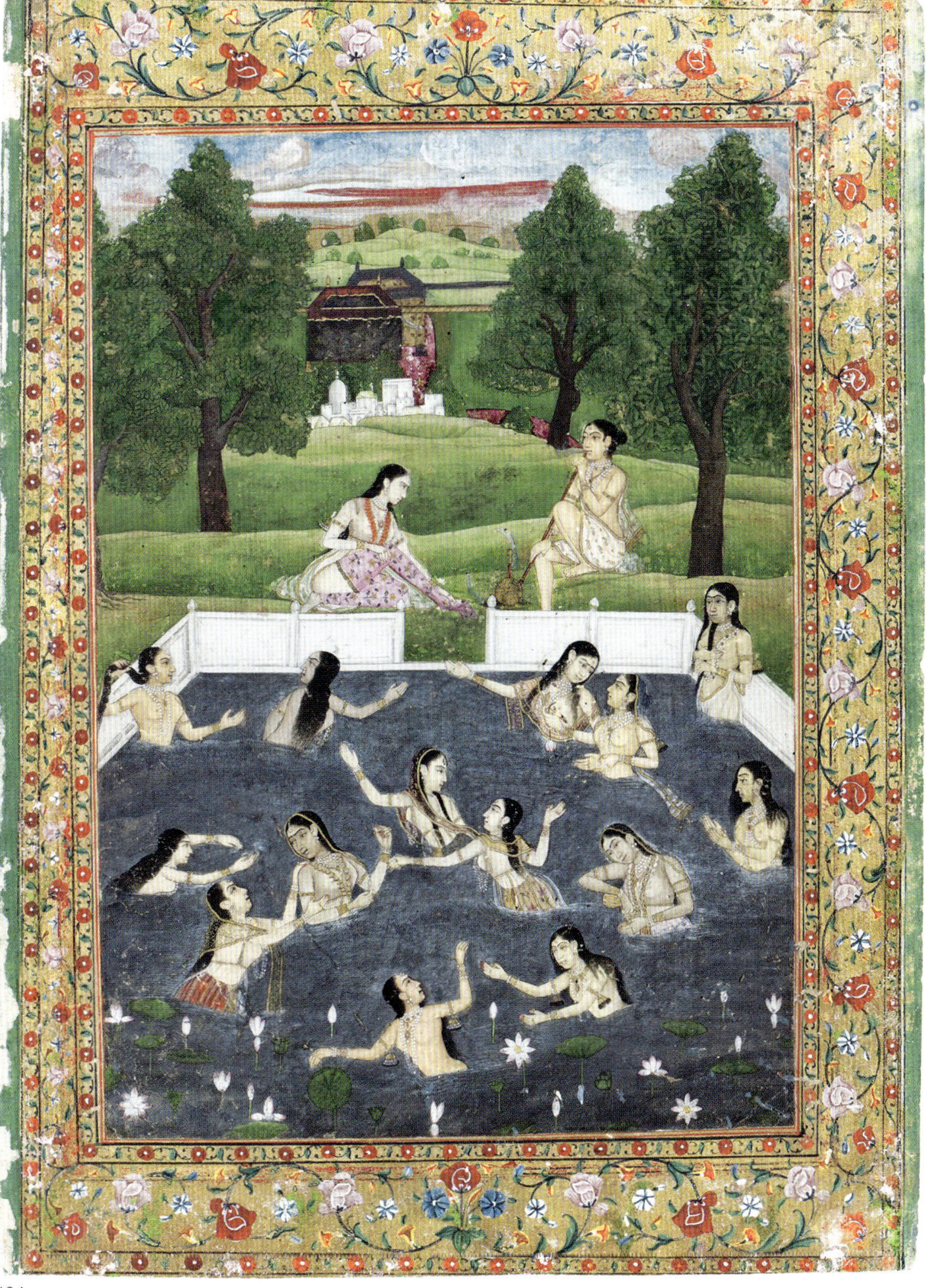

104

105
Velvet decorated with carnations

Turkey, Bursa, late 16th-17th century
Voided velvet decorated with metal embroidery
162 × 82 cm
Private collection, Brussels

A rectangular red madder velvet fragment embroidered with metal thread (*catma*), decorated with wide-open carnations arranged in a staggered pyramidal order, the stem with symmetrical, lanceolate leaves and the flowers interspersed with vegetal elements resembling pine cones.
Textiles like this are among the most characteristic productions in the Ottoman world from mid-16th to mid-17th century. They were often used as tapestries, curtains or antimacassars.
Carnations (*karanfil*) were among the most beloved flowers by the Ottomans and around the end of the 16th century, their representations started showing a fan-like shape (*yelpazeli*). Crimson red is the most common colour used for these textiles' background, but variations in green, blue, ivory and yellow also exist.

Provenance: antique art market.
Bibliographical references: Koechlin 1956, cat. n. 73; *The Age* 1987-1988, cat. n. 155, p. 222; Atasoy et al. 2001, cat. n. 342-348, pp. 316-317; *Jardin encantado* 2001, pp.144-145, n. 57; *Civiltà Islamica* 2010, cat. n. 114, pp. 146-147.

I.B.

105

106
Marble slab, part of a fountain

Northern India, 17th-18th century
Marble
h. 141 cm, w. 62 cm
Benaki Museum, Athens,
inv. n. GE 10805

Of rectangular shape, the marble carved in the typical *chevron* pattern with alternating small clovers, the upper and lower edges carved with scrolling vegetal tendrils. Similar panels were mostly located in the gardens of royal palaces. They were tilted upward and placed near fountains or crossways between one tank and the other to enliven the water's movement and simulate a waterfall.
Some panels are pierced with niches and when a candle was lit behind them, a mesmerising play of light would ornate the gardens at dusk.

Bibliography: unpublished. For a similar example, please see *Civiltà islamica* 2010, cat. n. 133.

I.B.

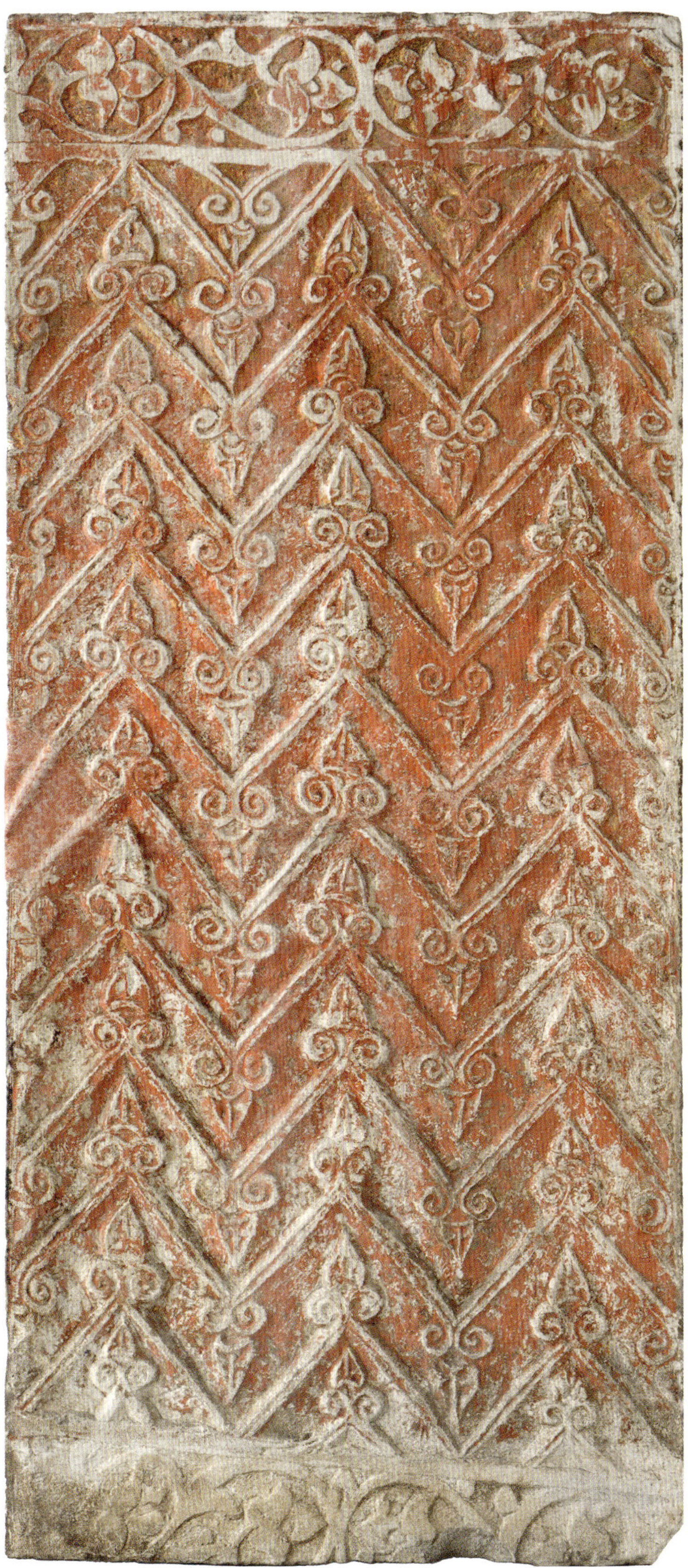

106

107

Cloth, decorated with tulips and pomegranates

Turkey, Bursa, 17th century
Voided velvet decorated with metal embroidery
107 × 63 cm
Benaki Museum, Athens, inv. n. 3801

Rectangular cushion cover (*yastik yuzu*), decorated with metal thread (*catma*) with floral patterns, the upper and lower edges ornate with bands of six petals filled with stylised flowers, the central panel decorated with a large rosette flanked by four tulips, two carnations and a prunus blossom, in the four corners flowers set in diagonals, two pomegranates and leaves on the short sides.
Similar velvets would have been woven in pairs. Their sizes, colours and decorative elements would often be limited and standardised. Nevertheless, it is rather rare to come by an exact matching pair. Notwithstanding the limited range of decorative motifs and materials the court would commission, Turkish craftsmen always managed to imbue their works with creativity and surprising variety.

Bibliography: unpublished. For analogous examples, see Atasoy et al. 2001, cat. n. 84, p. 132 and pp. 320-321; the Metropolitan Museum of Art collection, New York, inv. n. 30.95.66, and the Victoria and Albert Museum collection, inv. n. 101-1878.

Ottoman brocade fabrics

Flowers were among the primary decorative elements *en vogue* in the Ottoman Empire. Augier Ghislain de Busbecq, a naturalist and Ferdinand I's ambassador at the time of Suleiman I, describes in his *Turkish Letters* the multitude of hyacinths and narcissi, typical of those lands. He was also among the first travellers who brought tulips, lilac and horse chestnut back to Europe. From the second half of 16th century, tulips, hyacinths, roses and carnations soon became quintessential stylistic features present in every Ottoman decorative expression.
Bursa was elected first capital of the Ottoman Empire (1326 - 65) but its reputation as the pivotal centre for the international trade of textiles and silk lingered way longer. A primary textile centre, Bursa started developing its own industry and autonomous silk production already in the second half of 16th century, when it became unfeasible to supply the increasing demand for silk only with Far Eastern exemplars. A few documents, mostly purchase orders, testify that Bursa carried on supplying brocade and velvet panels to the court, especially for the upholstery, even when the Sultan moved to Istanbul. Documentary sources also certify that the court exercised a strict quality control over Bursa production, guaranteeing the best quality to each textile produced (*The Age* 1987-88, pp. 177-182 and Guru 1988, pp. 39-41). These fabrics became true status symbols at the Ottoman court, both in fashion and upholstery; they mingled the latest artistic tendencies and often ended up being exchanged and exported as diplomatic gifts and regalia.
Silk brocades are also mentioned in the Qur'an when speaking of the souls in Paradise:

... *They will rest on beds with silk brocade linings* (Qur'an 55:54).

The Persians and the Italians were among the best clients of Bursa's textile production. The Ottoman style was so sought-after in Italy that often Venetian and Florentine weavers replicated those silks and brocades with intertwining tendrils, wide-open carnations, tulips and *saz* leaves. In return, Turkish weavers started incorporating in their productions typically Venetians decorative elements, such as the crown.

I.B.

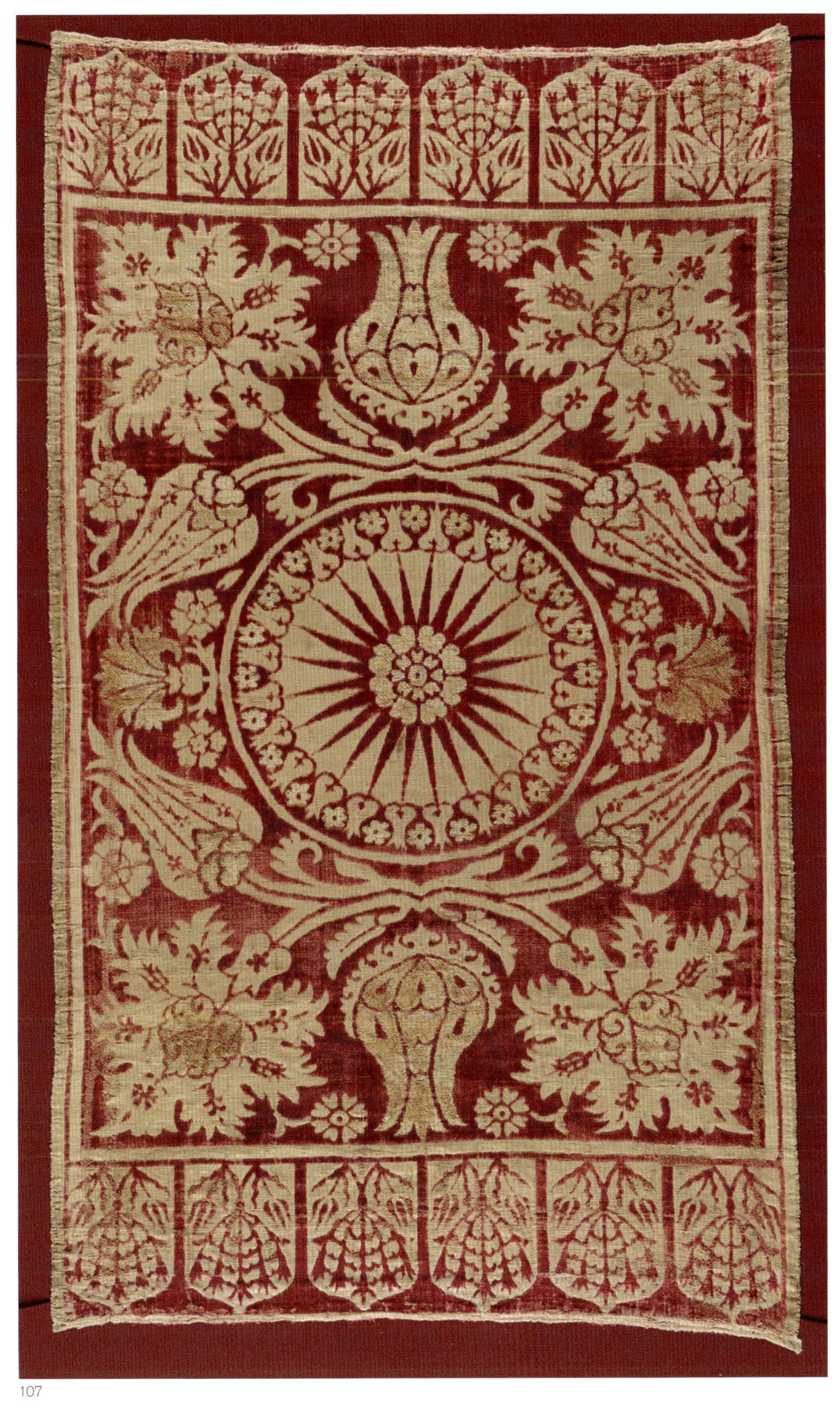

107

108
Garden rug

Southeast Caucasus, first half 19th century
Wool warp and weft, wool symmetric knot
298 × 138 cm
Moshe Tabibnia collection,
inv. n. 165776

The Central Asian origins of this carpet are evident in its rustic and pointed rendering of the garden, already seen in cat. nn. 2 and 102.
The decoration developing around a central axis with four fountains dividing the space in four *chaharbagh*, each of which is further divided in four gardens characterised by white flowers and little streams in herringbone pattern, the borders with stylised blossoming trees, the bold colours emphasising the swarming effect of the natural landscape.

Bibliography: Grote 1922, vol. II, pl. 38.

I.B.

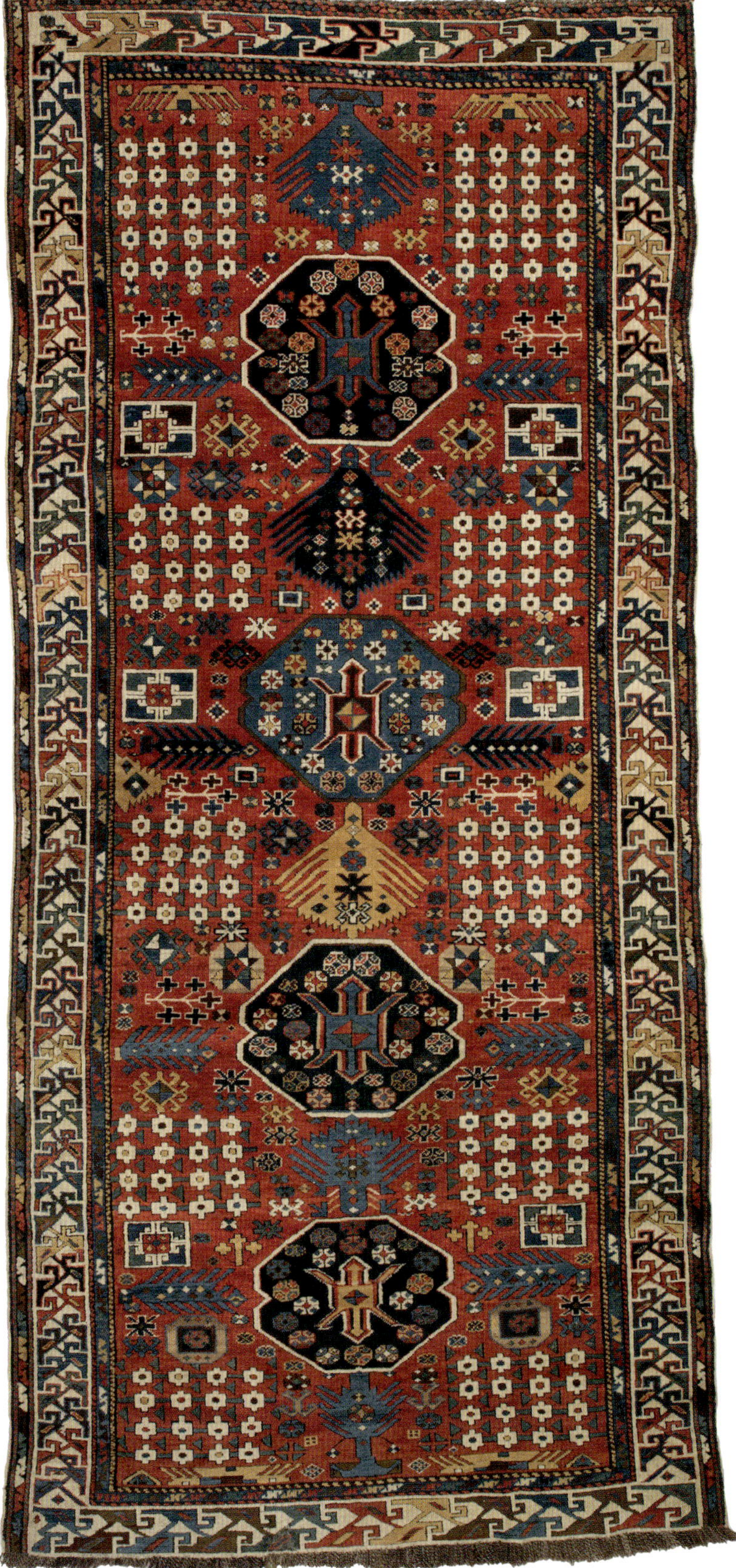

108

109
Ottoman silk cloth with floral decoration

Turkey, probably Istanbul, late 16th century
Silk brocade
52 × 58 cm
Benaki Museum, Athens, inv. n. 3901

Semi-square textile on madder red ground, embroidered with gilt metal thread, with repeating floral pattern with wide-open carnations on offset vertical rows, the border with tulip heads interspersed with arched medallions with central rosettes and floral bulbs.
The basic scheme sees the use of wide-open carnations in the centre with small variations in terms of numbers of petals, form and species of the other flowers and leaves in the composition. This is a second variation on the already-mentioned theme of cat. n. 105. Comparing both artworks, one can easily recognise similarities in the rendering of the carnations, the number of petals is also the same, but the elements in the background and frame vary. In cat. n. 105, the decoration looks cleaner with the pair of *saz* leaves and the pine cone motifs. In this example, the carnations are interspersed with arched medallions outlined by interlocking vegetal tendrils and floral trellis, a pattern which was sought-after and appreciated not only in Turkey but also in Italy. For an in-depth discussion on Ottoman cloths, see appendix of cat. n. 107.

Bibliography: unpublished. For similar examples, see Atasoy et al. 2001, pp. 316-317.

I.B.

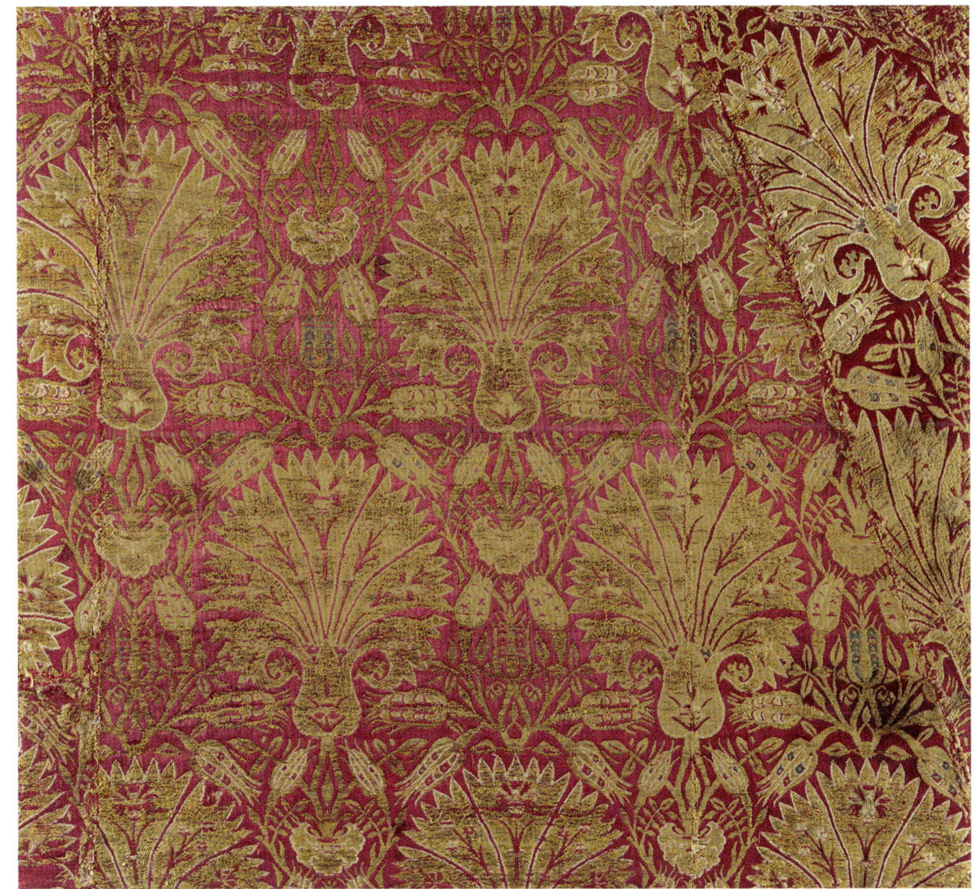
109

110-111
Pair of large pitchers

Iran-Afghanistan (Khorasan),
Ghaznavid period, 12th century
Copper alloy, cast and pounded, engraved and silver damascene
43 × 20 cm (inv. n. 8558);
43 × 19 cm (inv. n. 8859)
Weight: 2,294 g. (inv. n. 8558);
2,996 g (inv. n. 8559)
Museo d'Arte Orientale - MUCIV,
inv. n. 8558-8559

Of straight cylindrical shape, with a conical bottom, rising to a cylindrical neck, with flat shoulders, beak-shaped spout, and squared petal-shaped handle, the body modelled with both casting and hammering techniques, both jugs engraved and silver-inlaid but only one retaining the inlay work, the same decoration consisting of Arabic good-wishing and auspicious inscriptions within cartouches and polylobed and circular medallions filled with floral and vegetal motifs, the decorative patterns against a ring-punched or hatched ground distributed in a well-measured arrangement, most precisely on the spout, neck, shoulder and front body, leaving free of decoration a large portion of the exterior surface.

These two jugs are attributed to the metalware production of the Eastern area of the Iranian plateau during 12th century and it is likely to believe that they would have been produced in the context of the same atelier. In terms of form, these jugs should be considered a conjunction ring between certain spoutless ewers with similar cylindrical body and neck excavated in Nishapur (Iran) and in Maimana (Afghanistan), and the typical Khorasani ewers (North-Eastern Iran and part of Afghanistan) dating to the late 12th to early 13th century (Di Flumeri 2005, p. 232), which are characterised by a polylobed cylindrical body resting on a flared foot and with a beak-shaped spout, entirely clad in engraved, hammered and silver-inlaid decorations (Aga-Oğlu 1943, pp. 92-98; Scerrato 1966, pls. 24-26; Allan 1976; Allan 1982, pp. 41-42; Melikian-Chirvani 1982; Baer 1983; pp. 83-102).

Nevertheless, compared to the examples with simple cylindrical bodies (see Scerrato 1974, pp.198-199; Laviola 2016, pp.71-81), the two MAO jugs could possibly be linked to another category of refined production, an example of which is preserved at the Kandahar National Museum (Afghanistan), (Scerrato 1959b, figs. 14, 15; Scerrato n *L'Afghanistan* 1961, n. 157).

F.M.A.

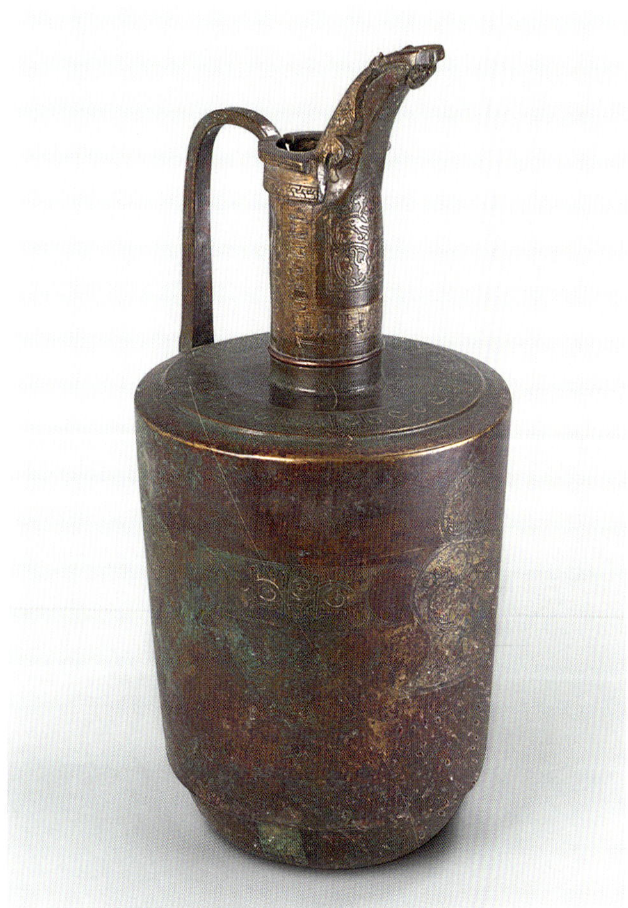

110

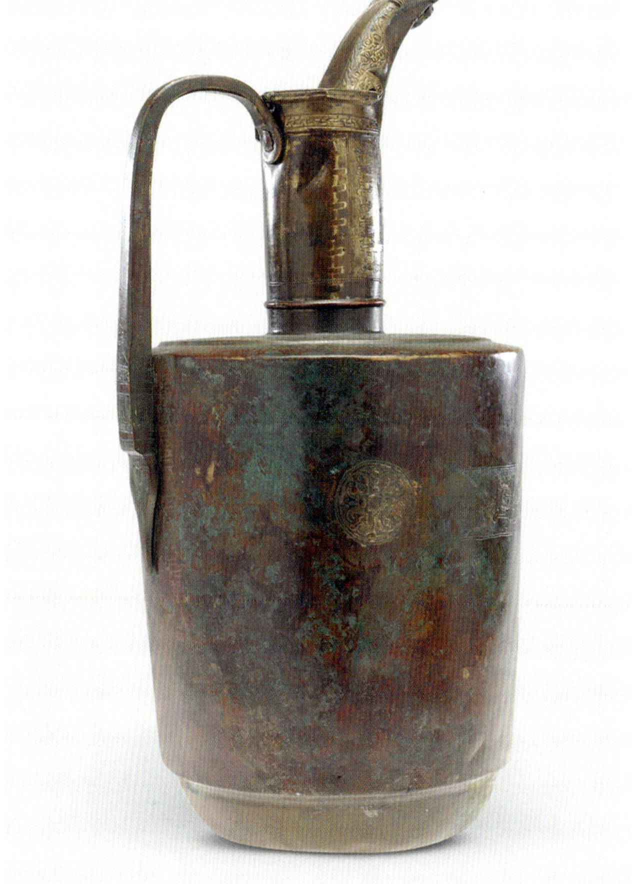

111

112
Small jug

Afghanistan, Ghaznavid period,
11th-12th century
Earthenware with engraved decoration
h. 17.5 cm, max w. 13 cm,
rim Ø 8.2 cm
Museo d'Arte Orientale - MUCIV,
inv. n. 7866

Of traditional shape, the body with double fairing, resting on a small labrum-shaped foot, rising to a slightly flared wide neck, with narrowing shoulders and curved handle on the side, the earthenware body covered in opaque white slip, the decoration mostly concentrated on the body and consisting of vegetal motifs in diagonal ribs, achieved through adding light pressure on the still humid earthenware, interspersed with X-shaped graphemes, horizontal mouldings and parallel strokes to the mouth, a decorative band with oval motifs interspersed with dense dotted pattern to the shoulder, enriched with circles filled with green glaze. The archaeological excavations in the city of Ghazni, conducted by the Italian Archaeological Mission in Afghanistan (1956-66), brought back to light numerous water ceramic vessels, which with little variants represent the most common types in the Islamic world. Ewers similar to our would have been produced in a variety of territories like Iran, Central Asia, Syria and Egypt between 9th-13th century. Both their shape and decorative techniques are indebted to the metalware tradition.

G.M.

113
Small jug

Afghanistan, Ghaznavid period,
11th-12th century
Earthenware with engraved and applied decoration
h. 12 cm, max w. 14.5 cm,
neck Ø 8.2 cm
Museo d'Arte Orientale - MUCIV,
inv. n. 8202

Of compressed globular shape, resting on a tall conical foot, rising to a large tall neck, with a vertical handle on the side, the buckskin-coloured earthenware with numerous inclusions and small elongated holes on the outer surface, the neck's base decorated with a wavy band filled with a large grapheme against horizontally hatched and milled lines, framed within two couples of parallel lines, on the body two rectangular sections interspersed with three medallions with moulded clovers applied with slip.
This ewer was purchased by the Italian Archaeological Mission in Afghanistan in Ghazni. Sadly, only the body is intact.

G.M.

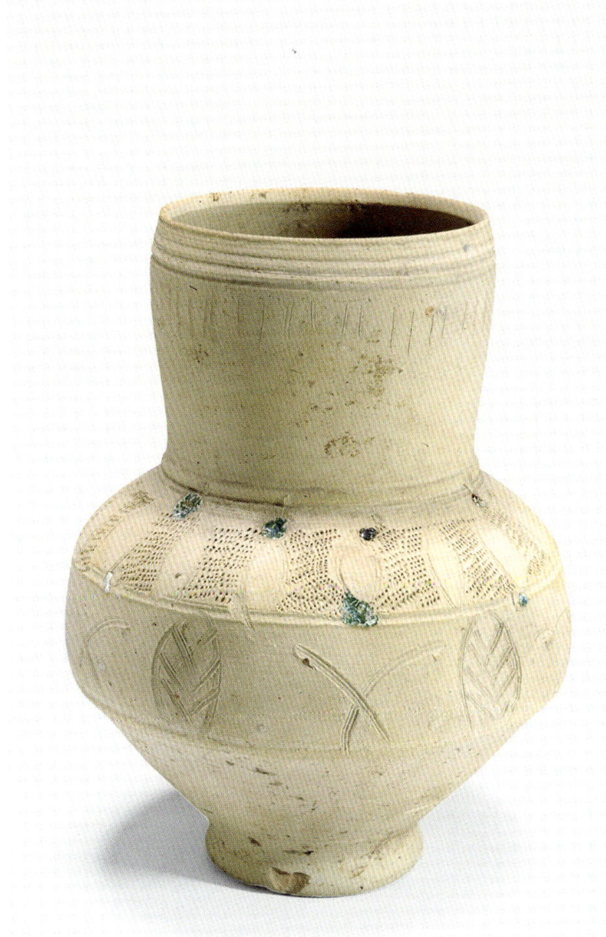

112

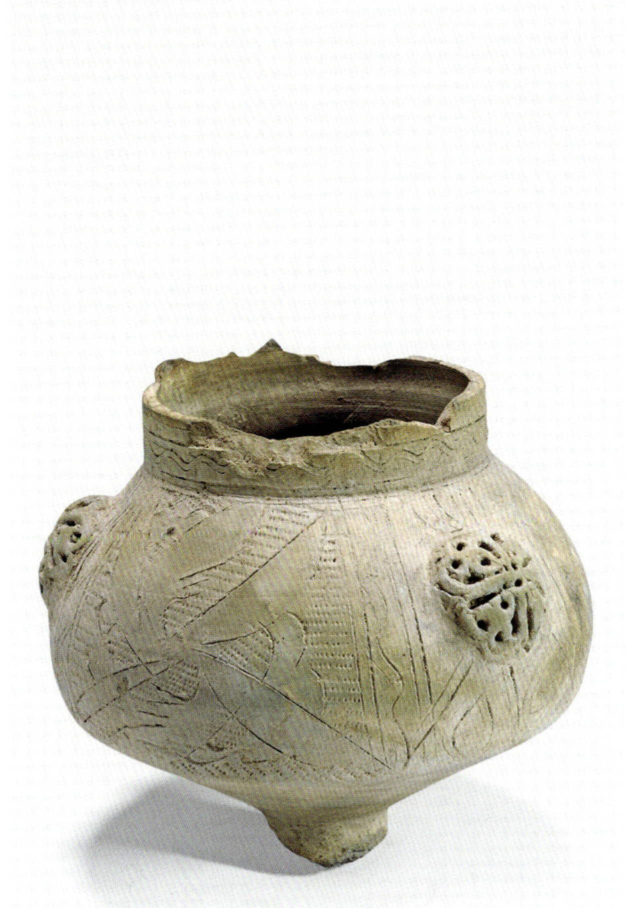

113

114

Water basin

Ghaznavid art, 11th-12th century
Sculpted marble decorated with bas-reliefs
70 × 74 × 15 cm
Museo d'Arte Orientale - MUCIV, inv. n. 8429

Shaped as an eight-lobed rosette, set within an octagon with a narrow band to the border, surrounded by a wide, plain and raised frame, the lobed petals contoured by an incised decorative band following their shape, the bottom of the basin engraved with an eight-pointed star, made of interlocking ropes surrounding the drain hole, in the corners between the outer frame and the octagon figural and vegetal decorations in relief, the other pair set in the diagonally opposed corner, comprising two couples of swans or ducks with interlocking necks; two with vegetal motifs such as palmettes and vine sprays emerging from fleur-de-lis; the basin sides, once set within a stand and barely touched.
This artwork is part of the rich series of marble basins, either in full or fragmented, which were bought by the Italian Archaeological Mission during their excavations and researches in Ghazni, in Afghanistan (1956-66; on their work and proceedings see Bombaci 1959, 1966, Scerrato 1959a). During the archaeological excavations on site, few finds were unearthed and several artefacts were found as spolia being reutilised in more modern structures. In the famous Ghaznavid palace, possibly founded already before the reign of Mas'ud III (to whom the construction of the palace is normally attributed), several fragments of basins were found and in the so-called *Lustre House* a full basin was brought back to light.
In the Linden Museum in Stuttgart, the visitors can admire another basin attributed to the same Ghazni series, possibly worked by the same atelier as ours (Kalter 1987, pp. 10, 65, fig. 3). The high number of Ghazni basins and tanks known and sharing similarities is rather significant. One could speculate they were in use in several different palatial complexes in the low land of the Dasht al-Manara. It is likely that they were primarily located in the gardens, such as the famous *Naw Bagh*, the new garden, within which Mahmud Ghazni, the greatest ruler of this dynasty, commissioned to build the *Turquoise Palace*.
According to the accounts of the 11th-century author al-'Utbi, this marvellous garden used to be vast: with an extension of a square mile, the garden was crossed by several water streams powered by the Ghazni river, whose water were channelled through covered canals. Bayhaqi (995-1077) mentions a different palace belonging to Mahmud in Afghan-Sal, located within the Sad-Hazara garden.
Ghaznavid art is characterised by a recurrent use of marble in both the decorative programme of several buildings and the composition of steles and funerary columns. Its use can be explained through manifold factors, but the most relevant was possibly the Ghaznavid sultans' will to emulate the fabulous Indian marble architecture and art they had the chance to admire during the military campaigns and looting in Northern India. The material was readily available given that there was a marble mine near the *ziyara* (pilgrimage site) of Saki, at a 5-km distance from Ghazni. The presence of several Indian stonecutters in the Ghaznavid capital also encouraged its use, which is confirmed by the carving technique where one can see the almost exclusive use of the flat chisel, similarly to the arts of Gandhara and in India. Finbarr Barry Flood (2009) tried to put together an encompassing synopsis and comparison of the different scholarly opinions so far expressed in terms of how much Ghaznavid and Ghurid art are indebted to the arts of India. The scholar believes that Ghazni hosted an entire Indian neighbourhood where the soldiers from the Subcontinent and their families were living. He is thus inclined to suggest that Hindu sanctuaries must have been built there and that their decorations must have inspired the local craftsmen.
The Indian influence is testified by not only the stylistic carving technique and the predilection for the use of marble, but also by the presence of artistic motifs and designs evident in the reliefs and in the architectures (e.g. the small earthenware columns of the Ghaznavid palace with typical Northern Indian *purnaghata* capitals in the shape of strongly flared vases). The inspiration is also present in the decorative vocabulary, including scenes with dancers (Bombaci 1959, figs. 2-3) or with a catcher with his monkey, on a slab now preserved in the Stuttgart museum (Fontana 2005).
All of the above considerations join into the analysis of the basin here exhibited, presenting a figural decoration with birds with interlocking necks. In her extensive study of Ghazni marbles, Martina Rugiadi (2012, pp. 1268, 1307-1308) suggested that the carved birds on this basin may well be peacocks. The fragment of another Ghazni polylobed basin presents the same specie (ibidem, p. 1273). The peacock, either on its own or depicted in a couple with intertwined necks, is a very common motif in Islamic art. However, we would like here to provide an alternative interpretation to our basin.
Johannes Kalter (1987, pp. 10, 65, fig. 3) briefly describes a basin, now in Germany, with decorative motifs typical from the Indian Middle Ages with birds with interlocking necks and another recurrent theme, the lion head with two bodies. The scholar however doesn't provide further information. We would like to suggest that the birds here carved should be interpreted as a representation of the *Hamsah*, a mythical swan or duck, symbol of the individual soul and the bird in the Hindu tradition that lays the cosmic egg from which Brahma rises and which subsequently becomes his vehicle (*vahana*). In Sanskrit, *hamsah* means swan / duck (on the macrocosmic duck, see Zimmer 1993, pp. 52-54).
Depictions of *hamsah* are frequent in Buddhist and Brahminic art since the time of the great king Ashoka (304-232 BC; see Vogel 1962, pp. 55-74, with numerous figs.; and also Coomarawamy, 1985, p. 50, figs. 88-89). In a small domed mosque (or funerary monument) in the mountainous region of Ghur, the Masgid-i sangi of Larvand, the entrance is richly adorned in pure Indian style (Scarcia, Taddei 1973). Even this monument, attributed to the Ghurid period and dating to the last decades of 12th century, presents on the eaves three couples of regardant birds and a duck to the feet of each jambs (Flood 2009, pp. 151-155, figs. 10-11). The question that remains here to answer is whether the Indian duck motif in our Ghaznavid reliefs was consciously chosen for religious or, most likely, aesthetic motifs, as in the case of the Ghurid monument, or whether, as we believe, it was chosen for its exotic flare, echoing the Ghaznavid victories of the military campaigns and sojourns in India.
Another perspective, which to our knowledge has yet to be tackled by academia, is the possible influence on Ghaznavid art of the sculptures produced under the Hindu Shahi, the rulers of Afghanistan and Ghazni

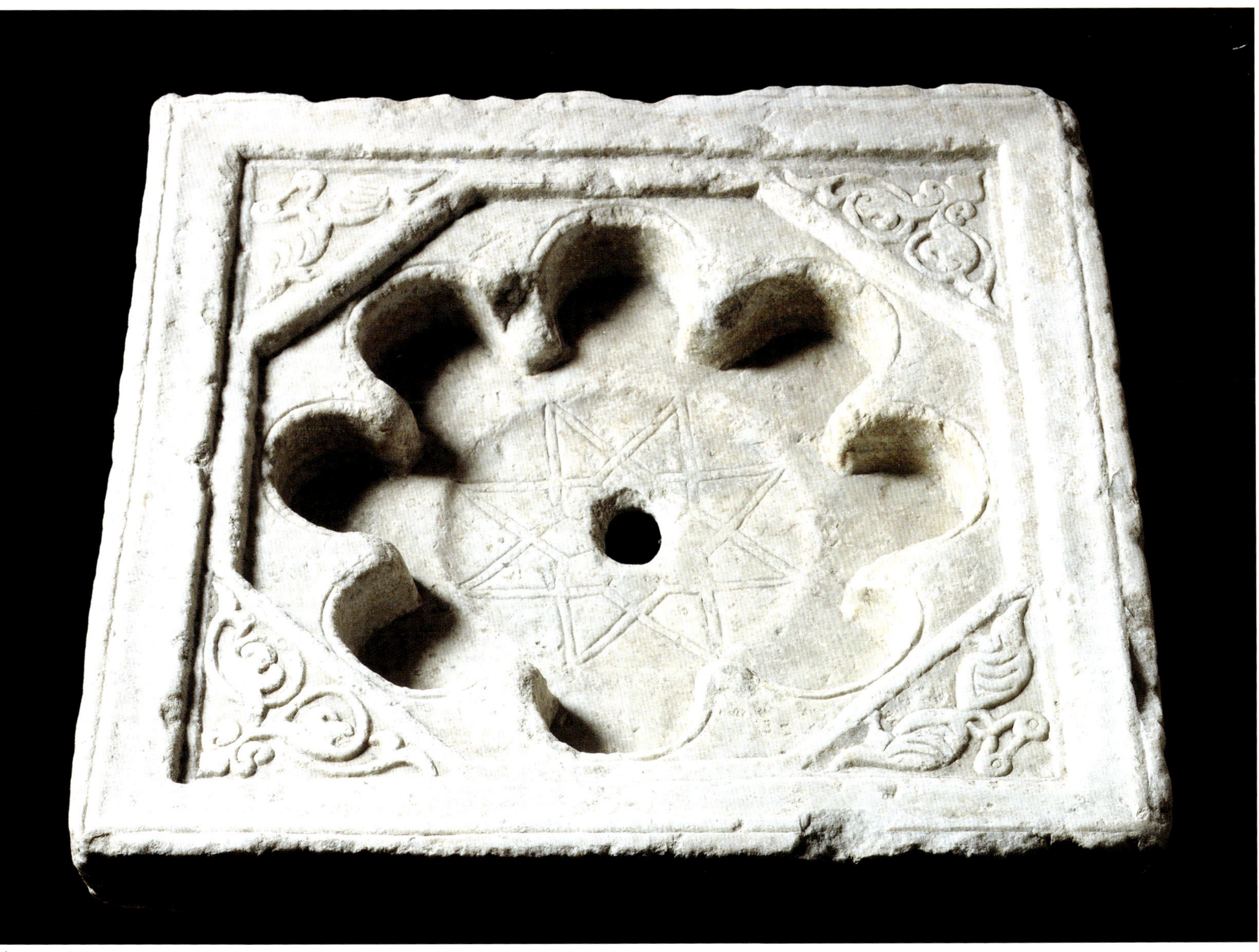

114

before the Turkish conquest with Alptigin in 961. Only one 7th-century relief has been attributed to this production, previously in the Doris Wiener Gallery collection in New York and lately sold at auction at Christie's New York, 20th March 2012. The relief presents on one side a couple of lotus flowers, on the other a horizontally-set lotus flanked by two birds, their bodies directed to the left and their heads facing each other.
One should also not forget the Hindu artefacts unearthed during the Italian Archaeological Mission in Ghanzi. Together with the marble sculpture of Brahma (Umberto Scerrato 1959a, pp. 39-40, fig. 39), voluntarily mutilated and used for the palace tile flooring, there are two more known though unpublished fragments, currently preserved at the Oriental Museum in Rome. One of these fragments is depicting Varaha, one of the avatars of Vishnu as a boar, and the latter Krishna lifting mount Govardhana.

M.J.

115
Tile

Iznik, Turkey, 16th century
Fritware, with polychrome underglaze painting
h. 24 cm, w. 20 cm
MIC, Museo Internazionale delle Ceramiche in Faenza, inv. n. 3852

An architectural tile fragment with underglaze red, blue and green-painted decoration outlined in black, the central medallion outlined in bole red and shaped as a *hamsa* or polylobed palmette, filled with carnations, tulips, rosettes and leaves, the left portion of the composition with rosettes, *hatayi* and blue *saz* leaves. The colours of this tile are typical of the mid-16th century. Similar tiles can be found in the Takkeci Ibrahim Aga Mosque (1592) in Istanbul. For an in-depth discussion on Iznik ceramics, see the appendix cat. n. 83.

Bibliography: *Le mille,* 1990, cat. n. 101, p. 136; Guida 2014, fig. 4, p. 84.

I.B.

116
Tile

Iznik, Turkey, second half 16th century
Fritware, with polychrome underglaze painting
h. 20 cm, w. 22.5 cm
MIC, Museo Internazionale delle Ceramiche in Faenza, inv. n. 3853

An architectural tile fragment with underglaze polychrome-painted decoration outlined in black.
In the centre an almond-shaped medallion, the borders created by intertwining blue *saz* leaves, the medallion filled with a floral bloom with four small red carnations, rosettes and interlocking vegetal tendrils, the four corners decorated with fragments of analogous polylobed medallions with blue crests and bole red outlines, filled with tulips and rosettes. The colours and the style of decoration are typical of the late 16th century productions and the design of intertwining medallions can also be seen on several textiles of the time (for an in-depth discussion on Iznik ceramics, appendix to cat. n. 83). Similar tiles can be seen in the harem area at the Topkapi Palace in Istanbul.

Bibliography: *Le mille*, 1990, cat. n. 105, p. 140; *Matisse Arabesque*, 2015, cat. n. 99, pp. 103-243.

I.B.

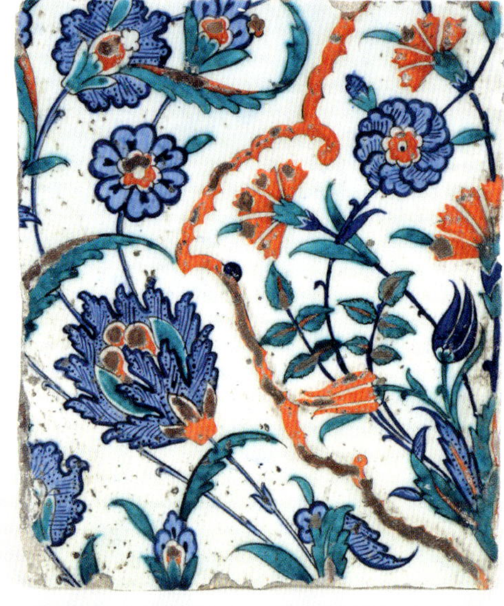

115

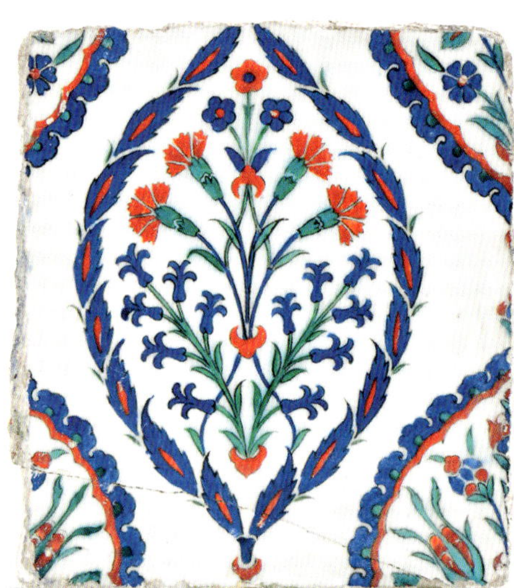

116

117
Duct

Alhambra, Spain, 14th-15th century
Carved stone
17 × 15 cm
Museo de la Alhambra, Patronato de la Alhambra y Generalife,
inv. n. R1388

A pipeline of the Alhambra, dating to the Nasrid period.

A.V.

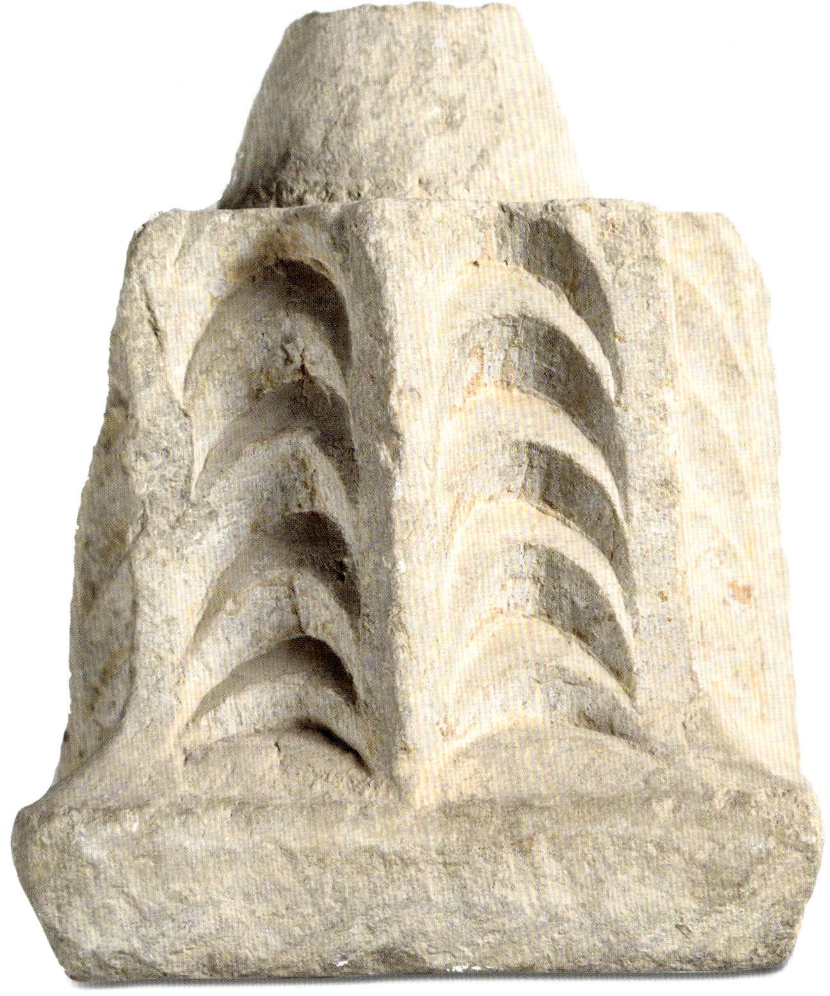

117

118
Tile

Iran, late 13th-early 14th century
Fritware, cast in a mold, enameled, painted and gilded
h. 19 cm, w. 27 cm
MIC, Museo Internazionale delle Ceramiche in Faenza, inv. n. 18913

A turquoise-glazed architectural tile fragment of rectangular shape, the moulded decoration consisting of alternating palmettes, the outlines, the minute vegetal tendrils in the background and the fretwork framing the composition all in red, heightened with gold. Tiles with features such as this are normally called *lajvardina* (*lajvard* meaning lapis in Farsi). Lajvardina wares are normally characterised by the presence of black, white or red decorations on a turquoise or dark blue background heightened with gold pigment. Typical of the Ilkhanid period, this type of production was abandoned shortly after.

Bibliography: *Le mille*, 1990, p. 113, cat. n. 79; *Eredità dell'Islam*, 1993, pp. 256-257, cat. n. 142; *Matisse Arabesque*, 2015, pp. 86, 242, n. 41.

I.B.

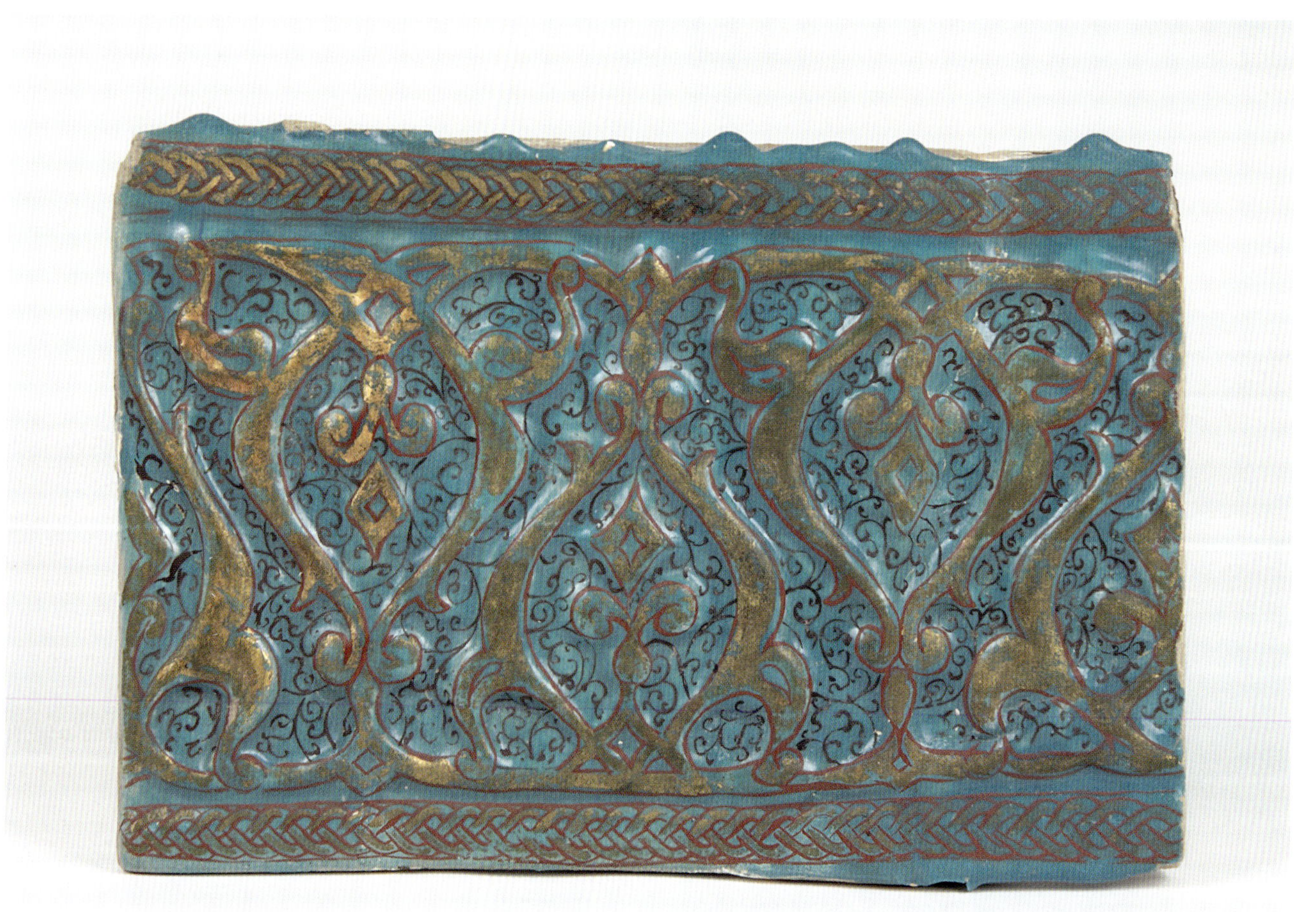

118

119
Model of home

Seljuk art, Iran 12th-13th century
Fritware, with turquoise blue underglaze painting
7 × 16 × 10.5 cm
Museo d'Arte Orientale - MUCIV, inv. n. 4044

A house model with flat roof and without a courtyard, with a wide veranda on the four sides, similarly to the precedent model showing a decorative band at the top used here also as a frame to the epigraphic inscription Allah, incised in cursive and glazed in turquoise, against a vegetal and arabesques ground, with pronounced grazings.

"The scope of these decorative artefacts is mysterious" wrote Hanna Erdmann (1965, p. 41) already more than fifty years ago. She was the first to publish a list of these enigmatic objects. These works, generally defined as house models, are moulded and thus seem to belong to a type of serial production. Similar to flat boxes, their parallelepiped shape always presents modest dimensions (on average a width of 14-15cm and a height of 5-6 cm). Usually, they are attributed to the Seljuq period (12th - 13th century), but their production possibly carried on until 14th century. The main country of origin is likely to be Iran, but a few models seem to have come from Afghanistan.

Bibliography: Torre 2010, p. 22, fig. 12; Scerrato 2014, p. 36, fig. 4; G. Manna, in *IRAN* 2015, p. 54, fig. 6.

M.J.

120
Model of home

Seljuk art, Iran 12th-13th century
Fritware, with turquoise blue underglaze painting
5.5 × 14.5 × 10.2 cm
Museo d'Arte Orientale – MUCIV, inv. n. 2712

A house model with courtyard, with ten human figures gathered around a round tray and two large vases of ovoid shape and with tall conical neck, the exterior with slits at the end of the long sides, turning the corners into pillars, small pyramidal cusps are placed on the corners of the roof, along its edge towards the courtyard a decorative band formed by small interlocked rings, the figures wearing their typical headdresses, worked in an approximate and stylised design, a flute to be noticed among the attendants, on the central tray a circle of small semi-spherical objects, possibly beakers, gathered around a central decorative element, on the outer walls incised figural decoration with animals, not very clear to see due to the thick glaze.

Bibliography: E.J. Grube, in *Eredità dell'Islam* 1993, p. 225; Torre 2010, p. 22, fig. 12; Scerrato 2014, p. 35, pl. III; Manna, in *IRAN* 2015, p. 54, fig. 6.

M.J.

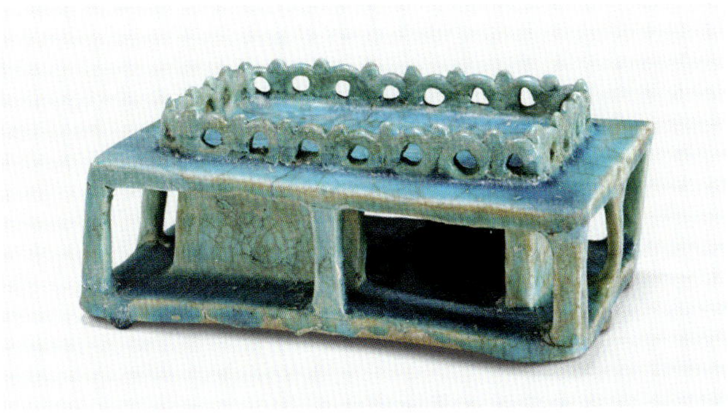

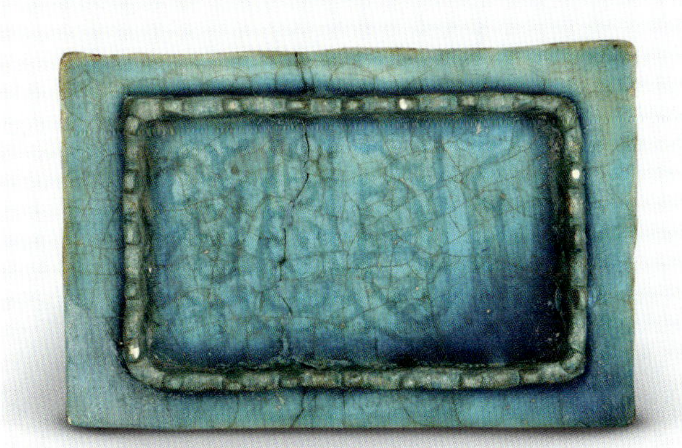

119

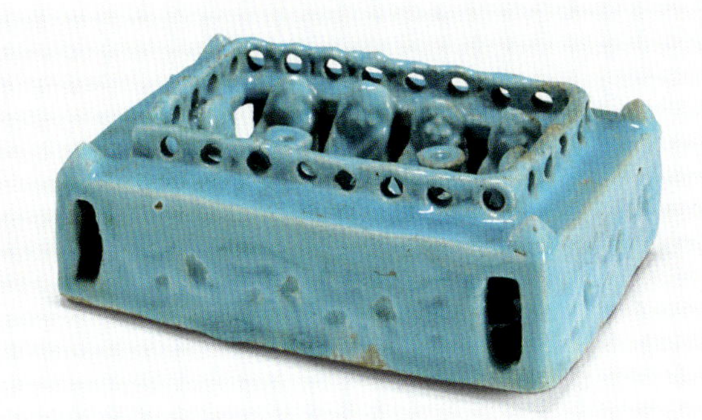

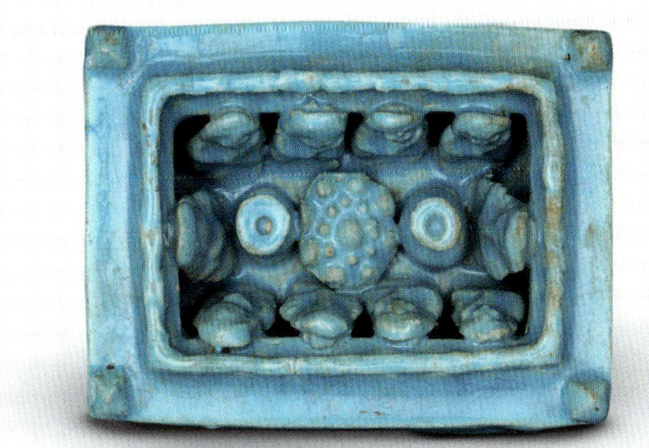

120

121
Flask

Iran, 17th century
Fritware, with blue and black painted decoration
h. 31 × w. 22 × d.12 cm
© The Ashmolean Museum, University of Oxford. Gift of Gerald Reitlinger, 1978, inv. n. EA1978.1696

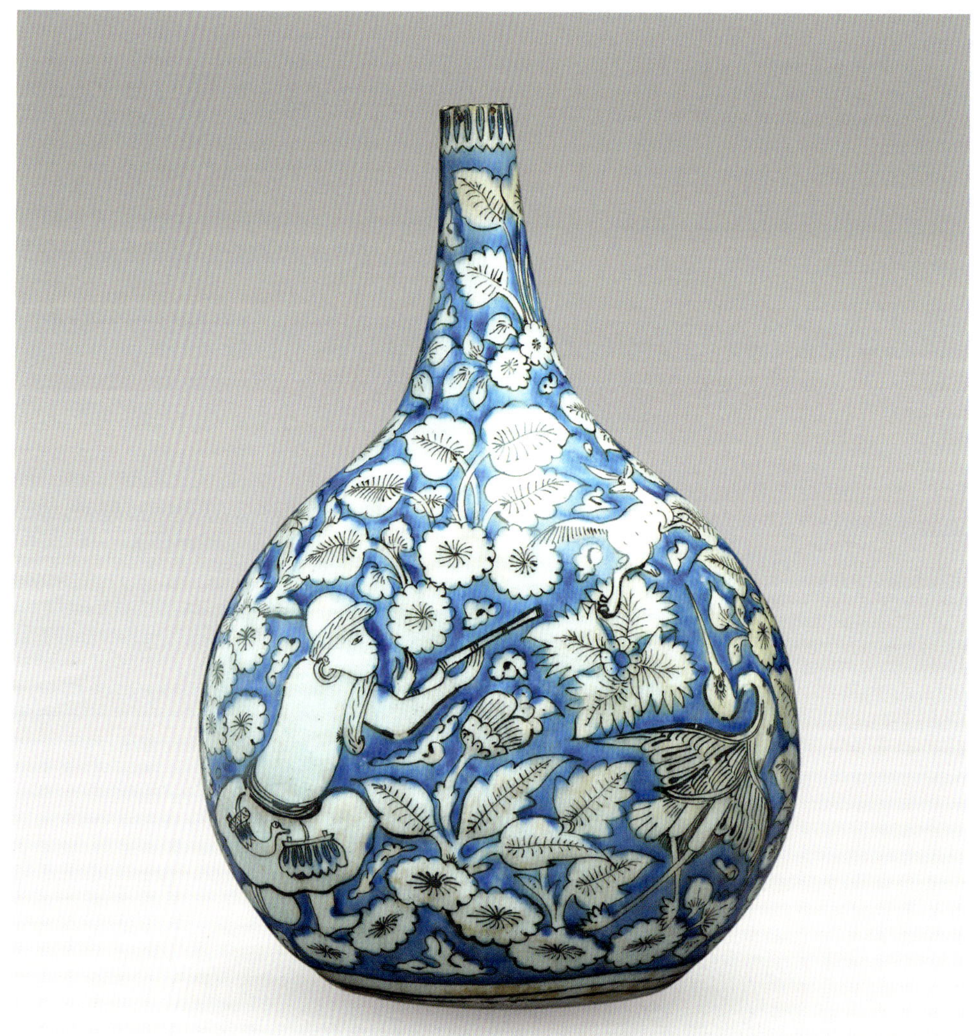

121

Drop-shaped with flattened sides, resting on an oval flat base, rising to a tapering neck, the body painted in the round in black and cobalt blue against a white ground, one side with a hunter targeting a deer with his rifle and a stork among floral and vegetal elements, the latter with a young maiden, seated under a tree, in front of her a drop-shaped flask and a ship-like vase, on the right a hunter approaching the scene with a gazelle on his shoulders.

The pictorial composition of this flask presents an almost miniature-like style. Each leaf is rendered with its own natural veneering and each flower with its petals, the feathering of the stork is very naturalistic and the hunter is not using any arm, but a specific long rifle which needs to be constantly refilled with gunpowder, contained in the flask hanging from his belt.

There are at least fifteen exemplars of this flask, each with different variations on this theme (*Beyond* 2006, p. 163); three are preserved at the Hermitage Museum in St. Petersburg (inv. nn. VG-294, VG-927 and VG-1023), one at the Louvre in Paris (inv. n. MAO 253) and four are at the Victoria and Albert Museum in London (Crowe 2002, pp. 150-151). These productions have normally been attributed to the kilns of Mashhad.

In Islamic ceramics, blue and white wares have often been considered imitations of Chinese porcelains. Indeed, during the Safavid dynasty, a large portion of the Iranian ceramic industry was devoted to imitate Ming prototypes in both decorative and chromatic terms. Chinese ceramics always had a special lure to the Islamic lands and were considered epitomes of luxury. Recurrent and intense trading relations between China and the Middle East, especially Persia, were catalysts of the import of new decorative motifs and tastes into the Islamic world. However, the Persians also played a crucial role in the artistic development of Chinese ceramic. Indeed, the cobalt blue used in so many Oriental ceramics exemplars is not a local resource to be found in China. It was most likely imported from Persia (often from Nishapur and Mashhad mines) and thus why it is often called "Persian blue" or "Mohammadi blue". Moreover, during the Transitional Period at the end of the Ming Dynasty, the Jingdezhen kilns got shut down and were thus unable to supply the market of both internal and external requests (mostly from Europe). It was then the turn of Persia to take over the leadership of the blue and white ceramic production. Around that time, Kirman, Mashhad, Nishapur, Tabriz and Isfahan's kilns produced magnificent exemplars of Chinese-inspired ceramics, both for the local market and for the European export market, as several Old Masters paintings testify, especially the Flemish ones. Emulating Chinese ceramics was the trigger to this new production, but the reinterpretation and stylisation carried out by Persian potters show a mature and skilful comprehension of the prototypes and the artistic creativity of the Persian genius, elaborating a truly unique design. The Ashmolean Museum's flask fits perfectly well in this context: its attention to details and its miniature-like quality of the painted figures is typically Islamic, whilst its elegance and sophisticated shape is a Safavid prerogative.

Bibliography: Welch 1973, cat. n. 89, p. 126; Canby, 1999, cat. n. 149, p. 156.

I.B.

122
Ewer (*aftaba*)

Brass
Lahore or Deccan, 16th century
h. 51 × l. 20 × w. 16 cm
 Presented by Miss Eleanor Butler, in memory of her father Dr A. J. Butler, 1976, inv. n. EA1976.43

Of globular shape, resting on a pierced splayed conical foot, rising to a tall tapering neck, with a domed lid, the thin elegant spout ending in a dragon head, the handle stylised at the top, the neck inscribed *Hajji 'Abd Rahim*, the body and spout worked in a spiral fluting pattern reminiscent of turbans (see also cat. n. 99), a decorative style typical of Islamic India. Also known as the *Butler ewer* due to the surname of its previous owner, this ewer had been attributed to Iran or Ottoman Turkey for a long time (see Petsopoulos 1982, cat. n. 48). It was later associated with the production of Islamic metalwares produced in the Indian Subcontinent due to its decorative elements. Indeed, the dragon at the tip of the spout looks more like a *makara* (mythical aquatic creature) rather than a Timurid dragon; the domed lid is reminiscent of Indo-Islamic architecture; and the pierced foot is similar to several Indian *lotas* (water jugs) (Zebrowski 1997, p. 142). For similar comparative exemplars, refer to Zebrowski, 1997, cat. nn. 177, 178, 179, 180, 186, 188, pp. 144-146.

Bibliography: Pope 1938-1939, pl. 1378 A; Petsopoulos 1982, cat. n. 48; Zebrowski 1995, pp. 159-172, p. 160 fig. 1; Zebrowski 1997, p. 142, cat. n. 189 and pl. 521; *Treasures: Antiquities*, 2008, cat. n. 220, p. 78.

I.B.

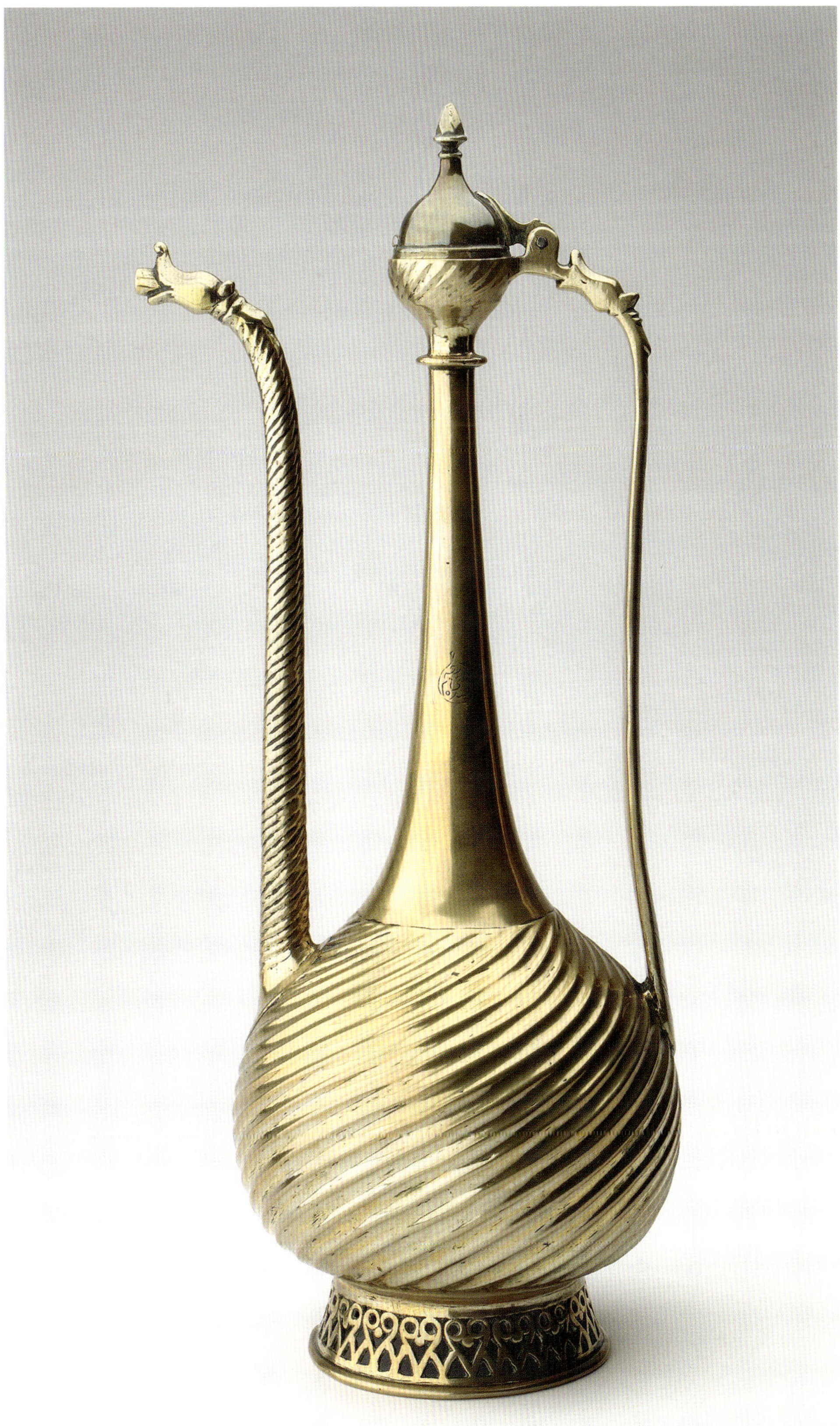

122

123
Tankard with peonies

Iznik, Turkey, late 15th century-early 16th century
Fritware, with underglaze painting in blue
h. 15 cm, w. with handle 12.7 cm
Ø 10.7 cm, foot Ø 7.8 cm
© The Ashmolean Museum, University of Oxford. Gift of Gerald Reitlinger, 1978, inv. n. EA1978.1736

Of compressed globular shape, on a circular straight foot, rising to a flared cylindrical neck with reinforced rim, on the side an S-shaped handle, the body decorated with blue underglaze-painted peonies, interlocking stems and spiralling vegetal tendrils, the decoration contained within two bands of geometric spiral-shaped fretwork on the rim and neck, the handle with *chevron* on a cobalt blue ground. This tankard can be ascribed to the first Iznik production due to its shape and colours. In terms of shape, it shows a strong affinity to Timurid metalwares (Iran, 14th-17th century), which seem to have been widespread in Turkey already in the 1520s. As far as the colours and the decorative repertoire are concerned, Chinese Yuan and Ming ceramics seem to be the source of inspiration for these Turkish ceramics exemplars. Chinese porcelain always exerted a strong fascination in the Islamic lands and was considered a lavish commodity both in Iran and in Turkey. The Ottoman victories followed by looting at Tabriz (1514), Damascus and Cairo (1517) led to a great influx of Chinese porcelains to the Turkish capital. These samples became the primary prototypes stirring the frenetic production of Iznik Chinese-inspired ceramics around 1520s. The use of blue and white underglaze painted decoration, also called *Baba Nakkas*, is present in Iznik ceramics from the late 15th to the early 16th century. The Chinese inspiration lies more in the conceptual idea than in the decorative details of these early samples. However, with the new models brought by the Ottoman looting, the imitation becomes more skilful and compelling. For all of the above reasons, the writer supports a dating slightly later than the suggested one, around 1520. For analogous examples, see Atasoy and Raby, 1989, cat. nn. 297 and 298.

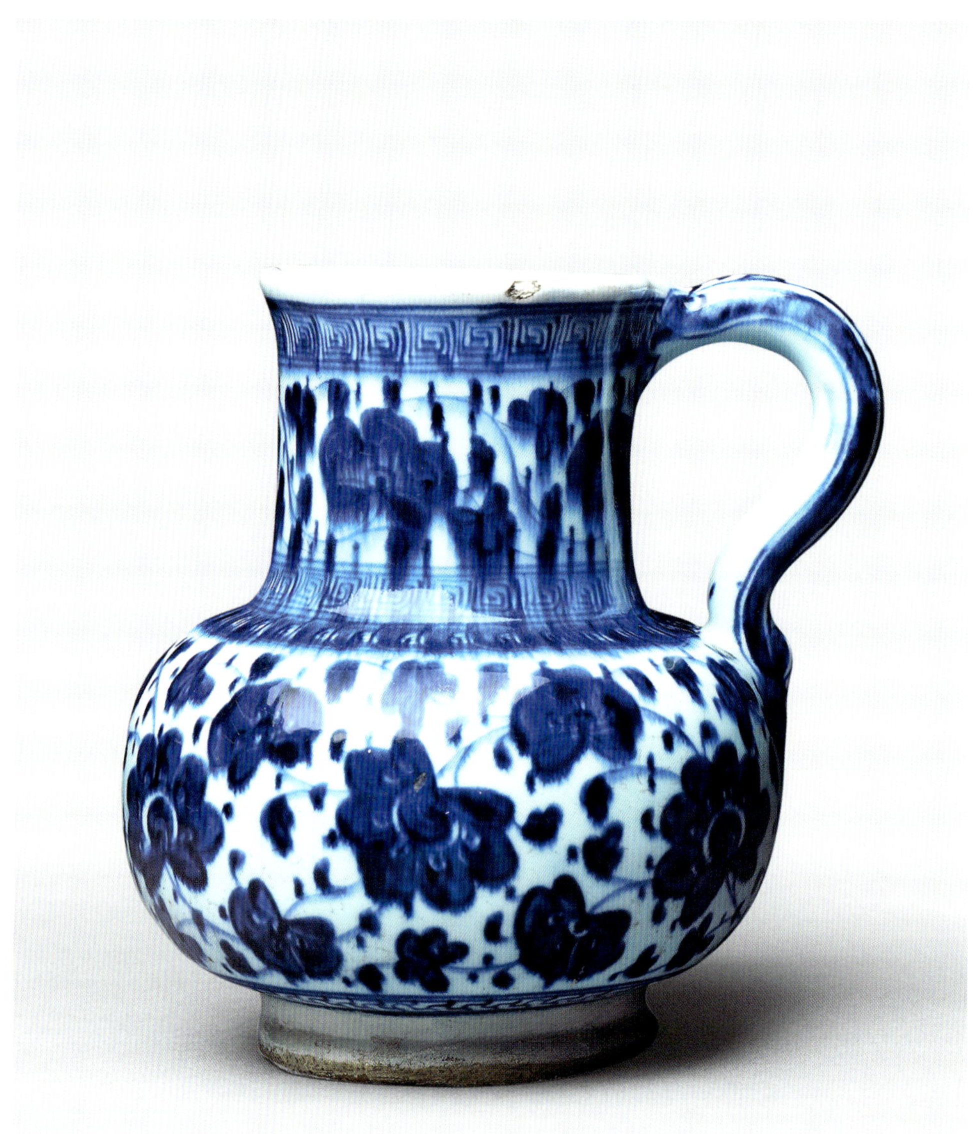

123

Bibliography: *Eastern Ceramics*, 1981, no. 376, p. 129; Allan et al. 1986, pl. 82.

I.B.

124
Tile panel

Multan, Pakistan, half 20th century
Pottery with underglaze painted decoration
160 × 67 cm
MIC, Museo Internazionale delle Ceramiche in Faenza, inv. n. 3843

Of rectangular shape, made from four rectangular tiles framed by twelve smaller tiles, underglaze painted in blue and turquoise on white ground, in the centre the floral and vegetal decoration consisting of a blossoming shrub with flowers and leaves worked symmetrically around the same axis, the composition of the central rectangle ending in a lobed architectural arch, the decoration on the tympani with fine arabesques on turquoise ground, the outer frame of tiles also on turquoise ground with intertwining palmettes interspersed with blue and white rosettes.

Multan is one of the most famous centres of ceramic production in Pakistan and in the 20th century, the major producer of blue and white wares (*kaashi gari*) in the Islamic lands. The tile production is normally reserved for local use in the regional architectural decoration, whilst wares are mostly produced for tourist export market.

Bibliography: Rye, Ewans 1976, pl. 275, p. 276.

I.B.

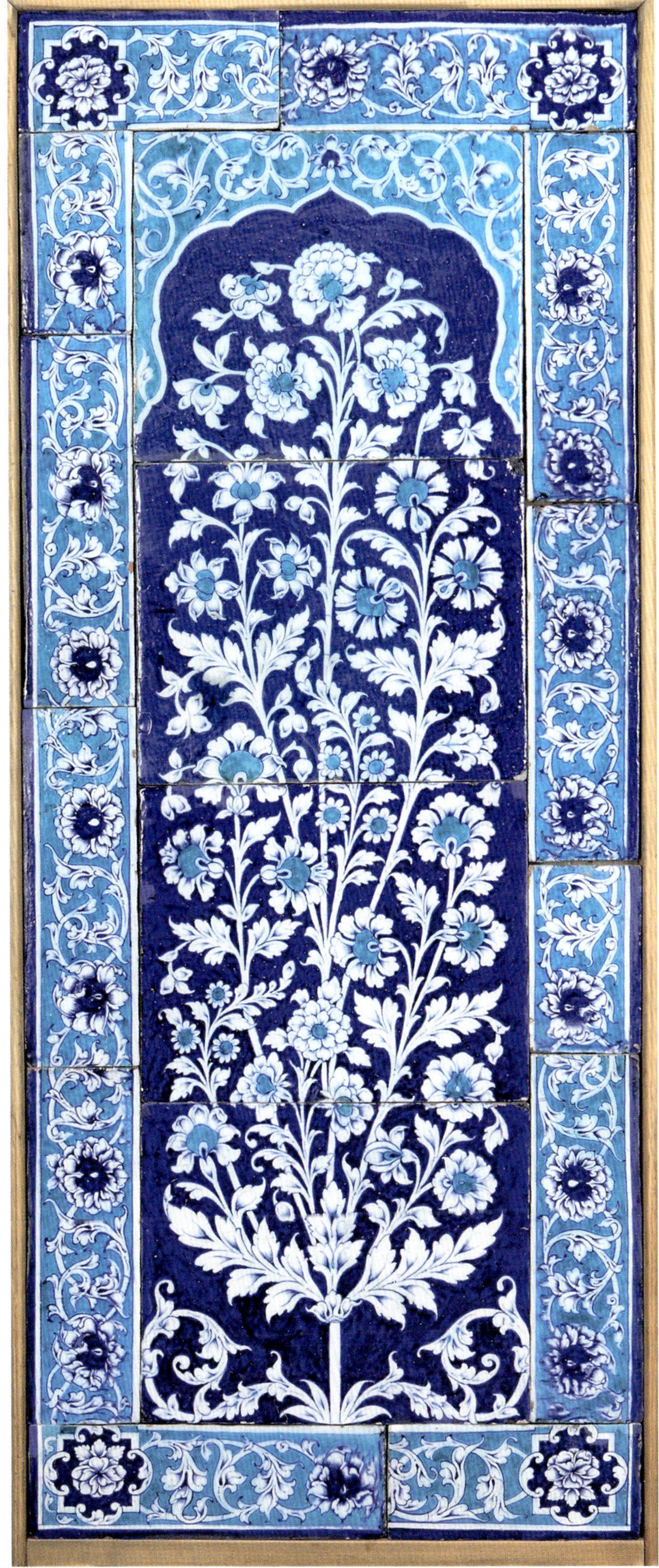

124

Damascus: the Lost Garden of Eden

Marco Galateri di Genola

On one of Muhammad's caravan journeys in Syria during his youth, it is believed that in the distance the Prophet caught a glimpse of the city of Damascus from the top of Mount Qasioun. This vision caused him to immediately divert his gaze, as he thought he was admiring Paradise itself and, being convinced that men are not allowed to enter Paradise twice, he refused to visit the city and decided instead to proceed on his journey.

It is with sweet nostalgia that I remember my numerous stays in Damascus, those spring and summer nights when we would climb up Mount Qasioun to have a drink or an ice-cream after dinner. I remember an uphill road which little by little, by getting higher, gifted us each time with a breathless vision: the vast city of Damascus laying at our feet in all its glory, degraded by an ongoing urbanisation but always magnificent.

Damascus, the most ancient city in the world, is renowned for its abundance of waters running through the city and for its surrounding lavish gardens. The city's main two rivers, Barada and El 'Awaj, rising from the Anti-Lebanon Mountains and branching out into a complex network of canals and waterways before disappearing into the desert, guaranteed a global and unanimous distribution of water to Damascene homes and almost two hundred public fountains. Every traveller's account records such lavish wealth: the ancient Arab merchants used to exaggerate, counting the number of Damascene gardens up to at least a hundred thousand; and the 19th century Western geographers, in tune with the Orientalist trends of the time, produced lithographs and prints where these gardens, though surrounded by the desert, were lush and evergreen.

Walking back down from the Mount into the city, my eyes too were filled with its richness. We used to enter the old town through the tall sturdy walls built by the Ayyubids and then, we would get lost in narrow alleyways with run-down old palaces' facades and small shops crammed with hidden gems and fascinating objects. At times, we were able to peek through rickety doors and unhinged gates to admire the beauty of ancient gardens, otherwise well-protected by foreign eyes through tall walls. And sometimes, with a little bravery, we were lucky enough to sneak into those gardens and stay there for a while, soaking in their past beauty in silence.

Damascene houses were structured to mirror local traditions. The most fundamental part of life – family life – took place in the interiors, where the different areas would be organised and divided to prevent guests from meeting the women, the children and the servants of the household. Instead, the areas facing the garden were dedicated to social life and gatherings, being an ideal place to rest, pray and meditate.

The centre would always feature an octagonal or circular fountain filled with water to the edges. Perfectly synced with the flooring, the central fountain would normally showcase a triumph of polychrome marbles and hard stones intaglios combined in different geometric patterns, such as squares, star and chessboard. Nearby, resting against the walls or hidden by the lush vegetation, one could find the daily rites tools, which although common they never lacked charm and aesthetic accomplishment; basins, buckets, bowls, ewers, jugs, ladles and beakers – all made of refined materials such as glass, ceramics, brass and bronze, each decorated with intricate arabesques and calligraphic compositions. I had learnt to appreciate their shapes and styles by often going to the souk and admiring some of the earlier models on sale there. They were often incised with exquisite calligraphy and at times with figural decorations, such as plants and animals, primarily fishes intertwining and chasing one another on the rim.

The fountain edges were enriched with spouts, from which the water flew freely and quietly, conveying all around a sense of refreshment and peace. The spouts came always in even numbers, but in the most varied shapes, such as fish heads, snakes or dragons, some of which seemed to have drawn their inspiration from distant lands in the Far East. It was as if one could see an entire world unfolding in those fountain spouts, from the deserts and the highlands, through all the commercial stops along the Silk Road.

During those night walks, it dawned to me how fountains and gardens were strictly interconnected as symbols of life, purity and spiritual rebirth.

Shape was also never left to chance, I knew this well. Whether squared or circular, gardens were divided in four equivalent parts, each separated by a path or stream of water which originated from the central fountain, an arrangement clearly inspired by the four rivers of Paradise described in the Qur'an.

Some people I met tried to explain this likeness in practical terms. They were convinced that the dryness of the soil, the boiling temperatures, and the lack of flourishing vegetation typical of the Arabic Peninsula and neighbouring countries led quite spontaneously to believe that Paradise would be a lush garden, crossed by fresh rivers and streams, filled with fountains, scented flowers, fruit-bearing trees and pleasant shade. There, one could easily spend hot afternoons and sultry evenings indulging in earthly pleasures and in a state of complete mental and physical wellbeing. But perhaps, there was more to it. Ancient traditions, religious practices, and relationships with different cultures all converged into one: looking at the world from a garden in Damascus, one really had the perception that it existed a profound link interconnecting lands and civilisations from Morocco all the way to India.

I still carry with me the memories of those gardens and of those years spent there. Damascus is today a metropolis weakened by war and thirst. The lack of drinkable water is a haunting risk, not only due to the now almost two million inhabitants, but also due to the progressive abandonment of the original hydric distribution system and the excessive exploitation of local rivers for industrial and agricultural purposes. Passing by the once magnificent abodes of the old town, one can often see neglected old public fountains, damaged and without water.

The Paradise that ancient travellers yearned for, and the gardens full of delights located in the innermost parts of these houses, all seem distant memories now. But those fountains gift us with an important lesson: water is a precious and yet frail good for humanity. Just a look at one of those fish-headed spouts should remind us all of the importance of keeping that subtle balance alive, because in the end we all yearn for an oasis, for Paradise.

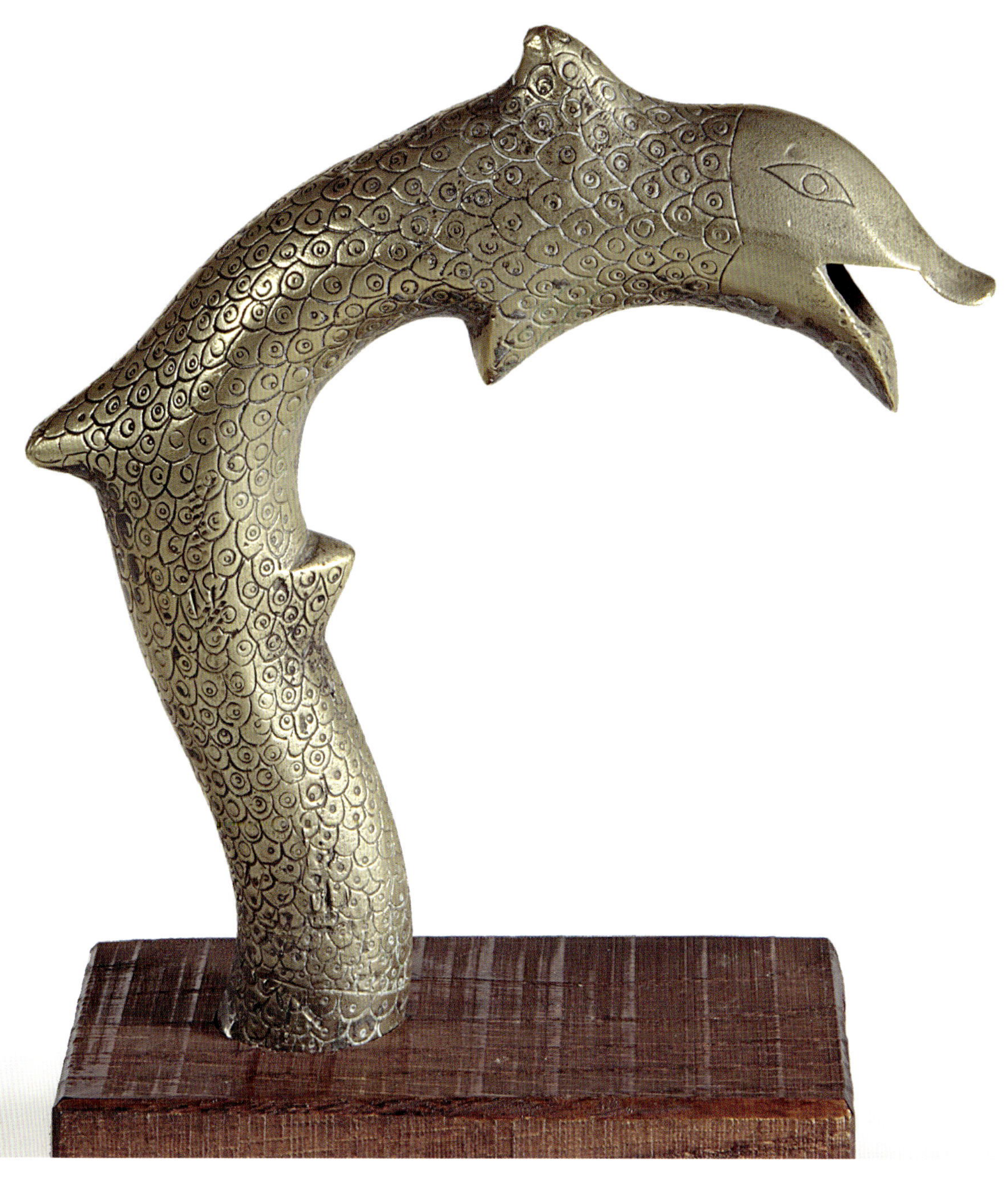

Bibliography

Abouseif 2005
D.B. Abouseif, *Veneto-Saracenic Metalware, a Mamluk Art*, in "Mamluk Studies Review", vol. IX, n. 2, 2005.

***A caccia in paradiso* 2004**
A caccia in paradiso. Arte di corte nelle Persia del Cinquecento, edited by S. Canby, J. Thompson, exhibition catalogue (Milan, Museo Poldi Pezzoli and Palazzo Reale, 10th March - 27th June 2004), Skira, Milano 2004.

Ádahl 2006
K. Ádahl (edited by), *The Sultan's Procession: The Swedish Embassy to Sultan Mehmed IV in 1657-1658 and the Ràlamb Paintings*, Swedish Rersearch Institute in Istanbul, Istanbul 2006.

Aga-Oğlu 1943
M. Aga-Oğlu, *The Use of Architectural Forms in Seljuq Metalwork*, in "Art Quarterly", 6, 1943, pp. 92-98.

Allan 1976
J.W. Allan, *The Metalworking Industry in Iran in the Early Islamic Period*, doctoral thesis, Oxford 1976 (http://ora.ox.ac.uk/objects/uuid:278c6978-9421-46af-af61-a062a2044591).

Allan 1982
J.W. Allan, *Nishapur: Metalwork of the Early Islamic Period*, The Metropolitan Museum of Art, New York 1982.

Allan 1986
J.W. Allan, *Metalwork of the Islamic World, The Aron collection*, The Metropolitan Museum of Art, New York 1986.

Allan 1991
J.W. Allan, *Islamic Ceramics*, Ashmolean Museum, Oxford 1991.

Allan et al. 1986
M. Vickers, O. Impey, J.W. Allan, *From Silver to Ceramic: The Potter's Debt to Metalwork in the Graeco-Roman*, Oriental and Islamic Worlds, Ashmolean Museum, Oxford 1986.

***Amos Gitai* 2014**
Amos Gitai. Ways, exhibition catalogue (Milan, Palazzo Reale, 2nd December 2014 - 1st February 2015), Giunti, Firenze 2004.

Anedda, Pala 2014
D. Anedda, A. Pala, *Acquamanili nella liturgia cristiana (IV-XVI secolo): il bronzo della pinacoteca nazionale di Cagliari*, in "Anuario de Estudios Medievales", 44/2, July-December 2014, pp. 689-731.

***Armenia* 2011**
Armenia impronte di una civiltà, edited by G. Uluhogian, B. Levon Zekiyan, V. Karapetian, exhibition catalogue (Venice, Museo Correr, Museo Archeologico Nazionale, Sale Monumentali della Biblioteca Nazionale Marciana, 16th December 2011 - 10th April 2012), Skira, Milano 2011.

Artan 2006
T. Artan, *Arts and Architecture*, in *The Cambridge History of Turkey*, vol. III, edited by S. Faroqhi, Cambridge University Press, Cambridge - New York 2006, pp. 408-480.

***Arte Islámico en Granada* 1995**
M. Casamar, *Arte Islámico en Granada, Propuesta para un Museo de la Alhambra* (La Alhambra, Palacio de Carlo V, 1st April - 30th September 1995), Editorial Comarws, Granada 1995.

Atasoy et al. 2001
N. Atasoy, W.B. Denny, L.W. Mackie, H. Tezcan, *Ipek, Imperial Ottoman Silk*, TEB, London 2001.

Atasoy, Raby 1989
N. Atasoy, J. Raby, *Iznik, La poterie en Turquie Ottomane*, Chene, Singapore 1989.

Atasoy, Uluc 2012
N. Atasoy, L. Uluc, Impressions of Ottoman Culture in Europe 1453-1699, Armaggan Publications, Istanbul 2012.

Atil 1973
E. Atil, *Ceramics from the World of Islam*, Smithsonian Institution, Washington D.C. 1973.

Atil 1981
E. Atil, *Renaissance of Islam: Art of the Mamluks*, Smithsonian Institution, Washington D.C. 1981.

Atil et al. 1985
Atil E., W.T. Chase, P. Jett, *Islamic Metalwork in the Freer Gallery of Art*, Smithsonian Institution, Washington D.C. 1985.

Baer 1968
E. Baer, *"Fish Pond" Ornaments on Persian and Mamluk Metal Vessel*, in "Bullettin of the School of Oriental and African Studies", vol. XXXI, part I, 1968, pp. 14-28.

Baer 1988
E. Baer, *Islamic Ornament*, Edinburgh University Press, Edinburgh 1998.

Baer 1989
E. Baer, *Jewelled Ceramics from Medieval Islam* in "Muqarnas", vol. VI, 1989.

Bahrami 1949
M. Bahrami, *Gurgan Faiences*, Cairo 1949.

Bailey et al. 1996
G. Bailey, L. Golombeck, R.B. Mason, *Tamerlane's Tableware: A New Approach to the Chinoiserie Ceramics of 15th and 16th Century Iran*, Mazda, Costa Mesa 1996.

Baldensperger 2010
Ph.J. Baldensperger, *Peasant Folklore of Palestine*, Palestine Exploration Fund Quarterly Statement, London 1893

Ballian, Moraitou 2006
A. Ballian, M. Moraitou (edited by), *Benaki Museum: A Guide to the Museum of Islamic Art*, Benaki Museum, Athens 2006.

Barrucand 1998
M. Barrucand, *Trésors Fatimides du Caire*, Institut du Monde Arabe, Cairo 1998.

Bashir 2008
M. Bashir, *The Art of the Muslim Knight. The Furusiyya Art Foundation Collection*, Skira, Milano 2008.

Bautier 1977
R.-H. Bautier, *Datation et provenance du "paon aquamanile" du Louvre à l'inscription bilingue, latine et arabe*, in «Bulletin de la Société nationale des antiquaires de France", 1977, pp. 92-101.

Benevolo et al. 2018
G. Benevolo, M.C. Costantini, C. Tovoli (edited by), *Tessere Giardini*, Bologna 2018.

Benkheira 2003
M.H. Benkheira, *La maison de Satan. Le hammam en débat dans l'islam médiéval*, in "Revue de l'Histoire des religions", 220 (4), 2003, pp. 391-443.

Benkheira 2008
M.H. Benkheira, *Hammam, nudité et ordre moral dans l'islam médiéval*, in "Revue de l'Histoire des religions", 225 (1), 2008, pp. 75-128.

Bertini 1881
G. Bertini, *Fondazione artistica Poldi Pezzoli. Catalogo generale*, Fondazione artistica Poldi Pezzoli, Milano 1881.

***Beyond* 2006**
Beyond the Palace Walls. Islamic Art from the State Hermitage Museum, edited by M.B. Piotrovsky, A.D. Pritula, exhibition catalogue (Edinburgh, National Museums of Scotland 14th July - 5th November 2006), National Museums of Scotland, Edinburgh 2006.

Bilgi 2005
H. Bilgi, *Reunited after Centuries. Works of Art Restored to Turkey by the Sadberk Hanim Museum*, Istanbul 2005.

Blair, Bloom 2009
S. Blair, J.M. Bloom, *Rivers of Paradise, Water in Islamic Art and Culture*, Yale University Press, New Haven 2009.

***Blue and White* 1985**
Blue and White. Chinese Porcelain and Its Impact on the Western World, exhibition catalogue, edited by J. Carswell (Chicago, The David and Alfred Smart Gallery - The University of Chicago, 3rd October - 1st December 1985), The Gallery, Chiacgo 1985.

Bombaci 1959
A. Bombaci, *Summary Report on the Italian Archaeological Mission in Afghanistan. Introduction to the Excavations at Ghazni*, in "East and West", 10, 1959, pp. 3-22.

Bombaci 1966
A. Bombaci, *The Kūfic Inscription in Persian Verses in the Court of the Royal Palace of Mas'ūd III at Ghazni*, in *IsMEO, Reports and Memoirs*, vol. V, Roma 1966.

Browne 1951-1953
E.G. Browne, *A Literary History of Persia*, 4 vols., Cambridge University Press, Cambridge 1951-1953.

al-Bukhari 1980
al-Bukhari, edited by M. al-Khatib, M.F. 'Abd al-Baqi, Q. al-Khatib, M. al-Babi al-Halabi, Cairo 1980.

al-Bukhari 2003
al-Bukhari, *Detti e fatti del profeta dell'islam*, edited by V. Vacca, S. Noja, M. Vallaro, Utet, Torino 2003.

Burke 2009
E. Burke, *Islam at the Center: Technological Complexes and the Roots of Modernity*, in "Journal of World History", 20 (2), 2009, pp. 165-186.

Burns 2002
J.D. Burns, *Antique Rugs of Kurdistan, A Historical Legacy of Woven Art*, published by the author, 2002.

Burzacchini et al. 2015
P.G. Burzacchini, G.P. Emiliani, M.G. Morganti, *Dizionario Enciclopedico della Ceramica. Storia, Arte, Tecnologia*, 3 vols., Polistampa, Firenze 2015-2017.

Canby 1998
S. Canby, *Princes, Poets and Paladins: Islamic and Indian Paintings from the Collection of Prince and Princess Sadruddin Aga Khan*, British Museum Press, London 1999.

Canby 1999
S. Canby, *The Golden Age of Persian Art, 1501-1722*, British Museum Press, London 1999.

Carboni 2001
S. Carboni, *Glass from Islamic Lands*, Thames & Hudson, London 2001.

Carswell 1972
J. Carswell, *Kutahya Tiles and Pottery from the Armenian Cathedral of St.James, Jerusalem*, 2 vols., Oxford University Press, Oxford 1972.

Carswell 1998
J. Carswell, *Iznik Pottery*, British Museum Press, London 1998.

Carswell et al. 1991
J. Carswell, A. Altun, G. Oney, *Sadberk Hanim Museum. Turkish Tiles and Ceramics*, Sadberk Hanim Müzesi, Istanbul 1991.

Casalini 2016
E. Casalini, *La collezione di filtri ceramici islamici del Museo di Faenza*, in "Faenza", n. 2, 2016, pp. 21-35.

***Catalogo dei codici* 2014**
Catalogo dei codici miniati della Biblioteca Vaticana, I. *I manoscritti Rossiani*, edited by S. Maddalo, in collaboration with E. Ponzi and the contribution of M. Torquati, 3 vols., Biblioteca Apostolica Vaticana, Città del Vaticano 2014.

Catalogo Poldi Pezzoli
Museo Poldi Pezzoli, *Catalogo generale* edited by Banca Commerciale Italiana, vol. VII, Electa, Milano 1987.

Cecutti 2013
D. Cecutti, *Una miniera inesauribile*, Maschietto Editore, Firenze 2013.

Christie's 2008
Art of the Islamic and Indian Worlds, London, King Street, 8th April 2008.

Christie's 2011
Art of the Islamic and Indian Worlds, London, King Street, 7th April 2011.

Christie's 2017
Art of the Islamic and Indian Worlds Including Oriental Rugs and Carpets, auction catalogue, London, King Street, 27th April 2017.

***Civiltà Islamica* 2010**
Arte della Civiltà Islamica, edited by G. Curatola, exhibition catalogue (Milan, Palazzo Reale, 21st October 2010 - 30th January 2011), Skira, Milano 2010.

***Civiltà Islamica* 2015**
Arte della Civiltà Islamica, la collezione Al-Sabah, edited by G. Curatola, exhibition catalogue (Rome, Palazzo del Quirinale, 25th July - 20th September 2015), Skira, Milano 2015.

Colonna 2011
V. Colonna, *La formazione delle raccolte d'arte islamica a Roma XVII-XX secolo*, in "Giornale di storia", 7, 2011.

Concas 1988
R. Concas, *Pinacoteca nazionale di Cagliari*, vol. I, Pinacoteca Nazionale, Cagliari 1988.

Concina 2006
E. Concina (edited by), *Venezia e Istanbul. Venezia, confronti e scambi*, Forum, Udine 2006.

Contadini 1998
A. Contadini, *Fatimid Art at the Victoria and Albert Museum*, V & A Publications, London 1998.

Coomaraswamy 1985
A.K. Coomaraswamy, *History of Indian and Indonesian Art*, Dover, New York 1985.

***Cora* 1985**
G.C. Bojani, C. Guidotti, A. Fanfani (edited by), *Museo Internazionale delle Ceramiche, La donazione Galeazzo Cora, Ceramiche dal Medioevo al XIX secolo*, vol. I, Fabbri, Milano 1985.

Crowe 2002
Y. Crowe, *Persia and China. Safavid Blue and White Ceramics in the Victoria and Albert Museum 1501-1738*, La Borie, London 2002.

Curatola 1989
G. Curatola, *Draghi. La tradizione artistica orientale e i disegni del tesoro del Topkapi*, Poligrafo, Venezia 1989.

D'Amora, Pagani 2011
R. D'Amora, S. Pagani, *Hammam, le terme nell'islam*, Olschki, Firenze 2011..

***Das Goldene Byzanz* 2012**
Das Goldene Byzanz und der Orient, edited by F. Daim, exhibition catalogue (Schallaburg, 30th March - 4th November 2012), Schallaburg 2012.

Di Branco 2009
M. Di Branco, *Storie arabe di greci e romani*, Pisa University Press, Pisa 2009.

Di Flumeri 2004
G. Di Flumeri Vatielli, *Large Ewer*, in *Crusades. Myth and Realities*, edited by Y. Toumazis, A. Pace, M.R. Belgiorno, S. Antoniadou, exhibition catalogue, Nicosia Municipal Arts Centre, Nicosia 2004, p. 232, fig. 116.

Di Flumeri Vatielli 2010
G. Di Flumeri Vatielli, *Metalli*, in P. Torre, G. Di Flumeri Vatielli, M. Jung, *Arte dell'Islam*, Città di Castello 2010, pp. 35-48.

Dodds 1992
J.D. Dodds, *Al-Andalus, The Art of Islamic Spain*, The Metropolitan Museum of Art, New York 1992.

Drake Boehm, Holcomb 2016
B. Drake Boehm, M. Holcomb (edited by), *Jerusalem 1000-1400. Every People under Heaven*, The Metropolitan Museum of Art, New York 2016.

***Eastern Ceramics* 1981**
Eastern Ceramics and Other Works of Art from the Collection of Gerald Reitlinger, edited by D. Willis, exhibition catalogue (Oxford, Ashmolean Museum, and Londra, Sotheby Parke Bernet, July-September 1981), Ashmolean Museum, Oxford 1981.

Eiland et al. 1999
M.L. Eiland, R. Pinner, *Oriental Carpet and Textile Studies, The Salting Carpets*, ICOC, Danville 1999.

***Eredità dell'Islam* 1993**
Eredità dell'Islam. Arte islamica in Italia, edited by G. Curatola, exhibition catalogue (Venice, Palazzo Ducale, 30th October 1993 - 30th April 1994), Silvana Editoriale, Cinisello Balsamo 1993.

Ettinghausen 1957
R. Ettinghausen, *The Wade Cup in the Cleveland Museum of Art, it's Origins and Decorations*, in "ArsOr", II, 1957, pp. 327-366.

Ettinghausen 1965
R. Ettinghausen, *The Uses of Sphero-Conical Vessels in the Muslim East*, in "Journal of Near Eastern Studies", 24, January-October 1965, pp. 218-229.

Falk et al. 1978
T. Falk, E. Smart, R. Skelton, *Indian Painting: Mughal and Rajput and a Sultanate Manuscipt*, P. & D. Colnaghi, London 1978.

Firat 2008
B.O. Firat, *Disorienting Encounters: Re-reading Seventeenth and Eighteenth Century Ottoman Miniature Paintings*, thesis, Amsterdam 2008.

Flood 2009
F.B. Flood, *Masons and Mobility: Indic Elements in Twelfth-Century Afghan Stone-carving*, in A. Filigenzi, R. Giunta, *Fifty Years of Research in the Heart of Eurasia. Proceedings of the symposium held in the Instituto Italiano per l'Africa e l'Oriente, Rome, January 8th 2008*, IsMEO conferences, 21, Roma 2009, pp. 137-160.

Fontana 1999
M.V. Fontana, *An Islamic Sphero-conical Object*

in a Tuscan Medieval Marble, in "East and West", vol. XL, n. 1/4 (December 1999), pp. 9-33.

Fontana 2005
M.V. Fontana, *La fortuna di un 'ağā'ib?*, in M. Bernardini, N.L. Tornesello (edited by), *Studi in onore di Giovanni M. D'Erme*, Università degli Studi di Napoli, L'Orientale, Dip. di Studi Asiatici, Series Minor, LXVIII, Napoli 2005, pp. 441-456.

Fontana 2014
M.V. Fontana (edited by), *Umberto Scerrato. Saggi inediti e opera minora*, 3 vols., Quaderni di Vicino Oriente, VII, Roma 2014.

Forthingham 1951
W.A. Forthingham, *Lustre ware of Spain*, Hispanic Society of America, New York 1951.

Gabrieli, Scerrato 1985
F. Gabrieli, U. Scerrato, *Gli Arabi in Italia*, Scheiwiller, Milano 1985.

Ghabin 1998
A. Ghabin, *The Quranic Verses as Source for-Legitimacy or Illegitimacy of the Arts in Islam*, in "Der Islam", 75/2, 1998, pp. 193-225.

Ghouchani, Adle 1992
A. Ghouchani, C. Adle, *A Sphero-Conical Vessel as Fuqqa'a, or a Gourd for "Beer"*, in "Muqarnas", vol. IX, 1992, pp. 72-92.

Giunta 2018
R. Giunta, *The Aron Collection I, Islamic Magic Terapeutic Bowls*, Ipocan, Roma 2018.

Goblot 1979
H. Goblot, *Les qanats, une tecnique d'acquisition de l'eau*, Mouton, Paris 1979.

Gómez Moreno 1951
M. Gómez Moreno, *El arte español hasta los Almohades. Arte Mozárabe*, vol. III, Plus Ultra, Madrid 1951.

González Martí 1952
M. González Martí, *Ceramica del levante español. Siglos medievales*, II. *Alicatados y azulejos*, Labor, Barcelona 1952.

Grote 1922
H.W. Grote, *Der Orientteppich. Seine Geschichte und seine Kultur*, 3 vols., Scarabäus, Berlin 1922.

Grube 1976
E.J. Grube, *Islamic Pottery of the Eighth to Fifteenth Century in the Keir Collection*, Faber and Faber, London 1976.

Grube et al. 1994
E.J. Grube et al., *Cobalt and Lustre. The First Centuries of Islamic Pottery, The Nasser D Khalili Collection of Islamic Art*, vol. IX, Azimuth Editions, London 1994.

***Guida* 2014**
G. Manna, U. Bongianino, A. Fusaro (edited by), *Guida alla sezione islamica. Museo Internazionale delle Ceramiche in Faenza*, Ediemme Le Guide, Misterbianco (CT) 2014.

Gursu 1988
N. Gursu, *The Art of Turkish Weaving*, Redhouse Press, Istanbul 1988.

Hasson 2014
R. Hasson, *The Museum for Islamic Art*, L.A. Mayer Museum for Islamic Art, Jerusalem 2014.

Heikamp 1980
D. Heikamp, *Catalogo dei vasi*, in *Il tesoro di Lorenzo il Magnifico. Repertorio delle gemme e dei vasi*, edited by N. Dacos et al., Sansoni, Firenze 1980, pp. 219-288.

Henderson, Raby 1989
J. Henderson, J. Raby, *The Technology of Fifteenth Century Turkish Tiles: An Interim Statement on the Origins of Iznik Industry*, in "World Archaeology, vol. XXI, n. 1, June 1989, pp. 115-132.

Hillenbrand 1999
R. Hillenbrand, *Islamic Art and Architecture*, Thames & Hudson, London 1999.

Ibn Hawqal 1938
A. Ibn Hawqal, *Kitab surat al-ard*, edited by J.H. Kramers, in *Bibliotheca Geographorum Arabicorum*, vol. II, Brill, Leiden 1938.

***Ibn Jaldún* 2006**
Ibn Jaldún. El Mediterráneo en el siglo XIV. Auge y declino de los imperios, edited by J. Páez López, exhibition catalogue (Siviglia, Real Alcázar, 19th May - 30th September 2006), Fundación José Manuel Lara, Sevilla 2006.

***Il Montefeltro e l'Oriente islamico* 2018**
Il Monfeltro e l'Oriente islamico. Urbino 1430-1550. Il Palazzo Ducale tra Occidente e Oriente, edited by A. Bruschettini, exhibition catalogue (Urbino, Palazzo Ducale, 23rd June - 30th September 2018), Sagep, Genova 2018.

Inventario
Inventario dell'eredità di Gian Giacomo Poldi Pezzoli, atto del notaio Rinaldo dell'Oro, n. 5486 di repertorio dell'archivio notarile di Milano, 26 aprile 1879.

***IRAN* 2015**
IRAN, arte e cultura. La civiltà dell'Iran attraverso ceramiche, calligrafie, miniature e immagini del presente e del passato, exhibition catalogue (Roma, Museo Nazionale d'Arte Orientale Giuseppe Tucci, 15th March - 19th April 2015), PS Edizioni, Roma 2015.

***Islam e Firenze* 2018**
Islam e Firenze. Arte e collezionismo dai Medici al Novecento, edited by G. Curatola, exhibition catalogue (Firenze, Gallerie degli Uffizi and Museo Nazionale del Bargello, 22nd June - 23rd September 2018), Giunti, Firenze 2018.

***Islam specchio d'Oriente* 2002**
Islam specchio d'Oriente, edited by G. Damiani, M. Scalini, exhibition catalogue (Firenze, Palazzo Pitti, 23rd April - 2nd September 2002), Bottega d'Arte, Livorno 2002.

Ivanov 2004
A.A. Ivanov, *A Second "Herat bucket" and its Congeners* (trans. by J.M. Rogers), in "Muqarnas", 21, 2004, pp. 171-179.

***Jardin encantado* 2001**
Un jardin encantado. Arte islámico en la Colección Calouste Gulbenkian, edited by J. Carswell, M.F.P. Leite et al., exhibition catalogue (Madrid, Fundación Santander Central Hispano, 27th February - 22nd April 2001), Fundación Santander Central Hispano, Madrid 2001.

Kalter 1987
J. Kalter, *Linden-Museum Stuttgart. Abteilungsführer Islamischer Orient*, Scheufele, Stuttgart 1987.

Knauer 1979
E. Knauer, *Marble Jar-Stands from Egypt*, in "Metropolitan Museum Journal", vol. XIV, 1979.

Koç, Bilgi 2005
Ö.M. Koç, H. Bilgi, *Reunited after Centuries*, Sadberk Hanım Müzesi, Istanbul 2005.

Koc et al. 2007
A. Koc et al., *Istanbul: The City and the Sultan*, Nieuwe Kerk, Amsterdam 2007.

Kœchlin, Mignon 1956
R. Kœchlin, G. Mignon, *Art Musulman*, Librairie Nationale d'Art et d'Histoire G. Van Oest, Paris 1956.

***La céramique médiéval* 1997**
La céramique médiévale en méditerranée: actes du 6. congrès de l'AIECM2, Aix-en-Provence (13-18 novembre 1995), edited by G. Démians d'Archimbaud, Narration, Aix-en-Provence 1997.

***L'Afghanistan* 1961**
L'Afghanistan dalla Preistoria all'Islam. Capolavori del Museo di Kabul, edited by G. Gullini, exhibition catalogue (Torino, Galleria Civica di arte moderna, July-August 1961), F.lli Pozzo-Salvati-Gros Monti, Torino 1961.

Lane 1938
A. Lane, *Early Islamic Pottery*, Faber and Faber, London 1938.

Lane 1957a
A. Lane, *Later Islamic Pottery*, Faber and Faber, London 1957.

Lane 1957b
A. Lane, *The Ottoman Pottery of Iznik*, in "Ars Orientalis", vol. II, 1957.

Laviola 2016
V. Laviola, *Metalli islamici dai territori iranici orientali (IX-XIII sec.). La documentazione della missione archeologica italiana in Afghanistan*, 2 vols., doctoral thesis, Venezia 2016.

***Le calife* 2002**
Le calife, le prince et le potier. Les Faiences à reflets métalliques, edited by J. Rose-Albrecht, exhibition catalogue (Lione, Musée des Beaux-Arts, 2nd March - 22nd May 2002), RMN, Paris 2002.

Lehrman 1980
J.B. Lehrman, *Earthly Paradise: Garden and Courtyard in Islam*, University of California Press, Berkeley - Los Angelese 1980.

***Le mille e una notte* 1990**
Le mille e una notte, ceramiche persiane, turche e ispano moresche, edited by P. Torre, exhibition catalogue (Faenza, Palazzo delle esposizioni, 15th September - 28th October 1990), Gruppo Editoriale Faenza, Faenza 1990.

***Le quattro parti* 2001**
La collezione Borgia. Curiosità e tesori da ogni parte del mondo, edited by A. Germano, M. Nocca, exhibition catalogue (Velletri, Palazzo Comunale, 31th March - 3rd June 2001 and Napoli, Museo Archeologico Nazionale, 23rd June - 16th September 2001), Istituto della Enciclopedia Italiana, Milano 2001.

***Les Andalousies* 2000**
Les Andalousies. De Damas à Cordoue, edited by M. Bernus-Taylor, exhibition catalogue (Parigi, Institut du Monde Arabe, 28th November 2000 - 15th April 2001), Institut du Monde Arabe, Paris 2000.

***L'étrange* 2001**
L'étrange et le merveilleux en terres d'Islam, edited by M. Bernus-Taylor, exhibition catalogue (Parigi, Louvre, 23rd April - 23rd July 2001), Musée du Louvre, Paris 2001.

Lettieri 1839
M. Lettieri, *Tazza e calamaio con caratteri arabici*, in "Museo Borbonico", XII, 1839, pp. 1-11.

Liverani 2018
M. Liverani, *Paradiso e dintorni. Il paesaggio rurale dell'antico Oriente*, Laterza, Roma-Bari 2018.

***Luz, Nur* 2013-2014**
Luz, Nur: la luz en el arte y la ciencia del mundo islamico, edited by K. Sabiha, exhibition catalogue (Siviglia, Fundación Focus-Abengoa, 26th October 2013 - 9th February 2014; Dallas, Museum of Art, 30th March - 29th June 2014), Fundación Focus-Abengoa, Sevilla 2013.

Madani 2008
T. Madani, *L'eau dans les villes islamiques médiévales*, in M.I. Del Val Valdivieso, O. Villanueva Zubizarreta (edited by), *Musulmanes y Cristianos frente al agua en las ciudades medievales*, Universidad de Castilla-La Mancha, Santander 2008, pp. 49-76.

Martínez Caviro 1978
B. Martínez Caviro, *Ceramica espanola en el Instituto Valencia de Don Juan*, Instituto Valencia de Don Juan, Madrid 1978.

Martino et al. 1996
L. Martino, P. Leone de Castris, R. Muzii, M. Utili, *La collezione Borgia*, Electa, Napoli 1996.

***Masterpieces* 2011**
Masterpieces from the Department of Islamic Art, The Metropolitan Museum of Art, New York 2011.

***Matisse Arabesque* 2015**
Matisse Arabesque, edited by E. Cohen, exhibition catalogue (Roma, Scuderie del Quirinale, 4th March - 21st June 2015), Skira, Milano 2015.

Mayer 1959
L.A. Mayer, *Islamic Metalworkers and Their Works*, Kundig, Genève 1959.

Mazzoli-Guintard 2003
Ch. Mazzoli-Guintard, *Vivre à Cordue au Moyen Âge*, Presses Universitaires de Rennes, Rennes 2003.

Melikian-Chirvani 1969
A.S. Melikian-Chirvani, *Cuivres inédits de l'époque de Qaitbay*, in "Kunst des Orients", 6, n. 2, 1969.

Melikian-Chirvani 1982
A.S. Melikian-Chirvani, *Islamic Metalwork from the Iranian World, 8th-18th Centuries*, Victoria and Albert Museum, London 1982.

Melikian-Chirvani 1987
A.S. Melikian-Chirvani, *The Transition to the Safavid Period: The Evidence of Metalwork and Its Epigraphy*, in *Transition Periods in Iranian History: Actes du Symposium de Fribourg-en-Brisgau, 1985*, Peeters, Leuven 1987, pp. 181-203.

Migeon 1907
G. Migeon, *Manuel d'art musulman*, 2 vols., Paris 1907.

***Moriscos* 1993**
Moriscos-Echi della presenza e della cultura islamica in Sardegna, exhibition catalogue (Cagliari, Pinacoteca Nazionale, 1993), Pinacoteca Nazionale, Cagliari 1993.

Mosland et al. 2015
S.P. Mosland, A.R. Petersen, M. Schramm, *The Culture of Migration: Politics, Aesthetics and Histories*, Tauris, London - New York 2015.

Norvelle 1980
M. Norvelle, *Water Use and Ownership according to the Texts of Hanbalī Fiqh*, tesi, McGill University, Montréal 1980.

Olmer 1932
P. Olmer, *Catalogue général du Musée arabe du Caire. Les filtres des gargulettes*, IFAO, Cairo 1932

Oney 1987
G. Oney, *Ceramic Tiles in Islamic Architecture*, Ada Press, Istanbul 1987.

***Orienti* 2018**
Orienti - 7000 anni di arte asiatica dal Museo delle Civiltà di Roma, edited by C. Rammasso, exhibition catalogue (Torino, MAO Museo di Arte Orientale, 20th April - 26th August 2018), Silvana Editoriale, Cinisello Balsamo 2018.

Pagliaro, Bausani 1968
A. Pagliaro, A. Bausani, *Letteratura persiana*, Sansoni-Accademia, Firenze-Milano 1968.

Pascon 1977
P. Pascon, *Le Haouz de Marrakech*, vol. I, Éditions marocaines et internationales, Rabat 1977.

Pasinli, Balaman 1991
A. Pasinli, S. Balaman, *Les faïences et les céramiques turques*, Cinili Kiosk, Istanbul 1991.

Petrasch et al. 1991
E. Petrasch, R. Sänger, E. Zimmermann, H. G. Majer, *Die Karlsruher Trkenbeute*, Hirmer Verlag, München 1991.

Petsopoulos 1982
Y. Petsopoulos, *L'art decoratif ottomane*, Denoel, London 1982.

Piemontese 2014
A.M. Piemontese, *La raccolta vaticana di orientalia: Asia, Africa ed Europa*, in C. Montuschi (edited by), *La Vaticana nel Seicento (1590-17009): una biblioteca di biblioteche, Biblioteca Apostolica Vaticana*, Città del Vaticano 2014.

Piotrosky 1999
M.B. Piotrovsky, *Earthly Beauty, Heavenly Art: The Art of Islam*, De Nieuwe Kerk - Lund Humphries, Amsterdam-London 1999.

Pope 1938-1939
A.U. Pope (edited by), *A Survey of Persian Art from Prehistoric Times to the Present*, 6 vols., Oxford University Press, London 1938-1939.

Pope, Ackerman 1967
A.U. Pope, P. Ackerman, *A Survey of Persian Art*, vol. IV, Oxford University Press, New York 1967[2].

Porter, Rosser-Owen 1988
V. Porter, M. Rosser-Owen (edited by), *Metalwork and Material Culture in the Islamic World*, Tauris, London 1988.

Powers 2002
D.S. Powers, *Law, Society, and Culture in the Maghrib, 1300-1500*, Cambridge University Press, Cambridge 2002.

Prudence 1961
O. Prudence, *Islamic Relief Cut Glass: A Suggested Chronology*, in "Journal of Glass Studies, Corning Museum of Glass", vol. III, 1961, pp. 9-29.

Rapoport 1975
I.V. Rapoport, *On One Group of Iranian Faïence Bottles*, in CSH, vol. XL, 1975.

Ravanelli Guidotti 1985
C. Ravanelli Guidotti, *Ceramiche occidentali del Museo Civico di Bologna*, Grafis, Bologna 1985.

Ravanelli Guidotti 1987
C. Ravanelli Guidotti, *Donazione Paolo Mereghi. Ceramiche europee ed orientali*, Grafis, Bologna 1987.

Raymond 1985
A. Raymond, *Grandes villes arabes à l'epoque ottomane*, Sindbad, Paris 1985.

Rice 1955
D.S. Rice, *The Wade Cup in the Cleveland Museum of Art*, Les Éditions du Chêne, Paris 1955

Rogers 1969
J.M. Rogers, *Aeolipiles again*, in *Forschungen zur Kunst des Asiens: In memoriam Kurt Erdmann*, edited by O. Aslanapa, R. Naumann, Istanbul 1969, pp. 147-158.

Rogers 2010
J.M. Rogers, *The Arts of Islam. Masterpieces from the Khalili Collection*, Thames & Hudson, London 2010, p. 111, cat. 126 = https://www.khalilicollections.org/collections/islamic-art/khalili-collection-islamic-art-house-model-pot1047/.

Roux 1977
J.-P. Roux, *L'Islam dans les collections nationales*, Éditions des Musées nationaux, Paris 1977.

Ruggles 2008
D.F. Ruggles, *Islamic Gardens and Landscapes*, University of Pennsylvania Press, Philadelphia 2008.

Rugiadi 2012
M. Rugiadi, *Decorazione architettonica in marmo da Gaznī (Afghanistan)*, doctoral thesis, Bologna 2012.

Rye, Ewans 1976
O.S. Rye, C. Ewans, *Traditional Pottery Techniques of Pakistan: Field and Laboratory Studies*, Smithsonian Institution, Washington D.C. 1976.

Sahin 2009
S. Sahin, *The Museum of Turkish and Islamic Art, Thirteen Centuries of Glory from the Umayyads to the Ottomans*, Blue Dome, New York 2009.

Santillana 1926
D. Santillana, *Istituzioni di diritto musulmano malichita con riguardo anche al sistema sciafiita*, vol. I, Istituto per l'Oriente, Anonima Romana Editoriale, Roma 1926.

Sauvaget 1932
J. Sauvaget, *Poteries Syre Mesopotamiennes du XIVe Siecle*, Leroux, Paris 1932.

Savage-Smith et al. 1997
E. Savage-Smith, F. Maddison, R.H. Pinder-Wilson, T. Stanley, *Science, Tools & Magic: Body and Spirit, Mapping the Universe*, Oxford University Press, Oxford 1997.

Scarcia, Taddei 1973
G. Scarcia, M. Taddei, *The Masǧid-i sangī of Larvand*, in "East and West", 23, 1973, pp. 89-108.

Scavizzi 1966
G. Scavizzi, *Maioliche dell'Islam e del Medioevo occidentale*, Fabbri, Milano 1966.

Scerrato 1959a
U. Scerrato, *Summary Report on the Italian Archaeological Mission in Afghanistan. The Two First Excavation Campaigns at Ghazni*, in "East and West", 10, 1959, pp. 23-55.

Scerrato 1959b
U. Scerrato, *Oggetti metallici di età islamica in Afghanistan. I: Antiquario di Kandahar*, in "Annali dell'Istituto Orientale di Napoli", n.s. 9, 1959, pp. 95-130.

Scerrato 1966
U. Scerrato, *Metalli Islamici*, Fabbri, Milano 1966.

Scerrato 1967
U. Scerrato, *Arte Islamica a Napoli. Opere delle raccolte pubbliche napoletane*, Istituto Universitario Orientale, Napoli 1967.

Scerrato 1974
U. Scerrato, *Nuove acquisizioni dei Musei e Gallerie dello Stato. Roma. Museo Nazionale d'Arte Orientale. Arte iranica pre-islamica. Arte islamica*, in "Bollettino d'Arte", 59 (3-4), 1974, pp. 196-199.

Scerrato 2014
U. Scerrato, *Hausmodelle*, in *Umberto Scerrato. Saggi inediti e opera minora*, I. *Quaderni di Vicino Oriente*, VII, 2014, pp.14-46 (the contribution appeared posthumously, updated by M.V. Fontana).

Schick 1999
L.M. Schick, *Ottoman Costume Albums in a Cross-Cultural Context*, in *Art Turc - Turkish Art: 10th International Congress of Turkish Art*, Fondation Max Van Berchem, Genève 1999, pp. 625-628.

Schick 2004
L.M. Schick, *The Place of Dress in Pre-Modern Costume Albums*, in S. Faroqhi, Ch. Neumann (edited by), *Ottoman Costumes: From Textile to Identity*, Eren, Istanbul 2004, pp. 93-102.

Şebnem, Bilgi 1997
A. Şebnem, H. Bilgi, *Delights of Kütahya, Kütahya Tiles and Pottery in the Suna and Inan Kirac Collection*, Research Institute on Mediterranean Civilizations, Istanbul 1997.

Shalem 1996
A. Shalem, *Islam Christianized, Ars Faciendi* vol. VII, Peter Lang, Frankfurt am Main 1996.

Sotheby's 1985
Islamic Works of Art, Carpet and Txtiles, auction catalogue, Londra, New Bond Street, 16th-17th April 1985.

Sotheby's 2017
Arts of the Islamic World, Londra, New Bond Street, 25th October 2017.

Soustiel 1985
J. Soustiel, *La céramique Islamique. Le guide du connaisseur*, Office du Livre, Fribourg 1985.

Soustiel 2000
L. Soustiel (edited by), *Splendeurs de la Cermamique Ottomane des Collections Suna-İnan Kıraç et du Musée Sadberk Hanım*, Musée Jacquemart-André - Institut de France, Istanbul 2000.

Spallanzani 1994
M. Spallanzani, *Ceramiche alla corte dei Medici nel Cinquecento*, Franco Cosimo Panini, Modena 1994.

Spallanzani 2006
M. Spallanzani, *Maioliche ispano-moresche nel Rinascimento a Firenze*, Spes, Firenze 2006.

Spallanzani 2010
M. Spallanzani, *Metalli islamici a Firenze nel Rinascimento*, Spes, Firenze 2010.

***Splendori a corte* 2007**
Splendori a corte. Arti del mondo islamico nelle collezioni del Museo Aga Khan (Parma, Palazzo della Pilotta, 31st March - 3rd June 2007; Londra, Ismaili Centre, 12th July - 31st August 2007), Olivares, Milano 2007.

***Sucre e Borja* 2000**
Sucre e Borja. La canyamel dels ducs. Del trapig a la taula, edited by J.A.G. Santonja, exhibition catalogue (Gandia, Casa de Cultura Marqués González de Quirós, 21st December 2000 - 23rd February 2001), Generalitat Valenciana, Valencia 2000.

***The Age* 1987**
The Age of Suleyman the Magnificient, edited by E. Asil, exhibition catalogue (Washington, National Gallery of Art, 25th January - 17th May 1987; Chicago, The Art Institute, 14th June - 7 September 1987; New York, The Metropolitan Museum of Art, 4th October 1987 - 17th January 1988), Abrams, New York 1987.

***Topkapi à Versaille* 1999**
Topkapi à Versailles. Trésor de la cour ottomane, exhibition catalogue (Musée national des châteaux de Versailles et de Trianon, 4th May - 15th August 1999), AFAA, Paris 1999.

Torre 2010
P. Torre, *Arte della ceramica islamica*", in P. Torre, G. Di Flumeri Vatielli, M. Jung, *Arte dell'Islam*, Città di Castello 2010, pp. 17-34.

Torre Balbás 1987
L. Torres Balbás, *Arte hispanomusulmán hasta la caída del califato de Córdoba*, in R. Menéndez Pidal (edited by), *Historia de España. España musulmana hasta la caída del Califato de Córdoba (711- 1031 de J.C.). Instituciones y vida social e intelectual*, vol. V, Espasa-Calpe, Madrid 1987[5].

Touwaide, Dendle 2008
A. Touwaide, P. Dendle (edited by), *Health and Healing from the Medieval Garden*, Boydell Press, Woodbridge 2008.

***Treasures: Antiquities* 2008**
Treasures: Antiquities, Eastern Art, Coins, and Casts: Exhibition Guide, edited by R. Frederiksen, exhibition catalogue (Oxford, Ashmolean Museum, 24th May 2006 - 23rd December 2008), Ashmolean Museum, Oxford 2008.

Tsigakou, Moraitou 2016
F.-M. Tsigakou, M. Moraitou, *Thomas Hope: Drawings of Ottoman Istanbul*, Benaki Museum, Athens 2016.

***Turks* 2005**
Turks. A Journey of a Thousand Years, 600-1600, edited by di F. Cagman, A. Locke, N. Olcer, N. Rosenthal, D.J. Roxburgh, exhibition catalogue (London, Royal Academy of Arts, 22th January - 12th April 2005), Royal Academy of Arts, London 2005.

Vanoli 2001
A. Vanoli, *I cammini dell'Occidente*, Cleup, Padova 2001.

Vanoli 2012
A. Vanoli, *La Sicilia musulmana*, il Mulino, Bologna 2012.

Vanoli 2014
A. Vanoli, *Miniatura ottomana e rappresentazione femminile in una raccolta di costumi orientali del XVII secolo*, in M.G. Muzzarelli, M.G. Nico Ottaviani, G. Zarri (edited by), *Il velo in area mediterranea fra storia e simbolo*, il Mulino, Bologna 2014, pp. 273-288.

***Venezia e Istanbul* 2009**
Venezia e Istanbul in epoca ottomana, edited by G. Bellingeri e N. Olcer, exhibition catalogue (Istanbul, 18th November 2009 - 28th February 2010), Electa, Milano 2009.

***Venezia e l'Islam* 2007**
Venezia e l'Islam 828-1797, edited by S. Carboni, exhibition catalogue (Venezia, Palazzo Ducale, 28th July - 25th November 2007), Marsilio, Venezia 2007.

***Venice* 2007**
Venice and the Islamic World 828-1797,

edited by S. Carboni, exhibition catalogue (Parigi, Institut du Monde Arabe, 2nd October 2006 - 18th February 2007; New York, The Metropolitan Museum of Art, 27th March - 8th July 2007; Venezia, Palazzo Ducale, 28th July - 25th November 2007), Zentralinstitut für Kunstgeschichte, Nürnberg 2007.

***Venise et l'Orient* 2006**
Venise et l'Orient 828-1797, edited by S. Carboni, exhibition catalogue (Parigi, Institut du Monde Arabe, 2nd October 2006 - 18th February 2007), Gallimard, Paris 2006.

***Verso Oriente* 2012**
Verso Oriente e ritorno. La pittura orientalista e gli scambi di modelli decorativi nel bacino del Mediterraneo, edited by M. Pasquali, exhibition catalogue (Montelupo, Palazzo podestarile, 22nd June - 14th October 2012), Noèdizioni, Firenze 2012.

Vidal-Castro 2001
F. Vidal-Castro, *Agua y urbanismo: evacuación de aguas en fatwa-s de al-Andalus y el norte de Africa*, in P. Cressier, M.I. Fierro, J.-P. Van Staëvel (edited by), *L'urbanisme dans l'Occident musulman au Moyen Âge, aspects juridiques*, Casa de Velázquez, Consejo Superior de Investigaciones Científicas, Madrid 2001.

Vogel 1962
J.Ph. Vogel, *Ther Goose in Indian Literature and Art*, Brill, Leiden 1962.

Ward 1993
R. Ward, *Islamic Metalwork*, British Museum Press, London 1993.

Ward 1998
R. Ward (edited by), *Gilded and Enameled Glass from the Middle East*, British Museum Press, London 1998.

Watson 1983
A.M. Watson, *Agricultural Innovation in the Early Islamic World*, Cambridge University Press, London - New York 1983.

Watson 1985
O. Watson, *Persian Lustre Ware*, Faber and Faber, London 1985.

Watson 2008
O. Watson, *Museum of Islamic Art Doha, Qatar*, Prestel, New York 2008.

Website of the Missione Italiana in Afghanistan
http://ghazni.bradypus.net/islamic_cat.

Welch 1973
A. Welch, *Shah Abbas and the Arts of Isfahan*, Asia Society, New York 1973.

Welch, Welch 1982
A. Welch, S.C. Welch, *Arts of the Islamic Book: The Collection of Prince Sadruddin Aga Khan*, Cornell University Press, Ithaca-London 1982.

Wiet 1932
G. Wiet, *Catalogue général du Musée Arabe du Caire. Objets en cuivre*, Institut Français, Cairo 1932.

Wilson 2007
B. Wilson, *Foggie diverse di vestire de' Turchi: Turkish Costume Illustration and Cultural Translation*, in "Journal of Medieval and Early Modern Studies", 37 (1), 2007, pp. 97-139.

Zebrowski 1995
M. Zebrowski, *The Butler Brass Ewer*, in J. Allan (edited by), *Islamic Art in the Ashmolean Museum*, parte II, Oxford University Press, Oxford 1995.

Zebrowski 1997
M. Zebrowski, *Gold, Silver and Bronze from Mughal India*, Alexandria Press in association with Laurence King, London 1997.

Zimmer 1993
H. Zimmer, *Miti e simboli dell'India*, Adelphi, Milano 1993 [ed. or. *Myths and Symbols in Indian Art and Civilisation*, Princeton University Press, Princeton 1946].

Cover
Ms Vat. Pers. 32, hammam scene,
15th century.
© Biblioteca Apostolica Vaticana

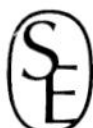

Silvana Editoriale

Direction
Dario Cimorelli

Art Director
Giacomo Merli

Editorial Coordinator
Sergio Di Stefano

Copy Editor
Noa Strada

Translation
Beatrice Campi

Layout
Denise Castelnovo

Production Coordinator
Antonio Micelli

Editorial Assistant
Ondina Granato

Photo Editor
Alessandra Olivari, Silvia Sala

Press Office
Lidia Masolini, press@silvanaeditoriale.it

Available through ARTBOOK | D.A.P.
155 Sixth Avenue, 2nd Floor, New York, N.Y. 10013
Tel: (212) 627-1999 Fax: (212) 627-9484

Silvana Editoriale S.p.A.
via dei Lavoratori, 78
20092 Cinisello Balsamo, Milano
tel. 02 453 951 01
fax 02 453 951 51
www.silvanaeditoriale.it

Reproductions, printing and binding in Italy
Printed by Tipostampa
Printed April 2019

Photo credits

The Aron Collection (photo Valerio Ricciardi, Rome)
The Ashmolean Museum, University of Oxford
Benaki Museum, Atene
© Biblioteca Apostolica Vaticana, Città del Vaticano
(Vat. pers. 32, Ross 878)
Biblioteca dell'Archiginnasio, Bologna
Cappelle Medicee, Florence (photo Antonio Quattrone)
Fondazione Musei Civici di Venezia, Museo Correr
(photo Archivio Fotografico - Fondazione Musei Civici
di Venezia)
Galleria Moshe Tabibnia, Milan
Instituto de Valencia de Don Juan, Madrid
L.A. Mayer Museum for Islamic Art, Jerusalem (Avshalom
Avital for 21, 49, 58, 104; Shay Ban Efraim for 59, 60, 61,
62, 63, 88)
MAO Museo d'Arte Orientale, Turin
MIC, Museo Internazionale delle Ceramiche in Faenza
Museo Civico Medievale, Bologna (photo Roberta Capaldi,
except for inv. nn. 1303; 2784)
Museo de la Alhambra, Patronato de la Alhambra y
Generalife, Granada
Museo del tessuto e della tappezzeria "Vittorio Zironi",
Bologna (photo Roberta Capaldi)
Museo d'Arte Orientale – MUCIV, Rome
(photo Fabio Naccari)
Museo e Real Bosco di Capodimonte, Naples
(photo Marco Pedicini)
Museo Nazionale del Bargello, Florence
(photo Roberto Palermo)
Museo Poldi Pezzoli, Milan
Polo museale della Sardegna - Pinacoteca nazionale
di Cagliari (photo Luigi Corda)
Private collection
Private collection, Brussels
Private collection, Genoa (photo Studio Vandrasch-
Bettega)
Private collection, Sanremo (photo Paolo Robino)